Mayfield Senior School
of the Holy Child

Ex Libris

Dr. Ann Gorman Condon

American History Scholar
Mayfield Senior School '53
UC Berkelely B.A. '57
Harvard University Ph.D. '75

Condon Library Collection
a gift from Dr. Thomas J. Condon
in loving memory of his wife

The Family
in the Western World
from the Black Death
to the Industrial Age

The Family
in the Western World
from the Black Death
to the Industrial Age

BEATRICE GOTTLIEB

New York   Oxford
OXFORD UNIVERSITY PRESS
1993

Oxford University Press

Oxford   New York   Toronto
Delhi   Bombay   Calcutta   Madras   Karachi
Kuala Lumpur   Singapore   Hong Kong   Tokyo
Nairobi   Dar es Salaam   Cape Town
Melbourne   Auckland

and associated companies in
Berlin   Ibadan

Published by Oxford University Press, Inc.,
200 Madison Avenue, New York, New York 10016

Oxford is a registered trademark of Oxford University Press

Library of Congress Cataloging-in-Publication Data
Gottlieb, Beatrice, 1925–
The family in the Western World from the Black Death to
the Industrial Age / Beatrice Gottlieb.
p. cm.   Includes bibliographical references and index.
ISBN 0-19-507344-4
1. Family—History.
2. Civilization, Western—History.
I. Title.
HQ503.c68   1993
306.85′09—dc20
91-42443

Pages 295–98 are an extension
of the copyright page.

1 3 5 7 9 8 6 4 2

Printed in the United States of America
on acid-free paper

In loving memory of Anna Slud and Joseph Gottlieb

ACKNOWLEDGMENTS

This book grew by slow accretions out of my graduate study in the history department of Columbia University, where I wrote a dissertation on marriage cases in fifteenth-century French ecclesiastical courts under the direction of J. W. Smit and Eugene F. Rice, Jr., at a time when family history was less fashionable in academic circles than it is today. My advisors were generous in their recognition of the fact that all three of us were learning from each other. I subsequently found moral and intellectual support in a group of women historians in New York City who founded the Coordinating Committee on Women in the Historical Profession, which in turn founded The Institute for Research in History. The Institute, which no longer exists, briefly provided a welcome center for men and women in all fields of history both in and out of the universities as the academic boom of the sixties was coming to an end. Two groups that originated in the Institute and are still in existence have been particularly helpful to me: the Family History Research Group and the Intellectual History Research Group. Parts of the book were read and criticized by them. I also presented an early version of Part V to the Columbia University Seminar on the History of Legal and Political Thought and Institutions. The overall plan of the book was the subject of helpful discussion in the seminar on social change conducted by Louise and Charles Tilly at the New School for Social Research. The idea for this book began in conversations with Joyce Seltzer.

Several people read parts of the book as it was being written. Each contributed a slightly different point of view, which I found valuable since I wanted to address a widely mixed audience. They were Betty C. Agree, Margaret Darrow, Alan Lessoff, and Hilah F. Thomas. Virginia L. Gross was also one of these readers, and I was deeply grateful for her perceptive comments, particularly on writing style. I miss her enthusiasm and a hundred other things since her death a little over a year ago.

I am grateful to Pamela Sheingorn for her insights on the Holy Kinship. Edgar Munhall, William Smith, and Leo Steinberg gave me some help with the illustrations. My old friend William B. Goodman has been an unfailing multifaceted resource and support. My thanks to everyone, especially for tolerance and patience.

New York   B. G.
February 1992

CONTENTS

CONTENTS

IV

Relatives Past, Present, and Future *177*

V

Ideas and Ideals *229*

I

A Place and a
Social Institution

The household is something tangible and physical, something that can be measured and counted, and something that was directly experienced by almost everybody. It is a good starting point. Ordinary people and scholars alike tend to feel that, in a way, the family *is* the household. It is certainly the place where most aspects of the family come into play.

The term "preindustrial" is especially applicable to the household, since industrialization brought changes in the subjects of both the chapters in this part: the people who made up households and the activities carried on in them.

1

The Members of the Household

One of the most widely held opinions of Europeans and Americans today is that households used to be very different. The traditional household conjures up images of warmth, bustle, shared activities, diversity, and, above all, size. It is a picture that leans heavily on the depictions of households in nineteenth-century literature, a counterimage to the small, parent-child households of restricted activities we believe we are surrounded by today. Historians have come to learn that, for the centuries preceding the nineteenth, this picture is mistaken in a number of ways. It especially needs to be modified by an appreciation of the fact that everyone did not live in the same way.

The most productive research in family history has been on the composition of households. It would be possible to fill this chapter with statistics—amazing statistics, considering that they are based on evidence left by people with a minimal interest in the questions we are now asking. I am not going to spew forth torrents of numbers, but having those numbers at our disposal gives us a certainty that we never had before. We know how many people there were likely to be in various kinds of households, and we also know a lot about who those people were.

Whether few or many, household members often were not relatives, either near or distant. We must pay attention to these nonrelatives if we are to get at the differences between families before 1800 and families of the present. As for the members of the household who were related, we need to ask whether the conjugal or nuclear-family household is as modern as we are so often told it is. There is, finally, the subject of the elderly—a burning issue today and not exactly an untroublesome one in the past. (Children are a subject unto themselves, and are treated in Part III.)

There was great diversity in households at any one time but amazingly

3

little change over the course of time. The kinds of households that existed in eighteenth-century Europe were similar to those that existed in fourteenth-century Europe, especially in the part of society that comprised the largest portion of the population, the tillers of the soil. By the eighteenth century a change had taken place in some households of the wealthy, one that seems to have started at least a hundred years earlier, and it chiefly involved nonrelatives. Although only a small number of people were directly affected at the time, this change was associated with an eventual transformation in the way people wrote and theorized about home life.

Many or Few

There were extreme contrasts in the size of households in the past, as there were in the size of houses. The extremes were so great in some places that an individual had almost as good a chance of living in a very large household as in a very small one. This is because the large households, while few in number, were so large that they absorbed great portions of the population. Most people, however, lived under the same roof with a handful of others in just about every part of the Western world. There may be some ambivalence today about whether a small, intimate household is better than a big bustling one, but there was probably total agreement in the past that, since it was desirable to be wealthy, it was desirable to have the kind of big household that went along with wealth. By the late twentieth century the contrasts of earlier centuries have diminished. In the course of the eighteenth and nineteenth centuries the small household got a little larger and the large household got much smaller.

The most striking examples of large households were those of royalty. A special case, huge royal households exist even today. It is helpful to think of royalty when we consider household size, because in the past the wealthy had a great deal in common with royalty. Their households were nearly as large and were the setting for similar rituals and formalities. According to a careful observer in the late seventeenth century, the household of an English lord would contain, on the average, forty persons. This is a clue to the size of wealthy aristocratic establishments elsewhere in the Western world, including those in the Spanish New World. The same English observer gave estimates of size for other kinds of upper-class households as well: twenty for bishops, sixteen for baronets, thirteen for knights, ten for squires, and eight for ordinary gentlemen.

Very large households in some rural areas were also associated with wealth, but not necessarily the same high social status and formal style. It is a simple fact that it took a lot of land to support a lot of people, so no holder of a small piece of land was likely to have a large household. One rural household in early-fifteenth-century Tuscany contained forty-seven people—a king-size establishment. They were apparently all related by blood or marriage, something that was unlikely in aristocratic households of similar size: five married couples of one generation, five couples of the next generation, twenty-six children of various ages, and the mother of some of the older men. As far as we know, this was the largest household in Tuscany at the time.

The average Tuscan household of the time was nothing like it. Keeping in mind that averages are sometimes deceptive, since they may result from mixing numbers that are very high and very low, it is nonetheless sobering to realize that the average fifteenth-century Tuscan household contained between four and five persons. Although about one individual in ten lived in a fairly large household, containing eleven to twenty-five persons, more than half the population lived in households close to the average size. Historians working on demographic data for France and England have established the same average for those countries for the whole span of time between the late sixteenth century and the early nineteenth century. Knowing that the average household contained four to five persons gives us a sense of scale, one that should put a rein on speculative fantasies all too easily nourished by stray bits of information about big families. It does not rule out the possibility that in the course of a lifetime an individual might live in households of various sizes, from much smaller than the average to much larger. In fact, this is very likely what happened.

One reason for the small average size of households is that most couples had far fewer children than we used to think they did. Some households even had only one or two persons in them. This was not as common as it is in the United States today, but it was certainly not unheard of, especially among the poor. In one small French village at the end of the seventeenth century, where everyone was on about the same level economically and socially, only three households contained as many as nine persons; all the others contained five or fewer. Seven had two persons each, and three had one each. This sort of pattern was repeated in many places. As for differences between rural households and urban households, there was no consistent pattern across Europe. All cities had several wealthy families, so there were likely to be some very large households. On the other hand, large towns with many wage earners had many one-person and two-person households. Rural areas with relatively large land holdings would, as we have seen, tend to have larger households than other kinds of rural areas and nearby small towns.

Even where there were large rural households, however, as in Tuscany, and where living and ownership arrangements could lead to gargantuan establishments, more modest households were usual. Instead of five married couples in one generation living together there was more likely to be a single couple. Instead of five married couples in the next generation, there was again likely to be only one, perhaps with one unmarried brother. In the third generation there would perhaps be two small children, and it was highly unlikely there would be an elderly matriarch or patriarch. Here, then, would be a household of seven persons with exactly the same structure as the one with forty-seven, but one closer, as it happens, to the realities of birth, marriage, and death in the fifteenth century. As those two small children grew up and married, one might move out, and their grandparents might die. That would reduce the household to four. It is not hard to see how the average of four to five came about.

In Europe's American colonies the average household was larger, having six to seven persons, an impressive difference. No one is sure why colonial households were larger, but some reasons seem obvious. There was more wealth to go around and it was somewhat more evenly distributed, there was more land available, and healthier living conditions increased both birth and survival rates. These factors were most apparent in New England and least apparent in the larger cities of the New World, where the average household size was closer to that of Europe. Rural slave-owning households in both North and South America were considerably larger than the average. All in all, the difference between New World and Old World seems to have been one of degree, not kind. When the European household was transplanted to more favorable soil it tended to expand, but not by very much. The difference could have resulted from only one or two more births, one or two fewer deaths, one or two more servants per family.

The facts of household size raise interesting questions about household structure. What kinds of people in what kind of relationship to each other populated those huge establishments of the wealthy? Were the relationships fundamentally different in small households? Were these relationships likely to follow different patterns in different places? Remember that the commonest experience of people in the past was of average-sized households, not so different in that respect from our own. It was not in size but in other respects that the ordinary household of the past contrasted with that of the present.

Relatives or Nonrelatives

Households in our own time may contain people who are not related to each other, but that is considered an unusual or temporary situation, whereas in the past Western households normally contained nonrelatives. Most of them were "servants"—a word whose changing overtones paralleled profound changes in social attitudes. The more we learn about servants in the past the more we realize how important they were to the lives of everyone. The study of the subject is in its very beginnings, but already some impressive theories have been advanced about the significance of servanthood for such diverse matters as the European marriage age and the development of the Western economy. We are still waiting for clarification of two big changes that seem to have taken place between the middle of the sixteenth century and the middle of the eighteenth century: the reduction of servanthood to a low-status occupation and the exclusion of servants from the notion of the family. The changes were not complete by 1800, but they were already clearly visible even as older patterns persisted.

The notions of household and family tend to overlap. Coresidence is often considered more important in defining a family than blood relationship. Now that we are looking at the nonrelated members of the household, it is worth pointing out that the very word "family" comes from *famulus*, the Latin word for servant. "Family" originally had nothing to do with being related by blood or marriage but rather referred to the live-in staff of a domestic establishment. European languages did not entirely shed this meaning of "family" until the nineteenth century. By now the meaning is not only obsolete but very strange indeed to modern ears. As the notion of kinship crept into the meaning of "family," the notion of household did not go away. The first definition of "family" in Samuel Johnson's dictionary of 1755 stated that it was a synonym for household. Furetière's French dictionary of half a century earlier called a family a household consisting of a head and his *domestiques*, whether "women, children, or servants." That is what Samuel Pepys was talking about in the seventeenth century when he noted in his diary that "I lived in Axe Yard, having my wife and servant Jane, and no more in family than us three."[1] A servant was thought of primarily not as a paid worker but as a household member, a "unit of production" that coincided with a "unit of consumption."

The presence of servants and other nonrelatives in the most typical household, the one of modest means located in the country, was about as likely in the fourteenth and fifteenth centuries as it was later. Even a small tenant who held land under the kind of customary lease that included near-servile obligations to work on the land of his lord—still common in France in the eighteenth century—would have a servant or two. Servants in farming households came from other farming households, and they were usually no poorer or humbler than their masters. Sometimes the servant's parents made the arrangements, with the understanding that the master would act in loco parentis, even sending wages home to the parents. Sometimes—just to confuse matters—master and servant were related, but this was not the normal situation, only a variation of the usual practice of servants working for social equals who were acquainted with their families. As a rule, servants were young. To put it another way, most young country people were servants. This was true of both boys and girls. They were sometimes as young as eight or nine, although more often they started in their teens, and they were likely to remain servants until they married. To be a servant was a combination of learning, working for a living, and boarding with a family. Servants resembled children in many ways. They took orders and were dependent. They were usually young, but even if they were in their thirties they were not yet full adults because they were not married. The married servant was an anomaly, only slightly less so in the last years of the period.

From the servants' point of view, the condition was full of ambiguities. It imposed restraints and kept them in the inferior position of children, and at its worst it exposed them to physical abuse and sexual exploitation. On the other hand, they were free of the responsibilities and burdens of adulthood. Ideally it was a time for courting, for dreaming of the future, and for saving a nest egg.

It was almost always a temporary condition. In the normal course of events, servants married and left to live on their own. They themselves would eventually have servants, as they would have children who went out to work as servants in other houses. The connection with a particular household was also likely to be temporary. Servants tended to move around a lot during the limited number of years in which they were in service. Variety may have been part of the attractiveness of the life, and they could always look forward to leaving an unpleasant master for a better one. It was also the case in most places that wages—which were regarded as less essential than upkeep—were not paid regularly but only at the end of the period contracted for, and then sometimes only if the contract was not being renewed. A year's contract was common, and there were customary times for hiring, like Michaelmas (September 29, effectively the end of the agricultural year) in much of England. A certain Richard Wood in late-seventeenth-century England moved about Staffordshire and Shropshire in the six years in which he was a servant, never working longer than two years in any one place.[2] A century later Joseph Mayett worked in eleven different places in the course of seven years, never for longer than a year at a time.[3]

The presence of nonrelatives in the household was so routine that there was a tendency to lump live-in relatives with servants. Quite often these relatives were really no different from servants, filling the same slot in the household structure. The situation could be confusing. Some Tuscan householders in the fifteenth century were well aware of this when they tried to pass off servants as foster children or indigent kinfolk in order to convince the tax collector that they were units of consumption and not units of production (which were taxable). The ambiguities were real enough. Poor relations—orphans, widows, old people—were sometimes taken in and given work in return for upkeep, but it was not always necessary work.

There were ambiguities about another category of person who might share the premises. This was the lodger, a person who was not really part of the household in which he slept and ate but who could not be said to have a household of his own. Some lodgers were simply lodgers: they paid for their accommodations and worked outside the household. Ambiguity about lodgers arose in the first place with servants who married. Although not "normal," servants did marry, in some areas more than others. Their work was the same as that of unmarried servants, but since their living accommodations were likely to be a little different—a room or a hut that was clearly theirs—they were sometimes not counted as part of the primary household. There was also an ambiguity about some relatives, who were called "sojourners" or inmates, even if they were quite closely related to the head of the household.

All of this may seem like a terrible confusion about categories, but it reflects a certain logic, in which the functioning of the household existed in a different realm from ideas about kinship. To be incorporated into a household meant to be part of a fairly clear structure of authority and dependency. Ambiguities were inevitable when those who were supposed to be childlike dependents (servants) became married adults or when those who had claims of kinship fitted into exactly the same structural slots as nonrelated servants.

Almost everything about nonrelatives in rural households held true for urban households. Servants were everywhere. They were, for the most part, young and unmarried and they moved about a great deal. But town life had its distinctive features, which became increasingly important as time went on and urban populations grew. For one thing, towns always drew people from the country, and town servants tended to be country people instead of coming from urban neighborhoods. This flow of young people into cities was a fact of preindustrial life that foreshadowed the even greater flow of later times. Urban servants tended to be female, since boys were more likely to stay in the country and do agricultural work. They might very well marry women who worked in towns, however, since the women, regarding servanthood as a temporary, premarital state, usually retained ties with their native villages. A very small urban household was more likely to have no servants than a similarly small rural household that worked the land. For the low- and middle-level urban household the staff often consisted of one maid of all work (like the Pepyses' Jane), although there are references to an ideal "modest" staff of three or four servants.

Households of urban artisans often had a special type of nonrelative living in them: the apprentice. Sometimes called a servant, the apprentice had a place in the household structure analogous to the servant's. In fact, whatever muddled notion we may have of apprentices nowadays probably comes fairly close to the older image of the servant. Apprenticeship placed people in a household-based master-servant, authority-dependency relationship. Apprentices were taken care of like servants, and they also did odd jobs like servants, jobs that often had nothing to do with the crafts they were supposed to be learning. The fact that an apprentice might eventually become a master himself was one of the clearest ways in which he was like the traditional servant. One difference was that an apprentice usually stayed in one place longer than a servant. An apprenticeship contract, almost always drawn up between parent and master, specified a term that usually ranged from three to seven years, depending upon location and craft. If, as sometimes happened, master and apprentice were related, that seems to have had little effect on the arrangements.

As far as we can tell, there were more lodgers in cities than in the country, because of the tendency of unattached people of all ages to flock there. An elderly widow who did handwork for a living was the kind of person who might not have a household of her own. She might be related to the head of the household she lived in and, although she paid rent, be expected to help out with chores. Since it did not always work out that everyone was either in service or established in a household of his or her own, young people in lodgings included unmarried artisans, journeymen who did not live with their masters, very poor day laborers, and the unemployed.

The city households of the wealthy were so different that it is easy to be bedazzled by them and forget that they were only a thin layer at the top of society. Contemporaries were also bedazzled by them and paid inordinate attention to them and their ways. Wealthy households were extremely large in both city and country, and many rich people had at least two residences. Most of the household members were servants. Although, as we have seen, it was not impossible to fill a house with forty-odd relatives, this was rare even in Tuscany. The true mark of wealth was a retinue of servants. If in the seventeenth century the household of an English lord was supposed to contain forty people and that of a truly great *seigneur* in France at least fifty-three, as one writer claimed,[4] an upper-class family (in our modern sense of family) could have been surrounded by several dozen nonrelatives.

The servants of the wealthy were in some respects altogether different from other servants. That is why it is misleading to generalize from their experience, which underwent transformations that may not have taken place in the population as a whole. Wealthy households were distinctive not only in degree but in kind. They were more like wealthy, powerful households in other parts of the world than their modest European neighbors. We all know that the very rich are different from you and me, but in the preindustrial world the rich not only had more money but also were the legally privileged, the lords and masters of the realm. The contrast between privileged and unprivileged, rulers and ruled, was reflected in the relationship between wealthy masters and lower-class servants.

These servants were in the main young and unmarried, who no more thought of their servant status as permanent than did servants in poorer households. On the other hand, their deference to their masters was a compound of their temporary dependency and what was expected of everyone from their background in dealing with the elite. They were usually country folk and they often formed networks to get employment for their relatives and neighbors. Whereas the typical city servant was female, servants in the wealthiest households were often male. To have menservants was a mark of high status. Young men were often chosen for their good looks, since their decorative value was symbolic and highly prized. Hence the handsome young footman, a familiar figure to readers of eighteenth-century literature. Young women apparently were not hired for their decorative value—they wore neither livery nor uniforms—and they were paid less, as women usually were. In the largest and wealthiest households there was a hierarchy within the staff. At the top were servants with special skills and duties, like stewards of estates, receivers of revenues, secretaries, and tutors. These men were often better educated and of higher social origins than the lower staff and were sometimes called "officers."

For ambitious people from the country a lifetime career in the service of a great household was a tempting prospect, since they could bask in reflected glory and might even rise in the household hierarchy.

This was the general situation from 1350 to 1800, but there were some striking changes in the period. Class differences in wealthy households became more pronounced, and "servant" became more and more pejorative. Through the sixteenth century, at least in England and France, the aristocracy practiced a form of lateral transfer. Boys were sent to the homes of the powerful by fathers who were sometimes not much less powerful. These "pages"—the word seems to be of Italian origin and suggests that the system also operated in Italy at one time—were servants in the traditional European sense. They did their masters' bidding, acted with deference toward them, were fed and clothed by them, and left them after a time to become either lords themselves or "officers" of high rank in the households of princes and nobles or in the armed forces. If they entered the courts of rulers, they were, of course, the courtiers. Pages were like apprentices to the craft of gentleman. By the end of the seventeenth century they were becoming an anachronism. So were gentlemen "officers." To be a servant in a great house in the sixteenth century was not at all a mark of low social rank, as the word "yeoman," which originally meant such a servant, indicates. If a man was well-born, it was an occupation with considerable prestige, and for the more lowly born it was an opportunity to rise into the higher ranks. To a well-educated seventeenth-century English gentleman it was still perfectly natural to say that his "best education" was under a wealthy lawyer "with whom I was a servant severall years," explaining elsewhere that he "served him as his Clarke."[5] In the same period the great French chef La Varenne referred to himself as the humble servant of his master, the king. A hundred years later another great chef was reluctant to refer to himself in that way, preferring to regard himself as a professional. At that same time Jean-Jacques Rousseau, ever the herald of new sensibilities, was at pains to point out that although he had worked in a great household and "ate the bread" of his master, he was no mere "valet."[6] Words like "valet," "varlet," and "knave," which originally meant "boy," acquired overtones of contempt as they came to imply a condition of permanent servitude.

The reasons why service in great houses declined in prestige (with the important exception of royal households) are probably to be found in the political developments of these centuries, as great lords lost much of their real power. There was another change of equal importance for which the reasons may be harder to sort out. The wealthy had ambivalent feelings about the lowborn people who served them. On the one hand they loved and protected them, on the other they felt that an insurmountable barrier separated them. There was ambivalence on the part of servants, too, but it took a while to come to the surface. In the eighteenth century Rousseau said confidently that "servanthood is so little natural to man that it cannot exist without some dis-

content," but behind that statement lay a revolution in social and political attitudes, attitudes about the worth of the individual and personal autonomy.
Many of the well-to-do were feeling a new kind of ambivalence. To have servants was desirable, even necessary, for any number of reasons, but there was
also a strong wish not to have them around. They were less and less thought
of as family and more and more as hired help. In listings of households drawn
up by Quakers in London in 1737 and again in 1762, children, servants, and
apprentices were included under the father and mother as constituting the
family unit, but in 1782 the servants and apprentices were omitted.[7] By the
nineteenth century nonrelatives were seen in a different light.

The changes in wealthy households eventually had an effect on how
everyone felt about servants, and industrialization eventually gave young people other things to do, but in 1800 the pattern I have described was still pretty
much in place. There were regional variations, to be sure. In the slave-owning
society of the New World, certain differences were inevitable, but even there
the tradition of apprenticeship flourished, and some lateral transfer of equals
continued to take place in frontier agricultural settlements, even into the nineteenth century, as in the practice of farmers' daughters working as maids until
they married.

A Nuclear Cell or an Extended Hive

Ever since the terms "nuclear family" and "extended family" entered the language they have figured as characters in a kind of morality play. Extended
Family is a bearded patriarch, the representative of the old days, who is confronted by Nuclear Family, a brash upstart or a young hero, depending on how
you feel about it. Sometimes all the virtue resides in one, sometimes in the
other, but Nuclear Family is always represented as modern, Extended Family
as old-fashioned. One of the surprises emerging from recent historical schol-
arship is that this picture turns out to be all wrong.

In the first place, we ought to define what we are talking about. The
nuclear family consists of a mother and father and their children. The term
itself tells us nothing about where they live, how old they are, or who is in
charge. The extended family means all the other relatives, but the definition
of relative is different in different societies. Extended family often includes
affinal relatives, that is, relatives by marriage rather than by blood. The morality play concerns the relatives who live together in a household and not the
nonrelatives who might be living there—the people I discussed in the previous
section. It focuses on the idea that in the past a household usually consisted of
more than a nuclear family and asks: Was that a good or bad thing? Nowadays
we tend to think of good and bad in terms of the benefit to individuals, so if
we bewail the supposed loss of the extended-family household, we imply that
growing up in such a household was good for children and turned them into

large-spirited adults. Those who do not bewail the loss and instead take the side of the nuclear-family household contrast its assumed closeness and affection with the authoritarianism they think was integral to the extended-family household.

Most of us live in nuclear-family households, whether we like it or not. I wonder whether knowing that such households did not come into being as a result of nineteenth-century industrialization but existed long before can reconcile anyone to an arrangement he or she considers narrow and stultifying. It may, however, be useful to realize that whatever ambivalence exists today about household structure probably did not exist in the past, because what was wanted of such arrangements was so different, as we shall see when we look at household activities, child care, and the ideology of the family. If there was ambivalence—we know very little about how people felt—it may reveal itself in the fact that there was a variety of types of households. It seems fairly clear that there were regional differences in the types of households newly married couples were expected to live in. There were also differences in the behavior of rich and poor. Broadly speaking, the poorer you were the more likely you were to live in a nuclear-family household. "Nuclear" and "extended" existed side by side instead of one following the other in a clear chronological progression, as the morality play would have it. There do not seem to have been moral values associated with household structure—certainly not values having to do with child development. Instead, status, economics, and custom were at the bottom of the contrasts and polarities.

The outstanding fact about nuclear-family households is that all through the past in the Western world, no matter where we look or how far back we go in time, they were extremely common. Their preponderance was overwhelming in England, the Low Countries, northern France, and the European colonies in the New World. The very earliest evidence about household structure in England, dated several decades before our starting point of around 1350, suggests that things were similar then. In some other parts of Europe nuclear-family households were less common, but when we take the trouble to count it turns out that even there they made up at least 50 percent of all households. Household structure probably reflected recognized norms, which seem to have been different in northern and southern Europe for those of modest means living off the land. In the north a household was supposed to be centered on a single married couple and headed by the husband or his widow. This structure could be modified by circumstances, such as the presence of an unmarried brother-in-law or an elderly parent, but it was basically what people seem to have expected a household to be like. In the south, where there was an even balance of nuclear-family households and extended-family households, people seem to have expected a household head to preside over more than one nuclear-family unit.

"When thou art married, if it may be, live of thyself with thy wife, in a family of thine own."[8] This advice from seventeenth-century England, which most of us follow today, encapsulates an attitude that helps explain the preponderance of nuclear-family households in northwestern Europe. Every marriage there was regarded as an occasion for establishing a new household. It was assumed that nobody would get married until there was a place for the couple to live and a way for them to have a livelihood. This almost always meant a separate house. The setting up of a new household was a positive step, by which the couple established themselves as adult members of the community. Both the practice and the attitude existed hundreds of years before the first stirrings of the Industrial Revolution. There is some possibility that the norm had an undue influence on census takers and other compilers of lists, who may have grouped people in ideal units instead of in the untidy combinations in which many of them actually lived. For, once past the first years of marriage, it was not easy for a household to keep the neat structure of father-mother-children. One of the parents might die, the children might die or leave, a second husband or wife might arrive, along with stepchildren, and an orphaned niece or nephew might take up residence as a foster child. Change and fluidity were the earmarks of the household in the past. Still, where the nuclear-family household was the norm, the changes always revolved around the nuclear core of one married couple, whether whole or truncated.

In other places the nuclear family appeared not as a norm but as one stage in a household's development. A French mountain village in the eighteenth century provides an example of a particularly speedy transformation from a truncated nuclear-family household to a very complex extended-family household. A certain Gabriel Perrot remarried after his first wife died, and he eventually had five children from his two marriages. Then his second wife died. Thus far he headed a nuclear-family household. He then married for the third time. His new wife was a widow with grown children, two of whom married two of Perrot's children at about the same time (an arrangement that was not so remarkable as it may seem). All these people—three married couples, sisters, brothers, in-laws—lived together in what was about as far from a nuclear-family household as it is possible to get. What happened later we do not know, but it is conceivable that this household one day again assumed a nuclear shape. No matter in what direction a household was going, it would probably pass through a nuclear phase at least once. Wealth had something to do with it. If Perrot had not had a big house and enough land (his third wife may have brought some wealth with her) he would not have been able to expand his household as he did, and so, even in a region where extended-family households were expected, his would have had to remain nuclear. The same series of marriages might have taken place, but each couple would have had to make its own way, presumably in its own little household.[9]

Large numbers of people on all levels of society in preindustrial times grew up in the immediate presence of the same constellation of relatives as their much-later descendants did. What happened to Afro-American slaves illustrates the combined effect of norm and need. Many of them came from societies in which household arrangements were very different from any found in the West, but in America they usually lived in nuclear-family households. The nuclear-family household was the norm that North American masters recognized, but even without this influence the straitened circumstances of slaves may have made it inevitable that they would adopt the simple household structure of poor people in many parts of the world. There is little doubt that owners' business decisions were responsible for the fact that small plantations frequently contained slave households without fathers, which were rarer on large, prosperous plantations.

Although not numerically overwhelming, households with more complex structures certainly did exist in the past. Complexity usually means two or more nuclear families living together—or, in basic terms, two or more married couples with or without their children. The commonest kind of complexity was generational extension, or what is sometimes called the stem family. Where stem families were found, every new couple was not expected to set up a separate household. In its simplest form the stem family worked like this: The son who was slated to inherit the house continued to live with his parents after he married and even after he had children. His sisters and brothers left to live elsewhere or else stayed on, but only as single people. When the father died, the son became the head of the household, and eventually his heir married and lived with him, continuing the pattern. Theoretically, there might be three or more generations living together in a stem family, but the only married couples were the head and his wife and the future head and his wife. In practice, there were rarely more than three generations: grandparents, parents, young children. Furthermore, in the course of its development the stem family would form a nuclear-family household several times. A young child growing up in what was supposed to be a stem-family household was more than likely to be living with just his or her parents and siblings, since the grandparents would no longer be alive, and aunts and uncles, if any, would have moved away. The stem family seems to have been most common in southern France and parts of Germany and Austria. It was a rural pattern, usually associated with a sizeable amount of property and with inheritance of land in one piece. Nowhere was it a universal pattern. In addition to the fact that stem families turned into nuclear families and back again over time, the "stem" was the main line of inheritance, so that the children who were not heirs to the land had to set up nuclear-family households when they married. They would do so even if they inherited land that was not the main piece containing the parental house. There were several variations on the father-son stem pattern, as there would have to be in a world where death took such a heavy toll. The commonest was that in which the heir was a daughter, who stayed in her parents' home after she married. In France this familiar yet irregular arrangement was called "son-in-law marriage" (mariage à gendre). It was the dream of non-inheriting sons to marry heiresses and, as a result, hook into just such a stem-family household.

Another kind of extended-family household appears in Western society from time to time, mostly in Italy and southern France. It is the so-called joint-family or multiple-family household. It is so different from what most of us are familiar with that it tends to excite our imaginations and make us feel that it must be ancient—the most likely contender for the role of Extended Family in the morality play. Joint families may have existed at all times, but they have also arisen in response to specific conditions. In eastern Europe, for instance, it is possible that the large joint-family household came in with serfdom in the seventeenth and eighteenth centuries and was not an institution of great antiquity. In western Europe there was a flowering of joint families in southern France in the fourteenth and fifteenth centuries, then a relative decline. They were extremely rare in northern France, England, and North America, less so in Latin America. Up to 1800 joint families were associated with land, and lots of it. In cities they were rare but invariably associated with great houses, great wealth, and local traditions that looked favorably on such arrangements, as in Genoa and Florence. If the poor extended-family household ever existed to any degree, it was at a later time, that of early industrialization. In England extended-family households increased in number after 1800 and reached a peak in the middle of the twentieth century!

A joint family is laterally extended. It is also often vertically (or generationally) extended, like a stem family. It differs from the stem family in that marriage is not a signal for sons (sometimes not even daughters) to move out. The Tuscan family of forty-seven is an extreme example. At the time of the census in 1427 it contained no fewer than ten married couples belonging to two generations, and there were in addition representatives of an older generation and a younger one—four generations in all. One reason we know quite a bit about such households is that they were often set up by legal contracts. What was set up was a community, sometimes between a father and sons, sometimes among brothers. The latter was called a frérèche in France. With the need that was felt for hierarchy and authority, there was almost always a clause indicating who was the head or chief. In a father-son arrangement it was usually the father, but it was traditional in some places to give equal authority to the father and all the sons at the time they assumed community ownership of the property. When only brothers were involved, sometimes the oldest was in charge, sometimes a head was elected, sometimes all partners were considered equal. Behind these neat-sounding arrangements could lurk great psychological tensions. Communities rarely lasted very long, and the contracts spelled out how the property would be divided when the inevitable breakup came. Apart from the tensions between brothers, there were of course practical limits to how long a family could stay together, continually adding offspring and in-laws. It was almost unheard of for adult cousins to be living together under the same roof.

Note the goings and comings of one prosperous peasant family in the

Upper Provence region of France in the early eighteenth century, its changing patterns, and the obvious capacity of one household to provide work and sustenance for many people. Antoine Collomp had six grown children at the time we hear about him—four sons and two daughters. Three of his sons and his younger daughter lived with him and his wife. Of these, the eldest son was married and had several children, the others were unmarried. The married son lived under an arrangement by which his father, as head of the household, had control over the property the daughter-in-law had brought as her dowry. The son who was no longer at home had married an heiress in the same village and was the head of his own household, working the land his wife had inherited in addition to some land Antoine had given him as his portion when he married. The remaining child, the elder daughter, had married a man from a nearby village and had gone to live there. After a few years the situation in Antoine's house changed (whether because of personal antagonisms or business calculation we do not know). Antoine made his two unmarried sons his joint heirs, and they stayed in the house after they both subsequently married. The eldest son moved out with his wife and children, having been given his independence by Antoine through the gift of a house and land and the transfer to him of his wife's dowry. The younger daughter's actions are not so clear, but it is possible that when she married she and her husband joined the household community, which was on the verge of turning into a frérèche at Antoine's death.[10]

For rural people who were lucky enough to own land or have some kind of customary title to it, providing for family members and preserving family property were evenly matched concerns. Someone like Antoine Collomp, with four living sons, had many options open to him, but it could happen that someone with his kind of property would be childless in his mature years. Some people set up fictitious family communities when they had no biological kin. In an area where it was normal for a sizeable piece of property to be occupied and worked by some kind of community, many kinds of arrangements were possible. Father-in-law and son-in-law might be equal partners in a frérèche, becoming fictitious brothers, and so might two friends who lived together with their wives and children under a similar contractual agreement.

In much of western Europe a household might have two or more married couples in it as a passing phase, not as deliberate policy. The kind of joint-family household that was most likely was one that would not be formally recognized as such. It was composed of fragments of nuclear families. Around the married couple at the core (which would often enough be half a couple) might be, among others, a young brother-in-law or sister-in-law who would have been part of his or her parents' household if the parents had been alive; the child of a dead sister or brother; the widow of an uncle or brother; a child of the husband's first wife's first husband; or a cousin, orphaned or not, working as a servant. Such a household was not likely to be large, and it was in a constant state of transition. If there was an extended family that was typical of the Western past, this was it. Compared to it, the present-day nuclear family is a model of permanence and consistency.

The Elderly: Dependent or Powerful

Part of the mythology of the extended family concerns old people. We think a lot about the old today, and no wonder, since there are now so many of them. Life expectancy has shot up in the past half century, and as a result more and more people are living beyond the time when they are economically productive or even able to look after themselves. Western society in the past, like some societies today still, had no such problem. Individual families may have had elderly parents to deal with, but the situation was likely to be of short duration and atypical. Another difference is that when possession of land was the key to almost everything, an old person with a sizeable piece of land continued to exercise power of a kind unknown to present-day wage-earners forced into retirement. We can romanticize past solutions if we like, but what we are dealing with today is a new problem.

The myth is that old people always lived with their children, were cared for by them, and shared in household activities—the extended family at its nicest. In fact there was not only great variety but considerable ambivalence as well. It was not the same ambivalence as that of the present. We agonize over whether to put our parents in institutions, and if we decide not to keep them at home we guiltily plead the lack of adequate facilities or the superior claims of nuclear-family harmony. In the past the contrast between the treatment of prosperous old people and that of poor old people was greater than it is today. The prosperous were far more likely to live with close relatives. When old people did live with relatives there was ambivalence about authority. As in *King Lear*, there was a conflict between a once-powerful, would-be-still-powerful patriarch and children resentful of prolonged subordination or, seen from the other side, between greedy children and a parent no longer able to protect himself.

The elderly rarely lived anywhere but in households. Although monasteries and convents could function as old-age homes to which persons of means might retire before the Reformation—and a few people of high rank in Catholic countries afterward—they were of minor significance. So the question is what kinds of households old people belonged to and what positions they held in those households. Some old people were the heads of households, others were not. In the eyes of contemporaries this was an important distinction— legally, economically, and emotionally.

Old people who were not heads of households in which they lived with their own children were mainly women. There were many widows and they were not necessarily very old, but that is a relative term, in any case. If a household was headed by a widow's adult—meaning married—child, she was cast in the role of elderly dependent. In the best of circumstances a widow could benefit from customs and laws that gave her back her dowry, let her have the use of a large part of the property that would eventually pass into the hands of her son, and provided her with a decent place to live, often a room in the house that was now under her son's authority. If the children were still young at the time of the father's death, a widow was likely to become the head of the household, but that would change once the heir grew up. His marriage contract became the occasion for spelling out the mother's and son's rights and obligations. Such contracts exude ambivalence. They gush with mutual love and concern on the one hand, but they are minutely specific on the other, leaving little to chance. A son in eighteenth-century Massachusetts, for example, paid his "honored mother" a security deposit as a guaranty that she would be provided for. It was common to list the precise amounts of meat, grain, and firewood that a mother was to be given each year. On one farm in Massachusetts where the mother's rights to one-third of the property (her dower rights under English common law) were being scrupulously observed, a traffic pattern was laid out: "The said widow is to have liberty to pass and repass from the road through the two thirds to her part of the barn yard for driving carts and creatures as there shall be occasion. The barn-floor is to be for the use of each. Joseph [the son] is to have liberty of passing and repassing from the road through the thirds to his part of the house the usual way for driving carts and creatures and other ways as there shall be occasion."[11]

It is reasonable to suppose that these contractual arrangements usually worked fairly well. Once in a while they did not. The yearly provisions were held back or not given in full, in some cases because they were really larger than was necessary for the mother's sustenance and were an economic burden to the son, making him feel that being head of the household was an empty distinction. A mother whose provisions were not so generous might chafe at her unaccustomed subordination, not to mention her displacement by a daughter-in-law. There were undoubtedly resentments on both sides. Though less common, we hear more about unhappy situations involving fathers than we do about those involving mothers. The dependent father was a disturbing image in a society where fathers were thought of as naturally powerful. Fathers became dependents when they were too sick and weak to remain in their own homes, especially if their wives were dead. Sometimes the father in a stem-family arrangement relinquished his control. The first case was bad enough. A very old man in a seventeenth-century English village said of himself that "his wife being dead, and his children grown upp, he now liveth as a sojourner with one of his sonnes"—a sojourner being a lodger, an outsider, a lowered status indeed.[12] The second situation was worse, because presumably the man had brought it on himself. A Scottish verse said he would be better off dead:

> Here is the fair mall [club]
> To give a knock on the skull
> To the man who keeps no gear for himself
> But gives all to his bairns.[13]

Proverbs expressed similar sentiments; "To hand over is no longer to live" and "Do not take your clothes off before you go to sleep."[14] All of this sounds like a complete absence of trust between fathers and sons. It is more likely that considerable anxiety was mingled with affection—which explains why prudent people tried to spell everything out in a contract.

So far I have been talking of people with property, of parents with living children, of households in which a dependent parent could be maintained, and of economic arrangements that were worked out in advance. Not everyone was so fortunate. People without property who worked for others, managing just to scrape by, often became destitute in old age. Even a person who had a little cottage, a tiny plot of land, and a cow barely had the means of self-support. The death of a husband or wife made it particularly hard to eke out a living. The elderly sojourner I just mentioned was better off than other sojourners who lived, not with relatives, but in the households of strangers. This common fate had its share of humiliations. In order to pay for lodgings, a really poor person had to continue working at menial tasks. The village, the parish, the county, or the lord of the manor often helped to pay for the support of the elderly as part of a system of poor relief. Then as now a large percentage of the poor were elderly. Public relief and more or less organized private charity of this sort existed all over the Western world. A common practice was to pay a household to lodge a pauper, who might or might not be a relative. According to English law, the children were supposed to be responsible for "every poor old, blind lame and impotent person," but it almost always happened that such a person became what we call a welfare recipient.[15] Some old people living as nominal heads of their own household were not necessarily better off than these poor lodgers. Their living space was often minimal—a hovel in the country, a garret room in the city—and they were just as likely to be dependent on charity.

At the other extreme were fathers who by virtue of wealth and longevity managed to wield power for many years. Mothers, no matter how wealthy, normally became dependents if they had grown children, but not so fathers. In northern Europe they either kept their unmarried children at home or sent them off to make their way in the world, giving sons sizeable portions on these occasions, just as they gave dowries to their daughters when they married. They remained in possession of house and land until they died and if they managed to avoid decrepitude their authority remained intact. The stem-family arrangement was a perfect example of a father's not only remaining in charge of a household but also getting a lot of help in running it from his son and daughter-in-law (or daughter and son-in-law). The eighteenth-century French writer Restif de la Bretonne described how his father had lived with and worked for his father-in-law for seventeen years. In southern Europe, with its joint-family arrangements, the authority of fathers was even more considerable. There it was not old people who were in a position of dependency but young and middle-aged adults. In fifteenth-century Tuscany, where there was only a fifty-fifty chance that a man and woman would form their own household when they married, the average age of heads of households was over fifty years (at least ten or fifteen years older than in northern Europe).

Between complete authority and utter dependency, between the power of wealth and the powerlessness of poverty, there was another possibility for old people: formal retirement. It is sometimes claimed that retirement was unknown in the past, that people worked until they became totally incapacitated. In one respect this is true. There was no commonly agreed-upon age for retirement, and employees did not get old-age pensions. In towns, craftsmen's guilds and religious confraternities had funds for people in need (that is, members who were too sick to work and members' widows and orphans), but old people received support only if they were also sick or feeble. In the countryside, on the other hand, parents with property frequently worked out retirement contracts with their heirs. These arrangements superficially resembled stem-family households, with the difference that the younger generation was in nominal control. We have already seen what such an arrangement with a widowed mother could be like. We have also seen how potentially dangerous it was to fathers, who were afraid of giving up too much. Most retirement contracts exacted a price from the heir for the privilege of taking over the household before his parents died. The arrangement that King Lear made with his daughters, in which he divided his property and was left with no home of his own, expecting to spend time with each in turn, reflects a very old custom in Scandinavian countries that was based on the principle of proportionality, each heir owing a share of upkeep that corresponded to his or her share of the inheritance. This was not a common custom in western Europe, but behind the more usual European retirement pattern was a similar notion that an heir's obligation was commensurate with what was inherited. It even showed up in New England in the seventeenth century, when there was land enough to go around. One elderly Massachusetts farmer worked out a separate arrangement with each of his sons, and the one who inherited the most took on the additional obligation of supporting his stepmother after the old man died.[16]

Retirees were not necessarily very old. Some could have been tempted by the prospect of having an abled-bodied couple on the premises to take responsibility and do most of the work, but there were probably many reasons why this pattern appeared all over the Western world. Landlords sometimes insisted on it to ensure continued productivity of the land, sometimes (as in eighteenth-century Austria, where young men without property were subject to military conscription) it was a way of helping out a child at a critical moment. And, in response to the grim facts of life, it was a way of getting a distant relative or a nonrelative to take over a son's duties when a couple was left without children. Of course, the amount of property and general economic conditions made a difference. If better opportunities beckoned it was not always possible to get even one's own son to take over a tiny piece of land along with the burden of supporting a parent.

There were wide differences in the amount of control a retired person might retain. At one extreme were the hapless farmers who "kept no gear" for themselves. At the other extreme were the prosperous villagers in southern France who adopted a strategy of holding on to part of the property, with the understanding that they might refuse to pass it on to the designated heir if he did not support them properly. In Austria, where retirement contracts were especially common, a parent might share meals with the rest of the household, but if he or she happened not to like them the heir had to furnish all the where-withal for separate meals, including staples, fresh produce, fuel, and a hearth. A wily old man of extremely modest means in a seventeenth-century English village managed to exact an obligation from his son, in return for possession of his cottage, that he would be completely taken care of as long as he lived, and that the daughter-in-law would continue to be "serviceable" to him even if the son died and she married someone else—an arrangement much more likely if there was a lot of property.[17] In Connecticut at the end of the seventeenth century a farmer and his wife in their seventies claimed in a court case that their two sons had not abided by their promise to provide "carefully and seasonably all things necessary for the sustenance of our ancient parents." The old couple declared the contract nullified and proceeded to take back the land they had given their sons.[18]

Like other people, the old lived alone, with a few strangers, with a married couple (related or unrelated), in huge households and in small ones. They were linked to the other members of the household by ties of affection, by carefully worked out legal obligations, often by extremely tense and ambiguous feelings. Only two generalizations are possible: old people were unlikely to be living in institutions and there were not very many of them.

The shape of households in the past, even the past of five centuries ago, was not radically different from what it is today. The household of relatively few members, with a nuclear family at its core, was familiar to almost everyone. Except for the rich, especially in the more southerly parts of Europe, large multiple-family households were rare. What was different about membership in households of the past was that it was so transient. This is the opposite of what most of us have imagined. Impermanence and discontinuity were common. Structures were ragged rather than neat, the result of constant erosion from death and accretion from remarriage. In addition, there was the presence almost everywhere of nonrelated members who came and went in accordance with the needs and capacities of the house. Who the members were is less important than what they did. Even if household members in the past fitted into a constellation that looked a lot like a modern household, they participated in a very different set of activities.

2

Life in the
Household

We do not think about the household today as something public or economically productive. Home is where you go to get away from the world and to rest from your labors. Even a housewife who feels that she never rests from her labors tends to think that her purpose is to maintain a setting for private activities. Exceptions are considered unusual—for example, the author of this book, who works at home. In the past, and not even the very distant past, it was difficult to separate household activities from other activities. A household was at one and the same time a family's private residence and a place in the public eye. More than any other aspect, the use to which the household is put differentiates the Western family of the present from the Western family of the past.

Every aspect of household life in the past was rife with ambiguities. From how rooms were furnished to what members of the household did in their leisure time, nothing was clearly delimited. The household was multipurpose and multivalent. It has pretty much ceased to be either. By 1800 households in the upper levels of society had already shed some of the household's ambiguities, but for those in the lower ranks of society in the countryside changes were too slight to be noticed. They were more noticeable in large cities, and even more so under the full impact of industrialization, which came well after 1800. The story to be told here is one of continuities and of gradual changes that foreshadowed the later, decisive changes. It is a story of contrasts between rich and poor, although rich and poor households alike had a multiplicity of purposes and values.

Before seeing what household members did, it helps to know something about the physical setting in which they did it. Not exactly a new subject for historical research, the study of the house is being stretched more and more to include the very humblest of habitations. The rest of this chapter deals with the work carried on in households, with the household's ambiguous public-private nature, and, finally, with a miscellany of matters related to the emotional content of household life, the ambivalence of which is suggested by the heading "Duties or Pleasures."

The Comforts of Home or Shelter from the Elements

The plain fact is that before 1800 most houses in the Western world were not very comfortable. Not even the houses of the rich were comfortable by modern standards. By now technology and industrialization have provided an adequate solution to the main problem of housing, how to protect us from cold and wetness. Modern notions of comfort include spaciousness, privacy, and what may be called aesthetic gratification (also known as interior decoration). For most of the period we are looking at, the houses of the poor and the not-so-poor lacked all three, except for a modicum of decorative detail. There was a tremendous contrast between rich houses and poor houses, but the contrast was not complete. The rich, like the poor, did not have privacy during most of the period.

One difficulty in discussing the houses of the past is that it is so hard to imagine them in use. Whether we look at beautifully preserved remains, at ruins, at artful reconstructions, or at plans and drawings, we have to fight the temptation to insert our own lives into those settings. Paradoxically, it is easiest to slip into anachronistic interpretations when there is physical evidence, which always appears so solid and incontrovertible. Old houses adapted to modern living are particularly misleading. A brick-floored room with a large fireplace that is used as a charming dining room today was likely to have had completely different functions, furnishings, and connections with the rest of the house.

The smallness of most rural houses in the past comes as something of a shock. Until 1800 and even after, the poorest country people made do with minimal space. For a long time a house meant little more than four walls and a roof, with no division into rooms, covering a space often no greater than that of a living room in many New York City apartments, to use one basis of comparison—a space of about 24 feet by 15 feet. Extremely low "ceilings"—actual ceilings were rare, since roof beams were exposed—were the rule. Country people tended to think of the house and the one room as synonymous. Called variously the "hall," "salle," and "chamber," the room was also known as the "house" in some parts of England. It remained the heart of the house for centuries. Many cottages of the very poor were eventually divided into two rooms, but the primacy of the main room, the hall, persisted. Those who could afford larger houses built rooms auxiliary to the hall on the same floor or added a "loft" or "chamber" on a second floor. By the eighteenth century, in both Europe and the New World, the typical house of a family that worked its own land and was therefore not on the very lowest social level might measure 50 feet by 24 feet and have a small upper story. There would also be space outside the house, some of it cultivated as a garden, some of it containing one or more outbuildings, perhaps arranged in a courtyard. Local variations were considerable, but interior space was cramped everywhere. European cottagers were not much better off than black slaves in the English colonies in North America. Houses still standing in southern Maryland show that around 1800 each slave family apparently lived in a room that measured 16 feet by 16 feet, sharing the roof with another family in an adjoining room. At about the same time agricultural laborers in England were housed in connected rows of similar tiny cottages.

Houses in cities were not very different. Buildings were sometimes larger because they were used as multiple dwellings. On the Continent the tradition of the urban apartment house is an old one, appearing in larger cities even before 1350. Five- and six-story examples from the sixteenth century are still to be seen in Edinburgh. Space was as cramped as in the country. A typical city house was basically a two-room country house with one of its narrow ends fronting on the street. The front room corresponded to the "hall." The pattern was repeated on the upper floors, with variations in which space was further subdivided or there was only one room to a floor. There was no general rule for dividing up the space among households. Since the really poor lived in only one room as they did in the country, there might be two or three households on a floor. Those who were better off, occupying three rooms or so, often lived on more than one floor, sometimes with the rooms connected to each other by means of a public gallery. Like houses in the country, city houses included outside space, usually located at the back, and it was put to the same uses— garden, storage, privy, and so on. These seemingly chaotic arrangements changed surprisingly little over the years. New houses built on the sites of old ones were fitted into the space in the same old ways, as were sheds and outbuildings, in Paris sometimes tucked into plots as small as 243 square feet.

Most urban dwellings straight through the eighteenth century were a microcosm of the social hierarchy. The vertical order in a single building was in approximately inverse relationship to wealth and social position. The ground floor contained an artisan's household, the second floor the household of a professional or some other reasonably well-off person, and after that one descended the social ladder as one went up the stairs, with the most wretched occupants at the top. The second floor was considered the best location, what the Italians call the *piano nobile*, and its occupant was often the building's owner. Larger and more elegant versions of such buildings erected in Paris and other continental cities in the eighteenth century contained apartments that were as spacious as some prosperous houses.

For those at the very top of the hierarchy separate houses were the rule, houses that twentieth-century Americans without hesitation would call mansions or palaces. What distinguished them in the first place was their size. In the country they were surrounded by open space and by distinctive structures, like walls, moats, dovecotes, and stables—all on a lavish scale. From the fourteenth to the eighteenth century the typical nobleman's house evolved from a fortified castle into a gracious residence, although not all aristocrats were able to live on the same grand scale. Still, to the extent that it was possible, aristocratic houses remained large and imposing. Sometimes their size was more image than reality, since turrets and crenellations continued to be built after they ceased to have any use beyond their martial appearance. Large houses in cities were also castlelike, until the shift to spaciousness and elegance in the eighteenth century.

Rooms did not usually have designated functions. In small houses the single room or the principal one of two rooms—the hall—had to serve many purposes: eating, sleeping, cooking, working, and storage. A principal room meant one with a hearth. The ordinary two-room cottage often had no hearth in the second room, not even a flue that shared the chimney of the principal hearth. The "other" room, although it may have had a name that sounds like a functional description, such as parlor or chamber, was as multipurpose as the hall. The earliest separation of functions was the use of the parlor or chamber for sleeping, but that did not necessarily keep some household members from sleeping in the hall. Urban artisans who lived on the ground floors of multiple dwellings used the front room as a combination workshop and store. A direct opening to the street had a horizontal shutter that could be raised to serve as an awning so that wares could be displayed and sold. In this seemingly specialized space the household nevertheless carried on all its functions except cooking, which was done either in the back room or in a separate building behind the house.

Although the equipment needed for cooking would seem to make the kitchen a likely candidate for the first specialized room, the separate kitchen actually evolved rather slowly. The evolution started in towns. Many Parisian buildings had a clearly designated kitchen, located behind the shop on the ground floor, for use by all the tenants. In the eighteenth century kitchens gradually began to appear in upper-story apartments. In the country the kitchen was, in effect, what was left in the hall after houses became big enough so that all the noncooking activities could be moved to other rooms. The parlor, for example, became the sitting room and dining room, sometimes with the ubiquitous bed in the corner. One moderately well-off French widow at the end of the eighteenth century lived with her two daughters and at least one servant in a house containing three rooms that were described in an inventory as two bedrooms and a room for cooking, eating, and living.[1]

In the earlier centuries the homes of the very wealthy also had multipurpose rooms in which eating, sleeping, and entertainment were indiscriminately mixed. The nobleman's hall was a larger version of the peasant's. Eventually, however, specialization of rooms became one of the differences between rich and poor. Sleeping chambers came first, then dining rooms, then that abundance of special spaces so characteristic of large houses in the late eighteenth century: morning rooms, breakfast rooms, libraries, music rooms, studies, dressing rooms. If an old-fashioned house still had something called a hall, there was often little use left for it other than as an imposing entrance area.

The kinds of rooms usually added on to the principal room, even in a noble house, were not for such elegant purposes. The greatest need was space for work and storage. In a one- or two-room house equipment had to be stored in rooms in which people spent time awake and asleep. In the two-room cottage of John Bevill, an English laborer in the early seventeenth century, the hall contained, in addition to some simple pieces of furniture, a shovel, two sickles, and an ax; in the chamber, along with two beds and two linen chests, were a kneading trough and two rolling pins.[2] Space was needed not only for tools but also for food and other provisions. Local traditions and expediency dictated whether storage rooms were placed on the ground floor, in a separate structure in a courtyard, or on the second floor. The commonest early use of upstairs rooms—which in England were often called lofts—was for the storage of grain and other food, such as apples. The larger the establishment, the more numerous and specialized the storage and service areas. There is a whole array of English words for them: buttery, pantry, larder, dairy, scullery, kitchen. The lean-to of a seventeenth-century house in Plymouth Colony, for example, has been identified as a "scullery" and such objects as a cheese press, a churn, mortars and pestles, agricultural implements, and containers of herbs and spices are now displayed in it.[3]

In the poorest of peasant houses one of its two rooms was sometimes used for animals. In larger houses there would be a barn, sometimes separated, sometimes attached to the main house. One of the signs of wealth was generous space for animals—great stables, for example, kennels, dovecotes, and fishponds. A German prince of the seventeenth century remarked that he wished he could be as well housed as Louis XIV's horses. Louis himself was of course housed at some remove from his horses, but most people were in almost constant contact with their livestock. In towns, too, many people kept chickens, cows, and pigs. In eighteenth-century New York, for example, pigs could be seen on Broadway, the best residential street. Wealthy town houses, like wealthy country houses, had stables. On all social levels much of what may look to us like living space was in fact set aside for animals and objects.

All social groups shared some of the same discomforts. In northern climates no house adequately protected its inhabitants from the elements. The basic construction materials of poor houses could not provide anything like adequate insulation. Most of them were built flimsily of wood, often wood lath in combination with some form of earth or clay, and for centuries they were covered with roofs of thatch. The very cheap and primitive construction of wattle and daub—basically twigs and mud, like the nests of some birds—was so insubstantial that thieves could enter by pushing the walls in. Wattle and daub were not much used after the fifteenth century, but really solid modest country houses did not appear before the eighteenth century except in areas with plentiful supplies of stone. Urban houses were built of the same materials as rural ones, so that until the end of the seventeenth century Paris and London were essentially made of wood. Houses sometimes collapsed for no apparent reason. Stone and brick, the materials used by the well-to-do, were eventually adopted by people of more modest means by the end of the eighteenth century. They were durable and they kept out the wind.

But even solid walls of stone or brick did not give good protection against cold and dampness. Interiors needed to be heated, and preindustrial technology was totally unequal to the task. The only method available to rich and poor alike was the open fire. In the earlier part of the period, and in poor cottages even later, the fire was in a raised open hearth in the center of the room. In spite of its many inconveniences, it may have done a better job of warming people than the later fireplace that was built into a wall and emptied its smoke through a chimney flue. People gathered in front of—or around—the fire because to be a little distance away from it was to feel uncomfortably chilly. That is why everyone wore so much clothing indoors in winter. If domestic comfort includes being able to relax in reasonable warmth while the winter winds blow, it can be said that nobody experienced domestic comfort in preindustrial times. Not only did clothing have to compensate for inadequate heating, but furnishings did as well. In addition to the tapestries and draperies that only the rich could afford, there were the bedsteads that only the very poor lacked. These elaborate constructions were like miniature houses, with a roof overhead and walls made of curtains that could be closed all around. No wonder they were regarded as precious possessions, mentioned in elaborate detail, bedding and all, in marriage contracts and wills. The chief heir got the best bed, and the widow often got the "second-best," as did William Shakespeare's.

The hearth—so important for warming people and for preparing food, a persistent symbol of domesticity and a convenient sign of wealth (tax assessments were sometimes made on the basis of the number of hearths in a house)—was for a long time practically a synonym for "household." It is ironic that something regarded so favorably should have been the source of so much discomfort. Smoke was a constant annoyance and fire an ever-present danger. The openings that were needed to get rid of at least some of the smoke caused drafts. Small houses had tiny windows to keep in the heat, so they were inevitably dark and smoky. There was an endless struggle between burning heat and smoke on the one hand and currents of cold air on the other. Benjamin Franklin's stove, his ingenious answer to the challenge of finding a more efficient way of providing heat, did not appear until 1740 and it was not cheap. The proverb about the burnt child who avoids the fire was undoubtedly based on everyday experience. It was all too easy for a child to get badly burned if a spark from the hearth ignited clothing or the wood of a cradle. Houses frequently caught fire and burned to the ground. In cities whole neighborhoods had to be rebuilt several times because of fires that spread quickly from one wooden structure to another. The Great Fire of London in 1666 was the Western world's largest city's version of what every city experienced.

Fireplaces were dirty as well as dangerous and added to the difficulty of keeping crowded dwellings clean. Some kinds of dirt were unknown in pre-industrial times, but in general the interiors of small country houses were hard to keep clean. As far as we can tell, frequent cleaning was not even attempted. In wealthier households the emphasis was on seasonal or periodic cleaning campaigns, and much of the written advice to housekeepers was about getting rid of vermin in furnishings and in stored clothing and linens. The supply of water was limited. Plentiful amounts of water were not available inside the house, since water had to be drawn from wells in both town and country. A well of one's own was obviously an advantage and was often a feature of the outside space of urban and rural houses, but there were public wells in many villages and urban neighborhoods.

Of plumbing there was only the slightest beginning in the wealthiest homes of the eighteenth century. Indoor privies were found in some large houses fairly early, but generous flushing with water was not one of their characteristics. The outdoor privy was what most people were used to, a structure that shared the space outside the house with the well and other outbuildings. Again, there was almost no difference between town and country. The very poor in the country had to do with even less—perhaps a discreet hole in the garden. What with all this, and the proximity of livestock, we can imagine what houses smelled like. In town the smells were less of a problem than the danger of contagion from unsanitary conditions and overcrowding. It was an easily observable fact that disease was worse and spread more rapidly in towns, a fact underscored by the recurrent outbreaks of plague. The very wealthy could escape to their country houses. Although they endured discomforts most of us would not appreciate, they were mercifully at a distance from the disease-ridden multitudes.

It may be hard to accept, this negative picture of houses in the past, since we have seen paintings of interiors that look not only comfortable but luxurious. Yes, the poor lived in wretched surroundings that barely served as adequate shelter, you may say, but that could not have been true of the middle class and the aristocracy. I have emphasized what life was like for the majority of the population because it is so easy to lose sight of them, but the mighty were also uncomfortable, and for many of the same reasons. The vast amounts of money they spent on their homes went only partly to achieve comfort. Much of it was spent for the symbols of wealth and grandeur. They built huge hearths with elaborately carved mantelpieces, but these hearths were also inadequate and smoky. The chilly walls of lofty halls were covered with rich tapestries, which were impressive to look at but not entirely successful as insulation. A member of Louis XIV's family wrote in her diary, with the merest touch of exaggeration, "At the king's table the wine and water froze in the glasses,"[4] and Madame de Maintenon, complaining that the Sun King refused to put in screens to shield a room from drafts because the room's proportions had to be maintained, remarked, "I must perish symmetrically."[5] The comforts of the rich and powerful were different from the relaxed domestic comforts that came to be valued so highly later. The very shape of chairs tells us that. It was hard to sit comfortably in any of the magnificently carved and upholstered chairs found in prosperous houses before the eighteenth century. The sitter looked impressive, full of dignity and show, dressed in stiff and opulent materials that matched the decor. Indoors or out, appearances alone left no doubt about who was on top of the social scale. A tendency to excess in decorative detail implied there was a lot more where that came from. One of the chief comforts of the rich and powerful was the ability to put on a magnificent display.

By the middle of the eighteenth century the houses of all but the poor were undergoing changes. Some changes were the culmination of a slow development, others seem to have appeared rather suddenly. Though kings still lived in public splendor and many people of modest means continued to carry on their lives in multipurpose rooms, a fairly large number in between tended more and more to have specialized rooms and to safeguard their privacy. New houses were built with rooms clearly designated as kitchens and sleeping chambers. Rooms were set aside for servants, a provision that had been rare earlier. Wealthy people who still felt they needed large rooms for public functions made sure they also had smaller rooms for more intimate gatherings and sometimes even more private rooms for individual use. The back stairs, the bell, and the dumbwaiter were new devices that kept servants out of sight until they were summoned. The pursuit of the aesthetic ideals of classical symmetry profoundly affected the look and shape of all houses. It was an influence that rapidly trickled down in the course of the eighteenth century. More and more farmhouses were built of solid materials like brick and stone; many of these buildings are still in use in the European countryside. They followed a similar symmetrical plan in both England and France, with a center stair-hall and an upper floor. Interior framed staircases, which had been extremely rare, became common, as did well-proportioned rooms and numerous windows made of clear glass. The style is familiar to us as American Colonial, which is still a living tradition. But these houses did not solve all the problems of shelter. It was still possible to "perish symmetrically" from cold, and crowded conditions got worse in towns. What was happening in domestic architecture was analogous to some other changes in the family in the eighteenth century, particularly among the rich and the moderately prosperous. They were adopting different notions of home life from those that had prevailed earlier. Surviving eighteenth-century *hôtels* in Paris and Georgian mansions in London tell us that grandeur and public display had certainly not disappeared, but formality of design was being made a little more compatible with a less ceremonial way of life.

Running the House or Making a Living

Consider the family farm. It seems to be slowly disappearing in the United States as agriculture becomes an economic enterprise separated from the household, like other kinds of work, but in the rest of the world the term "family farm" can still be applied to a large number of households. In the past it was the typical household in the Western world. On a family farm it is hard to separate the work of running the house from the work of the farm business. Although technology is making itself felt even in small-scale agriculture, the farmhouse is still a workplace and the people who live in the house work in it and for it. The farmer's wife is a special kind of housewife, very much like her preindustrial counterpart.

We twentieth-century, mostly urban, outsiders feel a certain ambivalence about a way of life that confounds and intermingles functions that for us are clearly distinct. For most people in the past there was no separation between producers and consumers or between places of production and places of consumption. Not only did many people consume what they themselves produced, but even those at the very top of the social scale, those whom we today tend to regard as consumers par excellence, lived in households in which production was as important as consumption.

There was almost no change in this respect in rural households up to the very end of the 450-year span we are considering. As early as the sixteenth century some very wealthy country homes were being slowly transformed into bucolic retreats for people who were mainly city-dwellers. It was in the cities that change was most apparent. City people were always more dependent on the production of others for their basic food supply, and there was a slow but steady shift from production to consumption even in lower-class urban households. Some of the rural wealthy had a long tradition of consuming in town what they produced in the country. The urban pattern has eventually come to dominate Western society, the culmination of the double process of urbanization and industrialization.

Making a living for some meant literally consuming what the household produced. For others it meant producing for a market, sometimes "producing" not goods but services. Running the house, a matter of secondary importance to most, chiefly meant some degree of maintenance of the premises and the preparation of meals. For a few households at the very top of the hierarchy, however, running the house, in this sense, was of primary importance and overshadowed everything else.

It was widely assumed that if you lived in the country and had not acquired luxurious tastes you could be self-sufficient. Many rural households attempted to be just that. They grew their own food, cut wood for fuel, and made their own tools and clothing from materials cultivated or at hand. All the members of the household did this work of production. Although there were different regional traditions as to what constituted man's work, woman's work, and child's work, there was practically no distinction between inside work and outside work. And, in general, servants did what other household members of the same age and sex did. Not only was it necessary to plant and harvest food crops, but equal effort had to go into preparing them for use. Hence the space given over to the storage and threshing of grain, cheesemaking, brewing, wine-making and cider-making, the smoking of meat, and the preserving and pickling of garden stuff. Complete self-sufficiency of this ideal sort was rarely achieved, and in any case was more like bare subsistence, partly because most households had so little land at their disposal. The degree of self-sufficiency for a large percentage of the population nevertheless remained high. Urban households also lived on what they produced, to a degree hard to imagine today. Ordinary houses in most towns had gardens, in which staple vegetables like cabbages and onions were grown, and sheds that housed animals like cows, pigs, and chickens. Like country people, townspeople had to spend time caring for all this "agricultural" production and preparing it for use. The disadvantages of living alone, especially for men, are all too apparent when seen in the light of what households were expected to provide for themselves.

Higher up the social scale the situation was remarkably similar, except that there was more of everything and most of the work was done by servants. Nobles, too, lived off the land. As time went on they tended more and more to collect money rents, but an older pattern persisted in which tenants paid in kind, delivering set amounts of grain and other produce to their landlords. Crops were also produced on land that nobles held directly. The noble household therefore functioned in large part as a huge warehouse and granary, and also as a processing center. It was just another rural household, in other words, but on a grand scale. The yearly routine of the greatest lords was for a long time dominated by a round of visits to their various estates in order to consume the production of each on the spot. Hence also the seasonal movements of royal courts from castle to castle, which happened to have public-relations and political benefits as well. The lord himself may have been at one or two removes from the actual labor, but he usually gave some attention to supervising his staff or consulting with a steward or majordomo. Noblewomen were engaged in preserving food, fabricating textiles and clothing, and preparing beverages, just like peasant women. Like the noblemen, they were often at one or two removes from the actual labor, although it was considered appropriate for an upper-class woman to do some kinds of manual work, like sewing and embroidery, and some kinds of food preparation, like the decoction of cordials. Southern plantations in the New World were run like these Old World establishments.

Although a large proportion of the population lived off the land—or, rather, scrounged for a living on a modicum of land—this was not the whole purpose of agriculture then, as it surely is not today. Any moderately well-off peasant had some kind of marketable crop, and this set him off from the land-less laborer or the cottager with a meager acre. From the point of view of life in the household, however, there was little difference between producing for subsistence and producing for a market. The manpower—or womanpower—always came from the household, which was, as we have seen, not necessarily made up of kin. Wives helped their husbands in the fields, and field work was common for peasant daughters, maids, and, in the New World, female slaves. Wives produced cheese for sale or worked alongside their husbands in larger-scale cheesemaking in cattle-raising areas. The size of the house and of the household was of course related to the scale of production. Large extended-family households were found where there was a lot of land, and usually where there was an important cash crop, like wheat or olives. In England, with its different traditions, a similarly large piece of land was likely to be worked by a household with a large number of servants.

The market for which most farmers produced was a weekly assemblage of stalls in a nearby town, with no benefit of wholesaler or other middleman. As often as not, wives were the ones who went to market. There were certain agricultural products that town dwellers could not do without but could not possibly produce for themselves in their little gardens and outbuildings. These were not, as our own experience would lead us to believe, dairy products, eggs, or meat, but, rather, the products that formed the foundation of Western com-merce before the industrial age—grain and wool. Grain was used for bread, which was the staple food, and wool was used for clothing. Already in the fifteenth century there was an international market in grain and wool, and the textile trade especially was responsible for the growth of important urban cen-ters like Florence, Bruges, and London. But much commerce remained local for a long time. The flour a baker in a provincial town used for his bread was likely to have been bought at a market stall from a woman who had helped to harvest the wheat and who may have brought it herself to the miller in her village for grinding.

The urban craftsman's household shows most clearly that the mere exis-tence of a cash economy had little influence on household functions. However professional a craftsman might be, however established in his trade as a skillful shoemaker, potter, tinsmith, or printer, he worked at home. His wife and chil-dren sometimes helped him and sometimes worked at those other things that kept a household going, like tending the garden, feeding the chickens, fetching water, making the fire, and cooking. If he had an apprentice or journeyman, that household member did a similar variety of jobs. Eating, sleeping, selling, working—sometimes at messy and noisome tasks—all took place in that one room that opened on to the street. To be better off meant only that there was an extra room or two for sleeping or storage.

Although full-time, top-quality craftsmen usually lived in towns and

formed the backbone of urban economic life together with their social superiors, the merchants, there were plenty of part-time craftsmen in the countryside. In their households production for home consumption and production for
sale overlapped. It hardly mattered whether a man called himself a farmer or
a blacksmith, for example, since many a farmer also did blacksmithing because
he could not make a living from his land alone and every village blacksmith
grew at least some of his own food.

There have been various estimates of the acreage needed for subsistence
before the Agricultural Revolution. Between thirty and fifty acres offered the
possibility of an occasional surplus, while ten acres was an absolute minimum.
Much depended on the quality of the land, of course. The hard fact is that
most holdings were under ten acres. Vast numbers of people had only one or
two acres, and perhaps half the rural population had no land at all. Things were
much better in the New World, something that accounts for a number of differences between European and American families in those times.

Most "family farms" of the past were the most mixed of enterprises. Many
country people set themselves up as independent craftsmen, providing iron-
work, carpentry, barrels, and beer for their fellow villagers. A housewife, using
the household as her base, might go into the business of brewing and selling
beer, or might earn something from her services as a midwife, and many poor
peasant women added to household income by selling a service that only a
married woman could legitimately provide: they became wet nurses. This
almost always meant having the infants live with them while they continued
to perform their other household tasks.

A large number of country people did piecework controlled by urban
entrepreneurs. The spinning wheel and weaver's loom, familiar features of
country houses, were used at least as much to earn money as to provide clothing for the household. The putting-out system, in which merchants in the
cloth trade provided the raw materials and paid for whatever degree of processing the rural household supplied—usually spinning, carding, or weaving—
operated in several parts of Europe from the fourteenth century onward. In
what is sometimes referred to as cottage industry it made almost no difference
who did the work. The household, in the person of its head, got the payment,
and everyone, even small children, contributed what he or she could. In a typical little village in northern France in the seventeenth century, 20 to 50 percent of the households were engaged primarily in the weaving of woolen and
linen cloth. They were *rural* households and, like their counterparts in the
Netherlands, Italy, and England, were engaged in agricultural tasks as well.
Early industrialization closely resembled this pattern. In the eighteenth century machines for frame knitting, for example, were at first located in workers'
houses in the Leicestershire countryside, and whole families worked on
them.

For those not comfortably perched at the top of the social pyramid it was
difficult to keep a household going in either country or town. The country had

an advantage because there were often things to be gathered, scavenged, and gleaned in woodlands or harvested fields, and there might be a common meadow in which a cow could graze; eking out a living was always precarious.

Exceptions to the rule that all work was household work were rare, even in the so-called middle class. Businessmen and professionals usually worked at home, as a few doctors still do today. There was no distinction between business premises and residential premises, even though the more well-to-do were able to keep parts of the house for private family use. The House of Rothschild was, in its eighteenth-century beginning, literally Meyer Rothschild's house in Frankfort, as four centuries earlier the Medici palace in Florence had been the base of a financial empire. It took a long time for cities to acquire their present division into residential and business districts; the process had barely begun by 1800. A mere handful of people on all levels of society went out to work. Sometimes they worked in someone else's home, although the general rule was that if you worked in a home you also lived there. Exceptions were government offices (originally part of royal households), already proliferating in the sixteenth and seventeenth centuries, and specialized settings like law courts. When a preindustrial merchant went "out" to work, he was either going on a journey to buy and sell or was on his way to a public square or a coffeehouse to deal with other businessmen. Economic life in these centuries could be quite complex and sophisticated, but it tended to operate from a domestic base.

Then what of housekeeping per se? The word did not have the restrictive meaning we give it. It was as common to refer to a man's housekeeping as a woman's, since it meant the undifferentiated mass of household concerns, especially those of a large establishment. The "house" in "housewife" originally paralleled the "hus" in "husband" and was a description of status rather than function. A housewife's duties, as we have seen, were manifold. In what was probably a minimal regimen of maintenance and repair, men would also have played a part. The cult of housecleaning was a late development, about whose beginnings we do not know a great deal. It may have been related to the eighteenth-century cult of domesticity in the upper classes. It is hard to believe that the large elegant houses of the rich in the eighteenth century were not constantly being swept, washed, and polished, but those activities were not mentioned among the duties of servants in writings of the period. Servants attended to the personal needs of their masters and mistresses, including dressing them and waiting on them at table. Servants were also on public display, visible extensions of the grandeur and elegance of the house itself. The members of that true leisure class at the top of the social pyramid, those who theoretically did no work, left the productive aspects of the household behind on their country estates. Their great town houses were primarily centers of consumption, where housekeeping was equated with keeping the place looking as grand as possible and providing sumptuous entertainment. It was consumption that the master and mistress presided over, as, on a much smaller scale, most urban householders do today.

A Private Place or a Public Institution

In our time the household is a private place. It lets in the outside world only when we choose to open our doors, usually on social occasions. The housewife in particular is thought of as spending her time in a private world, while her husband goes out to deal with the public world. To say that this distinction was unknown in the centuries we are looking at would be an overstatement. In certain places, especially at the top of the social scale, women were supposed to stay at home and remain shut off from public contact. But reality seems to have fallen short of any such ideal. For most households their great range of activities made it impossible to be cut off from the rest of society.

The way households interacted with each other inevitably reflected the structures and institutions of society. About our own time, especially in the United States, we can say that when a household interacts with a community—whether neighborhood, church, or government—it does so by choice. I am not speaking of obeying laws or paying taxes. I mean that nobody has to be a good neighbor or a member of the PTA or the Republican party, even if strong pressures are sometimes applied. Indeed, the pressures are less on households than on individuals. Furthermore, the interdependence necessary to keep society functioning physically is experienced most often as impersonal pipes and wires that feed into separate households. We push buttons, flick switches, and turn taps, easily deluded into feeling that the house is self-contained. Isolation is to many people a desirable feature in a house; "quiet" and "seclusion" are stock terms in the houseseller's vocabulary. By contrast, most of the activities carried on in households of the past had day-to-day links with larger communities of several sorts.

The rural household of moderate means was usually part of an estate or manor. Most land in Europe was owned by wealthy families and institutions, especially religious ones, and most of the people who worked the land did not own it, so our rural householder was almost surely a tenant of some sort. His relationship to the owner of the land could take any of a number of forms that changed slowly throughout the period. In the fourteenth and fifteenth centuries serfdom, with its unfree status and labor obligations, persisted in a few places, but there was a steady progression toward money rents and sharecropping. Whatever the household produced, some of it was earmarked for the owner of the estate. Either part of the actual crop was delivered to the landlord's storehouses on set occasions, or part of the proceeds from the sale of what the household produced was paid as rent.

For a long time the connection between lord and tenant was much more than a cash nexus. In many places the lord had a say in what crops were produced. Tenants might be obliged to work a certain number of days a year on the demesne, the land the lord kept for himself, and it was common to have tenants help bring in the harvest on demesne land. In France the owner of such necessary equipment as the grain mill and the baker's oven was usually the lord, who exacted a fee for their use. In some ways the owner of the land made his presence felt even more intimately. His approval was often needed for a marriage, especially if it meant that someone was going to move off the estate. "Approval" was often obtained by a payment, called *formariage* in French. Above all, the owner could not be overlooked when the head of the tenant's household died. By law or custom or economic pressure the lord had considerable control over the transfer of the holding, and it was not unknown for a lord to press a widow to remarry so that the land could be adequately worked.

A farm household worked in conjunction with neighboring households. The oldest and most pervasive rural organization in western Europe was the village. A typical household did not live in an isolated building surrounded by fields but in close proximity to other households, gathered in a cluster. The fields lay spread out beyond this cluster and were worked more or less in common. The system of open fields lasted in many places through the eighteenth century, and was the way agriculture was organized by the first settlers of New England. Open fields called for the antithesis of individualistic enterprise. Decisions about which fields to sow and which to leave fallow, when to plant various crops, and when to harvest were group decisions. An individual villager held strips of land scattered throughout the fields and was constantly coordinating his actions with those of his fellow villagers. Meadows and forests were often held in common, with everyone having an equal right to graze animals and gather nuts, fruit, and wood. There was sometimes a communal shepherd or cowherd. Life in rural England over these centuries was punctuated by events arising out of conflicts between the interests of landlords and the interests of villagers. For example, a lord would take over common grazing land for his own use, putting a fence around it so he could raise his own sheep for the profitable international wool trade. This upset the village economy, cutting into the productivity of moderately prosperous tenants and making life difficult for the great numbers of landless and land-poor country folk who were used to scrounging, gleaning, and foraging. The records of enclosures throw light on the underlying communalism in which the majority of rural European households participated. The village as neighborhood was more important to a rural household than an urban neighborhood was to a town-dweller.

There were exceptions to the village pattern. In some parts of Europe, especially where tillage was less important than the raising of livestock, farmhouses were more isolated or were grouped in tiny hamlets. Households like these were isolated in other ways, too. Because they tended to own their land instead of renting it, they were free of a landlord's control. In many cases, the land had originally been on the outskirts of settled communities and had been cleared by individuals. The pattern was repeated in seventeenth-century New England. There villages continued to exist and to maintain some common lands and common services, but since there were no great landlords and land was plentiful, even the moderately ambitious were able to carve out new territories over which they themselves had total control. The open-field system quickly disappeared in North America.

Most households in the past were not isolated. The peasant in Provence was isolated from the peasant in Scotland, just as he was isolated from the fisherman in Marseilles, but he knew all the people in his own village and they all knew a lot about him and his family. More of everyday life than its economic side was experienced communally. Village and parish were usually coterminous, and the symbol of the parish was of course the parish church. It was not only a place where the community participated in activities that could be called religious, like christenings, weddings, and funerals, but it also served as an assembly hall when community business of a secular nature was conducted and as a community refuge in times of war and natural disaster. It was not uncommon for the seating arrangement in the parish church to be a direct mirror of the social organization of the village. Households sat together, with the wealthiest and most powerful families occupying the best pews in front. As an English court decision put it, "a pew or seat does not belong to a person or to land, but to an house."[6] A meeting of villagers was usually a meeting of household heads and did not necessarily exclude women, who often headed households. The decisions made by the parish assembly may have been of less than earthshaking importance, but they were made by all the households and impinged on all of them. What went on in households tended to be everyone's business. The parish often assumed the burden of caring for the poor and the sick. It also cared about sexual morality and marital behavior. Snooping and rumor-mongering were taken for granted. Rumors of informal betrothal arrangements, premarital sexual relations, and adultery could lead to hearings before church courts, which had the power to fine, reprimand, and humiliate. To scandalize one's neighbors was a serious offense in church courts, and rumor was often accepted as evidence.

Urban neighborhoods had more diversity of interests and more mobility, but urban households were as exposed to public view as rural ones were, more so in the case of artisans living in ground-floor shops. Customers were constantly looking in or coming inside to place orders or be measured and fitted. Public access was a sign of prosperity rather than of poverty. Few bothered to climb several flights of stairs to look in on an impoverished laborer's quarters, but in the homes of middle-class businessmen and professionals there was a constant stream of customers, clients, patients, and other visitors.

The huge households at the top of the social scale were perhaps the most public of all. The servants at the entrance might keep some people out, but that was not their most important function. They were there to be seen, dressed in the livery of the house and serving as living symbols of the house's wealth and power. Receiving ceremonial courtesy calls of a kind we now associate with international diplomacy was a regular part of life in an upper-class household. In addition there were clients—the retinue of hangers-on that loomed so large in the perception of a household's importance—and suppliants, asking for a whole gamut of favors that only the powerful and well-connected could grant. Artisans and shopkeepers brought their wares to the houses of the great, who bought at home from people who, as we have seen, used their own homes to sell to lesser folk. Among the wares brought to great households were works of art. Dancing attendance on a patron was one of an artist's occupations, as Samuel Johnson's famous letter to Lord Chesterfield reminds us ("Seven years, my Lord, have now past since I waited in your outward rooms, or was repulsed from your door"[7]). Life in a royal household was especially public—something that will come as no surprise to a tourist who has seen the royal bedrooms at Versailles, the settings for the ceremonies of the *levée* and the *couchée*.

Not everyone lived in a fishbowl. For all the interactions of village life, the actual premises of peasant households were not particularly open, and as early as the fifteenth century rich people set aside private spaces within their generally public establishments. It is easy to believe that communities in town were not as closely knit as those in villages, because so many town-dwellers were newcomers, recent immigrants from the country. There was, however, considerable moving around in the countryside as well, not only by servants going from job to job but also by households that broke up or settled in other villages on larger or smaller properties acquired by purchase or inheritance. The permanence and inflexibility of village populations are part of the Western mythology about tradition. In fact, poorer people were less likely than richer people to stay put, in both town and country, and so less likely to feel the impact of communal life. Some peasants living in woodland hamlets, like those in Brittany, had never been part of a system of communal agriculture; a government official in 1750 complained that they would never agree to gather all their sheep into one flock and share the expense of a single shepherd.[8] The open-field system, which passed so quickly from the scene in New England, was on its way out everywhere. By 1800 the process had gone pretty far, although more time and the impetus of legal changes like the parliamentary enclosure acts in England and the abolition of church lands in France were still needed to make most rural households into private owners.

The transformation of the household into a private place happened most quickly where households ceased to be producers, yet even where their economic function did not change, a number of forces were pulling households in the direction of greater separation and seclusion. Religion was one of them. The village church had a narrower allegiance in places where some of the inhabitants belonged to nonconformist sects. Those sects themselves often worshiped, not in public, but privately in households. Even among establishment Catholics and Protestants there was a vogue for family prayers, which contributed a private spiritual dimension to household life. Among the wealthy, who could afford both a country house and a town house, there was a feeling that the country house could be a place to escape to for pleasure and recreation, freed of the pressures of public life. Country estates were in fact at least as busy and productive—and in touch with the outside world of the local community and the markets beyond—as any town house. Still, the urge to retreat was a feeling that was cultivated. The home as a place for the nurturing of individual spiritual fulfillment and personal relationships was an idea that fitted right into a new complex of ideas called Romanticism.

Duties or Pleasures

The duties imposed on household members nowadays are relatively few, if we except the duty to earn money for its upkeep (which almost always takes place away from the household). The most serious business in present-day households is bringing up children, which is considered a solemn obligation indeed. Yet even where children are concerned, a lot takes place outside the household; home is where children relax and enjoy themselves. This is merely to restate what we know: home is more a place of leisure than of work. What work there is falls disproportionately on one person—the wife and mother—who herself is likely to say that she "doesn't work" (except when referring to an outside job) and who tries to make the house a pleasant place "to come home to."

Since people in the past spent most of their time in the household, it was the setting for all of life's complexities and was therefore shot through with emotional ambivalence. The relationship between the "duty" side of household life and its other side is as good a way as any to get at the inner life of people in the past. It is, however, not so easy to separate the realm of the personal and the recreational from that of work.

Both the physical conditions in houses and the lines of authority in household organization fostered a tension between intimacy and distance. Most people lived in extremely close quarters and slept in close proximity to each other. Sharing a bed with a relative was routine, just as it was routine to share a bed with a stranger at an inn. The very wealthy might sleep alone, but they often had a servant in the room or right outside the door, ready to share in the intimate activities of getting out of bed, bathing, and dressing.

Modern readers are often shocked when they read about how people exposed themselves to their servants, seeming either to feel no shame or, by their disdain, to obliterate the servants' humanity. To some extent beliefs about social status erected barriers to intimacy. Sometimes a deep intimacy did develop between master and servant, perhaps more often between mistress and maidservant. It is hard to put one's finger on the exact nature of this intimacy, but, if literary examples mean anything, it could include sympathy, frankness, and loyalty on both sides. Shakespeare's fools and Molière's menservants and maidservants may have had sharper tongues than their real-life counterparts, but they fitted a familiar set of expectations. The one element that was absent was what some of us would consider essential for intimacy: equality. The servant was always a dependent and often of a different class. In literary works the blunt clearsightedness of servants is sometimes indistinguishable from the coarseness of the lowborn in general. The distrust and contempt that go with inequality seem to have cut both ways. Masters and mistresses liked to let their hair down with servants, but there were times when they wanted to keep servants out of their hair. Servants for their part might admire and respect their masters, but in varying degrees they also despised them for the failings they witnessed and the inability of the privileged to take care of themselves. Beaumarchais's Figaro, a famous literary servant, is less ambivalent than most. He comes late in the period and embodies a relatively new view of the comparable worth of common people and aristocrats, seeing little that is positive in the latter.

Inside more modest households there were other barriers to intimacy. Literature and correspondence offer hints that people behaved less formally at home than in other places, yet everyone seems to have had a strong sense of hierarchical structure, of a correct place for everyone. It was not only servants who were dependent, inferior, and obliged to obey masters. All the occupants of the household, including the mistress, were subservient to its head.

Sometimes close quarters and bed-sharing led to illicit sexual intimacy, but it does not seem to have been common. Physical place may have been promiscuous, but psychological place was apparently fairly rigid. It is almost impossible to say anything factual about the incidence of illicit sexual relations among close relatives in any period, let alone the undocumented centuries we are looking at, but it is safe to say that when this kind of incest occurred it was regarded as intolerable. Sexual intimacy between servants was more easily tolerated, even if officially disapproved of, and the sexual exploitation of female servants by masters was fairly widespread. Whether such a relationship constituted "intimacy" is open to question. The fact that bed-sharing was so routine and so public may partly explain puzzling customs like bundling. To permit a courting couple to get into bed together in a society in which premarital sexuality was officially discouraged makes no sense unless they were not necessarily compromised.

The tensions in households sometimes became unbearable. A belief in order and authority could not prevent family quarrels from flaring up, and the language used in those quarrels was drenched in resentment. This is familiar stuff: antagonism between kings and their sons and the rivalries of brothers that we read about in history books and Shakespeare's history plays. Whether it was the same lower down on the social scale, where the head of the household ruled over a meager patrimony, we do not really know. Without servants and without property, a "master" had little to ground his authority on, in spite of received opinions about paternal power, but no one can say for sure that poor households were warmer and more egalitarian. Then as now many murders were committed within households on all social levels, a fact that argues for a certain changelessness.

Something that has changed is the notion of leisure, which people in the past had little conception of. Most activity was multivalent in nature—and was reflected in the multiple functions of rooms. People undoubtedly had fun doing some things and preferred certain activities over other, but no chunks of "leisure time" were set aside. Both inside and outside the household fun and games had a way of being intertwined with serious functions. For a long time, for example, theater and festivals were connected with religious celebrations.

A few enjoyable, nonwork activities took place in the household, but, especially for poorer people, having a good time meant getting out of the house, if only to go to a tavern. Elaborate descriptions have come down to us of public celebrations that were occasions of great enjoyment—not only processions and carnivals and fairs but also, as we shall see, weddings, usually held out of doors in public places. The difference between rich and poor was considerable. The rich had more space, more time, and much more artificial light with which to make use of the evening hours at home. In most rural households the only season of the year in which the days were not full of unremitting toil was winter. There is an idealized image of the peasant family sitting in front of the fire, telling stories, playing games, and singing songs, but it appears that winter evenings were often spent in larger spaces, like barns, joining neighbors in group activities. Spinning was one of them. Women chatted with each other while they spun, and it was recognized as an occasion for young men to drop by and court single women. Whatever you call this, it is neither purely leisure nor purely a household activity. When people did sit in front of their winter fires they were often busy doing something useful. An English book of advice to husbandmen recommended that this time, "when the husband sitteth by the fire and hath nothing to do,"[9] be used to repair tools or make new equipment.

Meals were a source of some pleasure, but they were often rudimentary and bleak for the poor and a reminder of hierarchical arrangements for everyone. The staple food was bread, of which peasants ate large quantities (when they could). Meat was for special occasions, that is, Sundays and holidays. Sitting down together for a formal meal may have been almost as rare as eating meat. There are no descriptions of peasant meals before the eighteenth century, when it would seem that they were silent occasions in which people sat according to age and rank, sometimes with females sitting apart after serving the men. Only the master of the house was supposed to perform the ritual of cutting the bread. Servants and lodgers were of course included in such common meals—in their place. In very wealthy households the ritual of mealtimes could be extremely elaborate. In the earlier centuries books of etiquette were full of instructions for setting out food and implements with proper regard for rank. Seating reflected social position and relationship to the household head. There were changes in mealtime behavior during these centuries. Upper-class men and women began to sit all around the table, instead of just on one side, although everyone was still arranged in relation to the "head." Separate dining rooms became more and more common in the houses of the well-to-do, and of the moderately well-off as well, who had never made eating quite such a public ceremony.

Prayers, storytelling, and music were household activities. It was not only in Protestant countries that masters read from the Scriptures or recited a prayer at the end of the day in the presence of the assembled household; this was done everywhere after the Reformation, and was a reminder of the master's fatherly role. In many cases it must have been a duty that was pleasant and comforting for all concerned, though some literary accounts emphasize its coercive and joyless aspects. Exactly how storytelling was done in poorer households we do not know—for instance, whether everyone participated or just older women and young children. Some writers said they were frightened by these old wives' tales when they were little, and it has recently been shown that the versions in Perrault and the Grimm brothers were considerably toned down from what was recited by country folk. Frightening or not, stories were probably a welcome diversion, even among the upper classes. Solitary, silent reading did not take hold until printing had been around a long time. A book, whether printed or in manuscript, was a relative rarity and was meant to be read aloud. Chivalric romances like the *Morte d'Arthur* and *Amadis of Gaul* were the sixteenth- and seventeenth-century equivalent of present-day television, with the big difference that most households were too poor to own books. Literacy itself was a relative luxury.

Something similar can be said of music-making. We know little of the singing and playing in peasant households. Peasant music was often associated with public events, like weddings and village festivals. Wealthier people, on the other hand, seem to have had a lot of music in the home. Printed music was for a long time intended mainly for amateur musicians, and we know that some families sang and played together. How everyday an event this was we do not know, however, and it should be added that for some wealthy people music in the home meant having servants who could perform it.

Hunting, the favorite diversion of the upper classes, until rather recently had an important practical side, since it added to the household food supply in the form of venison, boar, partridge, and quail. In many places there was an ongoing conflict between lords and tenants over hunting—and fishing, too. Poor people also liked to hunt, and when they got a chance to speak about it they claimed that it was a necessity for them, which the lords were morally and legally wrong to restrict. Historians have long been aware of this issue of poaching, but it is not often discussed in the context of household activities.

The sheltering, feeding, and entertaining of guests—in short, hospitality—clearly involved both an element of duty and an element of pleasure. About the hospitality of the poor we know next to nothing, except that limited facilities would have set limits. Like the winter-evening recreation that often took place outside of individual halls and parlors, overnight shelter for strangers was likely to be provided outside the regular living quarters, in the barn or stable. But for the prosperous, and especially for the very prosperous, hospitality was at the heart of the whole notion of running a household. The tomb of an English aristocrat in the early eighteenth century summed up his virtues as follows: "A Generous NEIGHBOUR, An Hospitable ENTERTAINER of his FRIENDS at his TABLE, And a Constant Reliever of the POOR at his GATES."[10] Hospitality meant both generosity to the poor and good cheer for one's friends. Having a good time with friends and impressing equals and superiors may have been more agreeable than taking care of peasants and paupers, but the charitable aspect of hospitality was universally held to be an essential ingredient in the good reputation of a household head. There are numerous hyperbolic accounts of the daily "open table" of some aristocrats. A Scotsman in the early seventeenth century was said to have "thirty, forty, fifty servants, or perhaps more, every day relieving three or foure score poor people at his gate: and besides all this, can give noble entertainment for foure or five days together, to five or sixe Earles and Lords, besides Knights, Gentlemen, and their followers."[11] An eighteenth-century French aristocrat claimed that entertainment on this scale was obligatory for a man of his station, and so he had a staff of fifty-four liveried servants and a table permanently set for thirty-five to fifty diners.[12] Looking back from the vantage point of post-Revolution France, Madame de Genlis said that a great lord of the ancien régime wanted nothing more than to be able to give his friends theater seats, luxurious lodging, and lavish meals and also have plenty left over for the proverbial poor at the gate.[13]

The fact that the poor were always said to be "at the gate" gives an idea of how close they got. The public character of households diminished somewhat in the course of these centuries, but the tradition of letting down the barriers in periodic bursts of hospitality persisted for a long time at the top of the social hierarchy, sometimes radiating an anachronistic charm in a period when classic restraint was supposed to be the ideal. In the year 1799 the duke of Rutland still thought it appropriate to celebrate his birthday with such a burst, in three tiers: a ball for the local aristocracy in the upper chambers of the house, a dinner for the tenants in the hall (it was an old-fashioned house), and a meal that included four oxen, sixteen sheep and forty hogsheads of ale for everyone else on the grounds.[14]

We may be forever frustrated in learning more about what life in preindustrial households actually felt like. The upper-class homes we usually hear about are so often extreme in one way or another that we can easily suspect them of being exceptions. In any case, the feel of life in a peasant household is something that hardly anyone bothered to describe until the very end of the eighteenth century and it may not be safe to extrapolate backward. All we can do is juggle bits and pieces, which seem to form a pattern of obligations entangled with joys and sometimes outweighing them.

One way of looking at the evolution of household activities since 1800 is to think of it as a process of stripping away. The household lost one after another of its functions, but the few it retained took on increasing importance, particularly those connected with nurturing, love, and recreation. It is a convenient image, although the process was neither so simple nor so mechanical. It seems perfectly apparent that the household in the past was a place for activities that now take place in other institutions. In particular the separation of work from the household is by now a reality for almost everybody. It is equally apparent that some of the stripping away started quite early among the more privileged, who arranged the structure and use of their houses so that they could find privacy and recreation in them. There may be something to the often-heard characterization of domesticity (in the present-day sense of the word) as "bourgeois," since neither very poor households nor very aristocratic ones found it easy to slough off their multiplicity of functions. But much of the sentiment about domesticity as both private and enjoyable was voiced by aristocrats, and by the middle of the nineteenth century one of its best-known advocates was Queen Victoria herself. The very poor were catapulted into their version of the new domesticity—a household likewise stripped of many functions but not so charming—by becoming industrial workers.

II

Men and Women in a
Special Relationship

All societies recognize the special relationship of marriage. It gives a cultural shape to natural biological functions, separating couples who are married from all other pairings of men and women. Marriage is inseparable from "family," however it is defined. Getting married often starts a new family (household) and usually continues an existing one (kinship) that owes its existence to some marriage in the past.

This part is therefore not about sex as such but about a sexual relationship shaped by the contingencies, necessities, and beliefs associated with the family. The relationship is socially regulated and socially *perceived*. In the natural world (the world of animals and plants) males and females seem to be fairly equal in courting and mating. In some species the choice of mate is the female's, in some the male's. In the human culture described in this book there was an elaborate structure of sexual inequalities, one that still exists to some degree, since that culture has left us its legacy. The inequality in the past was too elaborate to be without its ambiguities, however—a fact that should have a special resonance today.

The chapters in this part are about choosing a mate, tying the knot, and living together—three aspects of a subject that no sensible person ever pretended was simple.

3

Preliminaries to Marriage

Marriage starts a family, but a lot has to happen before there is a marriage. In some ways premarital behavior epitomizes a society's whole culture. Just think of the services, equipment, institutions, personal energy, and artistic effort that are connected with the modern American search for a mate, the relationship of the courting couple, and the preparations for the moment of their transformation into husband and wife. At least as much was involved in the past. Furthermore, some of the salient features of the preindustrial family—ambivalences and all—are revealed in the preliminaries to marriage. The preliminaries can be seen as a series of choices, which raise issues that continue to resonate in somewhat different ways in the second half of the twentieth century: Should I get married or stay single? Should I marry someone I am in love with or someone who will benefit me and my family? Should I marry someone from my own background and neighborhood? At what age should I marry? Is premarital sexual intimacy acceptable? Should I marry again if my first marriage ends? The questions are familiar, but in the past some answers were arrived at through processes that are less familiar.

To Marry or Not to Marry

Not everyone gets married nowadays, not even everyone who wants to get married. In a vast oversimplification it can be said that there is one force pulling in the direction of the universal desirability of marriage and another pulling in the direction of remaining unmarried—because of other commitments, rejection of legal and religious conventions, a desire for freedom, or the unavailability of partners. During most of the four and a half centuries dealt with in this book there was a similar polarity, but the terms were slightly different. At one extreme was an even deeper acceptance of the inevitability of marriage as the normal condition, while at the other extreme were powerful institutions and social forces that promoted celibacy. Between the fifteenth century and the beginning of the nineteenth century there was a shift in the balance away from celibacy. The Protestant Reformation, starting in the sixteenth century, abolished monasteries and waged a propaganda campaign in favor of marriage. At the very end of the period we are looking at social and economic changes tended to lower barriers to marriage for poorer people.

A striking characteristic of the civilization of western Europe for centuries was the relatively high number of single people. Historical demographers have suggested that single adults made up at the very least 5 percent of the population and in many places 20 or 25 percent. This contrasts both with eastern Europe and with much of the rest of the world, where single people were hardly to be found. Nobody knows the reason for the Western pattern, especially since we are not sure when it started. What we are sure of is that it was very much in evidence throughout the centuries we are looking at, with the beginning flicker of a change in the eighteenth century.

In looking for the reasons for so much celibacy it helps to know who the single people were. Many were servants. As we have seen, they were everywhere, they were numerous, and they were almost always unmarried. Most of them eventually left service and got married, but not all of them. At any given moment there were a large number of single servants, and some of them would never marry. In towns, for example, where many women came from the countryside to work as servants, female celibacy was much higher than in the countryside, partly because there were not enough men to go around.

Others for whom marriage was unlikely were in general those who "could not afford" to be married. They were not necessarily poor. What mattered was their access to inherited property, mainly land. If only one son of a peasant inherited his father's land, the other sons might stay on as single workers. This happened in some parts of Europe, although in most places such disadvantaged sons left to find work elsewhere and eventually married. The phenomenon of the younger son who was relatively disadvantaged was more apparent in the upper ranks of society. There it required more wealth to make a suitable marriage. Younger sons often chose careers in which it was usual not to be married—like the military or the clergy (in Catholic countries). The Catholic clergy was the most concentrated group of single people—not only priests but also great numbers of monks, friars, and nuns. Their presence and their prestige were an argument for the superiority of the single life, and all Catholics were familiar with the idea that marriage, while respected, was a lesser condition. After the Reformation a married clergy helped eventually to modify this attitude in Protestant countries.

Marrying or not marrying presented itself to few individuals as a real choice, as far as we can tell. For most, circumstances and other people's decisions were what mattered. Still, if a peasant girl in the fifteenth century decided that a single life dedicated to God was what she wanted with all her heart she could expect to receive considerable approval, if not from the young men in her village at least from nobles at the royal court. This is what happened to Joan of Arc, who was as much admired for her virginity as for her other gifts. Not a few young French immigrants to Canada in the seventeenth century became nuns in spite of a government policy promoting marriage in the new colony—and also in spite of a large number of single men. At the other end of the social scale some scholarly Florentine patricians seem to have welcomed the opportunity to pursue what was called the contemplative life as opposed to an active life that included marriage and family.

To most people, however, then as now, marriage was almost as inevitable as being born and dying. An ordinary man like Martin Luther's father looked upon his son's decision to become a monk as an affront to practical common sense. In country villages single people were a rarity. This gave the celibate priest a special distinction, although before the Reformation not a few parish priests were "married"—that is, they had concubines, since legal marriage for priests was forbidden after the eleventh century. This may have caused scandal, or at least gossip, but it was not unusual. The great humanist Desiderius Erasmus, who was the son of a priest, included in his many complaints about how religious institutions worked in his day that the commitment to celibacy was imposed on boys and girls before they were old enough to decide for themselves. As a general rule, people who remained single did not stay in the country. They migrated to the cities, where they found work as servants or laborers and joined other typically urban unmarried people like monks and friars, nuns, soldiers, and prostitutes. The same city-country contrast was found in colonial Mexico and Brazil. Remember, however, that most people lived in the country. One urban group that married at a rate of almost 100 percent was the Jews. Jews were both inside European society and outside it. While they behaved in many ways like their Christian neighbors, theirs was a more restricted sphere of activity, and their marriage pattern was less varied than that in the greater world outside.

The inevitability of marriage was reinforced by numerous considerations. For the small farmer or peasant it was well-nigh impossible to get along without being married. Marriage made it possible to do the work that had to be done every day, and it was also needed to provide for the orderly transfer of property. In varying degrees this was so for those who ran small craft shops, for owners of estates with large domestic establishments, and for monarchs. The anomalous unmarried ruler in this period was Elizabeth of England. Unmarried she remained, but marriage negotiations were constantly carried on throughout her reign. For ordinary people full adult status was achieved only through marriage. The words for bachelor and spinster conveyed images of youth, dependency, and poverty, and were uttered with contempt or pity. Only married people had a legitimate right to sexual relations—not altogether a defunct idea today. Even as the Christian church was enthusiastically promoting celibacy, it proclaimed that for most people sexual abstinence was an impossible goal and that marriage was a positive good, having been instituted to prevent the sin of licentiousness. Popular attitudes seem to have gone along with this, especially where women were concerned.

People married because it was expected of them and because they wanted to, much as they do today. One appeal of marriage is much stronger today than it was in the past, however: the desire to have children. Wanting to produce an heir was not the same thing as the modern wish to experience parenthood or the modern postponement of marriage until children are desired. When twentieth-century historians discovered that there had been a huge increase in the rate of marriage in Marseilles after one of the last European outbreaks of plague in 1720, they jumped to the conclusion that the survivors were impelled by the need to replenish the population. A closer look showed that many of those who married were past childbearing age and that they, like those who were younger, married either because the plague removed obstacles that had previously stood in their way or because marriage had become necessary. That is, the shop needed a new master or mistress, the son inherited a means to a livelihood, the widow or widower wanted help or companionship. Empty slots had been created in the social structure that only marriage could fill.[1]

Love or Policy

Two contradictory assertions are often made about marriage in the past. One assumes that people must have met, fallen in love, and married exactly as they do now. The other, seemingly more sophisticated, assumes that love played no role and that all marriages were arranged for reasons of policy and practicality. Both fail to take into account the complexity of the world of the past. An honest look at our own world tells us that not every marriage nowadays is formed purely on the basis of love, even if people generally behave as though it should be. There is, in other words, some ambivalence on this point. There was also ambivalence in the past. Policy considerations tended to be strong among groups who had a lot to gain from advantageous marriage arrangements. A family already high in the social pyramid could catapult itself from a hilly little dukedom to the rule of more than half the world through a clever and lucky marriage strategy. "Let others wage war," went a verse about the Habsburgs, "you, O happy Austria, marry!" When great wealth and power were not at stake, love was allowed a bigger role. There seems to have been a gradual change over the centuries in the direction of more freedom of choice for the couple and hence of a greater acceptance of love as the basis of marriage. Most of the change may have taken place in the middle and upper classes, since there are signs that poorer people had been marrying for love for a long time. But there is no point in exaggerating the contrasts or the changes. Marriages for policy were still much in evidence in the nineteenth century, while love matches were heard of among the rich and powerful in the sixteenth century.

Arranging marriages was an important and time-consuming activity—"the weightiest business," someone said. The material benefits to a family could be considerable, since marriage was one of the occasions when property was distributed. If the Habsburgs could acquire an empire, a peasant family might acquire acreage and a merchant family might acquire capital. The enhanced family property would descend to an heir who in turn was expected to enlarge it, if possible, through subsequent marriage arrangements. There were also other than material objectives. The right family connections meant status and influence. Among all classes marriage was regarded as an alliance between two families. If a woman married a man of some distinction, for example, her parents and even her aunts and uncles shared in the honor. That is why they wanted to make the choice for her instead of leaving it to chance. A marriage made the two families kin. In some villages family connections were so valued that it is not always easy to tell whether people were trying to achieve greater wealth through marriage alliances or better marriage alliances through wealth. Marriage was also considered a good way to seal a peace between former enemies, whether they were peasants in the same village or the kings of France and Spain. Fifteenth-century Florentine patricians thought that making politically astute marriages was as important as making money. And in eighteenth-century England political power was largely in the hands of a small group of carefully intermarried aristocratic families who sent members to Parliament.

Parents often took on the double job of choosing their children's spouses and working out the details. In some circles the choice belonged so exclusively to the father that one French aristocrat cut off his son's questions about the woman who had been picked as his bride with, "Attend to your own business, sir!" This was not a universal attitude, however, or it would not have been remarked on. It was not at all unusual for the chosen couple to be asked what they thought, and in situations where single people were able to meet on their own it was the parents who were asked for an opinion. Still, parents' opinions carried great weight and their disapproval had consequences. We can only guess how many promises to marry were never carried out because parents withheld their approval, but we know that some children went to great lengths to win it.

The final choice of a mate was bound up with the process of working out details, which could be complicated. A marriage contract set up the conditions that made it possible for the couple to live on their own, but it could include a wide range of other matters. Bargaining resembled international treaty negotiations. The contributions of one side had somehow to match those of the other side, and future contingencies of various kinds were dealt with. The heart of the matter was almost always the dowry, the money or property the woman brought to the marriage. The size of a dowry depended partly on what the other side offered, partly on what nonmaterial assets the bride's family had. A particularly beautiful woman or one whose social status was higher than that of her husband might be able to offer a smaller dowry than usual. Sometimes months of bargaining came to nought, and the parents had to search for other prospects. To a greater or lesser degree there was parental control and involvement in marriage everywhere, even among small farmers in colonial New England. In some parts of Europe formal marriage contracts were common even for quite poor people.

To suggest that only parents cared about practicality would be misleading. Since the general rule was that nobody could get married unless he or she could afford to, even people who did not have to answer to their parents looked for "good" marriages, that is, ones with good material prospects. For a man in the country who had no prospect of inheriting land, the ideal wife was a woman who was in line to inherit her father's property (probably because she had no brothers). A craftsman in town improved his business prospects immeasurably if he married the daughter of a master in his own craft and could look forward to taking over the shop. Such ambition was recognized and generally applauded, although fathers of daughters tended to a bit of paranoia on this score. There was frequent talk, not only among the very rich, of fortune hunters. Women were sometimes more than passive participants. This was often the case with widows, and working women in towns were particularly likely to decide when the practical moment had arrived for them to marry. This could have been when they had accumulated a sufficient dowry from their earnings. For most people, marriage was in large measure an economic relationship, no matter how they felt about the people they married. The norm was what could be called the "two-person career." When a spouse died, a job opening was created, so to speak. The widow or widower remarried to fill the opening, or a son or daughter took over and almost simultaneously acquired a mate.

Love and marriage were linked in those past centuries, however. We should not let ourselves get too distracted by the weighty concerns of those at the top of society. Even as peasant fathers plotted their children's futures, the children were meeting members of the opposite sex at work in the fields and the threshing barn or at play in seasonal village festivities, at fairs, and on pilgrimages to local shrines. They singled each other out, exchanged words and caresses, and gave each other presents. It is fairly safe to say that parental choices were most often based on choices already made. It was accepted that parents or go-betweens did the negotiating at some point, but couples often said they had picked each other out and that they were in love. There were no surveys of popular attitudes in those days, of course, so we are guessing about what was going on in the minds of people who rarely wrote and whose statements were almost never recorded. When their attitudes were recorded, however—from time to time in court records and legal documents—love was very much in evidence.

A French peasant proclaimed his devotion to the woman he was courting by swearing by the place he hoped to have in Paradise.[2] A young English artisan exchanged promises with his sweetheart that they would "live privately and love firmly" and "be faithful till death."[3] People in love spoke of being "born for each other."[4] Even the illiterate knew love songs and ballads, many of which were about disappointment and cruelty but a good number of which were about the joys of love and the wish for the permanent companionship of marriage. Romantic love was the most popular of literary subjects throughout this period, and it was not always, as has sometimes been claimed, hopeless love, adulterous love, or idealized Platonic love. Shakespeare's audience, which was a pretty broad one, was apparently familiar with the kind of romantic courtship that appears in so many of his comedies. There was no moment in history when love suddenly emerged as a conscious motive for marriage; it was there all along. It was not always acted on, but it remained an attractive possibility to be realized when it could be.

The contrast with the late twentieth century is in the kind of lip service paid to freedom of choice, love, and parental control. Sensible, sober persons in the past tended to be suspicious of marriage based on love, and they gave excellent reasons for their suspicions. An English lady of the seventeenth century, Dorothy Osborne, who had herself insisted on marrying for love and apparently did not regret it, nevertheless said, "To marry for love were no reproachful thing if we did not see that of the thousand couples that do it, hardly one can be brought for an example that it may be done and not repented of afterwards."[5] Love matches simply did not work, or so the common wisdom went. So said Erasmus, Luther, Margaret of Navarre, Montaigne. Yet none of these people felt that parents should force their children into marriages they did not want. It was respectable to take the position that strife and unhappiness resulted from forced marriages. So said the very same Erasmus and Luther, so said Catholic and Protestant theologians of the seventeenth century, so proclaimed the title of a 1607 play, *The Miseries of Enforced Marriage*.[6] The correct position was that if parents behaved as they were supposed to, their choices would be best.

Everyone seems to have been poised for the possibility of conflict, however. Legal and religious institutions tended to back parents. There were laws that required parental consent. The Catholic church had no such requirement, although many clergymen argued in favor of it during the extensive debate on marriage at the Council of Trent in the mid-sixteenth century. Most Protestant church ordinances remedied this omission, which had been one of the targets of the leaders of the Reformation. Catholic countries—France and Spain, for example—had secular laws that made it difficult to marry without parental consent. Whether conflict was as common as all this would indicate we cannot tell for sure. The defiance of one nobleman's son, if the nobleman was powerful enough, could make quite enough of a disturbance. The battlefield for this struggle over power and sentiment was mainly the upper reaches of society. Lesser folk in the country villages meanwhile worked out their own accommodations with the ambivalence about love and policy, the sober and serious ones probably coming down on the side of policy, like their betters.

Marrying In or Marrying Out

Most of us take it for granted that we must marry out—that is, we cannot marry members of our immediate families. On the other hand, most of us marry in, to some degree. We marry people of the same nationality, race, and religion, and as often as not we marry people with the same kind of education and work experience. The technical terms for these two aspects of choosing a marriage partner are exogamy and endogamy. Every society has rules about what categories of people can and cannot marry each other, and anthropologists have found tribal societies with far more restrictive rules than those that operate in the Western world. People grow up understanding that there is a group they must or should marry out of and another group they must or should marry within. Nevertheless, there can be problems. This is partly because some rules are not entirely clear; in a complex society, such as exists today and such as existed in the 450-year period we are examining, rules stem from different sources and can be contradictory. It is also partly because rules are not always obeyed—a possibility that has stimulated the literary and mythic imagination nearly everywhere. Under names like incest and misalliance the breaking of exogamic and endogamic rules can arouse feelings of deep horror and fascination.

The rules about marrying out present few problems nowadays. The prohibition against marrying close relatives is generally accepted, and incest, which most people associate with illicit sex and not marriage, is regarded as pathological. Contemporary ambivalences and conflicts have more to do with not sticking to the groups we are expected to marry within. "Mixed marriages" are what we consider problematic. In the past there were ambivalences about both marrying in and marrying out. The most important changes over the centuries have been in the law, but most of the legal developments took place before 1350 and after 1800. The Reformation in the sixteenth century allowed marriage between closer relatives than earlier, but the Roman church had already made a major change at the beginning of the thirteenth century when it allowed very distant cousins to marry. The need to marry within one's own religion and social class was reduced only with the gradual appearance of religious toleration and the disappearance of a legally sanctioned social hierarchy.

Most people did not look far for their marriage partners. They married "close"—within their own villages or in villages within half a day's walking distance. If a peasant wanted to marry out of the manor on which he or she lived it was often necessary to get permission from the lord of the manor and pay him a fine. In towns neighbors married neighbors and, most often, people in the same occupation. Male servants married female servants. Most people did not marry outside their social rank. In the few places where there were vestiges of serfdom, servile status made it difficult to marry a nonserf, even though serfs and nonserfs may have lived and worked side by side. In addition to sticking to their own place and class, people did a considerable amount of close marrying within families, often pursuing deliberate strategies of intensifying family ties and keeping property from going to outsiders. Apart from marriages between cousins and second cousins, double marriages were a way of accomplishing this. For example, a brother and a sister married another brother-sister pair on the same day or (less romantic to our eyes) a father married the widowed mother of his motherless son's bride. In the marriage strategy of royal politics, brother-sister marriages were often included in peace treaties.

Popular opinion throughout this period was firmly on the side of marrying people near at hand. Youth groups in country villages—actually, groups of not-yet-married males—took upon themselves the job of monitoring matches made by village girls, expressing their disapproval of outsiders in public demonstrations, which went by the name of charivaris or some such term. An "outsider" could be from as little as five miles away. In towns, journeymen in some of the crafts used demonstrations and jeering songs to express their disapproval of the daughters of masters in their crafts who married wealthy, established men instead of men like themselves. They also disapproved of great differences in age, especially young women marrying much older men.

A strong current of disapproval of too much marrying in came from the Christian church. For centuries it waged a campaign for people to marry far afield. Whatever the theory behind this—to prevent the consolidation of powerful families or to promote love and charity by spreading the net of kinship as wide as possible—until the sixteenth century the church defined close kinship to include blood relatives up to third cousins, a wide range of in-laws, the families of godparents, and some other categories besides. It is not surprising that the tendency to marry within tight geographical and social limits came into conflict with the ecclesiastical rules against marrying such a great variety of kin. The conflict became one of the thorniest problems for the church's legal system. That there was considerable ambivalence on this score is manifest in the church's practice of granting dispensations. Marriage within some degrees of relationship were not absolutely forbidden if the proper authorities gave their permission. The Protestant churches made changes in this elaborate structure, but the Catholic church retained its system of many forbidden degrees of kinship, some of which were not always forbidden and a smaller number that were. In the eighteenth century a single diocese in France issued between 70 and 150 dispensations every year.[7] An example of how fraught with ambivalence the subject might be is one of the most famous cases of a dispensation that backfired, the one granted to Henry VIII to enable him to marry his first wife, Catherine of Aragon. The dispensation was needed because she was technically his sister-in-law. He welcomed it at the time, but years later, when Catherine failed to produce a male heir, Henry was said to have agonized over the forbidden incestuous nature of the marriage, which he feared a mere papal parchment had not been able to wipe out.

When people left the countryside, as many did, to find work in town, they could anticipate marrying immigrants from other places, thus abandoning the tendency to close marriage. Those in the higher reaches of society could find marriage partners in their own social rank only by choosing them from far away. If an ordinary peasant usually married within a radius of ten miles, say, a lesser nobleman would have to extend his range to the next diocese or even the next province or country. But even the strict limitation to social rank was not always observed, as the fuss over requiring parental consent suggests. Marrying into another social group was, in fact, the recognized path of social mobility in this rigidly stratified world. In some measure this was what parental strategy meant: trying to inch upward or put the seal on other achievement by acquiring a family foothold in a higher rank. Though there was something shocking—I suppose there still is—about great gaps between the social ranks of marriage partners (the dreaded misalliance), narrow movement across social lines excited almost no comment. The ideal case was prestige marrying wealth. The rich commoner became the son-in-law or daughter-in-law of an aristocrat, for example, and among Jews a rabbi's son or daughter lent prestige to a merchant's family, whose wealth was welcomed in turn by the rabbi. Between religions and races the barriers were well-nigh impenetrable throughout the period, partly because they were enshrined in law. Minorities did not necessarily welcome intermarriage. One reason that the Jews maintained their identity through centuries of oppression was their adherence to religious endogamy (often necessitating a certain amount of geographical mobility); conversely, the Huguenots who stayed in France after their religion was outlawed in 1685 saw their numbers dwindle as a result of intermarriage with Catholics. Quakers worked hard at enforcing their rules against marrying non-Quakers, without total success. Where racial intermarriages took place—in some far-flung colonial territories—wide gaps were, again, unacceptable. In colonial Brazil, for example, whites married persons of mixed race, not blacks.

The extreme case of marrying one's own kind was found in royal marriages, where many of the tendencies found in the lower ranks of society appear magnified. Ideally, royalty married royalty, so the marriage market had to be geographically very wide, practically embracing the whole world. Differences of nationality could not count and, surprisingly, religious differences were often not the barriers they were for lesser folk. The symbolism of marriage as an instrument of peace was so powerful that rulers were often willing to convert or make little fuss. The invasion of the Spanish Armada was preceded, some time before, by marriage overtures to Queen Elizabeth by Philip II of Spain. This intermarriagiability of all Christians, which in principle existed on all levels, is an interesting contradiction to the bitter religious struggles of the sixteenth and seventeenth centuries. On the matter of near relations, it almost seems as if the aim in this period was to unite all of European royalty into one family. In the seventeenth century two French kings in succession married Spanish princesses of the House of Habsburg, which was related to the Habsburg rulers of Austria, while a French princess was married to one of the English Stuarts, another of whom was married to the German king of Bohemia—I could go on and on. The wife of Louis XIV was his first cousin, an extremely close relative. But Spain and France remained enemies, except for brief periods, so marital strategy was obviously not the perfect solution to the problems of war and peace. It nevertheless continued to be pursued as such, straining the limits of both nearness and distance in the forging of alliances.

Marrying Early or Marrying Late

What is the right age to get married? There is not much agreement about that these days, although most of us have feelings about what is "too young" or "too old." Attitudes range all the way from strong approval of early marriage as an antidote to sexual promiscuity to advocacy of late marriage as a guarantee of family stability. Throughout the period we are looking at there were the same extremes, but certain groups of people consistently married "young" or "old," and in some groups there was a difference between when women married and when men married. Not much changed over the years. Most of the change was in groups at the very top of the social scale, in which the youngest marriages had taken place. In the bulk of the population the marriage age fluctuated slightly in response to local conditions and started to show signs of getting lower toward the end of the period, especially in England with the beginning of industrialization. In North America ages were generally lower than in western Europe, a pattern that continued from colonial times into the twentieth century.

Both men and women married at a much later age than our long-held notions about traditional times may have led us to believe. Juliet's age— "Come Lammas Eve at night she shall be fourteen"—may have seemed as startling to Shakespeare's audience as it does to us. He himself married a woman of twenty-six.

That is relatively late when we think of the age at which human beings reach sexual maturity (roughly between twelve and seventeen). It is also late when we compare it with other parts of the world, including eastern Europe. Like the small but significant proportion of permanently single people, this late marriage age had been a characteristic of Western civilization for a long time. The average age hovered around twenty-five, women generally being a little younger, men frequently older. In *first* marriages—a distinction we must constantly keep in mind—the difference in age between husband and wife was usually not great, and it was not at all unusual for wives to be a little older than their husbands. If one of the partners was marrying for a second time, there was likely to be a greater age gap, but it should not be assumed that it was invariably the man who was older. Such patterns were found among rural people who could not set up a household until they had a house and the means of making a living. There was a connection between the deaths of fathers and the marriages of sons. Someone has calculated that the average marriage age was roughly the same as the number of years the average father could expect to live after he reached the middle of his reproductive period—in other words, when a father died his children married.[8]

Things did not usually work out so tidily, but there can be no doubt that marriage was closely associated in people's minds with economic independence. Servants, for example, were not economically independent; the marriage ages of this important group were close to the Western averages. The distinctive western European servant phenomenon is not found in parts of the world where early marriages are common. When it became possible for people to earn money without having to go through a stage as servants, they tended to marry a bit younger. The need to wait was always less for those who never expected to have land or achieve prosperity—agricultural workers, unskilled day laborers in towns, and, as time went on, a growing number of wage earners in industrial manufacturing, whether in town or countryside. Economic independence was a relative matter, of course, but it was undoubtedly related to a couple's perception of whether they could afford to have children. An eighteenth-century observer commented that Europeans avoided marriage "till they can see how they shall be able to maintain a Family,"[9] whereas "marriages in America are more general. . . . Marrying early is encouraged from the prospect of good subsistence."[10]

Marrying very young was certainly not unheard of, especially for women. In southern Europe a considerably lower marriage age for women prevailed among all classes. At the same time, men tended to marry even later there, so that gaps of nine or ten years between husbands and wives were standard. Longstanding custom, household arrangements, and inheritance patterns were sufficiently different in northern and southern Europe to account for these differences. The two areas were alike, however, in having a similar range of variations: the poor tended to marry later, people in cities to marry earlier. When people emigrated to more distant places—to other continents rather than to nearby towns—the skewing of the population balance between the sexes was sometimes more extreme than in European cities. In seventeenth-century French Canada, for example, men far outnumbered women. As a result, a woman could expect to be married at fifteen or sixteen to a man who was likely to be twenty-eight or thirty. The situation was similar in the earliest days of Maryland and Virginia. In colonial New England, on the other hand, there seems to have been a far closer approximation to the European sex ratio and, probably for that reason, to European social arrangements. People there married at ages close to the European average, if slightly younger. For European Jews there was a strong commitment to get everyone married off early, and Jewish men married much earlier than Christian men. But even among Jews the rich were younger than the poor when they married.

Aristocrats and urban patricians in particular married young. Historians used to pay exaggerated attention to so-called child marriages in a few extremely high-placed families. Most of these were agreements on paper, the result of intricate negotiations to forge family alliances, and not every such "marriage" became a reality. Still, where the need for alliances rather than the more modest aim of economic self-sufficiency triggered marriages, parents tended to strike while the iron was hot, if only to give themselves enough time to try again if things did not work out. King Louis XIII was married at age fourteen and a half, and Venetian patricians often married their daughters off at fourteen. Juliet was an Italian patrician herself, although the Italian story-teller who first wrote about her made her somewhat older than Shakespeare did.

Can these interesting numbers give us an inkling of how people felt? We have very little in the way of actual opinion, most of it from moralists who linked their opinions to the venerable idea that since one of the chief ends of marriage was the containment of the libido—what they called the remedy for fornication—early marriage meant less opportunity for sin. Most of the population was not paying attention, apparently. What they thought is hinted at by the pattern of changes in marriage age. Where the age was high, it tended to get lower as social and economic conditions made that possible. But where the age was extremely low, it tended to go up over time. Only the first wave of French Canadian wives were so young and so much younger than their husbands. European aristocrats tended to marry at progressively higher ages. Industrial workers were able to get married earlier than their late-marrying peasant forebears. In New England, people got married younger in the eighteenth century than in the more "European" seventeenth century. It is tempting to make a grand generalization and say the Western world was edging toward universal agreement on a perfect marriage age, say somewhere between twenty-one and twenty-five. But all we can see, rather dimly, is that when young people—or their parents—felt free to change prevailing patterns, they retreated from two kinds of behavior that they may have perceived as unappealing: the imposition of marriage before the partners were fully grown up, on the one hand, and the postponement of marriage longer than the partners wanted, on the other.

A pattern of late marriage had many social consequences. For one thing, sexually mature men and women had to deal with their sexual impulses outside marriage. They seem to have coped with deferred licit sexual gratification in every imaginable way, but not by engaging in uninhibited extramarital sexual intercourse. How this was managed is not yet fully understood. Late marriage has consequences for the status of women. Not only were young unmarried women faced with the challenge of their sexual impulses, but many of them were also self-supporting and making their own way in the world. They did not lead sheltered lives, even if technically they were nominal and legal dependents of their fathers and masters. Another consequence of late marriage is that women made use of far less than the full span of their fertile years, so the number of children they had was reduced. This may or may not have been a reason they married late, but the effect was there nonetheless.

Courtship Hot or Courtship Cool

The subject of courtship is closely related to the issue of sexual restraint raised by late marriage. Courtship today is in every respect hotter than it used to be. Nowadays, even if people who are courting are not sexually intimate, they seek each other out, spend time together, and get to know as much as they can about each other. This is not the place to take stock of what has been called a sexual revolution, but obviously there is no universal agreement on courting behavior today. It is much easier to see that there was a polarity in the historical period we are looking at. At one extreme was a pattern of arranged marriage and no premarital contact, a pattern that was the ideal for many. At the other extreme was something not very different from twentieth-century behavior, even including premarital intercourse. Never regarded as ideal by anyone who expressed himself or herself on the subject, it nevertheless was widely accepted. The main change that can be detected over the span of time is that the ideal was considerably modified—a development that went along with changes in the way parents controlled the marriage of their children. By the nineteenth century the positive value of personal, fairly intensive courtship was almost universally accepted. The polarity about sexual intimacy persisted, however.

The two poles of courtship behavior were linked to social status. It is not simply that aristocrats behaved one way and peasants another; there are too many variations and exceptions to allow such a sweeping generalization. Rather, the determining factors were how much was at stake for the respective families and what opportunities there were for the couple to be "hot"— or even warm.

Courtship in the wealthiest and most powerful circles of society was curiously lopsided. The would-be husband seemed to be courting the woman's father rather than the woman herself. Often he too played almost no role, since most of the preliminary steps before a formal betrothal would be taken by members of the two families—not just the fathers of the prospective bride and groom. This weighty business involved meetings of whole delegations, preceded by exploratory contacts made by family friends or other go-betweens. Even when things went smoothly they could take a long time. At some point in the deliberations the couple met in fairly formal and public circumstances and exchanged gifts. They might then be allowed to converse in private, but it goes without saying that they were expected to be decorous. In upper-class circles, especially if the woman was very young, she might be kept from any but the most formal contact with her future husband, even if he was expected to sing courting songs to her (or hire musicians for the purpose), as was the case in Italy. Cool courtship fitted in with marriages arranged as family alliances and with severely restricted freedom of movement for young women.

Certain aspects of cool courtship existed at every level of society. All men were expected to ask a father or a master for permission to marry a woman or even to court her, and both families entered into negotiations as soon as possible, even if the couple had met on their own. But courtship tended to be less cool when there were opportunities for it to be warmer. A traditional youth culture, which has come down to our times in bits and pieces of rural folklore, both encouraged courtship and controlled it. Village life provided many social occasions for unmarried people. These were often public events like festivals and fairs, sometimes with older people present. In any case they were opportunities to look, to talk, and to touch. They could lead to a warmer stage, in which a man called on a woman at home—although this too might not be entirely private, since her family might be present and the man might have brought some friends. Young working people in towns had at least as much freedom of movement as their counterparts in the country, and they were more likely than anyone else to form attachments based on personal inclination—after, it can be assumed, a period of warmish courtship. It was considered desirable in all such situations to use the services of go-betweens at the beginning. Men demonstrated their friendship for each other in this way, as in the courtship of Miles Standish. A certain proportion of those for whom warm courtship was possible turned it into something very warm indeed, but sexual intercourse does not seem to have been common. Nor was it likely to occur very early in the relationship. And while it is true that girls were sometimes seduced by men who pretended to be courting and then abandoned them, they may not always have been the passive victims they were expected to portray themselves as. A lower-class woman might easily find herself in circumstances in which she was a willing partner: close sleeping arrangements in the household or, in the countryside, the excitement of an outdoor celebration in the woods and fields on festivals like Saint John's (Midsummer's) Eve.

Behind this wide variety of behavior lay what at first glance appears to be an ambivalent attitude bordering on outright self-contradiction. I am speaking of the attitude toward virginity. It is no exaggeration that the loss of virginity was considered a misfortune and that there was well-nigh universal agreement on all social levels that a single woman who was not a virgin could not expect to marry well. Western culture has been almost obsessive in condemning women's premarital sexual activity. Can this possibly jibe with hot courtship as I have just described it?

"Courtship" is in fact an ambiguous term. It can apply to the early stages of acquaintanceship (or negotiation), or it can include the whole period up to the moment of marriage. A characteristic of Western marriage in earlier times was the long interval between the decision to marry and the actual marriage. This meant not only what we call a long engagement but also a series of stages strung out over weeks or months before the engagement, which was an event of legal and religious significance beyond anything most of us would assign it today. In many respects a formally betrothed couple was as good as married— which could be a troublesome ambiguity. In addition, although betrothal was expected to be a formal, public ceremony, informal betrothals were thought to have the same force. Being betrothed could be based on something as modest as the exchange of a daisy or a pear or even an inner conviction derived from speech and manner. (Normally, a formal engagement would follow in due course.)

Put these ambiguities together and you get a logical foundation for excusing some kinds of premarital sexual intercourse. A couple that was as good as married was not doing anything very wrong, even a couple just a few tiny steps away from being as good as married. In other words, while there was ambivalence about the wrongness of *extramarital* sex, premarital sex—sex on the unswerving path to marriage—could be excused. The Catholic church was willing to overlook certain impediments to marriage if a couple had slept together. Even so, upper-class people asking for dispensations almost never cited sexual intimacy as their reason.

Premarital sex was not particularly admired or promoted, but it was acceptable. The pregnant bride was a familiar phenomenon in the lower classes. On the other hand, we are fairly sure that most brides were not pregnant. It was not so much that pregnancy triggered a marriage as that the strong expectation of marriage triggered a pregnancy. The surest way to be a successful seducer was to make a woman believe you wanted to marry her. Since irregularities and misfortunes are what leave the most traces in historical records, we have a surprising lot of information about illegitimacy from the fourteenth century on. From it we can conclude that, in the first place, illegitimacy was rare, and in the second place, it usually resulted from broken promises of marriage. I would only add, as another way of reminding the reader that times have changed, that sometimes it was the parents who broke a couple's promises.

To Remarry or Not to Remarry

Not all marriages are first marriages, nor were they in past centuries. It has been estimated that a quarter of all marriages were ones in which one of the partners had been married before. Of these, as many as half were likely to be remarriages for both partners. Second, third, and even fourth marriages were not uncommon. None of this had anything to do with divorce, which for all practical purposes was nonexistent even where it was allowed. It had to do with death. The unmaking of marriages was one of the ways death was a driving force in the historical family.

In spite of the great number of remarriages in the past, there was ambivalence about them, both in ideas and behavior. Today the idea of remarriage seems to be regarded favorably, except by those who disapprove of breaking up marriages by means other than death. On the other hand, the contemporary world is full of widows who do not remarry. The ambivalence in the past had to do with widows, too. They did not remarry nearly as much as widowers did, and attitudes toward the remarriage of widows reflected an intricate set of ambivalent attitudes about women and sexuality. Since widows and remarriage have never received the attention they deserve from either contemporaries or historians, it is difficult to assess changes that may have taken place over time. An eventual decline in the death rate gradually raised the age of widows, but not before the nineteenth century. Not until the twentieth century were there significant numbers of remarriages by people who were divorced rather than widowed.

The proportion of widows who did not remarry was always high. Permanent widowhood was therefore a familiar state, especially in towns. "Widow" was a title affixed to a name, like "Mrs." (as in Widow Brown, Veuve Cliquot), for which there was no masculine equivalent. The proportion of widows in a population was directly related in most places to the numerical balance of the sexes. Almost everywhere in Europe women outnumbered men, and they tended to outnumber them even more as they grew older. This situation was less extreme in the countryside, possibly because those who did not have a place in the rural economy tended to migrate to a town. New colonial settlements overseas were almost like laboratory tests, exceptions that proved the rule. In seventeenth-century Canada and Maryland, for example, where men greatly outnumbered women, widows almost always remarried rather quickly, and they not infrequently married bachelors, something that was less likely in the Old World. As the colonies became more settled, widows remarried less. The life of a woman in Mexico City or other large urban center, like that of a contemporary in Spain, was, by the age of sixty, spent one-third single, one-third married, and one-third widowed.[11] No matter where a widow lived, however, she was more likely to remarry if she was fairly young. Wealthy widows were supposed to be especially susceptible to the wiles of fortune hunters, but the facts do not lend much support to this popular fantasy. It is true that women who had inherited their husbands' farms or craft shops often married men who could help them carry on the business—marrying the boss's wife being as good a strategy as marrying the boss's daughter—but really wealthy widows, well provided for in ways that we will look at later, did not have to marry and in fact did not remarry at a great rate. For the first time in their lives they had the means to be somewhat independent, with an identity no longer derived from either father or husband. It should be pointed out, however, that most widows then, as now, were poor, and they were the chief objects of public charity—they and their orphan children.

The contrast with what happened when a man became a widower is dramatic. He remarried as soon as he could, and his own age made little difference. If he had small children, he might move with blinding speed, installing a new wife in a little over three weeks. The man who married many times was a familiar phenomenon. This somewhat distorts our perception of the death rates for men and women. The rate for men was higher—hence the large number of widows. But the most vulnerable time for women was during the years of childbearing, so a man might go through a succession of young wives. This pattern was to be seen among the rich and powerful as much as among the poor. To look no further than one of the most powerful monarchs of the period, Philip II of Spain was married four times, always losing his wives from natural causes, unlike the father of one of his wives, the much-married Henry VIII of England. Philip was closer to statistical reality than Chaucer's fictitious Wife of Bath, who, "sith I twelve yeer was of age . . . Housbondes at chirche dore I have had fyve." Widowers often chose to marry widows, sometimes as part of a strategy in which they arranged simultaneous marriages between their children.

Attitudes toward remarriage were more ambivalent with regard to widows than widowers. The Wife of Bath's *apologia pro sua vita* is a tissue of such ambivalence, and it is not hard to show that she comes out of a strong misogynistic tradition in Western literature. The popular disapproval expressed in charivaris overlooked this distinction for the most part, however. They implied that any remarriage was objectionable, indeed any marriage that could be regarded as a mismatch according to the impossibly rigid standards of the youth groups, who, needless to say, managed to keep busy. Though they had no effect on the remarriage rate, they probably reflected the discomfort that remarrying couples could not help but feel. Christianity was nothing if not ambivalent. On the one hand, the Catholic church respected every marriage as a sacrament and church authorities issued condemnation after condemnation of the charivaris' mocking obscenities but, on the other hand, the church tended to place remarriage in a lesser category, reducing the ceremonial requirements, imposing a certain interval between widowhood and remarriage, praising the chaste widow, and sometimes implying that there was no difference between remarriage and bigamy. In the fourteenth and fifteenth centuries it allowed its own lesser clergy—a large and varied group that later disappeared—to marry, but only once. A cleric who remarried was "bigamous" and lost his clerical status; it is interesting that he was also called bigamous if he married a widow. Secular laws and customs could be read as delivering a similarly ambivalent message. In some circumstances widows were generously provided for even if a husband left no will. They might enjoy independent ownership and authority such as they had never known as wives, and they usually did not need anyone's consent if they chose to marry again and bring their property into a second marriage. Not surprisingly, lawyers and moralists fretted about this, calling it self-indulgence at the expense of the children of the first marriage. And it is also not surprising that men often wrote wills providing that their widows would have to give up what they had been left if they remarried. That such a provision was not simply a matter of hard-nosed common sense but may have expressed ambivalence about widows' sexuality is suggested by the wording of many of these wills, in which immoral or licentious behavior was equated with remarriage as grounds for the loss of an inheritance. Most of this ambivalence was just as evident in Protestant countries as in Catholic ones.

People did not consciously choose between the opposite poles of behavior described in this chapter. Most of them, as a matter of course, got married, married within a narrow socioeconomic range, obeyed their parents, and behaved with relative decorum. At the same time, they were, to a greater or lesser degree, aware of the tensions and tugs between the poles. They may have thought about them, and they may even have nurtured their fantasy life with them. The subject matter of literature suggests that they did. We cannot, from this distant vantage point, ask them what was going on in their minds, but we should at least recognize the cross currents swirling about them. We can also recognize the possibility of eventual changes in the direction of the currents.

4

Weddings

A wedding, as I will be using the term, is whatever transforms a man and a woman into a married couple. One might think that a history of weddings would be only a description of customs, some of which have disappeared and some of which have lingered on as charming survivals. Historians of law and of religion have long known otherwise. Between 1350 and 1800 important changes in legal and religious institutions had an effect on marriage, which is both a legal condition and one traditionally connected with religion. There was an evolution from complexity to simplicity in weddings, and the confusions that accompanied this process touched the lives of many people. Like so much else about the family that has changed, the confusions and ambivalences about weddings tell us a good deal about modes of thought and feeling, most of which we no longer share but some of which we retain in vestigial form.

A Religious Ceremony or a Civil Contract

Most of my married readers, I am sure, had a religious ceremony of some kind, licensed or attested to by a government document. In some parts of the Western world the government document is the essential instrument and the religious ceremony is optional. In any case, the state regulates and records weddings, and for all those people for whom a wedding is one of the few occasions on which they go to church there is no conflict between church and state but rather a smooth and self-evident cooperation. It took a long time to get to this point, however. For hundreds of years the Christian church had struggled to assert its role in weddings, and it was still doing so in the fourteenth and fifteenth centuries. What seemed like its final victory in the sixteenth century started to erode in the seventeenth century with the first attempts to establish civil marriage, and throughout the period between 1350 and 1800 there were striking contrasts in the way weddings were performed in different places.

The church had already gained considerable control over the institution of marriage before 1350. The authority of church courts to hear cases about contested marriages and marital discord, for example, was universally recognized, but there was still some disagreement about its role in weddings. Even so, most people accepted a connection between weddings and churches. In northwestern Europe a priest usually officiated when the couple exchanged their vows, and the place for the exchange was just outside the church—"at chirche dore," as the Wife of Bath put it. In some parts of southern Europe the ceremony took place inside the church in front of the altar. Weeks before the ceremony a forthcoming wedding was announced by the priest at Sunday services, in obedience to a papal decree; this proclamation or posting of the banns was meant to elicit information about the possible existence of what the church considered impediments to the marriage. Bishops kept issuing decrees and orders affirming the priest's role. The Council of Florence in 1439 officially declared marriage to be the seventh of the church's sacraments. Although it had been generally regarded as a sacrament before, this was a reminder that the spiritual nature of marriage necessarily made it a concern of the church. Actually, marriage was somewhat different from the other sacraments, since its ministers were the man and woman exchanging vows, not the priest who heard them or blessed them. The priest's role, so much insisted on, was thus ambiguous and was widely misunderstood. An ordinary churchgoer was likely to think that the priest was essential to the sacramental nature of the ceremony.

Marriage was an important issue in the Protestant Reformation of the sixteenth century. Reformation leaders rejected the notion of marriage as a sacrament, but they nevertheless helped to strengthen the religious character of weddings. In Protestant countries a clergyman was required to participate in a wedding, and he was expected to talk about the spiritual nature of Christian marriage. The Catholic church in the same period, partly in response to the Reformation, partly in response to internal criticism, made some important changes at the Council of Trent, which adopted a number of decrees on marriage in its last year, 1563. After centuries of allowing local variations, the wedding ceremony was to be uniform throughout the area of the Roman church's jurisdiction, and the presence of the parish priest was declared essential. (He still had no role in the sacrament, the concept of which was unchanged.) So it was not until the late sixteenth century that a church wedding was required everywhere, but it became rapidly entrenched as normal practice. This became a problem for nonconformists (Christians who were not members of the official church of the countries in which they lived). One reason for the undercover travels of Jesuits in sixteenth- and seventeenth-century England

and Huguenot ministers in eighteenth-century France was the need for them to preside at weddings. In places where Jews were allowed to live, their weddings were assumed to be part of their separate religious life, regulated by the Jewish community and of no interest to the outside world. A strong association between weddings and religion was fixed in people's minds.

What had been overcome was an attachment to very old practices in many parts of Europe. In some parts of Germany in the fourteenth and fifteenth centuries weddings normally took place in private homes, presided over either by persons of secular authority or by family elders. Southern Europe had strong traditions going back to ancient Rome that included reliance on the services of a notary, a highly respected professional who had the important job of drawing up all kinds of legal documents and keeping a record of them. In fifteenth-century Florence a couple normally exchanged their marriage vows in front of a notary. This might take place in or near a church, especially if the people were not rich, but tradition favored the home of the bride's family or the office of the notary. No priest was present. Weddings had absolutely nothing to do with priests, in the opinion of Paolo Sarpi, a sixteenth-century Venetian writer who was among those angered by what happened at the Council of Trent.[1] By that time his was a minority opinion. Trent was the culmination of a long campaign that bishops had waged against this variety of practices, a campaign that went on for so long partly because of the church's tendency to accept what people were accustomed to and adapt it to Christian use rather than root it out.

While directly strengthening the participation of the clergy, the religious changes in the sixteenth century indirectly created a situation in which a new version of secular weddings eventually became necessary. European Christians were now divided into Catholics and several kinds of Protestants. In the few places where there was toleration of religious pluralism an effort was made to give marriage a validity that did not depend on denominational requirements. In the seventeenth century the Netherlands had a procedure for civil marriage, and Oliver Cromwell introduced one in the English Commonwealth. In the late eighteenth century the Austrian emperor Joseph II, devoted to ideas of enlightenment and toleration, ordered the use of civil marriage; a few years later in France there were even more far-reaching developments. There, in 1787, Huguenots were finally allowed to have their marriages recognized as legal if they went through an optional civil procedure, and the constitution of 1791 declared categorically that marriage was a civil contract.

In countries with a single established religion, as most countries were, the interests of growing government bureaucracies contributed to the rise of civil marriage. Secular authorities had always been unwilling to leave marriage entirely in the hands of clergymen and the church did not handle all aspects of marriage. Cases about the property of married couples, for example, were handled by lay courts, and many places had secular laws on adultery, sometimes existing side by side with church laws, thus making malefactors subject to double jeopardy. In spite of the church's apparent victory on weddings, competition between church and state continued. After the Council of Trent there was considerable reluctance in France to go along with its decrees, which the French church, always more Gallican (insistent on its administrative independence from the pope) than ultramontane did not officially adopt for some five decades. French kings meanwhile issued a series of royal decrees requiring parental consent and raising the age of those who were able to marry without it. Technically speaking, because the established churches in Protestant countries were agencies of the state, their laws on marriage were state laws. This was a step in the direction of civil marriage. Because of the need of bureaucracies for good records, governments made increasing demands on clergymen and notaries to keep information about the weddings they officiated at or even to transmit it to the state. Civil marriage brought with it, in addition to the benevolence of religious toleration, the advantage to the state of being able to keep better track of its subjects.

Civil marriage was not very rapid to develop, nor has it ever achieved anything like total victory. England rejected it after the Restoration of 1660 and along with many other European countries did not adopt it again (as an option, not a requirement) until well after 1800. The New World practice paralleled the Old. Most of its colonies started out with established churches, toleration spread slowly, and in the early United States there were thirteen different marriage laws, only some of which accepted weddings not performed in a religious setting.

Spoken Words or Written Document

Today if you want to prove that you are married you can refer to a document on file in a government office, just as there is a document recording your birth and there will ultimately be one recording your death. But it is not the document that transforms a man and woman into a married couple. A marriage certificate is not the same as a wedding, any more than birth certificates and death certificates are the same as being born and dying. What the certificate does is to record the speaking of certain words on a solemn occasion. While merely speaking the words is not enough for a legal marriage in the Western world today and the record of the wedding must be put into writing, the spoken words nevertheless have the operative force. This is true whether a wedding is in a British registry office, a French *mairie*, or an American church, city hall, or private home. There is a historical continuity here that can easily be lost sight of in our highly literate culture. In the past the spoken word was often all there was, and it had a power beyond anything it has today. Over the four centuries we are considering, that power gradually diminished and there was an accompanying rise in the use of writing to support, record, or supplement the words.

For centuries there was a contrast between northern and southern Europe. Reliance on the spoken word was almost total in Germany, England, and the parts of France north of the area that followed the written, Roman law. The verbal formulas that were used resembled each other, but we would hardly expect uniformity when, as we have seen, there was such diversity about where weddings took place and who officiated at them. Bishops tried to impose particular rituals in their own dioceses, but up through the fifteenth century their decrees were more often aimed at making sure a clergyman was present than specifying what should be said. In some places considerable importance was attached to the words spoken by the bride's father, with which he transferred his authority over her to her husband. In most church formulas, however, the focus was on the exchange of consent between the couple, in the form of two little speeches that took many forms but whose drift has changed little down to the present. "I take thee for my wedded wife," said the man, adding his promise to be faithful, to provide sustenance, and to keep her until death. The woman said, "I take thee for my wedded husband," and went on to make parallel promises. Having said these words, they were married, it was believed, in the eyes of God and of the legal system that at the time had primary jurisdiction over marriage, that of the Roman church, based on canon law.

Church courts were constantly hearing cases in which there was a dispute over whether words like these had been spoken. Sometimes a case turned on the tense of the verb. If the meaning was, "I shall take thee," rather than, "I [now] take thee," there had been no wedding, although there was a solemn commitment to get married eventually. Promises "in words of the present" were synonymous with a wedding, while promises "in words of the future" were synonymous with a betrothal. Since the words themselves were what counted, it did not matter where or under what circumstances they were spoken.

A common kind of case in church courts was one in which a single woman who was pregnant charged that the man who seduced her had spoken "words of marriage." A male strategy that still sometimes works today was all the more effective at a time when spoken words were endowed with legal force. If he admitted to the court that he had spoken the words, it meant that they were married. Since there were usually no witnesses, the man could say whatever he pleased in court and get off scot-free. But that did not change the fact that if words of marriage *had* been spoken it was believed that a real marriage existed until death in the eyes of God. The church was obliged, however, to let the man off if it could find no proof that he had spoken the words. In an effort to rid itself of such troublesome cases, it set up requirements for proper wedding procedures in each diocese and punished those who did not comply.

For example, the words were always to be spoken in the presence of witnesses, and the parish priest in particular was to be there to hear them. The solemnity of the words was to be honored by the place in which they were spoken, preferably in or in front of the church. The cases persisted, however, and it remained a paradox that a couple could at one and the same time be penalized by a church court for disobeying the diocesan requirements for marriage and be declared truly married.

The changes in weddings in the sixteenth century did not diminish the force of spoken words, but church legislation sharpened the requirements for the circumstances in which they were spoken—a step that seemed revolutionary at the time. The Council of Trent decreed that unwitnessed words no longer had any validity and that the speaking had to be done in front of a priest. Protestant regulations were similar, but not nearly so restrictive as the fulminations of early Reformation leaders against the canon law's paradoxes would lead one to expect. In England the situation remained ambiguous, because the Anglican church, unlike the Protestant churches on the Continent, continued to recognize the old canon law. England was of course unaffected by the Roman Catholic Council of Trent's decrees, so that throughout the seventeenth century Anglican archdeacons' courts continued to hear cases that won them the appellation of "bawdy courts." By the middle of the eighteenth century the British Parliament had come around to the view that it was all right to impose requirements for valid marriages, as the rest of Europe had done, and in 1753 it passed a law that was similar to laws on the Continent. There were some in Parliament who thought this was wrong, maintaining, as some of the diehards at Trent had done, that true words of marriage were enough in the eyes of God and that it was presumptuous of man to intervene. In typical eighteenth-century language, a member of Parliament called the new law "one of the most cruel enterprises against the fair sex that ever entered into the heart of man."[2]

In southern Europe there was altogether a greater reliance on written documents. This was also so among European Jews, for whom a wedding almost always meant, in addition to a highly public spoken ceremony in front of a rabbi, an elegantly drawn-up paper. As we have seen, it was quite common in Italy before the sixteenth century for the exchange of vows to be made in front of a notary, who kept a written record of the event. This document was sometimes referred to as a contract.

When people spoke of marriage contracts, however, they usually meant something else. They were referring to the common sort of written agreement, drawn up before a wedding took place, about material arrangements. Although it was not what made a marriage, it was nonetheless held to be a sign and symbol of a marriage, as well as its written record. In Italy and southern France quite poor people used the services of a notary to draw up a contract even when the amounts involved were trifling. For wealthy people all over Europe marriage contracts could be the most important legal documents in their lives, usually far more important than wills, which were less common. Among Florentine patricians in the fifteenth century, weddings involved a virtual orgy of document-writing. Not one but three documents were drawn up, signed, and registered with a notary. The first was the betrothal, the second the property arrangements, and the third the record of the exchange of vows and whatever else constituted the wedding ceremony. Except for the last, these documents preceded the wedding, and marriage contracts normally represented the outcome of the bargaining between families that laid the foundation for most marriages.

Even after the legal requirements for weddings changed in the sixteenth century, the making of marriage contracts continued, not only as a practical business matter but also because they were still considered integral to the act of getting married. The interval between the signing of the contract and the final tying of the knot got progressively shorter, reflecting a general tendency to tighten wedding procedure. In the seventeenth century an interval of eighty-four days was common in southwestern France, thirty days among French immigrants in Canada. By the end of the eighteenth century the interval was likely to be ten days or less, and in some places the contract-signing was intertwined with the festivities of the wedding itself, taking place the evening before or on the same day.

A marriage contract could be short or long, simple or complex, with considerable variations within regional legal traditions. Every contract contained a statement in which the couple declared themselves ready to marry—before God, in accordance with custom, in the Roman Catholic church, or whatever—and committed themselves to certain actions "in the name of marriage" (as a common formula had it). The most important item was the dowry, which in one form or another was considered essential to marriage all over Europe. The contract spelled out the amount and nature of the dowry, which varied with the wealth of the bride's family and the local laws and customs. A servant girl's dowry might consist of a little cash that she had saved or her master had saved for her, with a small contribution of his own thrown in. In Florence there was a dowry fund under municipal management that worked like certificates of deposit: a girl's father or other family head made a deposit when she was a child, and at the time of the wedding a sum that had been determined at the time of the deposit was paid to her husband. Dowry gifts for poor girls were a favorite form of Christian charity; such were the gifts brought by Saint Nicholas in the early versions of his legend. Rich women's dowries could include substantial amounts of real estate and were in effect their inheritances. Usually, however, dowries did not consist of land or houses but rather of cash, jewelry, furniture, and, in the case of country people, farm implements and livestock.

Almost as important as the dowry in many contracts were agreements to feed and care for parents, especially if the groom was going to take over the family farm. As in the contracts that set up joint household communities, there was always a section on the disposition of property when one of the parties died. This especially meant arrangements for the support of the widow. Among very wealthy families in England the signing of a marriage contract was recognized as the occasion for anticipating what would happen to property not only on the deaths of the husband and wife but also on the marriages and subsequent deaths of their children and sometimes their children's children, resulting in what was called a "strict settlement."

The marriage contract was clearly a multipurpose document. That such a document figured so largely suggests what people thought getting married meant. While spoken words were indeed what made you married and, in the highest spiritual sense, were all that you needed, you were encouraged to believe that marriage required something besides words to give it substance.

Regular records of weddings were not kept to any extent until the seventeenth century and in some parts of Europe not even then. Notaries kept registers in southern France and Italy, but in the rest of Europe the only record of a wedding was likely to be in people's memories. Some parish churches began to keep registers in the sixteenth century, but rarely in a systematic and consistent manner. Requiring priests to keep marriage registers was one of the Council of Trent's modernizing measures, and several governments, including that of England, imposed the same requirement on Protestant ministers. The vital statistics we associate with the modern state were therefore first kept by clergymen, and this collaboration between church and state continued until the same pressures that gradually led to civil marriage led the state to take over the whole job of record-keeping. We would know a lot more about marriages in the past if record-keeping had started earlier and been as thorough as it is today. All those troublesome marriage cases in the past make it clear that written records would have been useful, but institutions were slow to do anything about it. Documents tended to be special rather than routine. A contract, for example, was a particular arrangement for a particular set of circumstances. A priest might on occasion issue a written "license" permitting a parishioner to marry in another parish, or a couple might obtain another kind of license, as William Shakespeare did, that allowed them to do without the publishing of all or some of the banns. If a dispensation from an impediment was needed, it always came in written form. The association of written papers with weddings was not rare. What took a long time to evolve was the automatic and unvarying association of every wedding with a routine piece of writing.

A Single Act or a Process

The idea that a wedding is a single act has also taken a long time to evolve. No matter how many preliminaries and festivities we surround a wedding with, it is clear to us that before the wedding a couple is not married—not even a little bit. Yet, in most places in the period we are looking at, getting married was treated as a process, one that unfolded in stages, with mounting degrees of obligation. The legal developments of the period were pulling in the opposite direction, however, and sooner or later behavior accommodated itself to the law.

The most important stage on the road to marriage was betrothal. A betrothal was much more than any engagement is today. The relationship it established could be broken only with great difficulty and the expectation of profound disapproval. Like a wedding, a betrothal was normally a ceremonial occasion, involving the two families and climaxing negotiations that may have gone on for weeks or months. It was often associated with the signing of the marriage contract—not always, it should be pointed out, with the participation of the future bride. In Florence in the fourteenth and fifteenth centuries, breaking a betrothal was such a dangerous thing to do that—among the upper classes at least—political enmity or even outright warfare might result. So strong was the legal obligation of betrothal that it was usually impossible for one side to get out of it without the agreement of the other side. Refusing to marry someone you were betrothed to could mean that you would never be allowed to marry anyone else. Jewish practice was similar: there was usually a written betrothal contract, and a heavy fine had to be paid to have a betrothal broken. Betrothals were not lightly entered into, and they represented a fairly advanced stage of the marriage process.

There was huge diversity in betrothal ceremonies before the reforms of the sixteenth century. Where written contracts were the rule, betrothals were usually put in writing. In other places it was enough for the parties, or even the parents of the parties, to give solemn spoken promises. Almost everywhere there was an exchange of gifts, or at least a gift from the man to the bride or her family. A common accompanying gesture was the couple's drinking wine out of the same cup. In some places the church made a strenuous effort to participate, just as it tried to strengthen its role in weddings. Some bishops prescribed a betrothal ritual at the church door in front of a priest. The exchange of promises by the man and woman in a public religious ceremony was in stark contrast to the meeting between family representatives in a private home that was so common elsewhere. But behind the lack of uniformity lay universal assent to the necessity and power of betrothal.

It should be no surprise that in this complicated situation betrothal caused problems. If the process went smoothly no one had to think about the precise degree of commitment reached at each stage, but there was a plenitude of ways in which things might go wrong. Then the question of the exact relationship of betrothal to marriage had to be addressed. The church kept issuing regulations about the length of betrothals, in an attempt to tighten the temporal relationship and speed up the process. There was a common tendency for betrothals to stretch out for months and even years. During that time circumstances—and minds—might change. Another danger, as the church saw it, was that the couple might consider themselves as good as married. Sexual intimacies were, as we have seen, tolerated if not actually approved of. There was no little confusion about how much more was needed to make betrothal into a complete marriage. One of the puzzling threads in Shakespeare's *Measure for Measure* is the way in which the wicked Angelo is trapped into legal marriage through his illicit lust for Isabella. Because he is still legally betrothed to Mariana, whom he jilted, he does not commit fornication by sleeping with her when she is substituted for Isabella under cover of darkness. In such a case canon law presumed that the sexual act was that of a married couple and therefore considered the couple validly married from then on. This was one more instance of the church's recognizing the validity of something it profoundly disapproved of.

In real life Mariana might have considered suing for breach of promise. This was one of the commonest kinds of cases in church courts that operated under old canon law—up to the middle of the sixteenth century in most of Europe and up to the middle of the eighteenth century in England. Unlike later breach-of-promise suits, they were not civil suits for damages. If the promise could be proved, the court would rule that the marriage had to be completed. The courts were obliged to recognize every variety of "betrothal," formal or informal, public or private, and they had to listen to all kinds of strange evidence. Everyone familiar with these cases admitted that they were richly productive of perjury, like the seduction cases described in the previous section, which were based on the same legal principles.

The doctrine alluded to in *Measure for Measure*, that of "presumptive marriage," had always bothered many right-thinking persons and it did not survive the sixteenth century, but the awe in which betrothal was held by Protestants as well as Catholics persisted well into the eighteenth century. In some places betrothals were still celebrated in church. It continued to be necessary for couples to ask church courts for permission to break their engagements if they wanted to avoid obstacles to future marriage with others. And in some remote mountain regions betrothed couples lived together with community approval while the final wedding preparations were being made.

Betrothal was the most serious and consequence-laden step in the process of getting married, but it was not the only one. There were the contract negotiations and the formal signing of the contract—sometimes two contracts. There was the series of three banns posted in church, preferably over a period of only three weeks immediately before the wedding, although sometimes the pace was slower. Dowries were often paid in installments, the last one coinciding with the wedding day, but there were also arrangements under which a dowry was to be paid through the first year or more of marriage, raising the possibility of sticky litigation if the payments stopped. In the eyes of the church the last step in the process was the formal exchange of vows together with the priest's benediction, what it referred to as "solemnization." Yet in a sense solemnization was no more important than some of the other steps. A couple could be validly—if not quite respectably—married without it, as Angelo and Mariana were. It was even possible to be respectably married in some places for a whole year before receiving the priestly benediction. The process as a whole was what really mattered.

Confusions abounded before the sixteenth century. Jurists and commentators on canon law, ever in search of basic principles, had always desired clarification and simplification. Their attempt to reduce to a single moment what in practice was a long, drawn-out process produced the paradoxes of marriage law, in which neither view of marriage wholly ceded to the other. Most legal authorities agreed that the moment of the wedding's completion occurred as the words of consent were exchanged. *Consensus facit nuptias:* consent makes a wedding. This was said to be the heart of the matter, everything else being merely reinforcement, decoration, and ceremony, however laudable. Faced with the power of betrothal, however, the lawyers had to make concessions, and their biggest theoretical disputes were over the difficult distinction between betrothal and wedding. The distinction most widely accepted was the one based on the tenses of the verbs used in the two instances: the future tense meant a betrothal, the present tense a wedding. This was a way of backing into an outright elimination of betrothal, since words of the present were operative in and of themselves and did not have to be preceded by words of the future. But betrothal continued to have legal force, even as it was being chipped away at. Canon lawyers sometimes used another distinction, one that seemed to be grounded in common sense: between a marriage *begun* (everything including betrothal and the exchange of words of the present) and a marriage *completed* by sexual union (*matrimonium consummatum*). The more "spiritual" distinction based on tenses had greater currency, but it also had its critics, especially among opponents of the church's legal system, like Erasmus and Luther. They conjured up images of entrapment, of vows exchanged in a drunken transport, of confusion about grammar. ("Ordinary people know nothing of such grammatical subtleties," said Luther, pointing out that the future tense was not the same in German as in Latin.)[3] The canon lawyers' attempts at simplification and clarification seemed to these critics to make a mockery of a serious matter. There is no evidence to suggest that the lawyers' bare-bones definitions had any effect on the usual patterns of getting married. Since lawyers appear on the scene when there are problems and disputes, it was only at such times that the legal paradoxes were evident.

Betrothal began to lose its legal standing in the sixteenth century. The situation was most clear-cut in the Catholic countries that adopted the decrees of the Council of Trent. Betrothal as a separate step no longer had a clear place in Catholic ritual or canon law. In Protestant countries there was a more uneven development, but there too church and state tended to take less and less notice of betrothal. Still, betrothal died hard. Its former importance is reflected in its ritual survival in many church wedding services, in which the first part is actually a betrothal ("Will you have this woman . . . ?"), followed by the more significant words in the present tense ("Repeat after me: 'I, John, take thee . . .'"). Jewish weddings followed exactly the same development—certain kinds of isolation do not keep a group from participating in general trends. In earlier times Jewish betrothal had been a separate transaction months before the wedding ceremony, but by the seventeenth century it had been incorporated into the ritual under the canopy. Weddings were on their way to being compressed into a single act in practice as well as law.

Words or Deeds

There is another aspect of weddings in which a complex set of practices contrasts with a simple legal definition. Gestures and rituals not essential to weddings would be deeply missed even today if they were omitted. Besides words, the formal ceremony includes things like the business of the ring, drinking wine, smashing a cup, holding hands, and kissing. The wedding day usually includes a feast after the ceremony, with a cake, music, and dancing. People express ambivalence on this matter when they sometimes regret that they did not have a "real" wedding even though all the legal requirements were satisfied. In the past, when the wedding day was the culmination of an intricate process, even more significance was attached to the traditional gestures and acts that filled the day and sometimes spilled over to the next day and the day after that. Some of these nonverbal elements have survived, others have fallen into disuse. In general they were treated seriously, even cropping up in the discussions of legal theoreticians who would have liked nothing better than to strip the whole process down to a few words. There seems to have been a pervasive feeling that a good deal besides words was necessary, but there was tension between the need to reinforce an action in manifold ways and the need to simplify and purify.

Weddings were public events—something required by custom as well as the church. All the group activities connected with weddings guaranteed that the marriage would become known to the community, and the community was often not only spectator but also participant. It was common to have an outdoor wedding procession, for example. It might take a roundabout route through the village or town to the church before the ceremony or it might take place afterward, bringing the couple to their house, the house of the groom's father, or the house of the bride's father for the feast. Loud music and the shooting of guns often accompanied the march, drawing maximum attention to what many people thought of as the quintessential symbol of a wedding. The symbolism was especially pointed when the procession led the bride out of her father's house and deposited her in her new home. Only slightly less public was another symbolic act, in which a priest blessed the marriage bed and then, in view of the wedding guests, the bride and groom were placed in it.

These customs varied widely, and most of them eventually disappeared. A custom still observed is a feast attended by a large number of guests. The wedding feast, like the wedding procession, has at times stood as a symbol for the whole wedding. To have a crowd and to share a meal were both important, and the food itself took certain traditional forms, almost always including a cake of some sort. Dancing has also had a long association with weddings. There were special wedding dances, and there was traditional dance behavior, such as the bride's dancing with every guest who asked her. At weddings in Rome in the sixteenth century a customary dance, whose meaning was probably clear to everyone who participated, had relatives lined up according to their degree of kinship with the groom and moving through a pattern of complicated figures in which they "recognized" and greeted each other, as if in a solemn square dance.[4]

In the Middle Ages a number of nonverbal elements had made their way into church rituals, some to stay, others to be purged in various efforts at purification and Christianization. The purging reached a peak in the seventeenth century, under the influence of puritanical Protestantism on the one hand and Counter Reformation Catholicism on the other. At least three ritual gestures have withstood all these efforts at reform, having achieved a religious authenticity of their own: the handclasp, the ring, and the kiss. Not only were they integral to the wedding ceremony, but each of them has at one time or another been treated as the sole symbol of a wedding. In England "handfasting" was a synonym for a wedding. Jan van Eyck's famous wedding portrait shows Giovanni Arnolfini and his bride with their hands touching, the groom seeming about to place his right hand on the bride's right palm. As for the ring, fifteenth-century lawyers sometimes argued that, in the absence of other material evidence, a ring on a woman's finger was a plausible indication that a wedding had taken place. The kiss, whatever its sexual overtones, was one of the earliest Christian symbols of community, the recognized conclusion to all medieval pacts and ceremonies of personal attachment, like the act of homage between vassal and lord. These associations assured the kiss its honored place in the wedding ceremony.

In the evolution of weddings since the fourteenth century there has been a constant tug of war between those in power, religious and secular, and those who, for one reason or another, remained attached to certain practices. Time after time what some regarded as absolutely necessary was labeled by others as pagan, obscene, disgusting, or just plain annoying. The best example of this is the charivari. There is a theory that at one time a charivari (or *Katzenmusik* or rough music or *mattinata* or shivaree) was part of all wedding celebrations. By the fifteenth century it was becoming limited to weddings that were considered vulnerable to criticism, like remarriages—which, of course, were very common. Still, elements of the charivari persisted as a feature of all weddings, even in parts of the United States, where groups of young men would sometimes sing raucous songs and make loud noises outside the bedrooms of newlywed couples. The charivari's distinctive contributions were noise, ridicule, and obscenity, and if the charivari itself was no longer an inevitable part of the wedding, those elements survived either by being incorporated into the wedding procession, which in many French villages became a substitute for the charivari, or by becoming part of the wedding feast.

It is perhaps easier to understand the objections to noise, obscenity, and ridicule than the tenacity with which people clung to them. Weddings are an odd phenomenon in Western society, the repositories of an extraordinary amount of ritualistic behavior that is only dimly understood but nevertheless eagerly engaged in. Anthropologists point out that, apart from weddings, our culture has no common rites of passage. Getting married has been the traditional way to move into adult status, and it is understandable that the community should participate, since public recognition of the new status is so important. A rite of passage does more than celebrate a change. It also protects against the dangers of transition—the kinds of dangers we unconsciously try to ward off when we knock wood or say "God bless you" to someone who sneezes. Spirits and ghosts were supposed to be especially threatening at vulnerable moments like weddings. There was a ritual sanction to the noisemaking that helped to publicize a wedding, just as there was to the breaking of the glass from which the bride and groom drank wine—still traditional in Jewish weddings and a common Christian practice in earlier times. Such gestures were based on a belief, shadowy but potent, that they would frighten and confuse threatening evil spirits.

As for erotic language and sexual explicitness, which could easily be transformed into obscenity or interpreted as such, they had a certain appropriateness for a rite of passage that was also a fertility rite. Ridicule fitted both aspects of the rite. It helped to confuse malevolent spirits, and it also went along with sexual innuendo. Charivaris, processions, and the songs and verses at wedding feasts mocked and teased the couple, especially if the bride was suitably reluctant and innocent. The archetypical wedding was the first wedding of young people, and this set the ritualistic pattern, even if remarriage was extremely common. The theory that charivaris were originally part of all weddings has yet to explain how they shifted their focus to "atypical" ones; it looks as though the shift was still going on in the fourteenth and fifteenth centuries.

The authorities who tried to change the way weddings were celebrated were ambivalent about some of these gestures and rituals. Everything was not equally condemned as disrespectful or pagan. For a long time the priest's nuptial blessing was held to be necessary for a virgin bride but not for a widow, and not even for the groom or the marriage itself; this suggests that the blessing's function was to protect the bride in her passage from maidenhood to womanhood, a notion that is not particularly Christian. Another example is the blessing of the marriage bed. As late as the seventeenth century French priests were still expected to carry out this dubious ritual, but it had become suffused with Counter Reformation sobriety and instead of being an occasion for public merriment became one for a homily on the seriousness of holy matrimony. In the wake of the religious upheavals of the sixteenth century, Christians pursued with renewed vigor the centuries-old process of making weddings more solemn and Christian, which they did both by adapting and by excising. Protestant and Catholic authorities alike tried to put an end to large, noisy processions, even outlawing the use of musical instruments. In an age of missionaries, the conversion of the common people to a simpler, purer wedding ritual was undertaken with something like missionary zeal.

It was among the common people that the effort apparently needed to be concentrated, since the upper classes had already moved away from much of this traditional behavior. Many of the rich and powerful had lavish weddings, but out-of-door displays in full view of everyone were becoming an embarrassment, as were all practices that could be considered coarse and vulgar. The boisterous peasant weddings depicted by Pieter Bruegel were probably nothing any patron of the artist would want to emulate. The peak of refinement in aristocratic weddings may have been reached in England in the eighteenth century, where it became fashionable to fly in the face of nearly every one of the hoary traditions. Weddings were held quietly at home, the number of guests was kept small, the wedding feast was a relatively modest lunch, and "publicity" was achieved by sending out simple announcements—to rely on writing was a sign that times had indeed changed. Weddings by license—dispensing with the publication of banns—went along with this apparent desire for privacy and intimacy. Genteel Fanny Burney wrote in 1770: "I don't suppose anything can be so dreadful as a public wedding—my stars! I should never be able to support it."[5]

The trend seems to have started early. In the fourteenth century, and probably earlier, aristocratic weddings sometimes took place in the middle of the night, often not in church but in private chapels. This was a practice that ecclesiastical authorities inveighed against for reasons that are not absolutely clear, perhaps because such ceremonies were not sufficiently public or solemn. Nor do we know how widespread they were. They may not have resulted entirely from a yearning to avoid exposure to the vulgar mob but rather from fear of the very same baleful influences that the loud noises of traditional wedding celebrations were supposed to ward off. One of the things most dreaded was a magic spell that would render the groom impotent. This was done by someone at the wedding secretly knotting a leather cord in a certain way and uttering the words, "Whom God hath joined together let the Devil separate." Any man with enemies or rivals could expect such mischief to be tried against him. One way to prevent it was to keep the wedding as inconspicuous as possible—an opposite tactic to the one usually followed and apparently justified only by exceptional circumstances or very high rank.

There were many other good reasons for quiet, private weddings. The trend was unmistakably toward the elimination of obscenity, embarrassing talk, and rough behavior; it started early and was helped along by the developments in Christianity over these eventful centuries. One transitional moment of ambivalence was in 1502 at the wedding in Ferrara of the legendary Lucrezia Borgia and Alfonso d'Este. Plans had been made for the usual shivaree-like *mattinata*, thoroughly justified by the fact that this was Lucrezia's third marriage and her husband-to-be's second. High rank, political power, and personal sensitivity combined to quash the plans, however—something that would not have been possible for lesser folk, unless they paid a stiff fine to the would-be revelers, and a fine may indeed have been necessary in this case. At any rate, that elegant lady, Isabella d'Este, sister of the bridegroom, expressed disappointment that custom had been tampered with and commented that the wedding was "rather cold."[6]

Weddings were indeed cooling down. Even the temperature of lower-class weddings gradually dropped, but the contrast between upper-class refinement and peasant vulgarity persisted, to serve as a reminder of deeply felt class differences. Those in the middle class sometimes strove for even more refinement than the aristocrats did. Along with refinement went the tendency to simplify the gestural elements and reduce their number, since they were increasingly thought to be merely decorative.

To Conform or Not to Conform

In every society there are couples who want to get married but find it impossible to follow the usual procedures. Before the seventeenth century procedures varied so widely in the Western world that "usual" makes sense only when speaking of particular localities. Departing from the usual did not mean doing things that might have seemed odd elsewhere but things that were different from what was expected in one's own region. These couples might have had any of a number of reasons, especially in view of the church regulations about impediments, which caused weddings to be delayed until dispensations were granted in a costly and time-consuming process. The most important reason, however, in the past as in the present, was parental opposition. Whatever form the usual procedure took, it always included the participation of parents and relatives. Anything else was in and of itself unusual. "Elopement" is the modern term. It has acquired rather benign overtones, but even when used to express stern disapproval it always implies that the couple becomes no less married than by the approved method.

Elopements have always been exercises in ingenuity. The history of elopement is the story of how people have learned to make use of a succession of legal and institutional loopholes. As the recourse of a minority of people in exceptional circumstances, elopement is never common. In the past it seemed a worse infraction than it does today, at least from what we read in works by moralists and theologians. This is hardly surprising, since marriages were ideally supposed to be controlled by families. Paradoxically, however, there were more loopholes in the earlier centuries than in the later ones. The varieties of elopement throw light on the development of marriage law and wedding ritual. If exceptions prove rules, elopements are good tests of a marriage system.

Ambivalence about elopements is pretty much the same everywhere and at all times. They defy normal expectations and so are disapproved of, but at the same time they are accepted. According to anthropologists, there is no system so rigid as not to provide some possibility for elopement. In Western society from 1350 to 1800, considerable effort was expended in closing loopholes, but no perfect answer was ever found. The sixteenth-century Reformers believed that the legal structure actually caused elopements—a notion that was the basis for one of their strongest attacks on canon law. With hindsight we now recognize that most people preferred to conform, and the possibility of a small amount of permitted nonconformity may have provided a safety valve that kept the system going.

Before the changes in marriage law in the wake of the sixteenth-century Reformation and Counter Reformation movements, loopholes abounded in what was an intricate and paradoxical legal system. The canon-law definition of marriage as something resulting from the exchange of consent between the two parties was an open invitation to do without the services of a clergyman when the need arose. If a couple stubbornly maintained that they had pledged themselves to each other, an ecclesiastical court was likely to back them up, and it really made little difference whether the words had been "in the present" or "in the future." In the records of fourteenth- and fifteenth-century church courts there are accounts of dramatic confrontations in village churches, when, upon the reading of the banns, a man steps forward and claims to be the true husband of the woman whose wedding is about to take place. This could have been the first that anyone had heard of the earlier "marriage," but sometimes it turned out that a handful of friends had been present when the couple exchanged consent. The woman often denied the man's claim at first but later admitted in court that her parents were forcing her to marry a man she did not care for and that, yes, she had exchanged promises with someone they disapproved of. The upshot was that the court forbade her to commit the "bigamy" demanded by her parents, who had no choice but to accept the unwanted son-in-law. This perfectly legal, indissoluble marriage was based on nothing but the few words that the law regarded as essential.

When people spoke of clandestine marriage this was the kind of thing they usually had in mind. A famous case of clandestine marriage occurred in the mid-sixteenth century at the very top of the social pyramid in France, intensifying the alarm many people already felt about the dangers inherent in the legal loopholes. The king, Henry II, had arranged to marry his daughter to the son of the duke of Montmorency, the Constable of France. The young Montmorency revealed to his shocked father that he had already exchanged words of marriage with a young lady-in-waiting at the royal court. The case was eventually brought before a papal court, which to the chagrin of the king and his constable found that words "of the present" had been exchanged and therefore no man could put asunder whom God had joined together. The prelates of the French church subsequently circumvented the papal ruling—a manifestation of the politico-religious struggles of the period—but the principle on which it rested nevertheless remained intact for the time being.

There was a widespread feeling that the most effective way to make a clandestine marriage unassailable was not to rely on words alone but to consummate it by sexual intercourse. Pregnancy has always been a way to break down parental resistance to a marriage, and under the old canon law copulation made the form of the words irrelevant, so long as the couple maintained that *some* words had been spoken. It is interesting that in fact few so-called clandestine marriages involved copulation. Young couples seem to have intended merely to put pressure on their parents to agree to the marriage. This was how Montmorency's son later explained what he had done. Clandestine marriage of this kind was closer to betrothal than marriage and is another indication of the awe and confusion surrounding that step in the process.

A slightly different kind of clandestine marriage used the services of a clergyman. In spite of the minimalism of the law, people seem to have wanted some such formality when they had an actual wedding in mind instead of a negotiating tactic. Parish priests could be punished if they officiated at weddings that had not been preceded by banns or attended by witnesses, but they were not impervious to persuasion or even bribes. In addition, one of the complexities in ecclesiastical organization before the sixteenth century was the existence of enclaves scattered throughout Christendom that, unlike ordinary parishes, were not subject to the discipline of local bishops. These were known to would-be eloping couples, as such information usually is. For instance, most mendicant orders were not under a bishop's rule, so a friar would have been the natural choice for a quick wedding, like that of the eloping Romeo and Juliet.

Much ink was spilled on the subject of clandestine marriage in the fifteenth and sixteenth centuries. Lawyers and theologians defined it, explained its intricacies, and generally condemned it. Others condemned the laws that made it possible and anyone with a taste for reform demanded that the laws be changed. The subject was debated for weeks at the Council of Trent. Most of the agitation for reform came from those who thought that parental consent should be an essential requirement for marriage, at least for the first marriage of a legal minor (in some places this could mean someone twenty-five or even thirty years old). To read these reformers one would think that at least 50 percent of all marriages were elopements. This was far from the case, but the fact that the mere possibility was so alarming says a lot about the prevailing view of marriage. The upshot of the agitation was a change in marriage law, taking different forms in different places. Clandestine marriage as it had been known was virtually eliminated. The options for elopement were thus transformed.

Clandestine marriages of the old sort were still heard of in some places—in parts of Switzerland as late as the eighteenth century, for example, and in England, where up until 1753 the old canon law on marriage was still in effect. After that, elopement in England had to tailor itself to restrictions similar to the ones in most countries of the Continent.

Elopement was still possible. France was the setting for ingenious evasions called *mariages à la gaulmine*. The minimal Tridentine requirements for a wedding specified the presence of the parish priest and "two or three" witnesses. As before, banns were supposed to be proclaimed and, if not, the priest was supposed to refuse to participate; but the absence of banns in itself did not invalidate a marriage. French royal legislation made similar requirements. When a certain learned and brilliant Gilbert Gaulmin encountered obstacles to his intended marriage, he devised a scenario in which his priest was forced to hear him exchange vows with his bride in the presence of two friends. This technically fulfilled the requirements for priest and witnesses and the scenario was adopted by a number of French couples up to the middle of the eighteenth century, to the continuing distress of the upholders of parental authority. Sometimes the wedding party rushed in and caught the priest by surprise, and sometimes notaries were used as witnesses, so that the whole episode would be duly recorded. In England and other Protestant countries eloping couples could still find clergymen who, for one reason or another, were willing to officiate at weddings that were, one might say, improvised on the spot, preceded neither by banns nor by parental consent. Some chaplains in England in the seventeenth century were still not under episcopal jurisdiction, so places like Lincoln's Inn, the Southwark Mint, and Newgate Prison were known to offer possibilities to eloping couples. In the eighteenth century the best-known route was the one over the northern border, because the rules of the Church of Scotland remained less demanding than the newly revised rules of the Church of England. The village of Gretna Green was famous as a place where complaisant ministers could be found, and it became almost synonymous with elopement.

The age-old complaint of those who demanded ever-stricter regulations was that elopements were common and that it was too easy to find clergymen who sided with rebellious children against their parents. What is closer to the truth is that elopements were not only rare but also risky. Not every village girl who pledged herself to a man her family opposed was able to withstand their pressure to renege on her promise. Her conscience might be tormented for years to come, but it was not easy then, any more than it has ever been, to be a romantic heroine.

Pierre Bayle's account in his *Historical Dictionary* treats Jeanne de Piennes, the young lady-in-waiting to whom the Constable Montmorency's son was pledged, as a heroine, for all the good it did her. She never wavered in her version of what had happened, in spite of being held in a convent against her will and subjected to repeated grilling. In the end her "husband" went

FIGURE 1   A seventeenth-century Dutch family poses for a formal portrait. At this stage of the family's existence the number of children matches the precise average for the period. The ratio of girls to boys (3 to 2) is also close to the average. Note the wide range of ages. The book the father's hand is resting on is undoubtedly the Bible.

FIGURE 2　A wealthy English family at tea around 1720. The maidservant is at the center, but it may be that the focus was intended to be on the tea, a new and fashionable commodity. She is part of the "family," in any case.

FIGURE 3　Old women receive charity in Durham, England, in the 1770s; the ration for each recipient includes bread and a clay pipe. It was at least as common for old people to be fending for themselves as paupers as for them to be living in households with their own children.

A Scheme of the Income and Expence of the feveral Families of England, calculated for the Year 1688.

Number of families	RANKS, DEGREES, TITLES, and QUALIFICATIONS	Heads per family	Number of perfons	Yearly income per family l. s.	Yearly income in general l.	Yearly income per head l. s.	Yearly expence per head l. s. d.	Yearly encreafe per head l. s. d.	Yearly encreafe in general l.
160	Temporal lords	40	6,400	3,200 0	512,000	80 0	70 0 0	10 0 0	64,000
26	Spiritual lords	20	520	1,300 0	33,800	65 0	45 0 0	20 0 0	10,400
800	Baronets	16	12,800	880 0	704,000	55 0	49 0 0	6 0 0	76,800
600	Knights	13	7,800	650 0	390,000	50 0	45 0 0	5 0 0	39,000
3,000	Efquires	10	30,000	450 0	1,200,000	45 0	41 0 0	4 0 0	120,000
12,000	Gentlemen	8	96,000	280 0	2,880,000	35 0	32 0 0	3 0 0	288,000
5,000	Perfons in greater offices and places	8	40,000	240 0	1,200,000	30 0	26 0 0	4 0 0	160,000
5,000	Perfons in leffer offices and places	6	30,000	120 0	600,000	20 0	17 0 0	3 0 0	90,000
2,000	Eminent merchants and traders by fea	8	16,000	400 0	800,000	50 0	37 0 0	13 0 0	208,000
8,000	Leffer merchants and traders by fea	6	48,000	198 0	1,600,000	53 0	27 0 0	6 0 0	288,000
10,000	Perfons in the law	7	70,000	154 0	1,540,000	22 0	18 0 0	4 0 0	280,000
2,000	Eminent clergymen	6	12,000	72 0	144,000	12 0	10 0 0	2 0 0	24,000
8,000	Leffer clergymen	5	40,000	50 0	400,000	10 0	9 4 0	0 16 0	32,000
40,000	Freeholders of the better fort	7	280,000	91 0	3,640,000	13 0	11 15 0	1 5 0	350,000
120,000	Freeholders of the leffer fort	5¼	660,000	55 0	6,600,000	10 0	9 10 0	0 10 0	330,000
150,000	Farmers	5	750,000	42 10	6,375,800	8 10	8 5 0	0 5 0	187,500
15,000	Perfons in liberal arts and fciences	5	75,000	60 0	900,000	12 0	11 0 0	1 0 0	75,000
50,000	Shopkeepers and tradefmen	4½	225,000	45 0	2,250,000	10 0	9 0 0	1 0 0	225,000
60,000	Artizans and handicrafts	4	240,000	38 0	2,280,000	9 10	9 0 0	0 10 0	120,000
5,000	Naval officers	4	20,000	80 0	400,000	20 0	18 0 0	2 0 0	40,000
4,000	Military officers	4	16,000	60 0	240,000	15 0	14 0 0	1 0 0	16,000
500,586		5½	2,675,520	68 18	34,488,800	12 18	11 15 4	1 2 8 Decreafe.	3,023,700 Decreafe.
50,000	Common feamen	3	150,000	20 0	1,000,000	7 0	7 10 0	0 10 0	75,000
364,000	Labouring people and out-fervants	3½	1,275,000	15 0	5,460,000	4 10	4 12 0	0 2 0	127,500
400,000	Cottagers and paupers	3¼	1,300,000	6 10	2,000,000	2 0	2 5 0	0 5 0	325,000
35,000	Common foldiers	2	70,000	14 0	490,000	7 0	7 10 0	0 10 0	35,000
849,000		3½	2,795,000	10 10	8,950,000	3 5	3 9 0	0 4 0	562,500
	Vagrants; as gipfies, thieves, beggars, &c.		30,000		60,000		4 0 0	2 0 0	60,000
	So the general account is								
500,586	Encreafing the wealth of the kingdom	5½	2,675,520	68 18	34,488,800	12 18	11 15 4	1 2 8	3,023,700
849,000	Decreafing the wealth of the kingdom	3½	2,825,000	10 10	9,010,000	3 3	3 7 0	0 4 6	622,500
1,349,586	Neat totals,	4½	5,500,520	32 5	43,491,800	7 18	7 9 3	0 8 9	2,401,700

FIGURE 4 Gregory King's list of probable household sizes in England, 1688. Note that "temporal lords," at the top, have twice as many people in their households as "spiritual lords" (bishops). A large group of the middling sort have households containing 4 to 5 people. Only the lowest of the low, including "thieves" and "beggars," have households with fewer than three.

FIGURE 5 Floor plan of a sixteenth-century English farmhouse constructed of wood and mud. It has three rooms on the ground floor and a "chamber" above, which is the size of "house" and "buttery" combined. The "house," the main room sometimes called the hall, which has the only fireplace, is 15 feet square. A buttery was a storage room.

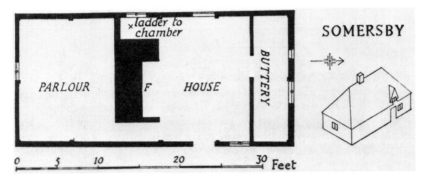

FIGURE 6 *(left)* A farmyard in November. These fifteenth-century Flemish peasants, male and female, are preparing dried flax to be made into linen. Note the various structures, including a dovecote, all with thatched roofs. Pigs and chickens were inevitable in any such domestic scene.

FIGURE 7 *(right)* Interior of an eighteenth-century Scottish cottage. A lot is going on. The room, probably the "house" or "hall," has an old-fashioned brazier type of fireplace. There is a curtained built-in bed in one corner at the back, and the inevitable chickens are above and below.

FIGURE 9 *(facing, below)* The village of Feckenham, Worcestershire, in 1591, with its open fields. The letters and symbols indicate the ownership of the various parcels. "A+" means the lord's demesne, "*" means "the Common Fields, Meadows and Closes." Enclosure and consolidation of individual strips had already begun. Few owners had less than five parcels of land, and a handful had more than a hundred each. The single street and the village church are clearly depicted at the center.

FIGURE 8   Shop fronts in a fifteenth-century town. The artisans do
their work and sell their wares out in the open, in front of their living
quarters. There is a barber in the middle, flanked by an apothecary
and a tailor with his apprentice. The white cone in the right
foreground is a sugarloaf—sugar was then chiefly for medicinal use.

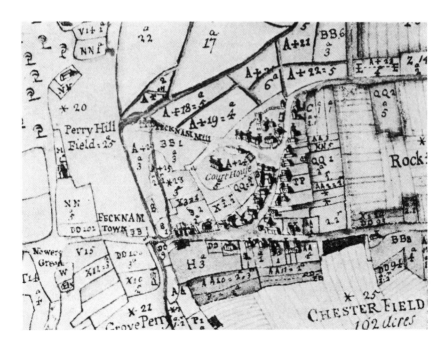

FIGURE 10   The arrangement of pews by households in a village church in 1701. The front of the church is at the top, with the pulpit on the left. The best pews are in the front. Note that No. 5 north is "for servants" of Shotton, the holder of No. 1 north. Similarly, No. 2 south (right) belongs to Balderton Hall and No. 8 north (left) to "Balderton Hall for servants."

FIGURE 11   The celibate ideal paradoxically expressed in nuptial imagery. In this fifteenth-century painting by Andrea del Sarto, St. Catherine as the mystical bride of Christ extends her finger so that the Infant Christ can put a wedding ring on it.

Heyrath durch Zuneigung
Mariage par Inclination

Heyrath aus Eigennutz
Mariage par Interet

FIGURES 12 AND 13   Although the choice between "love" and "interest" was still a very hard one to make for many in the eighteenth century, popular opinion was on the side of love. These engravings are typical of how that opinion was expressed.

FIGURE 14   Charles I of England and his French Catholic wife, Henrietta Maria. The royal status that they shared counted for more in the making of this match than the difference in religion, in spite of the fact that Protestant-Catholic antagonism was then at its height.

FIGURE 16 (facing)   Like St. Catherine, an elegant Jewish bride of the fifteenth century extends her finger for the groom to put the ring on it. If this picture were not part of a Hebrew manuscript it would be impossible to identify the ceremony as Jewish. The man with the gray beard may be the officiating rabbi.

FIGURE 15 Courting in public. Peasant women are gathered in what looks like a barn to spin and make lace, observing with approval a young man who has arrived to declare his affection for his chosen one.

לא טוב

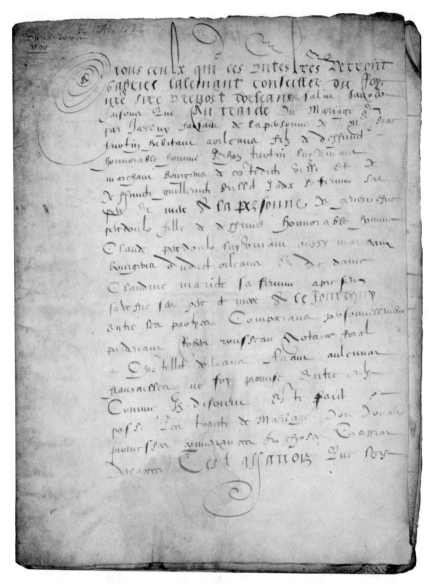

FIGURE 17   A sixteenth-century French marriage contract. This is only the first page of an impressive document on vellum detailing the property arrangements made between two merchant families of Orleans. The fathers of the couple were both dead.

FIGURE 18   The symbolism of marriage. The bride and groom touch hands in this famous fifteenth-century double portrait by Jan van Eyck of a wealthy Italian couple (she with the receding hairline, protruding belly, and tiny waist required of a fashionable fifteenth-century maiden). The artist acts as witness to the exchange of vows, inscribing that fact over the mirror: "Johannes de Eycke fuit hic 1434." The lighted candle and the dog symbolize fidelity; the room is a bridal chamber. Other details reinforce the message that this is a nuptial occasion.

FIGURE 19 A village wedding procession in seventeenth-century France. A large motley group, including children and musicians, accompanies an elaborately coiffed bride to the church door, where the groom is probably already waiting. This would be the last time she would wear her hair loose, since to do so was a sign of maidenhood. Note that men and women walk in separate groups.

FIGURE 20 A 1785 print by Thomas Rowlandson ironically entitled "Filial Affection, or a Trip to Gretna Green," in which an irate father tries to prevent an elopement.

FIGURE 21   A sixteenth-century couple depicted as sharing in the business from which their wealth derives: the picture is said to be of a money lender and his wife. While she watches him weigh coins and jewels she fingers the pages of a book of devotions (itself a jewel-like object).

FIGURE 22   A wife spanks her husband with a broom in what was probably intended as an amusing decoration on the seat of a choir stall in a French church.

FIGURE 23   An English charivari or skimmington ride in an eighteenth-century illustration. Amid the symbolism of trousers, skirt, horns, etc., a couple is made to ride back to back. The husband is either henpecked or a cuckold or both.

FIGURE 24 *(left, below)*   In this drawing from one of Leonardo da Vinci's notebooks, the partial view of the anatomy of a woman engaged in sexual intercourse shows a blood vessel going from the uterus to the breasts. This inaccuracy reflects the belief that milk and menstrual blood were the same substance.

FIGURE 25 *(right, below)*   A woman in labor using a birthing chair and attended by two other women, one of whom is probably a midwife. The illustration appears in the first printed manual for midwives (1513).

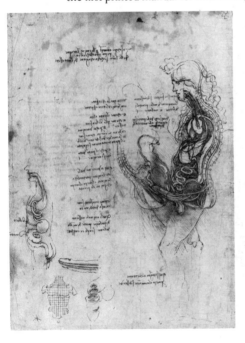

FIGURE 26　The community of women: St. Elizabeth is depicted as a fifteenth-century Florentine patrician who has just given birth, attended by female friends and relatives. The infant is already being suckled by a wet nurse.

FIGURE 27   A male midwife depicted as a monster, and who "for my own use" has a shelf of aphrodisiacs to administer to unsuspecting patients. Note the frightening instruments and, by contrast, the benign absence in the right half of much equipment.

back on his word, changing his story to make the plausible claim that they were only betrothed and that they had betrothed themselves in order to soften parental resistance. He had changed his mind, he said, because of his father's wishes. But for the betrothal to be legally terminated her agreement was needed, and to induce her to agree he lied to her, saying that the pope had ruled that their pledges were not binding. Her response was, "It seems that he did not mean what he once told me, that he would rather lose his life than change his mind. . . . I see that he prefers being rich to being a man of honor." She therefore agreed not to insist on the obligation.[7] At the time there were certainly some who admired her, but it must be pointed out that the dutiful son, though he seems to have suffered from a bad conscience in later years, also had his admirers.

A few years later there was a famous case in England, that of the earl of Hertford and Lady Katharine Grey. Theirs was the other kind of clandestine marriage. Unlike the French pair, they had a clergyman and consummated the marriage. They may have decided to go further because the resistance they were facing was not merely parental. Their situation was far more desperate and precarious because Queen Elizabeth opposed their marriage for political reasons. Although the marriage was theoretically unassailable under the old canon law, which was supposedly in effect, the queen used every legal device, taking advantage of the wedding's secrecy. The wedding was declared never to have taken place. The couple were detained in the Tower, found guilty of the crime of fornication, and then kept under what amounted to house arrest, far apart from each other. As far as they were concerned, they had lost their gamble, although two generations later the marriage was retroactively recognized as valid.

It may not have been easy for parents to remain obdurate, however. Whether because of affection for their offspring or unwillingness to let a family disintegrate, many of them seem to have come around—which may explain why French kings found it necessary to issue a whole series of decrees throughout the seventeenth century and why the question of clandestine marriage was discussed with such intensity in England until the middle of the eighteenth century. Upper-class parents seem to have been calling on the law to accomplish what they were unable to do themselves.

The literary treatment of elopement had a lighter side as well, especially when there was more and more public approval of marrying for love. David Garrick's 1766 play, *The Clandestine Marriage*, was a popular depiction of the familiar conflict between love and wealth. Its brave eloping couple won their gamble, and it is perhaps appropriate that a little later they even got an opportunity to sing of their triumph in an Italian opera based on the play, Cimarosa's *Il matrimonio segreto*.

Comedy and tragedy are not realistic descriptions of life, of course. Most couples were not faced with the difficult choices of characters in plays and, when they were, they chose neither the sufferings of tragedy nor a gamble on comic reversals. They held out for parental approval and they got married in the public eye, in the presence of clergy, and with all the festivities and rituals they and those around them expected at weddings.

The complex variety of weddings in the past, the confusions about their legal significance, and the literary attention paid to the unusual have given some people the impression that the form of weddings did not matter and the general attitude toward them was rather casual. All that is needed to destroy this impression is a closer look at the evidence. Money, time, energy, and a whole gamut of emotions were poured into weddings. They were central social events, and they were the highly charged prelude to the formation of a central social institution, the household. Little wonder that not only individuals and local communities cared about them, but church and state as well.

5

The Married Couple

Saint Paul's Epistle to the Ephesians says: "This is a great mystery (5:32)." Paul is speaking of the relationship between husband and wife, which for him is a metaphor for the relationship between Christ and the church. His words are constantly used in Christian discussions of marriage. "Mystery" is rendered as *sacramentum* in the Vulgate—one reason that marriage is included among the Catholic sacraments. For historians the relationship between husband and wife is a mystery for a different reason. It is, after all, mainly a private matter. Its most interesting aspects are hidden from us and we must make do with maddeningly contradictory hints. Those who speak to us from the past on this subject either express personal feelings, which we should think twice about before taking them to be representative, or are engaged in polemics and sermonizing. Recent research has thrown some light on the material conditions of marriage and new questions, based on modern psychological and sociological theories, are being applied to familiar texts. Apart from these slight advances, however, we are not much better informed than we ever were. And what a pity, since so many of us today consider the married couple to be the essence of what a family is, and nearly everybody feels that the personal relationship between husband and wife determines the quality of family life.

Such contradictory hints as we have suggest ambivalences that may get us at least to within calling distance of certain knowledge about married couples in the past. The questions are obvious. The first is about power: Who, if anyone, was boss? Then there is the question about emotions: How did husbands and wives feel about each other, and what kind of sexual intimacy did they share? Closely related to these questions are the issues of sexual fidelity and the durability of marriages, but it is useful to treat them separately because we happen to know quite a bit about them and can even see the kind of historical evolution they went through.

Partnership or Hierarchy

The current cliché is to call marriage a partnership. That it is an absolutely equal partnership is not, I think, universally accepted. The belief persists that what women do is less important than what men do and that big family decisions should be made by husbands. So there is some ambivalence today whether to retain a comfortably familiar image of power in the family or to overhaul it by totally embracing our society's ideal of equality.

The notion of equality as a fundamental principle did not have much currency in the past. It did not even start moving to the forefront of accepted ideas until the late eighteenth century, when, for instance, equality was combined with liberty and fraternity in the slogan of the French Revolution. Realizing equality is harder than talking about it, and even in the United States, where equality was officially proclaimed a self-evident truth two hundred years ago, we are still trying to attain it.

While it is probably no surprise that inequality was rife in earlier centuries, it is important to recognize that what we see as a blemish was for a long time considered to be positive. True, Christianity proclaimed the equality of all souls—depicted in art as the equality of all social ranks in the face of death—but the Roman church was itself a hierarchy, organized in layers of ascending authority. All society was hierarchical, and so, it was believed, was the natural universe. Hierarchy was the natural order and its opposite was chaos. The famous speech of Ulysses in Shakespeare's *Troilus and Cressida* is a paean to hierarchy, or "degree," which, when neglected, leads to discord, cracking "the unity and married calm of states":

> O, when degree is shak'd, . . .
> Then enterprise is sick! How could communities,
> Degrees in schools and brotherhoods in cities, . . .
> Prerogative of age, crowns, sceptres, laurels,
> But by degree, stand in authentic place?

Husband and wife each had an "authentic place." Reality is rarely so neat, however, as our own struggles with racial and sexual inequality remind us. If there was next to no ambivalence about what the power relationship in marriage should be, there seems to have been a wide range of possibilities and attitudes in actual marriages. The ambivalence in the past arose from the contrast between a simple theory and a complicated, sometimes disturbing, reality.

The main elements of the theory appear in Paul's Epistle to the Ephesians, where they are treated as long-established ideas:

> Wives, submit yourselves unto your own husbands . . . for the husband is the head of the wife, even as Christ is the head of the church. . . . Let the wives be to their own husbands in everything. Husbands, love your wives, even as Christ also loved the church. . . . So ought men to love their wives as their own bodies. He that loveth his wife loveth himself. . . . For this cause shall a man leave his father and mother, and shall be joined unto his wife, and they two shall be one flesh. . . . Let every one of you in particular so love his wife even as himself: and the wife see that she reverence her husband. (5:22-33)

This idea of a loving despotism was buttressed by the idea of the natural inferiority of women, an idea whose antiquity argued for its truth. It was stated clearly in Aristotle and obliquely but unmistakably in the Old Testament. Worshipers in Anglican churches were regularly reminded that the woman is "the weaker vessel, of a frail heart." Frailty justified control, but a control that should not be too harsh. "Although she is inferior," said a handbook for French confessors in the sixteenth century, "yet she is not a slave or a servant but the companion and flesh of the flesh of her husband."[1]

Popular wisdom echoed the philosophers and theologians, with fewer nuances. An English proverb said, "A woman, a spaniel, and a walnut tree, the more they are beaten, better they be."[2] Wives who talked back and were disobedient were shrews, and, according to another English proverb, "it is better to marry a sheep than a shrew."[3] The French favored the imagery of roosters and hens, one proverb declaring, "When the rooster crows the hen should fall silent."[4] These ideas were enforced in charivaris, which commented on the relations of people already married, just as they did on those about to marry. As time went on, charivaris in some parts of Europe were organized almost exclusively to express disapproval of husbands and wives who did not know their "authentic place." One of the English words for charivari, "skimmington," was a synonym for a woman who beat or henpecked her husband, and it sometimes also meant a husband who allowed this to happen.

The legal systems of the Western world supported the theory. When a woman married, her identity was swallowed up in her husband's. As William Blackstone pithily put it in the eighteenth century, summing up the thrust of English common law, "The husband and wife are one, and the husband is that one."[5] What this meant was that, with a few exceptions, a wife could not bring a legal action in a court, make a contract, or own property. If she technically had title to property, it was controlled by her husband. The commonest way of looking at the property of a married couple saw it as a community of pooled resources, to which the wife sometimes made a major contribution in the form of her dowry. As long as the marriage lasted she had next to no say in how it was managed or spent. There were national and even regional variations, to be sure, but the similarity in the legal disabilities of wives outweighed any differences. Where the influence of Roman law was strongest, as a continuing tradition in southern France and Italy and as a learned development that gathered force in the sixteenth and seventeenth centuries elsewhere, the dowry was supposed to be preserved as a separate entity that the husband could use but not use up. Even in theory this had little to do with the wife's independence, but rather with making sure that she would be provided for after her husband died. The dowry was supposed to help the husband support the household; it did not make the wife an equal partner.

The law assumed, furthermore, that the husband as the ruler of the household had the right to use discipline to enforce his rule. In this respect, wives were subjects of the same loving despotism as servants and children. There were laws all over Europe giving men the right to beat their wives. The appalling behavior of Petruchio in The Taming of the Shrew was at the very least legal, and it was apparently expected of those who wived it wealthily as well as those who wived it poorly, although this seemed to be changing in the eighteenth century. Abuse and cruelty were always frowned on, but a man was expected to do what he had to in order to be obeyed.

When we turn from law and theory to practice, one of the things about these centuries that is striking is the outward formality of married couples. Other times, other customs: it is not safe to deduce too much from style. Still, style is important. When a wife referred to her husband as "my lord" or "Mr. Bennett" instead of "Jim" she was not only conforming to the way her world categorized individuals—the antithesis of our compulsion to democratize relationships by using first names and nicknames—but she also implied that the rules of authority and subservience were not suspended for her just because she was the man's wife. Although her husband referred to her as "my lady" or "Mrs. Bennett," everybody knew that Mr. Bennett gave the orders to Mrs. Bennett ("the husband is the head of the wife"). There do not seem to have been wide class differences in this regard. A French proverb said, "If you have a husband you have a lord." In the eighteenth century in the south of France, a relatively backward area, it was expected that a peasant wife would refer to her husband as "our man" (the head of the household, that is), attribute jealous suspicions to him, and express fear of physical punishment. Wives usually stayed in the background, and on the rare occasions when husbands mentioned their wives it was in a tone of paternalistic indulgence, accompanied by a shrug of the shoulders.

The work that wives did, whether it consisted of distinctively female tasks, as defined by the prevailing social conventions, or was no different from what men did, was assigned a lower value. It was almost invariably thought of as assisting the primary work of the husband and, if it happened to be done outside the household, it was paid for on a lower scale. In the south of France, for example, in the fifteenth century, women were paid precisely half what men were for picking grapes and by the end of the sixteenth century, as the labor supply grew, the differential became even greater. Since the husband's role was to do the supporting, if he did not do so he was a failure both as a husband and as a man. The wife's role was theoretically to manage the husband's resources in a helpful and obedient manner, even if she was in fact contributing to the household's income.

There is another side to this picture. Wherever it may have fitted on the scale of values and however it was remunerated, women's work, as we have seen, was essential. In a rural household living on a modest amount of land, it was impossible to do without women's work. There was something close to a partnership in the complementary relationship of rural men's and women's chores—a reality that considerably modifies what at first glance appears to be an absolute commitment to hierarchy and deference. The husband's territory was the field and the forest, the wife's the house and the farmyard. She produced—and often sold—eggs, butter, and cheese. At times husband and wife collaborated on the same territory, more often the wife on the husband's. She helped at harvest time, gathering the grain he cut with his scythe and later winnowing what he flailed. In the woods, where he hunted rabbits and birds, she picked berries and collected kindling. In town, where the wives of artisans were part of the business operation, they not only did necessary female things like feeding the apprentices but also sold the bread the baker baked, the meat the butcher cut, and the pots the tinsmith made.

Wives also did things that were not merely complementary to their husbands' occupations. The wife of a poor day laborer in a town could not afford to pay attention to the theory that men's proper role was to support their families. She did whatever work she could find, sometimes on her own selling fish or fruit in the market, sometimes in the employment of entrepreneurs who paid her for sewing, spinning, or embroidery. The terms "fishwives" and "alewives" have preserved in the English language the notion of certain traditionally independent female occupations. Not only did women in England frequently engage in brewing on their own, but the running of a tavern or inn could come very close to being an equal partnership of husband and wife, in which the tasks were interchangeable.

These patterns could be found all over Europe, and in Europe's American colonies as well. In the colonies they were perhaps even more noticeable because of the relative absence of the highest levels of society. To live "like a noble" meant to depend on the labor of others and be a lavish consumer. An aristocratic wife was, ideally, a household manager and so, in a way, close to the image of domesticity promoted as a middle-class ideal in the nineteenth century. An aristocratic husband could be a lot of things—estate manager, judge, soldier—all distinctively male and all endowed with the highest status. This clearly hierarchical division of "labor" in aristocratic couples was highly visible in a status-conscious society and got disproportionate attention from theorists. We are only now learning how often the behavior of people lower down on the social scale did not match the theories. In the middle class (that fluid and changing concept), urban artisans and their wives at its lower reaches were likely to form partnerships with complementary tasks, as we have seen. At its upper reaches, the bourgeoisie—urban merchants, financiers, and professionals—had a tendency to measure their success by their ability to act like aristocrats. In the newer middle class already becoming visible in the eighteenth century, which would blossom in the nineteenth century as industrial capitalists, family firms were common. Wives were often active participants in every aspect of business, like artisans' wives. Later on this became rarer, as the aristocratic notion of elegant domesticity took over. This development really belongs to the period after 1800, but it can be partly understood in the light of the longstanding contradictions between aristocratic ideal and lower-class reality.

On all levels of society even wives' control over property was not a completely one-sided situation. In some parts of Europe wives could not only possess but also control certain property of their own. In Roman law this property was called "paraphernalia"—that is, things above and beyond the dowry. It did not usually amount to much, although it could theoretically include anything, even valuable real estate. In practice the tendency was for wives to sign over control to their husbands, converting all possessions, no matter who the legal owner, into a common fund. What is more important is that wives had some power at law to protect their property if it was being badly managed. They were not utterly helpless. A wife could sue for a legal separation of goods (a right that gained strength in France) or to halt the wasting of the property that was to be hers in her widowhood. Such power says little about marriage as a partnership, of course. As in so much of the law about conjugal property, it should perhaps be seen more as protection of the weak than as an assertion of equality. It operated only in abnormal situations, and had little to do with the ordinary functioning of marriage.

A number of legal systems, however, required both spouses to participate whenever a piece of property was sold. This was especially true where all the property or at least the property acquired during the marriage belonged to the couple jointly (a system widely followed in the parts of France under customary law, as distinct from the written law under Roman influence). Even in England wives participated in some sales and they were required to do so in the first decades of the Plymouth Colony, which was essentially under the same common law. Using the vocabulary of partnership when setting up community property became more common in France in spite of the commitment of lawyers to Roman models.

Admittedly, the evidence for true partnership is not very strong. But we have not yet considered second marriages. Not every bride was a girl who came fresh from her father's house bearing her dowry or portion. Widows who had retrieved their own property from their first marriages and had inherited additional wealth from their husbands sometimes made contracts with new husbands in which they kept control of at least part of their own property, and they sometimes also insisted on exclusive authority over their own children. Widows were not always as powerful as they theoretically could be. Some widows lost their inheritance if they remarried, and sometimes a widow agreed to give up her inheritance in return for being allowed to remain in her house and be supported by her husband's heirs (normally his and/or her children). The potential power of widows was commonly realized in the more fluid atmosphere of New England.

The fact that widows emerged from their first marriages with so much authority hints at the sort of relationships they may have had with their first husbands. It was not at all rare in seventeenth-century England, for example, where wives were nominally incompetent, for husbands to name their wives in their wills as executors of their estates and to give them full control of their property and total responsibility for bringing up their young children.

Alongside conventional praise of the docile wife and fantasies of the perfect gentleman's wife, like those in Molière's *School for Wives,* was a reality that these wills bear witness to. John Calvin may have appreciated his wife mainly for the fact that she was never a hindrance to him, but other men wrote of their deceased wives in much more positive terms. A number of upper-class widowers recalled how much they missed their wives' companionship and help, saying that they now had to deal with matters they used to leave to their wives and admitting that their wives had been more competent than they were. There is less written evidence lower down on the social scale, but with the very real responsibilities borne by women it is not unlikely that most children would have seen their mothers and fathers as equally powerful presences. "It is better," said an English proverb that seems to have circulated as widely as its reverse, "to marry a shrew than a sheep."[6]

The almost pathological fear of "shrews" points to an extreme disjunction between ideal and reality. We can be sure that some wives abused their husbands, but how far a woman had to go to be considered a shrew is not clear. The ideal was threatened by the merest hint of superiority or dominance in a wife and, although charivaris often punished a "shrewish" wife, the man bore the shame for not adequately filling his role as husband. In French and English villages throughout this period (and also in large towns in earlier centuries) a jeering and outraged crowd of neighbors made such a victimized husband ride a donkey mounted backwards. This "skimmington," "riding," or "*chevau-chée*" was the commonest form of charivari. Whatever wives were supposed to be like, it is obvious that they sometimes had an opportunity to be strong, active, competent, and dominant. And sometimes their husbands appreciated it, especially if it could be hidden from the outside world under the mask of convention.

Love or Duty

The most intimate part of the relationship between husband and wife is of course the greatest mystery of all. Even today, when there is so much public discussion about sex, it remains a somewhat shadowy subject. Attitudes have greatly changed since 1800, especially the attitudes of those who write and preach, but whether there has been as great a change in the attitudes of ordinary couples is less clear. This subject evokes all sorts of hypotheses and explanations, since we are all tempted to project our own feelings onto the murky background of a few facts. Perhaps historical research will one day reveal how husbands and wives acted (and felt) in bed—but I doubt it. The very fact that someone would write openly about such things in the period we are concerned with makes his or her information suspect. To do so was entirely atypical; what has changed most is the level of frankness. Remember that I am talking not of pornography or eroticism, which were not rareties, but of descriptions of marital relations.

An ambivalence that has by now lost much of its meaning is that between marital sex as a pleasure and marital sex as a duty. Today any ambivalence on this score is obscured by our tendency to approve of pleasure. It was otherwise in the past, although toward the end of the period there were signs of change. We are dealing mostly with attitudes expressed in writing, some of which was extreme and highly theoretical. Throughout most of this period the notion of a married couple as a pair of lovebirds was quite unacceptable, but from the early seventeenth century on the harsh view of marriage as a solemn duty was considerably softened.

The Judeo-Christian attitude toward sexuality is, to say the least, cautionary. Centuries of Christian theological writing praised virginity as the highest state a human being could attain. Sexuality within marriage was justified on two grounds: it channeled potentially dangerous impulses and it produced children. Saint Paul was as often quoted on this subject as on that of power in marriage: "It is good for a man not to touch a woman," he said in the First Epistle to the Corinthians. "Nevertheless, to avoid fornication, let every man have his own wife, and let every woman have her own husband. . . . It is better to marry than to burn" (7:1-2, 9). What Christians heard from the pulpit and in the confessional was that marriage was the remedy for fornication and that husband and wife each had a duty to the other to provide relief for lusts that might otherwise run out of control. The word "contract," which was so often used in connection with marriage, meant that, whether there was a written document or not, the parties had mutual obligations. Sex was often called the *debitum conjugale*. Not infrequently the delicate question was broached as to how much one party was entitled to demand of the other, and there were actually some efforts at quantification. When ecclesiastical judges in the fifteenth century, for example, had to decide whether complaints about nonperformance of duty were justified they tended to regard intercourse two or three times a week as reasonable. Marital duty involved not only the notion of what was enough but also of what was too much. Clergymen constantly warned against "adultery" in marriage, insisting that when married people had sexual intercourse it should not be wildly passionate, neither a legalized surrender to base instincts nor a kind of idolatry. Many secular writers—Montaigne among them—supported this idea.

The second justification for sex, procreation, was overlooked by Saint Paul, but it became firmly established in theology, if always in a slightly uneasy balance with the first justification. Throughout this period a Christian was unlikely to be told that sex was *only* for procreation. There were theories about "natural" and "unnatural" sex, natural being defined as what was likely to lead to conception, but it is not so clear that the emphasis was on having children rather than on avoiding behavior that was sinful. Catholic theologians in the seventeenth and eighteenth centuries wrote profusely on the subject of marital sexuality and dealt with extraordinarily complicated matters. An example is the case of a woman who was afraid of having more children because it would be a danger to her health. Continence being her only recourse (anything else being unnatural), the problem was whether there might not be a greater danger to her husband's soul if she did not fulfill her marital debt. There was no easy solution. Protestant theologians—perhaps because they were not faced with the regular challenge of the confessional— had much less to say on the subject of sex in marriage, except for the English Puritans, who, while praising marriage wholeheartedly in a way that Catholics could not, also spoke of obligations and warned of the temptations to sensuality in the marriage bed. The Jewish attitude to marital sex was apparently similar.

Duties are rarely thought of as pleasurable. If people really believed what they were told about sex in marriage they might very well have been resentful, and some people were. But whether women resented men more than men resented women is hard to say. This is not the place to go into the picture of women's sexuality that appeared fully elaborated in the nineteenth century, which included the notion that nice women did not enjoy sex but had a duty to their husbands, who did. Certainly there was a widespread belief earlier that men were more aggressive and less able to control themselves. Upper-class women sometimes complained obliquely of their husbands' lack of consideration, as Madame de Sévigné's beloved ailing daughter seems to have done when her mother kept urging her not to get pregnant again. We can probably assume that lack of consideration was also found among lower-class husbands. Sexual performance among the poor was further complicated by the fact that so many of them were overworked and undernourished—perfect conditions for both resentment and lack of desire. On the other hand, the notion of marital duty allowed the woman to make demands of her own, and there were some court cases brought by wives complaining of their husbands' nonperformance or impotence.

When it came to expressing their feelings in writing, however, men complained about marriage more than women did. This is not surprising, since almost all writers were men. A whole genre of writing going back to the Middle Ages and extending through the seventeenth century bitterly attacked the burdens of marriage. One fifteenth-century French work was ironically entitled *The Fifteen Joys of Marriage*, and other titles included *Why Not to Take a Wife* and *The Purgatory of Married Men*. The real subject of these works was hatred and resentment of women. As a sixteenth-century Frenchman chillingly put it, "Marriage is a way of learning how to hate women."[7] Women were said to be fickle, sly, unreliable, and, above all, the quintessence of sensuality. Women were the daughters of Eve, who had caused the fall of man. To say that the opinions in these works were contradicted by other works, as well as by what many people did and said, does not minimize their significance. These works were respectable and popular. They hint at a great deal of confusion about sexuality and the institution that legitimized its expression. They tell us that at least some men longed to be free of their sexual impulses, which in their minds they transferred to women and blamed them for. We know misogyny never died, but it eventually took different forms. By the middle of the eighteenth century this genre of misogynistic writing had become quite unfashionable. The Protestant Reformation is often given the credit for the change, because Protestantism promoted a positive view of marriage, but the influence was not immediate and there were Protestant misogynists as well as Catholic ones. One of the components of a married couple's relationship in these centuries must have been the fear and suspicion that men and women had of each other, intensified by a somewhat greater gulf than now between men's and women's worlds and hardly diminished by the method of choosing spouses in certain parts of society.

Love is an ambiguous concept in the Western world. By the fourteenth century it bore the weight of two traditions—an older one that equated it with sexual desire and a newer one that saw it as an exalted spiritual state. Poets and writers of romances tended to put more and more emphasis on the latter—a dominant characteristic of Western literature. Theologians tended to regard love as a danger in both of its aspects. Let no one think, however, that because married couples were advised to be restrained, love was not taken seriously. It was taken very seriously, not as something bland but as one of those hard realities of life that human beings had to come to terms with. Again, I am speaking of what was written. In addition to the familiar theological opposition of carnal desire and spiritual purity there were secular works that spoke of the struggle between love and honor, an ancient theme that became a particular favorite of seventeenth-century dramatists.

Reflective people generally agreed that to fall in love and get married for that reason was a bad idea. On the other hand, they just as generally agreed that husbands and wives should love each other and they sometimes suggested that sharing sexual pleasure was an expression of that love. Puritan writers in particular praised the delights of married love. Love was supposed to develop in the course of marriage and was not to be confused with either infatuation or lust. Most people were probably unable to make such distinctions, or if they did they might assume that "real" love—whether sexual passion or spiritual exaltation—could only be found outside marriage. That there was an inherent contradiction between marriage and love (however defined) was a not uncommon idea. But the opposite idea—that marriage and love naturally went together—seems to have been at least as common, and whatever concept people had of love was in varying degrees incorporated in the marital relationship. By the middle of the eighteenth century Wetenhall Wilkes, an English writer of "moral advice to a young lady," could proclaim that marital affection was "the completest image of heaven we can receive in this life."[8]

Even if we cannot marshal a lot of evidence showing that married people were "in love," we have no difficulty finding examples of great affection, warmth, and devotion at all times and in all social groups. The very warnings against going too far are evidence. William Gouge, a seventeenth-century Puritan divine who said that a wife should always address her spouse as "husband," seems to have often heard otherwise, since he gives a rather long list of terms to be avoided, including "sweeting," "sweetheart," "love," "dear," "duck," and "chick."[9] We do not often hear peasants and artisans of the past speaking for themselves, but on rare occasions when they were asked to explain why they wanted to get married—such as when they put in requests for dispensations—they used expressions like being "made for each other" and wanting to enjoy the happiness of each other's company. Some of these people were marrying for the second time, so one might suppose they knew what to expect. That they expected their words to meet with approval from church authorities is another indication that love in marriage was not so narrowly conceived as some theoretical works would lead us to believe. There seems to have been a gradual change in the tone of these documents, with more and more emphasis on personal happiness in the late eighteenth century. But even in the fifteenth and sixteenth centuries there is an occasional glimpse of something akin to passion between husbands and wives. A German burgher described (approvingly) in his journal the emotional scene at the deathbed of his young sister-in-law as her bereaved husband clasped her in his arms, kissed her, and said "good night" to her over and over again.[10] Even the most upper-class of aristocrats could have affectionate, companionable marriages. Frenchmen sometimes claimed that this was far more common in England than in France, but they made the comparison in order to criticize their own countrymen—holding up the English as a model was a familiar device of the eighteenth-century philosophes, a device that could not have worked if the values had not been shared.

The mystery remains, probably never to be pierced. We are free to speculate that, in spite of outward manner and the prescriptions of those in authority, some husbands and wives enjoyed considerable sexual intimacy and respected each other's needs. On the other hand, who can say what effect oft-repeated strictures and the social gulf between the sexes had on private behavior and inner feelings?

Fidelity or Infidelity

Although fidelity is an aspect of a couple's sexual relationship, there are good reasons for treating it separately. We actually have some facts about adultery, the opposite of fidelity, and so we can move a bit beyond theory and speculation. Adultery was quite often a matter of public knowledge. It is now no longer prosecuted as a crime in Western countries (although it is still a "fault" under some divorce laws), but between 1350 and 1800 religious and secular courts dealt with it in a variety of ways; court records and other official documents provide considerable information about it. Attitudes toward adultery were abundantly expressed in all that was written about it over the centuries by poets, dramatists, novelists, moralists, and lawyers.

Central to the subject is the persistent and pervasive belief in a double standard—one code of conduct for wives, another for husbands. Women's behavior should be seen in the light of the fidelity that was expected of wives and men's behavior in the light of the greater latitude that was allowed to husbands. There has always been some ambivalence about the double standard, however preeminent it may have been. And today, when the pendulum seems to have swung so far in the opposite direction, it remains a sturdy relic. In the centuries we are considering, the double standard gained strength, reaching what may have been its high-water mark, at least in the law, around 1800.

Most women seem to have been faithful wives, as they were required to be. It was risky to be otherwise. Under whatever law she was subject to, an adulterous wife could be repudiated by her husband. She might also be punished as a criminal. Although the canon law of the Roman church treated the adultery of wives and husbands as equally criminal, secular laws generally penalized only wives. In England, in the brief period when adultery was a secular crime, during the Commonwealth in the mid-seventeenth century, it was specifically a crime only wives could be punished for. In French secular law it was always so. The court of public opinion was also hard on female adultery. The widely held notion of honor—a complex concept midway between inner probity and public image—was tightly intertwined with the notion of female chastity. A wife who committed adultery damaged not only her own honor but that of her husband and family as well. The "authentic place" assigned to wives included this duty of embodying and preserving family honor, so that women were also expected to cover up any wrongdoing by their husbands. A French proverb described wives as staying close to home "like dogs," while husbands roamed the streets "like cats."[11]

Along with this strict code of behavior for wives went a literary preoccupation with the subject. Female adultery was already well established as an important theme in Western literature before 1350. While it is extremely dangerous to use literature as an accurate description of behavior, it must be taken into account if we want to understand values and attitudes. Men looked at the sexual nature of women with extreme ambivalence. On the one hand, women were like Mary—pure, passive, humble. On the other hand, they were the daughters of Eve—untrustworthy, sensual, insatiable. The awful thing about married women was that, once they had sexual experience, the floodgates might open and the potential Eve in every woman might emerge. Men seem to have been both repelled and fascinated by this possibility. In Western literature the adulterous wife is found on every social level and treated in a great variety of ways, from the cynicism of Boccaccio's bawdy tales and Brantôme's gossip about French court ladies to the delicacy and awe of courtly-love poetry and chivalric romances. That the whole structure rested on powerful male fantasies is buttressed by the fact that some of the best works in the genre are not about adultery itself but rather about the obsessive fear of it. Shakespeare has given us a comic version in the character of Master Ford in *The Merry Wives of Windsor*, a play in which the wives are chaste to perfection. He has also given us the tragedy of *Othello*, in which Iago works the fertile ground of a nightmarish fear that even a Desdemona might have hidden depths of depravity and deceit.

Side by side with the tendency to put the blame on the wife went a powerful current in Western thought that minimized her responsibility. The blame fell rather on the man with whom she committed adultery. An enraged southern French peasant in the eighteenth century would feel perfectly justified in thrashing his wife's lover to within an inch of his life while he did no more than severely reprimand his wife, perhaps sending her away until he was ready to forgive her. The same secular laws that punished adulterous wives sometimes punished their lovers as well. A case of what to some eyes might seem to be double adultery—a married woman and someone else's husband—was likely to be treated in secular law as single adultery, an offense against the woman's husband only. To be known as a cuckold was a horrible humiliation. Calling a man a cuckold or making the sign of horns on the head was the worst of insults. To be cuckolded was also in large measure supposed to be one's own fault. A real man was supposed to be able to control his wife's behavior, and, it was darkly hinted, satisfy her sexual needs. Charivaris, which could be rather cruel popular demonstrations against marital relations perceived as abnormal, often mixed up power relations and sex. A man who allowed himself to be mistreated by his wife was assumed to be a cuckold.

Compared to the complex, contradictory view of female sexuality, male sexuality was a simple matter—in theory. Men needed sex and a real man was a sexually potent one. This is hardly an unfamiliar idea, which in its more exaggerated form we nowadays call machismo. In the past much everyday behavior was based on this idea. Upper-class girls and wives had to be chaperoned and protected against the predations of unattached men. Prostitutes were regarded as a necessary evil to deflect male lust from respectable women. While the official church attitude praised chaste and ascetic men, it recognized how difficult the struggles to maintain chastity could be. The ascetic triumphs of Saint Anthony, Saint Jerome, and Jesus himself were admired as beyond the capacity of ordinary men. In the earlier part of the period one of the "abuses" in the Roman church frequently pointed out by reformers was that priests, who were supposed to be celibate, often had concubines and held on to them even after being repeatedly fined and reprimanded. Rome, the city of clerics, was a city full of prostitutes. Both before and after the Reformation, conventional wisdom had it that the only licit outlet for sexual activity was in marriage, but everyone knew that illicit sexual activity abounded. Although the very purpose of marriage was to channel the sexual impulses of men, the danger of a husband's straying from the conjugal bed was always imminent. To say that no one was surprised when it happened is an understatement.

Of faithful husbands we know next to nothing. There may have been great numbers of them, but they were not particularly noticed or singled out for praise. Their fidelity, unlike the fidelity of wives, was, in a way, irrelevant. We know much more about unfaithful husbands. The cult of machismo promoted a certain amount of openness and even vainglory, with the adulteries of monarchs and great nobles serving as public models. Since, according to church law, both Catholic and Protestant, the infidelity of husbands was considered adultery, there are records of cases in which adulterous husbands were prosecuted. Finally, there is information about the people men committed adultery with. This is our main source of information for adultery at the lower end of the social scale. It was the sexual misconduct of women, most noticeable when it led to pregnancy and illegitimate births, that attracted the attention of authorities and caused them to find out about the married men who, it often happened, were the fathers.

The occasional husband who fell in love with another woman and wanted to marry her need not concern us here. Unfaithful husbands typically went about their adulteries with no thought of destroying their marriages. There was almost always a woman available under one's own roof: a servant. Sexual relations between masters and maids were common—not universal or universally approved of, but unexceptional. Where slavery existed, as it did in Spain, Italy, and the New World, women domestics were, if anything, even more unprotected and available. It could not have been easy for a servant, who was subject to her master's authority, to resist his sexual importunities.

The master-servant pattern continued all the way up the social scale. But above a certain level there was also another pattern, one that sometimes even appeared in the relationship of master and servant. It was something like concubinage, the keeping of an auxiliary "wife," without legal standing but with a degree of permanence. To keep a woman required money. It was sometimes done by rich and not-so-rich urban merchants, but to have a mistress was preeminently associated with the aristocracy.

The word "mistress" is itself an interesting study in ambiguity. It was used in French and English at least since the fifteenth century to mean both "a woman one wants to marry" and "a kept woman." The first meaning continued as the primary one almost to the end of the eighteenth century, when it fell away and surrendered the field to the second meaning. (The title "mistress" to indicate a married woman stems from a related but separate set of meanings.) That two such different meanings could coexist in the same word is best explained from the standpoint of the man. Whatever his true feelings, he was called a "lover" both when he was courting and when he kept a concubine. The convention was that his mind was on love in both cases. But when he married, the lover was transformed into a husband. A mistress came to mean someone who, so to speak, specialized in love, which was separable from what a husband got from or gave to a wife.

Kings had mistresses almost as though there was an unwritten rule that required it. The subject of royal mistresses has fed a whole genre of popular history, but it does not hurt to repeat here what has often been said: the typical European princeling of the late seventeenth and early eighteenth century took a mistress to ape the glories of Louis XIV, just as he did when he built a miniature Versailles. The tradition of having a mistress is far older, of course. It went along with being powerful, rich, and virile. We have already seen that a wife's embraces were supposed to be lukewarm. We may never know to what degree the keeping of a mistress was personally satisfying rather than a perfunctory way of conforming to the assumptions of the double standard.

Not everyone approved and not everyone felt compelled to imitate the royal and aristocratic pattern. Preachers of all persuasions attacked illicit sexuality, and in some political controversies the corrupt, licentious courtier was compared unfavorably with the upright citizen who kept an orderly control over his appetites. In seventeenth-century England especially, during the Civil War, there was an exaggerated contrast between two stock figures, the stolid burgher and the pleasure-loving Cavalier. These were stock figures indeed, but they stood for a real polarity of attitudes. It was possible to identify oneself proudly with one or the other extreme.

And the extremes sometimes met in odd places, like the court of the Sun King himself. All the while that Louis XIV was forming his collection of mistresses, he made conciliatory gestures to respectability. Call it hypocrisy, if you will, but there is, after all, no greater tribute to an idea than the hypocritical effort to mimic conformity to it. Not all his liaisons were intentionally exposed to public view. When a mistress achieved a sort of official status, she found herself under attack in sermons preached in the king's presence. When the king took a married woman, Madame de Montespan, as a mistress, the eloquent Bishop Bossuet intensified his criticism. The mistress's husband had, after all, accused the king of causing the wife's adultery, which was, as we have seen, thought to be a worse offense than the king's. It must be pointed out that Louis, like most other adulterers, was not a religious libertine but a practicing Christian, so he could not avoid having mixed emotions. In middle age, after his wife died, he secretly married a religious, almost straitlaced woman and followed quite a different pattern of life. Was this bourgeois virtue? Such behavior was sometimes called that and it certainly was often praised by those who questioned the prerogatives of the aristocracy in the eighteenth century. Nonaristocratic Frenchmen apparently pursued more discreet adulteries than they had done earlier, tending to keep women outside the home rather than having affairs with their servants.

Penalties for adultery varied widely, from a small fine to death. These extremes display all the ambivalence about sexuality and the double standard that permeates European culture. Before the Reformation, adultery came into church courts either because it was presented as grounds for legal separation or because it was an offense against public decency. Known adulterers were punished, but secret ones were not tracked down in any systematic way. The worst punishment meted out by diocesan judges was excommunication, almost always temporary, or public humiliation. These punishments were regarded as severe, but they were usually imposed only on repeat offenders. First offenders got warnings, usually coupled with fines.

After the Reformation, Protestant theologians claimed to have higher standards of marital conduct than the pre-Reformation church; they not only encouraged more surveillance but also pushed to make adultery a capital crime, on the model of the Old Testament. The resistance to this is a clear testimony to ambivalence. Capital punishment for adultery was indeed the law of many Protestant governments, including those of Zurich, Basel, and Boston. But it was only for the *fifth* adultery conviction in Zurich and Basel; earlier convictions were punished (as they had been in earlier times) by fines and brief jail terms. In seventeenth-century Boston no court ever ordered an execution for adultery; instead, the worst punishment imposed was exile. John Calvin's own Geneva imposed penalties that were relatively mild.

A woman fined and reprimanded by a church court might also be arrested and imprisoned by the state. This would not happen to a man. One of the indications of the solid entrenchment in the law of the double standard is the church courts' loss of power. Their jurisdiction became more and more restricted after the sixteenth century. Nowhere could this be seen more clearly than in France, where decisions on marriage matters by church courts were frequently overturned by royal courts, which in the course of the seventeenth century attained a near-monopoly on adultery cases. It became virtually impossible for a charge of adultery to be brought against a husband.

What most women thought of the double standard of marital fidelity we cannot say. We know what they were supposed to think. The marquis of Halifax in 1700, in a distillation of the best advice he could offer his daughter on the subject, put it this way: "Remember, that next to the danger of committing the fault yourself, the greatest is that of seeing it in your husband. . . . Such an undecent complaint makes a wife much more ridiculous than the injury that provoketh her to it."[12] That is the double standard in a nutshell.

Permanence or Fragility

"Till death us do part." These familiar words, expressing deep, permanent commitment, are taken with a grain of salt nowadays. It is a commonplace that marriage has become fragile, and it is easy to assume that, by contrast, marriage was permanent in the past. But in fact it was no more permanent than it is today. It is a paradox of changing conditions in the Western world that marriage has become both more permanent and more fragile. The likelihood of growing into old age along with one's husband or wife is far greater today than in the past, when a couple that was still together after the age of fifty was a great rarity. On the other hand, the likelihood of splitting up after a few years by getting a legal separation or a divorce has increased tremendously in the twentieth century. It almost looks like a balancing act: a high rate of separation by death goes along with a low rate of separation by legal action, and vice-versa. In the past when a couple got married they could not help but have ambivalent expectations about the durability of their relationship. They were tightly locked into it and could not easily get out of it by legal means, but they knew very well that the time was probably not far off when death was going to part them.

Before the sixteenth century it was impossible to divorce and remarry in Europe unless you were Jewish or Muslim or unless you had the means of manipulating legal machinery so that divorce appeared under a different guise. Christendom was unlike the rest of the world in this respect and notably different from the pagan world it grew out of. The Christian church's struggle to achieve authority over marriage had taken centuries, but for a few centuries its authority was well-nigh complete. The only continuing obstacle to its authority was at the very top of society, where dynastic considerations sometimes made dissolving a marriage in order to form another alliance seem an urgent necessity. When Henry VIII first tried to shed Catharine of Aragon he went about it in the time-honored way, not by asking for a divorce (which was impossible) but by claiming that the marriage was not really valid. This was not the first time a pope and a ruler clashed over the permanence of a marriage, but the pope stood fast this time, reaffirming the church's doctrine that a marriage lasted until death.

It is well known what political and religious consequences followed from this clash, but one thing that did not happen as a result of England's break with Rome in 1534 was the sudden wide availability of divorce. The situation in the rest of Protestant Europe was not so different, in spite of the fact that Luther and other leaders of the Reformation were in favor of permitting divorce. The Protestant rejection of the sacramental character of marriage removed the theological objection to divorce, and Protestant theologians tended to agree with Erasmus that there was a terrible contradiction in canon law between the ease of getting married and the impossibility of getting divorced: "It is extremely easy to get into a trap, and there is no way out."[13] Real divorce—legal dissolution and permission to remarry during the lifetime of the first spouse—was written into the laws of Protestant countries. The pattern of local variations in divorce laws in this period is extremely varied, but there were underlying consistencies. Nowhere was divorce made easy. Everywhere it was something exceptional. In England there was not even a straight-

straightforward new law, something John Milton argued for under the Commonwealth in the mid-seventeenth century. There was instead a slow accumulation of legal precedents, mostly after the Stuart restoration, limited to the aristocracy and granted by the House of Lords only on the grounds of a wife's adultery. About one hundred such bills of divorcement were granted before 1800, averaging fewer than one a year. On the Continent, too, it took a long time for divorce to become anything but extremely unusual. Adultery was almost the only grounds and it was usually the man who sued. Although theorists wrote about the importance of compatibility in marriage, there was almost no recognition of this in divorce laws. The notion of guilt prevailed.

Even though divorce was legal, it was regarded with extreme suspicion. The divorced person who was guilty of adultery was usually not allowed to remarry. The city of Zurich did not have such a prohibition, but it put the guilty party on probation; a woman was given three years of probation before being allowed to marry again. There was a common bias against granting divorces to women. Even though it was possible under Zurich law for a woman to obtain a divorce on the grounds of her husband's adultery, the husband was given only one year of probation. Among European Jews, for whom divorce was not a novel idea, there was also a tendency to make the process slow and difficult, and the grounds were almost as limited as those in Christian law. Most of the North American colonies replicated the English situation and as a consequence allowed no divorce whatsoever, since they did not even possess the machinery for bills of divorcement. Massachusetts was an exception, adopting a regular divorce procedure and becoming almost the only place in the English-speaking world where a poor person could get a divorce. But even there the tendency, especially before the middle of the eighteenth century, was to avoid actual divorce and revert to the more traditional legal separation (without permission to remarry), especially if the wife brought the suit.

Where real divorce is impossible, as it was in so much of the Western world throughout this period, there are other possibilities for those who are really determined to escape from a marriage. One possibility—not to put too fine a point on it—was murder. This extreme step was not often resorted to, as far as we know, but it was one that could plausibly be achieved, given the feelings about female adultery. Of course, people could *wish* their spouses dead. Many a married man in the process of seducing a single woman promised he would marry her after his wife died. A common method of self-divorce was for husbands to abscond. They would sometimes settle elsewhere and get married again. This combination of desertion and bigamy was not too difficult to effectuate in a world where written records were few and communication from diocese to diocese and even from parish to parish was minimal. It happened in all parts of the Western world, not least in less-developed areas like New England. Bigamy was severely punished, but it was probably not discovered very often. Desertion and bigamy were mainly options for men. A deserted wife was trapped in the uncomfortable ambiguity of having no husband and yet not being free to marry. She might go to great lengths to resolve her situation, looking for witnesses who would be willing to testify, truly or falsely, that her husband was dead. The outbreak of plague in Marseilles in 1720 was something of a boon to deserted wives, who could claim that their husbands had died in the epidemic.[14]

The old church courts, operating under canon law, allowed women to sue for legal separations. This was almost the only recourse for women in wretched marriages. In principle a wife could accuse her husband of adultery, but in practice women tended to limit their complaints to severe physical mistreatment. This does not necessarily tell us what their marriages were like. People made use of whatever legal machinery was available to them. In the eighteenth century in France, for example, there was a dramatic contrast between the marriage cases in Cambrai, where the old form of church court continued to operate, and those in the rest of the country. Most of the suits for separation in Cambrai—75 percent of them, in fact—were brought by women. In the rest of France women rarely brought such suits, for the simple reason that it was difficult to do so and unlikely that the suits would succeed. Legal separation ("from bed and board," as the phrase went) was a release from the pains of a marriage, not from the marriage itself. It was not uncommon for a separation to be granted for some finite period—say, three months— in the hope that matters might improve.

For those who wanted to dissolve a marriage and be free to marry again legally, in the absence of legal divorce there was the possibility of annulment. It remained a remote possibility for all but the rich and powerful. In the face of a bias in favor of the sanctity of marriage, it was necessary to prove in a court of canon law that there had been something intrinsically wrong with the marriage from the beginning. This was what Henry VIII claimed about his marriage to Catharine of Aragon. Her relationship to him as the widow of his older brother made their marriage impossible, he said, even though there had been a dispensation from the pope. There was a lot of complex legal lore about grounds for annulment, mostly connected with the intricacies of kinship— consanguineal, affinal, and spiritual. Ecclesiastical judges had to hold in delicate balance their commitment to the permanence of marriage, their wish to enforce the rules against incest, and their suspicions of perjury. Once in a while a couple found their marriage threatened with annulment against their will, because they had not taken the precaution of getting a dispensation for an impediment caused, say, by the fact that the husband's stepmother was the wife's godmother. One basis for annulment was the inability to have sexual relations. Claims of impotence and frigidity were carefully investigated in church courts, using whatever medical and anatomical knowledge was available. If the claim was fraudulent the court did not want to be tricked into saying a valid marriage was null; if sorcery was at work the proper remedy was exorcism rather than annulment. There is not the slightest doubt that fraudulent claims were made in order to annul marriages, just as adulteries were faked to get legal divorces.

It was not until long after the period covered by this book that divorce became acceptable. The beginnings of the process can be detected in the eighteenth century, especially in a place like Massachusetts, where divorce had been established for some time and where there was a clear shift in the 1760s to more divorce petitions by women. They often had to settle for legal separations, but they apparently felt freer to initiate such actions than they had earlier. The idea that someone was entitled to a degree of personal satisfaction in marriage came to be more openly expressed in court records in this pivotal period.

Most marriages broke up after about ten or twenty years, not because of desertion or legal action but because of death. Things seem to have been a little better in the New World, with marriages lasting an average of twenty to thirty years in some places in the English colonies. If most people married in their mid-twenties, it is easy to see that widowhood was likely to occur in the middle and late forties. Husbands tended to die first, in spite of the very real hazards of childbirth to young women.

The fragility of life was something no one could be unaware of. Any sensitive reader of late-medieval and early-modern literature knows what a presence death was, something matched in our own century only by the literature of war and holocaust. The fragility of marriage was also something deeply embedded in the consciousness of all, not least because hardly anyone grew up with a full set of either parents or grandparents. From the point of view of the married couple, this meant that however fond they were of each other they were likely to feel it was necessary to make provisions for a future without each other. Marriage contracts were primarily provisions for widowhood. For couples who were not particularly fond of each other, it was not unrealistic to dream of deliverance by death. Catholic priests were told to warn husbands not to give voice to such hopes. It is interesting to speculate about the emotional consequences of such a common family pattern. The dead spouse was sometimes almost physically present in the persons of the children from the earlier marriage, but surely memory and associations had their own power. The ambiguities of monogamy are not a recent phenomenon. Law, religion, and literature may proclaim the exclusiveness of the marriage bond and extol the ideal of one man and one woman linked through eternity, but marriage as lived in the real world has always been something else.

It is disappointing not to be able to shed more light on the mysteries of the relationship between husband and wife. On the other hand, once we accustom ourselves to the idea that the relationship was in many important ways not a personal one, not a private emotional bond closed in on itself, our eyes are opened to many things we do know. To speak of the family necessarily means to speak again and again of husbands and wives, if not in the terms most familiar to us. Some married couples in the past loved each other and were whatever we mean by "happily married," but it is a mistake to overlook the context in which they lived, which included a legal system in which husbands were masters and a social atmosphere that proclaimed the double standard at every turn. In any case, marriage was only the beginning, not the whole story.

III

Procreation and Education

Many people today would say that children are the heart of the matter. People get married to have children—or so many of them claim. The household we think of as ideal is child-centered. In the past, children played a different role in the family and carried a different sort of weight. Most people assumed that children would arrive in due course, and they were integral to the notion of inheritance. But the household, as we have seen, was not centered on them. There was too much else going on.

Still, children were much in evidence in households and got considerable attention from adults, particularly women. In spite of the different weight carried by children in the past, we have a surprisingly lot of information about them. The chapters that follow look at children from three different angles: how they were born, how they were cared for in infancy, and how they were prepared for later life.

6

Conception and
Birth

The moment of conception and the process of birth are biological events, which are much the same for all mammals. But bringing children into the world involves more than biology. Birth is a social drama, with a cast of characters dictated by cultural notions of what is necessary and appropriate. Even before a drama of birth is enacted, impregnation and pregnancy are accompanied by all manner of social expectations and personal attitudes. That is why the subject has a history.

It is a history that in many ways parallels the history of humanity's view of its physical environment—the history of science and technology. Between the middle of the fourteenth century and the end of the eighteenth century there were important changes, and by the twentieth century the Western world had gone through three "revolutions" related to biology: the agricultural revolution, the scientific revolution, and the population explosion. Before these revolutions, the physical environment was thought about differently and the actual environment was different because it had not yet been affected by the revolutions.

We expect people to have complicated, ambivalent feelings about matters as fundamental as conception and birth. Today birth control, abortion, and childless marriages are highly charged moral issues. Having many children is a positive good to some, a positive evil to others. Where and how to give birth have increasingly become subjects of controversy. There seems to have been a range of attitudes in the past, too; there was certainly a wide range of behavior. But present-day ambivalences have little in common with the ambivalences of the past, because the three revolutions have created a different setting for our present-day dilemmas: world population is rapidly increasing, life expectancy is high, children outlive their parents, mothers rarely die in child-birth, and artificial birth control is effective and available.

Two of the paired alternatives in this chapter—"Passivity or Control" and "Doctors or Midwives"—may sound like ones we face ourselves, but birth control in the past involved different options and a different attitude toward the control of natural processes, and neither doctors nor midwives were like their present-day counterparts. The two other pairs of alternatives—"A Baby Every Year or Spacing of Births" and "Dying in Childbirth or Living into Old Age"—may not seem like real alternatives. We have so often heard that frequent pregnancies and death in childbirth were the lot of women in the past that we may be surprised to learn that the picture was not nearly so simple. On the other hand, is it surprising that a complex, stratified society should have had a multitude of ways to deal with reproduction?

Passivity or Control

A few people today may believe that conception is entirely a matter of chance or nature, but they are exceptional. Although there are still some mysteries, most of the physiology of human reproduction is understood. It has been shown to respond to various kinds of intervention, which are now done as confidently as intervention in any of the other natural processes of which modern science claims to know the laws. The same medical profession that gave us vaccination, anesthesia, antibiotics, and heart transplants has given us the diaphragm, the rhythm method, the pill, and the IUD. Most of us take for granted this ability to control nature through science and accept the structure of cause and effect that science is based on. We have seen technology march in step with scientific knowledge and affect our daily lives. We may have ambivalent feelings about how technology is used—not only in reproduction—but we do not doubt its effectiveness.

People who live without modern science and technology have their own ways of dealing with nature. The alternative to modern technology is not passivity. Our ancestors may have been passive about certain things that we like to control, but they were not passive about everything. They had a strong wish to take charge of their lives and not submit blindly to fate. The wish was manifest in the handful of clever men in the sixteenth and seventeenth centuries who became the pioneers of modern science, but their motivation was not novel. Only their methods were. Ordinary people were constantly exploiting nature and interfering with its processes, using windmills and watermills, draining wetlands, pollarding trees, digging metals out of the earth.

They also controlled their own reproduction, although not until the eighteenth century were there any hints of the family-planning pattern familiar to us today: limiting the number of children to two or three and restricting childbearing to a relatively few years, usually at the beginning of marriage. A quick first look suggests that people in the past were passive, limiting the number of children only through the mechanism of an appallingly high death rate over which they had no control. Demographers used to assume that it was possible to observe "natural" conditions of fertility in preindustrial populations, but when they took a closer look they learned that the absence of modern contraceptive technology did not mean passivity. Some aspects of reproduction were not interfered with, but others were manipulated. For example, there were efforts at promoting fertility, rather than limiting it, and at influencing the sex of offspring. Even prevention of births was attempted—sometimes successfully—but usually under the guise of something else and without today's programmatic approach.

The subject presents quite a challenge and requires a method akin to refined snooping. Historians have used spotty birth and marriage records and census lists to ferret out possible patterns of conception and contraception behind statistics of known births. There is no record of pregnancies that never happened, of course, or of pregnancies that did not eventuate in births. They show up only as spaces, which need to be interpreted. Were some of the spaces miscarriages? Were some of the miscarriages intentional? As for people's attitudes toward the control of reproduction, we would not get very far if we relied on a straightforward reading of formal writing, since there was a gulf between the men who did the writing and the women who were having—or not having—the babies. On this subject, perhaps more than others, the polemical nature of so much that came from the pens of moralists and theologians can be seriously misleading. Still, in spite of the intractable nature of the subject, we know more today than we ever did before.

Throughout these centuries most women had certain experiences in common. Once they started having sexual intercourse they became pregnant at more or less regular intervals until menopause. The first child nearly always arrived by the end of the first year of marriage. Marriage, sexual intercourse, and pregnancy were closely intertwined. Even more striking than the inevitability of childbirth soon after the start of sexual relations is the average age at which women had their last babies. On most levels of society just about everywhere it was forty—which means that some women were even older than that. They apparently continued to conceive as long as they were able to.

Adding to the impression of passivity is the seasonal pattern of conceptions. Decisions about when to get married seem to have had little to do with nature but were probably influenced by the timing of contract negotiations, the relaxation of the demands of agricultural work, and the precepts of religion, which forbade weddings in Advent and Lent. The commonest months for weddings in France, for example, were January and February, the least common March and December. Once past the first conception, however, couples tended to fall into a seasonal rhythm. The high point of the year for conceptions was the time the poets sang of. Sweet lovers loved the spring, and married couples apparently loved late spring and what they called midsummer (around the time of the summer solstice) best of all. Contemporaries were aware of the pattern, especially the near absence of births at certain times of the year. One sharp-witted medical man named François Rabelais investigated parish registers in his neighborhood because he was curious about this phenomenon.[1] Another Frenchman, Moheau, two centuries later, attributed it to the fact that in June "a sort of sap spreads and extends itself through the whole body."[2] The pattern was primarily a rural one, but that was important in a predominantly rural world. With the passage of time the pattern faded. It was still visible in the eighteenth century but is totally absent today.

We can only assume that, then as now, people frequently acted without giving any thought to conception. But that is not to say that people *never* gave any thought to conception. Far from it. It was obvious to them that not every sexual act resulted in pregnancy. There was a widespread idea that the couple's behavior and attitude during intercourse affected the outcome. Women were believed to have at least as much of the responsibility as men, and simultaneous orgasms were sometimes said to be a sure sign of conception. This was only one of the ways in which people tried to make sense of a process that was all the more mysterious before anyone had any inkling of a mechanism involving microscopic sperm and eggs. By the end of the eighteenth century, some medical men knew that conception could occur without sexual intercourse. A Scottish surgeon, John Hunter, in 1776 oversaw the first successful artificial insemination of a woman, but he was reluctant to publicize the case during his lifetime because it flew in the face of entrenched ideas.[3]

We have only hints of the ideas of ordinary men and women, but we can read in books what learned men thought. In a work on medical jurisprudence written as late as 1815 Samuel Farr claimed that "without the enjoyment of pleasure in the venereal act no conception can probably take place."[4] This was the reasoning behind a common assumption in law that a woman who bore a child could not have been the victim of rape; if she had been truly unwilling she would not have conceived. It was almost always the woman who was blamed if a marriage did not produce children: the fault was in her body or her attitude. A range of apparently contradictory ideas had wide currency. The timing of intercourse was thought to be important, sometimes on the basis of astrological principles—still taken seriously by some in the highest circles in the seventeenth century—sometimes on the basis of medical lore. When the court physician of Henry II of France gave advice about the part of the month in which women were most fertile, he followed a hoary tradition that it was immediately after menstruation. What the king made of this information we do not know, but his wife, Catherine de' Medici, finally conceived after twelve years of barrenness and went on to give birth to a passel of future kings and queens. A reason sometimes given for the taboo against intercourse during menstruation was that such intercourse resulted in deformed and defective children. There were also theories about how the timing and mode of inter-

course affected the sex of the child. The best conditions—variously interpreted—would produce a boy. As the story of Henry VIII's marriages suggests, however, the inability to bear sons was often regarded as a permanent
disability of some women.

Learned men approached the subject of fertility by way of the theories that
underlay their understanding of the human body—the humors and sympathetic magic. These theories died hard. Ever since antiquity they had offered
a plausible, harmonious explanation of bodily functions and the body's relationship to the rest of the physical world and the heavens beyond. Nicholas
Culpepper's *Directory for Midwives* (1656) was still giving advice on achieving fruitfulness that drew partly on the idea that certain combinations of
humors, with their various properties of warmth, coldness, wetness, and dry-
ness, provided the right conditions for conception, and partly on the idea that
substances associated with fertility could make human beings fertile. Women
were advised to wear a lodestone or the heart of a quail as an amulet, to drink
certain herbal potions, to ingest a powder made of the dried wombs of hares,
and to eat crabs, lobsters, and prawns, which had the reputation of being especially fecund.[5]

Popular and learned ideas often met on common ground. For centuries
learned and unlearned alike blamed male impotence on witchcraft. It was the
convenient hypothesis to fall back on when no other explanation could be
found. If a man was capable of having sexual relations and the marriage nevertheless remained barren, the woman became the focus of attention. She, too,
might be the victim of witchcraft. But some popular notions about barrenness
diverged from those of the learned. Both highborn and lowborn women continued to resort to magical practices like incantations and spells. Women used
the church for their own purposes, praying to saints associated with motherhood, going on pilgrimages, and visiting places that were said to dispel barrenness, like certain hallowed fountains, streams, and rocks. Some of this activity
had the approval of religious authorities, but some lost that approval in the
course of time as both theologians and secular thinkers attacked "superstition." Some had always been suspect and remained underground.

With high death rates, especially high infant mortality, the emphasis on
promoting conception rather than preventing it seems to make sense. We
have already seen, however, that the average number of children per family,
while larger than today, did not begin to approach the shoeful of the old
woman in the nursery rhyme. People did in fact limit their fertility. They did
it by marrying late or by not marrying at all. Whether or not directly connected with a wish to control births, decisions about late marriage and celibacy
were made consciously and deliberately. If a couple with moderate means did
not marry until they could support themselves, the woman might be at least
twenty-five years old, which was rather late in the natural childbearing period.
In times of bad harvests and other disasters, couples postponed getting married
until conditions improved. Contemporaries often commented on what looked

like a rush to marriage after a disastrous event; to them it looked like an increase in the total number of marriages, but it was more likely that marriages had been postponed. Not getting married at all could also be a conscious policy, especially among those with a lot of property. Italian patricians and English aristocrats, among others, tried to keep wealth from dribbling away into dowries and multiple inheritances by putting some daughters into convents and encouraging some sons not to marry. Religious institutions were convenient allies, but they were not essential. After the Reformation there was little difference in the strategies of French Catholics and English Protestants.

The gradual lowering of the marriage age for large numbers of people helped to push the population up in the eighteenth century. It was clearly happening among the English settlers in the New World. In 1798 Thomas Malthus used what he believed was the American experience as the foundation for his famous formula: "Population, when unchecked, goes on doubling itself every twenty-five years, or increases in a geometrical ratio."[6] Malthus thought that population needed to be checked, since he believed the supply of food could not increase at the same rate. What he recommended was precisely what seemed to be going out of style: late marriages.

Most contemporaries of Malthus were not worried about runaway population growth and there had been no advocates of birth control as public policy before him. A few years later, however, the French writer J.-B.-P. de Sénancour indignantly exclaimed, "It is imprudent, blameworthy, and senseless to have as many children as chance may happen to produce."[7] This idea could not have been newly minted in 1806, when he recorded it. We now know that some individuals had been thinking along these lines for about a hundred years and had been acting accordingly, but it is not easy to get at the facts of a private matter between husbands and wives. Just as we know more about sexual practices in illicit relationships, we know more about birth control outside of marriage. Ideas about birth control were for centuries mixed up with ideas about immorality and unnatural behavior. The arguments and opinions of theologians and philosophers, while interesting in themselves, do not shed much light on what married couples were doing.

The primary method of birth control used by women was abortion. We cannot say with any confidence that it was widely used. Miscarriages and stillbirths were extremely common, and only a tiny fraction may have been intentional. We do know that some husbands voiced concern over being burdened with too many children, and it is possible that some couples made decisions about abortions together.

A lot of information about what caused abortions was available. A number of herbs—rue, for example—had the reputation of being abortifacients. When theologians and physicians warned pregnant women about too much physical labor or sexual activity they were simply repeating the accepted notion that those were ways in which fetuses could be aborted. Stillbirths and abortions were often spoken of in the same breath and were believed to have the same causes.

What we call early abortion was something else. Since we are not privy to the world of women in the past, the subject is extremely murky. The historical record rarely sheds any light on it except when it was part of some famous scandal, like the one in the reign of Louis XIV when sorceresses in the pay of promiscuous ladies of high rank were said to have performed abortions by the thousands. One thing that contributes to the obscurity of the subject is the fact that for a long time both medical men and ordinary women believed that the fetus was not really alive in the first months of pregnancy, that something called quickening happened only when the woman began to feel movement. The early months were thus regarded only as a kind of preliminary phase in which the menstrual flow stopped. Women often tried to restore menstruation. Ending pregnancy may not have been their aim, since amenorrhea was considered a serious ailment, but the womens' efforts would have had the same result as intentional abortion. By the eighteenth century physicians were performing therapeutic abortions to save mothers' lives, but it was not until much later that we find them performing abortions to prevent births.

The man's method was coitus interruptus, or premature withdrawal. Those who wrote about it in the past had nothing good to say about it. Theologians through the centuries attacked it as sinful and secular thinkers in the eighteenth century called it a trick on nature. It was regarded as a way of indulging one's sexual appetites while avoiding the natural consequences. Mixed up with arguments about its use in marriage was its association with illicit sex and occasional confusion with the use of abortifacients. In contrast to this verbiage is silent evidence that its use spread little by little among the most moral, most responsible, most prosperous, and best informed segments of society. What may at first have been done only in the demimonde was taken up by respectable people, through a process that is so far hidden from us. Nobody can be absolutely sure that what looks like the result of systematic coitus interruptus did not have other causes—perhaps even planned periods of abstinence—but there is a strong argument in the fact that, by the middle of the nineteenth century, contraception and coitus interruptus had become practically synonymous. Protestant couples may have adopted the practice earlier than Catholics. The earliest signs of families taking a more or less modern "planned" shape have been detected in the upper class of Protestant Geneva in the seventeenth century, and there are hints as well from some places in England and Germany. In the next century, however, the strongest signs were in France. In marked contrast to upper-class Englishwomen, French noblewomen, who married fairly young, were having the last of their progressively smaller broods (an average of only two children by 1799) at younger ages, often by their mid-twenties. As an English noblewoman, the countess of Sutherland, remarked in 1791, "The French ladies are all astonished at how anybody can be *si bête* as to have *trois enfans*."[8] Analogous developments were taking place in prosperous French families of lower rank, and there are indications that the practice gradually spread to those even further down on the social scale.

Moheau, an observer of population trends in France, wrote in 1778, "They are playing tricks on nature even in country villages."[9] Like so many of his articulate contemporaries, he believed that people were practicing coitus interruptus because they had lost sight of their moral and social obligations. These observers were convinced that the population of France was declining at a precipitous rate and that national survival was at stake. This is one of history's clearer examples of the unreliability of contemporary witnesses. We now know that the population of Europe, France included, shot up in the course of the eighteenth century. It may have looked to the educated elite as though people around them were having fewer children, and in the course of time even lower-class Frenchmen began limiting the size of their families, but it was not happening to any great extent when these cries of alarm were being sounded. The detective work on this subject may not be finished.

Some kind of psychological turnaround seems to have taken place in the eighteenth century in a growing number of married men, culminating in Sénancour's 1806 statement about imprudence and senselessness. Many men now felt it was they who had the responsibility for the number of children they had (or, it may be, the number of pregnancies their wives had to endure). An eighteenth-century futurist, Louis-Sébastien Mercier, supposedly looking back on his own time, said somewhat ambiguously, "People avoided bringing children into circumstances in which they would be burdened with hardship, as husbands guarded their transports to avoid having a child in the home."[10] Coitus interruptus is not the most self-indulgent way to enjoy the "transports" of sexual pleasure. It requires considerable self-control and a rational concern for consequences. In any case, it was not until men took charge of contraception that it started slowly moving along the path to respectability and having noticeable effects. In all this time, however, there was extreme ambivalence and there was hardly any open acknowledgment of what was going on.

The idea of limiting births—or pregnancies—was not total anathema to the moralists who fulminated against abortion and coitus interruptus. Catholic theologians in particular wrestled with the problem of balancing the health of the wife, the welfare of the children, and the salvation of the husband's soul, which was endangered if he sought sexual gratification outside of marriage. It had always been respectable to leave one's wife alone, if one could manage it. In that sense men had always been responsible for the number of children they had. When they eventually took the step to separating sexual relations in marriage from procreation it may therefore not have looked like such a big one, even if it represented a leap in thought when seen against the background of centuries. Men remained in charge until twentieth-century technology made it possible for women to exercise effective control over contraception. It was men who eventually appropriated for the marriage bed a notorious accessory for the prevention of venereal disease in illicit sexual encounters: the condom. Condoms of one sort or another existed at least since the sixteenth century, but by the eighteenth century were still not spoken of as contraceptives.

The control of conception was bound up with the understanding of conception, and both changed from the fourteenth century to the eighteenth century. The development remains less than clear because much was hidden by the smoke surrounding two emotionally incendiary subjects, sexuality and the relative power of men and women.

A Baby Every Year or Spacing of Births

It is usually assumed that in untampered natural conditions married couples will have a child approximately every year. While the Western world in recorded time never provided anything like natural conditions, the most effective way of reducing the number of births—late marriage—was not directed at controlling reproduction within marriage. We would therefore expect frequent births to have been common. Anthropologists caution us, however, that living in a technologically and economically undeveloped society does not guarantee frequent births; women in some African and South American tribes give birth to only two or three children in their lifetimes and at widely spaced intervals. As usually happens when we examine the evidence closely, the pre-industrial West turns out to have been complex and full of contrasts. Some women did spend their childbearing years being pregnant almost all the time, but for large numbers of women there were always intervals of several years between births. The question raised by this polarity is how, in the absence of family planning as we now know it, this could have been so.

From the end of the fourteenth century to the middle of the seventeenth century the population of western Europe rose steadily, slowly making up for the steep and sudden decline in population around the time of the Black Death in 1348. From the late seventeenth century to about the middle of the eighteenth century the increase slowed down, and in many places there was near-zero population growth. In this period, which has been studied quite thoroughly, there was no significant change in the birth rate. What happened was that births and deaths canceled each other out. A dramatic change occurred around 1750, when the population began to shoot upward, and the upward movement has not stopped yet. The change looks dramatic on a graph, but it did not feel particularly dramatic at the time, except in big cities, which were getting more crowded. That was not because more children were being born in cities but because more people were coming to live there. As we have seen, French writers were afraid that the population was declining, but the French population rose from about nineteen million in 1715 to about twenty-six million in 1789. Parallel to the sharp increase in population was a reversal in the sizes of rich and poor families. Before the Industrial Revolution, poor people as a rule had fewer children than rich people. In the nineteenth century it could be said that the rich got richer and the poor got children, but this pattern was barely evident in 1800. The older pattern is what demands our attention.

Poor women were just like rich women in having babies throughout their married lives up to menopause. They had fewer children than rich women for three main reasons. Their husbands were likely to die before their childbearing years were over and they would not marry again—a common experience in all parts of society but especially common at the lower end of the social scale. They were likely to be in poor physical health, so they conceived less easily and miscarried more often. Finally, they breast-fed their babies.

It is a fact of human physiology that breast-feeding extends the intervals between births. In addition to the normal infertility right after childbirth, lactation causes prolonged infertility in most women lasting at least a month and sometimes much longer. Local customs varied in prescribing the age at which babies were to be weaned, but it seems that two years of breast-feeding was common. Evidence from many different places shows that the average interval between births was about two and a half years. Baptismal and burial records tell us that a woman typically produced a baby every two or three years, except when a baby died before the age of one. Then the rhythm was broken and the interval before the next birth was shorter.

The connection between breast-feeding and birth intervals may have been more than physiological. It was widely believed, and stated in medical books, that sexual intercourse had a bad effect on the mother's milk—for example, the milk would curdle. People may have observed a taboo against resuming sexual relations until the mother stopped nursing. If my readers are skeptical about the observance of this taboo, I do not blame them, but it should be pointed out that becoming pregnant put a nursing mother into a difficult bind. Her milk supply was likely to diminish. It was thought that the milk consumed by the child was exactly the same fluid that nourished the fetus, and sexual intercourse was believed to cause the fluid from the breasts to be diverted to the womb even before conception took place. It is not easy to put ourselves in the place of a nursing mother of the past, but we can recognize that if she wanted to postpone her next pregnancy it might not have been because she was committed to the idea of spaced births. She could have been concerned about her own immediate comfort and energy and the nursing baby's health, not to mention her own spiritual health with regard to sexual indulgence. Whatever their motive, nursing mothers conceived less often than mothers who did not nurse.

The circumstances in which the poor lived raised obstacles to a rapid series of pregnancies. While the early death of an infant might shorten the interval before the next birth, high death rates of adults cut down the possibility of conception. Low resistance to disease caused the early death of many a potential father, and poor living conditions made women start menstruating late, stop early, and have amenorrheic episodes throughout their lives. Not having enough to eat was something poor people experienced time and again, and this had a direct effect on fertility. Add to this the effect of hard times and hard work on libido and psychological health and the image of strong, lusty peasant women producing bouncing babies year after year evaporates.

Almost the exact opposite of what I have said about poor women was true of women who were better off, some of whom were amazingly prolific. The duchess of Leinster, who died in 1814 at the age of eighty-three, gave birth to twenty-one children,[11] but that was unusual, even for a duchess. A UNESCO report has shown that the highest average fertility ever found in any large group of people anywhere in the world is about eight births per woman.[12] This was precisely the average among English noblewomen who were contemporaries of the prolific duchess and is what we should have in mind when talking about the large families of the past. When the French government in 1669, in an effort to build up the population of Canada, offered a generous cash award to all married men in the colony who had at least ten children, there were few takers.[13]

Life expectancy was only slightly higher in the upper classes, but rich women unquestionably ate more and worked less than poor women. Because they were in better general health, they were able to conceive more easily, whether or not they had sexual relations more frequently. Another prolific English noblewoman, Charlotte, duchess of Beaufort, who got married in 1791, gave birth twice in 1792—in February and December. Her own mother, the marchioness of Stafford, had had four children in four years.[14]

The clearest difference between rich women and poor women is that rich women did not breast-feed. There is irony in the fact that the women who came closest to the "natural" rhythm of having a baby every year were the ones who abandoned the natural practice of suckling their young. The use of wet nurses affected the mother and father as well as the child. The mother was free to resume sexual relations after giving birth and, since she had only a short infertile period, she would be able to conceive again fairly quickly.

The reasons women did not breast-feed are not particularly clear or simple, but it is clear that for certain women in every part of Europe it was routine not even to consider breast-feeding as an option. It had been so for centuries. There was an occasional brief vogue for breast-feeding among upper-class women, notably at the end of the eighteenth century in line with Enlightenment—and Romantic—ideas about Nature. In some places there were women of lower social rank who also did not breast-feed. They were among the minority of the population that lived in towns, especially the wives of artisans, whose work in shop and household was their main concern. In France the practice of using wet nurses grew as towns grew. In the colonies of North America increased wealth and aristocratic styles of living went along with the use of wet nurses. There was a continuing contrast between poor country women and city women, wealthy and not so wealthy, throughout the period. Almost always it was country women who did the nursing for city women.

Written opinions about breast-feeding were marvelously ambivalent. Rarely was anything said about its effect on fertility, although the learned theories of conception all made some sort of connection on the basis of the fact that the "menstruous" fluid was not available for conception when it took the form of milk. A somewhat unusual eighteenth-century duchess of Devonshire wrote of her in-laws after she had her first baby, a girl, that they "abuse suckling" because of "their impatience for my having a son and their fancying I shan't so soon if I suckle."[15] Since antiquity some authors had spoken about the debilitating effect of breast-feeding, which might interfere with future childbearing. Most writers, however, were in favor of breast-feeding by the mother. It was assumed to be the natural thing to do, although medical treatises always also gave advice on how to choose a wet nurse. Theologians and moralists attacked what they believed to be the reasons why mothers did not nurse: vanity and sensuality. They did not want their bodies deformed or to deny themselves sexual pleasure. One did not have to be a Saint Bernardino of Siena in the fifteenth century to say that. An eighteenth-century Quaker minister in South Carolina, Sophia Hume, angrily asserted that when women claimed they had insufficient milk it was usually not true; they were guilty of sinful pride, not wanting to endure discomfort or the loss of their "shape."[16] On the other hand, the problem of the husband's unsatisfied libido was something that bothered Catholic theologians. Rather than risk the sin of adultery, it was better, they said, for the wife to put her child out to nurse and keep herself available to her husband. Although the fulminations of moralists were directed against the sensuality of women, it was to the husband that advice about choosing a wet nurse was usually addressed.

Breast-feeding was a subject surrounded by contradictory ideas and deep feelings. Written opinion always made a connection with the parents' sex life. The reader will have noticed, in addition, that a class bias runs through this material, one that speaks volumes about preindustrial society. Whatever the benefits of not nursing, whether for the wife or the husband, they were obviously not available to the humble country people who provided the wet nurses.

Doctors or Midwives

There has recently been a revival of interest in midwives in the United States. Some women nowadays object to the clinical, impersonal atmosphere of hospitals and to the limited empathy between mostly male doctors and female patients. The controversy of sorts that is now going on bears only a superficial resemblance to the controversy between doctors and midwives before the latter part of the eighteenth century, when doctors started to gain the upper hand. In all that span of time, midwives delivered most babies. Doctors were not entirely out of the picture, but to say that women had a choice—as many women do today in America, where the situation is completely reversed—is inaccurate. The women whose babies were being delivered played a very small role in this history. It is a history best known as a chapter in the development of modern medicine, the story of a battle for the minds of men and for the support of institutions. We know least about what is perhaps most important to our present purpose: the deeply embedded way of doing things that was being undermined from the sixteenth century onward.

Childbirth was for centuries reserved to the world of women. As late as 1708 a French physician, Philippe Hecquet, wrote a book entitled *The Indecency of Men Attending Women in Childbirth*.[17] In the early sixteenth century, a German physician was convicted of a capital crime for pretending to be a woman in order to be present at a delivery.[18] Women depended on other women for advice about conception, pregnancy, and childbirth to an extent that we can only imagine. Women seem to have inhabited a full and active world of their own, which occasionally intersected with the world that is visible to historians. There were saints of the church, like Saint Margaret, to whom they prayed for a safe delivery, and a village church would often contain a chapel dedicated to one of these saints, used by village women for, among other things, christening a stillborn infant to whom the saint might grant one more breath of life. These religious practices, like the ones connected with fertility, were not all officially recognized. On the other hand, a number of traditional church observances reflected the rhythms of women's lives—for example, the ceremony of "churching" or purification, which took place a month or so after childbirth. Works of art show women in childbed surrounded by a crowd of women. They were neighbors and relatives, qualified by virtue of sharing the female condition. The one person among them with anything like professional qualifications was the midwife. She was a respected personage in that world and, to a degree, in the world of men as well. In seventeenth-century New England, for example, several prominent Puritan ministers were the husbands of midwives, and midwifery was regarded as an appropriate activity for "gentlewomen" in the Old World as well.

Unfortunately, what was a secret from men remains pretty much a secret from history. Respectable or not, midwives often practiced informally. Regulation and licensing were rare until the end of the period, although more common on the Continent, especially in German cities and in France, than in Britain and New England. The legacy of the midwives is an oblique one.

In spite of their wide experience and a level of competence sometimes grudgingly admired by medical men, their practices were not treated in the earliest textbooks. For a long time, in fact, their practices seemed mysterious and suspect—easily associated with sorcery at a time when witches were seen as a constant threat. The oath taken by English midwives in order to get a license stated that they would use no sorcery and that they would properly baptize the infant if death was imminent. The license was granted by the church, not a government office or professional organization.

The invasion of this women's world by men started slowly. The privacy of women was generally respected, and before the sixteenth century the interest of the medical profession in the subject of childbirth was mainly theoretical. Most of the theories came from Greek and Roman antiquity, as did almost all medical learning. Doctors approached most conditions through the theory of the humors, relying to some extent also on ancient forms of sympathetic magic. An eaglestone was supposed to have the property of assuring a safe delivery, for example. No less a personage than Anne Boleyn wore one on her left wrist, and there is every indication that her husband, Henry VIII, saw to it that she had the best and most up-to-date care. In the first printed book to go into detail about childbirth, which appeared in 1513, the attitude toward midwives of the author, the German physician Eucharius Rösslin, was an uneasy mixture of contempt and trust. His book became the standard European work on the subject; in English it was called *The Birth of Mankynde*, published while Henry VIII was still on the throne. Rösslin thought of his book as a guide for pregnant women and a manual for midwives. He did not expect doctors to replace midwives; he only wanted midwives to be better informed and to abandon some practices he thought dangerous or useless. He provided them with a compendium of ancient lore that had been preserved through the Middle Ages, couched in terms of the humors, along with a few shrewd observations of his own.

The relationship between doctors and midwives continued more or less on this basis into the nineteenth century, with midwives delivering most of the babies and doctors telling them how to improve. The doctors' tone became more strident as they came to identify themselves with new scientific learning and the midwives with benighted ignorance and superstition. It seemed indefensible to the doctors to leave women to the limited capacities of their traditional closed world and deprive them of the benefits of men's knowledge. A medical textbook in 1800 stated flatly that midwives were "as ignorant of their business as the women they deliver."[19] By the middle of the eighteenth century the science of obstetrics had made considerable advances. André Levret in France and William Smellie in England, building on the improved understanding of the anatomy of parturition, perfected the design and use of the forceps. Obstetrics became part of the curriculum of colleges for physicians and surgeons (although many medical men did not attend school and continued to get their training through apprenticeship). From the end of the seventeenth century, French midwives could study at the Hôtel-Dieu in Paris and were required to take an examination before they could be licensed. In England, which was characteristically less bureaucratic, teaching hospitals gave instruction to midwives. In both countries, doctors continued to write handbooks for midwives in which "the art of midwifery" was brought "to perfection upon scientific and medical principles"[20] and midwives were encouraged to study under physicians.

In theory, midwives continued to take care of what was called the "lying-in," with the traditional assemblage of women usually in attendance, and sent for a doctor if things did not proceed normally. Only surgeons were permitted to use instruments. This collaboration existed mainly in cities and mainly for women of means. But men were also beginning to take on normal births. Their pretension were mocked by Laurence Sterne in his depiction of Dr. Slop, the "accoucheur" who lords it over the midwife in attendance at Tristram Shandy's birth and is all too eager to use his "new-invented forceps," with which he manages to crush the infant's nose. In America there was a rapid transition in the course of little more than one generation at the turn of the nineteenth century to the total replacement of female midwives by male obstetricians in prosperous urban circles. The crowd of women companions disappeared along with the midwife, transforming what had been a female social occasion into a professional encounter. It was not long before a physician, Walter Channing, expressed the opinion, in a work entitled *Remarks on the Employment of Females as Practitioners in Midwifery*, that since only trained physicians could properly deliver babies and females were not suited to medical training, women were totally unsuited to be midwives.[21]

What happened when Mary Wollstonecraft had her second child illustrates the ambivalence that surrounded the question of who should preside at births. The year was 1797, when the transition from midwives to doctors was well on its way. The early monuments of modern obstetrics, books by Jean-Louis Bardelocque and Charles White, had already been published and five maternity hospitals had been functioning in London for several decades. Mary Wollstonecraft was an intelligent, independent woman, who associated with some of the most advanced thinkers of the time—many today regard her *Vindication of the Rights of Woman* as the first feminist manifesto—and her husband, William Godwin, was a writer in the forefront of radical political thought. In opposition to him, she insisted on being attended by a midwife because she thought it was improper and immodest to have a male doctor. This had long been the prevailing attitude, even among doctors, and there was a rash of prurient speculation in the eighteenth century about the advantage male midwives could take of their patients. The midwife Mary Wollstonecraft hired was at the top of her profession, the chief midwife at the Westminster New Lying-In Hospital. Two other women were in attendance—a watered-down version of the traditional crowd of friends and neighbors. After a healthy baby girl had been born the midwife was confronted with a problem she knew she could not deal with: there was no afterbirth. So she did what she was trained to do. She sent for a doctor, the chief obstetrician at her own hospital. The doctor did what *he* was trained to do, but this was before the days of antiseptics, which were to make such a difference in the chances of recovering from birth complications. In other words, the doctor supplied skills the midwife did not have, but he was severely restricted himself. The appearance of a medical man in the birth room had long been taken as a sign that either mother or child would die. About two weeks later Mary Wollstonecraft did die, of septicemia. During a brief period in which she seemed to be improving, she had felt pleased with her use of a midwife and thought it had been justified. She and those around her seem to have taken this delivery as a kind of test. A doctor friend of hers told a number of his colleagues how remarkably well she had done with only a woman midwife.[22]

The story of Mary Wollstonecraft is symptomatic of a process that was moving ahead quickly in prosperous circles. Poor women, especially country women, continued to depend on midwives. And for all women the place to have a baby was at home. The final step in the break with the tradition of a female community, giving birth in a hospital, was as yet taken only by an unfortunate few, the charity cases who made up the clientele of the early maternity hospitals.

Dying in Childbirth or Living into Old Age

Childbirth is always risky, and was much riskier in the past. In spite of this, men do not as a rule outlive women nor did they in the past. In modern Western countries life expectancy is greater for women than for men, but this is neither a new development nor the result of improvements in obstetrics. Although female infants are almost always outnumbered by male infants, a more equal balance of the sexes was very soon reached in the past because male infants had a higher death rate. Whatever is said about women dying in childbirth has to be put in this context of female survival.

General life expectancy has increased tremendously in recent times. Old people are becoming the most visible sector of our population. In contrast, the population of the past was a young one because of a high birth rate along with shorter life expectancy. This was the situation throughout the human past, as far as we can tell, and not just the 450-year segment we are focusing on. Old people—men and women alike—were always a rarity.

Young adults of both sexes faced life-threatening situations, death in childbirth being only one of many young women faced. The notion that women ran a disproportionate risk because of childbearing and that they were more likely than men to die in early adulthood turns out to be mistaken. The sad fates of particular women may cause us to overlook the happier fate of women in the aggregate, if indeed being left a widow with young children is a happier fate. As we have seen, it was a common one. Provided that we keep in mind how women fared in all the dangers of life, it still makes sense to single out the danger of childbirth as an important experience of families in the past. If statistics were everything, we could dismiss the polarity that is presented to us—some women dying very young in childbirth, others outliving men by many years—because the two extremes nearly cancel each other out. For the women themselves and for those around them, however, the difference mattered a lot.

The vulnerability of women in childbirth was a favorite theme of clergy-men. After Mary Wollstonecraft died, one of them observed that that stren-uous fighter for equality of the sexes "had died a death that strongly marked the distinction of the sexes, by pointing out the destiny of women, and the diseases to which they were peculiarly liable."[23] Some years earlier Cotton Mather, addressing pregnant women, had said in his inimitable style, "For ought you know your Death has entered into you, you may have conceived that which determines but about Nine Months more at the most for you to live in the World."[24] To contemporaries the dangers of childbirth were glar-ingly apparent, highlighted by the travail and pain of even the healthiest births. *The Book of Common Prayer*, in the liturgy for the churching of women after childbirth, spoke of "great danger," the "snares of death," and the "pains of Hell."[25]

Everyone had ample opportunity to observe the dangers. In the middle of the sixteenth century a king of England, Edward VI, like thousands of his sub-jects, had lost his mother shortly after his birth. A contemporary French dia-rist, Guillaume Versoris, duly recorded the deaths of four wives over a period of four years, probably all because of childbirth. I say probably because he did not always give the cause of death and did not record miscarriages or still-births. But he gave telltale dates. He married his fourth wife in June of 1526, and she died the following March—nine months later. His two previous wives had died within a month of giving birth, like Mary Wollstonecraft.[26] The prob-lem for all these women was that little could be done if there was any kind of abnormality or mishap. Retention of the placenta, as in Mary Wollstonecraft's case, or abnormal positioning of the baby invited the risk of infection from attempts to rectify the situation by inserting a hand or instrument into the birth canal. A problem that today would lead to a routine cesarean section was nearly always a disaster. Not only were midwives not surgeons, but surgeons themselves regarded abdominal incisions as justified only if the mother was already dead or nearly so. Cesareans had been known from antiquity, but were used only as a last-ditch effort to salvage the baby. The violence of Shake-speare's image—"Macduff was from his mother's womb untimely ripp'd"—expresses something of the horror and desperation people felt about the perils of birth.

It is still not clear whether women are particularly susceptible to disease during pregnancy or particularly resistant to it. The evidence from the past is utterly inconclusive because so many people who were not pregnant, female and male, succumbed to diseases whose periodic outbreak was a characteristic feature of Western life. A child ran the constant risk of losing a father and an almost equal risk of losing a mother, whether because of childbirth or some-thing else. The Black Death at the beginning of the period we are looking at raged for three or four years, killing perhaps a third of the population in a single year in some areas. Plague returned with slightly reduced intensity to almost every part of western Europe throughout the next three centuries. In 1599 the city of Valladolid in Spain lost almost 20 percent of its population. In 1665 London lost about 25 percent of its population. The last big plague epidemic was that of 1720 in Marseilles but as late as 1800 there was plague in Cadiz. The major epidemics were no respecters of persons, striking the wealthy with almost as much intensity as the poor. A measles epidemic in 1712 carried off the heir to the French throne at the age of thirty, along with his wife and oldest son, leaving a two-year-old son who as Louis XV succeeded his great-grandfather to the throne three years later.

Other diseases, which came in the wake of bad harvests, were harder on the poor. Periodic subsistence crises were as characteristic of these centuries as plague epidemics were. Sometimes only a local area was affected, sometimes a whole region. The toll might be as high as a quarter of a village's population. France is said to have had between eleven and sixteen general famines in every century from 1500 to 1800. The great Irish famine of the nineteenth century was an old-style subsistence crisis. No one knows why such crises and major epidemics gradually subsided in the course of the eighteenth century. Their end, in any case, marked the end of an era in which adults died at almost the same rate as children.

After the death of his wife, William Godwin was left with a newborn daughter and a stepdaughter, in a "forlorn and disabled state with respect to the two poor animals left under my protection."[27] He soon did what most widowers did: he looked for a new wife. The woman he married a few years later had a son and a daughter. Godwin and his new wife soon had a son together. The result was one of those households whose structure was so typical in the past: five children by three different fathers, one of them an orphan, three of them half-orphans. The corollary to the death of a woman in her childbearing years was the arrival of a stepmother. It mattered little *how* the woman had died.

A remarkable number of women survived. It has been estimated that life expectancy in general throughout this period was no more than twenty-five or thirty years (compared to seventy-five in the United States today). Once a person reached the age of twenty or so, however, the chances of surviving until fifty or sixty were pretty good. Much depended on who you were and where you lived. British peers, for example, had a higher life expectancy at birth than people at the lower end of the social scale; it rose from thirty-seven years in the late sixteenth century to forty-eight years in the late eighteenth. Life expectancy was higher in the country than in towns. In New England, where the crises and diseases of the Old World were generally absent, life expectancy was higher than in the peerage. Many of the first settlers of Massachusetts lived into their seventies. Things improved very slowly in Europe, first becoming noticeably better in the middle of the eighteenth century. Even cities became less hostile to the prospects of longer life. At the same time, the New World was becoming less benign than it had been, and life expectancy declined somewhat from the remarkable heights of the seventeenth century.

It was only in the New World that men tended to live as long as women. It seems that in relatively small populations, like those of New England and New France (Canada), where people lived in particularly healthful conditions, women may have lost their usual biological advantage, becoming slightly more vulnerable than men because of childbirth.

Most of the women who survived were mothers. Widows with children, including elderly widows with grown children, were the commonest of phenomena. They had come through the perils of childbirth apparently unscathed. Normal childbirth seems to have been—statistically, anyway—less dangerous than the other vagaries of life. Women of childbearing age who had normal deliveries could reap all the biological benefits of having survived to adulthood.

In 1681 John Locke, a man of intelligence, integrity, and great powers of observation, made a note in his diary about a woman named Alice George, who was, "as she said," 108 years old. She was, in any case, a very old woman. Locke wrote: "Her condition was but mean, and her maintenance her labour, and she said she was able to have reaped as much in a day as any man, and had as much wages. She was married at 30, and had 15 children, viz. 10 sons and 5 daughters baptized, besides 3 miscarriages. She has 3 sons still alive, her eldest John living the next door to her, 77 years old the 25th of this month."[28]

Alice George was hardly typical, but her case is instructive nonetheless. Time and again it was the women who had the most children who lived to old age. The very toughness that pulled them through their deliveries kept them alive later.

The experience of conception and birth in many parts of the world today is not so different from what it was in the preindustrial West. The great contrasts with the past in our part of the world are the result of changes that took place mostly in the twentieth century. Change was under way, however—if slowly and ineffectively—much earlier. The mental world we live in, while different from that of the period from 1350 to 1800, had its beginnings in that period, especially from about 1650, when the scientific view of nature was becoming a clear and conscious attitude. The female social environment surrounding reproduction functioned with amazing vigor throughout the period and continued to do so in backwaters until very recently, but the privileged were quick to abandon it as the price of more scientific care for mother and infant. The plot thickened in the nineteenth century, but I leave it in 1800, with the male obstetrician entering the quiet bedroom of his patient and discreetly poking around under the covers.

7

Early Childhood

The subject is babies. There may be nothing in the modern Western world on which there is more unanimity. Apart from a few pathological monsters, we all, it seems, adore babies. If they get on our nerves or present us with problems, we make generous allowances for them and get back as quickly as possible to positive feelings.

Scholars differ widely about how babies were treated in the past and how adults felt about them. Some say that at best babies were regarded with indifference and were often handled with considerable harshness. Others think there was the same tenderness we see today. One reason for the disagreement is the tricky business of interpreting long-discarded ways of caring for babies. We have to do a lot of guessing about motivations, and it is often hard to believe that people who treated babies the way they did were not deficient in tenderness. Further complicating the issue is the fact that educated opinion changed during the period, and inevitably some of the evidence comes to us filtered through the critical attitudes of writers who were bent on reform. In contrast to the present, the past knew many polarities in the treatment of babies. The picture is incomplete, however, and historians may never be able to fill it all in.

The three sections that follow are about a single polarity, that of love on the one hand and indifference on the other. The first section considers it in reference to the extremely precarious hold on life that babies had in the past. The second section looks at care, handling, and attitudes in general. The third section focuses on the most important aspect of infant care, feeding.

Loved Persons or Passing Acquaintances

There is a certain logic to the idea that people would not invest much emotion in small creatures they knew might be around for only a short time. A common way of dealing with human disasters, and a most effective one, is by becoming anesthetized to shock and grief. That reasoning is behind the opinion of some historians that parents in the past did not love their small children with anything like the intensity of parents in the present. Of course, mere logic is inadequate to explain the workings of human behavior and thought, as we see over and over again in the ambivalence and contradictoriness that keep forcing themselves on our attention. It is one thing to be anesthetized to the death of children in general, or even the death of one's neighbor's children, and quite another to be confronted with the death of a being one has conceived and borne oneself. Furthermore, there is no necessary psychological link between how one reacts to death and how one treats a baby who is still alive. When we look at how people responded to the death of an infant—a banal event, to which everyone had countless opportunities to become inured—we do not see a one-sided picture. The evidence allows us to come to any conclusion we want to, but only if we are willing to shut out the evidence to the contrary. The emotional reaction to infant deaths was not discussed very often in the past, but by the end of the period we are looking at it was talked about more and it was also talked about differently. Looking back over the whole period, we can see that there was always a wide range of responses to the young child's fragile existence. In the course of time certain responses faded as others came to the fore.

The facts were grim. Apart from stillbirths and deaths due to the immediate circumstances of parturition, which could be at least as dangerous for the child as for the mother, an infant in the first months of life had in general a 20 to 40 percent chance of dying before his or her first birthday. That means that of every ten babies born an average of only six to eight survived. In stark contrast, in advanced industrial nations nowadays at least 98 percent of all babies are assured of living through the first year. To say that babies survived their first year of life is to say very little when speaking of the past. In many places an average of two or three more out of the original ten would be dead before the age of ten. In brutal summary, it took two births to make one adult, since the chances of surviving to age twenty were in general no better than fifty-fifty.

Babies and little children died of a variety of diseases, especially diseases of the digestive system. A commonly attributed cause was "worms," which may have meant parasites like the roundworms that infested drinking water or may have been a vague term for a whole range of stomach and intestinal disorders, including malnutrition. When epidemics raged, the very young were particularly vulnerable. Although smallpox and measles were not exclusively childhood diseases, they were frequent killers of children. Children suc-

cumbed to many other diseases that were still known and feared by our forebears in the early twentieth century: mumps, diphtheria, whooping cough, and
scarlet fever. There was no known cure for any of them. Once they struck,
the child's recovery was a matter of luck. Some steps were taken against smallpox in the eighteenth century, at first by a few upper-class people who had
their children innoculated, then with the discovery by Edward Jenner at the
end of the century of the efficacy of cowpox innoculation.

Some children were luckier than others because of geography or class.
Their chances of living to adulthood were slightly enhanced if they were very
well off, probably because of better nutrition, which increased their resistance
to disease. Children in North America, in both the French and English colonies, had a higher rate of survival than the European average. In a rural area
like Andover, Massachusetts, in the seventeenth century, for example, the
chances of reaching adulthood were remarkably good for the time, something
like 5 to 1, as against the even odds faced by European babies.

Dead babies had little individuality. In the early days of record-keeping
some parish registers did not even list their deaths. Family portraits show that
they were not forgotten, but in earlier times they were remembered as abstractions rather than as persons. A portrait was not so much a picture of a family
at a particular time as a record of its history, including the children, living and
dead, who had been born to a couple. The lack of individuality implied in
images of stiff little swaddled bodies may have carried over to living infants
during their first months and perhaps into their first years, when they were
helpless, vulnerable, and only provisionally committed to life. Only the well-
to-do could afford to pay for portraits. How the poor remembered their dead
infants we cannot say. They had no portraits and often no written records
except those that might have been kept in the parish church. Most people
were vague about dates, so they were not likely to retain even a simple fact
like a dead child's birth date. Only those at the upper end of the social scale,
important people who paid to have horoscopes cast and who kept family trees,
knew their own birthdays, those dates that are so important to us as attributes
of our individuality.

Religious beliefs contributed to the tendency to regard babies as without
individuality. Their deaths could be seen as part of the mysterious workings
of evil in the world and were sometimes taken to be punishment for the sins
of the parents, helping to displace grief over the death of a little person with
concern about the state of one's own soul. This encouraged a strangely for-
ward-looking attitude, a resolve to go on and do better next time.

It was an attitude compounded in equal parts of fatalism and resilience,
often expressed in terms that can sound cold and heartless. A woman who was
being considered as a wet nurse by a wealthy Italian merchant's wife in the
fifteenth century promised her prospective employer that since she expected
her two-month-old to be dead that very night she would report for work as
soon as the baby was buried.[1] In a seventeenth-century French book, entitled

Childbed Chatter, a young mother got the following retort when she complained about the trouble it would be to take care of children: "That's all foolishness, my girl. Before they get to the point of giving you much trouble you will have lost half of them, maybe all of them."[2] The names of dead babies were often re-used. A fifteenth-century Italian farmer explained to the census-taker that his son Antonio, who was at present living in his house, was not the same Antonio who had been there during the previous census: "He died, and I made him over again."[3]

Men frequently reassured themselves that they had the wherewithal to make more babies. And make more babies they did. Demographers have been struck by the correlation between high death rates and high birth rates, not only in the preindustrial world in general but also in particular localities. In the eighteenth century infant mortality was highest where the birth rate was highest—usually among poor wage earners, both urban and rural. Understanding the phenomenon is a chicken-and-egg proposition. There is not much evidence that people were consciously replacing babies who died, in spite of the Italian farmer's remark. It may be closer to the truth that the same fatalism and passivity that surrounded procreation surrounded death. But it would be arrogant to say this with certainty. All we have is an impression, backed by statistics, that the more inevitable the birth of babies was taken to be, the more inevitable was the likelihood of their death.

On the other hand, the religious rituals connected with the death of infants suggest profound concern for them as individuals, or at least for their individual souls. Catholics and Protestants alike believed it was important to baptize babies as soon as possible, especially if they were not long for this world. There was a universal dread of consigning them to limbo or whatever uncertain afterlife lay in store for the unbaptized. The laws and regulations on this matter, however much they varied throughout Europe and the New World, all prescribed that baptism take place either the same day as the birth or very shortly thereafter, usually no more than a week later. Since most of the records give only the date of baptism and not the date of birth, we do not know how closely the rules were followed, but there are signs that observance was scrupulous. Midwives were prepared to perform the ceremony themselves if it did not look as though there would be time to get the baby to church before it died. The church's licensing of midwives in England was connected more with this matter of spiritual health than with physical health.

People were not even willing to leave stillborn babies unbaptized. In some places they were "baptized" in church without being given names and then buried in consecrated ground; in other places they received church burial without any sort of baptism. Widespread collusion in a kind of fraud to obtain true baptism occurred in France throughout the period. A dead newborn would be quickly taken to the village church, usually by a group of women, into a chapel that had a reputation for its efficacy in such circumstances, usually one dedicated to the Virgin Mary or a female saint. There the women prayed for a moment of life for the child. They would later claim that they had seen the infant stir its limbs, and often insisted they had seen blood come from its nose. These signs of life lasted only long enough for the baby to be baptized. Whether real or imaginary, the miracle owed its existence to the desperate concern of some adults for at least one aspect of a baby's well-being.

We get occasional glimpses of parents' grief. Sometimes it took extreme forms, setting off extended periods of depression in a few bereaved fathers who have left written testimony. The incidence of death among Martin Luther's offspring was fairly typical. Of his six children, two died before he did, one at eight months, the other at thirteen years. He was upset about both deaths, especially that of his thirteen-year-old daughter, going so far as to express profound doubts about the God whom he otherwise saw as a mighty fortress.[4] The loss of older children was understandably harder to take than that of infants, and the fact that one fifteenth-century diarist, Giovanni Morelli, was haunted for a year by the death of his first-born son at the age of eleven, feeling that nothing would ever go right again, may not be the slightest clue to how he would have felt if the boy had died at eleven months instead of eleven years.[5]

Another fifteenth-century Italian, Leon Battista Alberti, observed the intense grief of bereaved fathers and had the characters in a dialogue discuss whether it was a good idea to take pleasure in the behavior of tiny children; the pain would be all the worse if they died.[6] Something of this attitude was expressed all through the period, a simultaneous outpouring and holding back, an attempt to balance the impulse to cherish babies against the knowledge that they might be snatched away at any moment. The chatty duchess of Orleans, a member of Louis XIV's family, remarked that having babies was hard, and to see them die, "as I have had the sad experience of doing this year," made the whole enterprise quite devoid of pleasure.[7] In the late eighteenth century the English historian Edward Gibbon expressed the painful balance in nonreligious, rational terms: "The death of a new-born child before that of its parents may seem an unnatural, but it is a strictly probable event."[8]

Parents may or may not have exercised restraint toward their own mortal babies, but there was one baby about whom they could indulge their feelings to their hearts' content. That was the Infant Jesus, depicted in high and low art, on stage and in song. In painting, the stiff icon of earlier centuries turned into a recognizable, animated, chubby baby at the hands of fifteenth-century Renaissance artists and their successors. I doubt that the change in painting style had much to do with a change in attitudes toward babies. Artists were honing their skills at making images lifelike—"so lifelike that he seems to be breathing," as Vasari said of a portrait by Giotto[9]—and rendering the familiar recognizable. When the Holy Infant was depicted as a responsive, almost reflective individual, it may have been partly idealization, but it may also have been a distillation of observed babyhood. People may have been used to looking at babies as appealing persons before artists began painting them that way.

The Holy Family was always imbued with considerable humanity, and perhaps never more so than in the early part of the period we are looking at. The convention of portraying little Jesus and his family in contemporary surroundings, engaged in familiar activities, helped to drive home the point. This was done not only in elegant church paintings but also in the mangers set up at Christmastime and in the popular Nativity plays, in which the Mary figure would sing lullabies not very different from those the mothers in the audience sang to their babies. Many female saints described having visions of the Infant Jesus, in which he was put into their care and allowed himself to be fondled by them, like any human child. The maternal tenderness in these visions often overshadows the feelings of religious awe.

Tenderness and fascination, long hidden in the shadows, seemed to emerge into the light in the eighteenth century—part of that apparent transformation in family attitudes and human relations that I have talked of before, a phenomenon we are wrong to ignore but must resist making too much of.

It is possible that the rise in the practice of birth control among married couples around this time was connected with a wish to do something about the death of babies, if only indirectly by giving each baby the most favorable allotment of the family's resources. The circles in which domestic affection was most openly expressed were generally the ones committed to limiting births. Leaving the number of children to chance was something J.-B.-P. de Sénancour would call "imprudent" and "blameworthy." It certainly was out of harmony with the idea that individual babies were important and interesting. Such "new" attitudes were most visible among people who were well off and articulate: the urban middle class and the aristocracy.

Some changes in the eighteenth century did not bring improvements in the welfare of babies. For lower-class people, increased urbanization meant earlier marriages and less breast-feeding. While the prosperous may have limited their families and given their offspring a more secure hold on life, a growing landless proletariat was having more babies than ever and burying them at the old rates.

The Enlightenment ideas current in the eighteenth century were in perfect accord with the new—or newly visible—attitudes toward babies. A concern with "humanity" emphasized the individual worth of human beings apart from their place in the social hierarchy. The attendant cultivation of tenderness and kindness soon grew into a cult of sentiment that was embraced by quite a few, although ridiculed by some. Religious ideas about eternal punishments and predestination were softened, and beliefs tended to be accommodated to the test of rationality. All of this made it less easy to take the death of tiny babies for granted. In fact, it made death in general harder to accept. There was, at least in some circles, more mourning over the loss of a loved one and less attention to dying well and preparing for the next life. Unfortunately, babies continued to die at pretty much the same rates. As Gibbon said, their death was "strictly probable." To regard it, in his words, as "unnatural" was to open oneself up to considerable pain. It was in this century that there was more writing of personal letters than ever before, and in them tenderness, pain, and grief over babies were often expressed.

The puzzle is, as always, whether these were new feelings related to the new ideas in the eighteenth century or old, familiar feelings newly expressed. How much difference does a change in vocabulary signify? I am predisposed to resist hyperbolic statements about a complete turnaround in attitudes. Science began to offer a little hope for the treatment of children's illnesses, but the hope remained unrealized for a long time. When Enlightenment thinkers discussed babies they usually sidestepped the issue of mortality and characteristically accentuated the positive, concentrating on the development of children's potential humanity. Like men in the preceding centuries who wrote about children, they were more interested in what children would eventually become than in what they were like when they were very small and very fragile.

Concern or Convenience

Although a pall of death hung over early childhood, people in the past concentrated on less momentous matters in the everyday care of children. Some historians think "carelessness" may be a more accurate word. Because there have been many changes in the last two centuries in the way small children are treated, the differences in detail and style in the past could imply a corresponding difference in attitude. No one can say for sure.

A family's first concern in our own times is supposed to be the welfare of its children. In a conflict between the well-being and happiness of a child and the convenience of an adult, the child takes precedence. We know this does not always work out in practice, but the ideal is clear and unambiguous and the law tends to back it up. Any ambivalence in our time about the kind of care children get is in the realm of personal psychology, an aspect of parents' inner conflicts. There is almost no general ambivalence. We do not willingly admit to doing anything that is not in a child's best interests.

Before the nineteenth century, when child-centered talk proliferated, childhood was barely recognized as a distinct time of life, except in negative terms: a child was not an adult. Writing about the first seven years of life was very vague, especially before the eighteenth century. Interest picked up only as children reached the age for training and schooling, so that we learn little or nothing about really young children from formal treatises, whether moral or medical. The little we know about how people behaved suggests that they had rather ambivalent motives. A lot that parents did seems to have been for their own convenience and they seem to have done little that caused them inconvenience. They also put considerable effort into doing certain things that look downright cruel and hostile to us. To gauge whether those things were intended for the care of the children or the convenience of the parents we need to know more than the surface facts.

It is not hard to amass evidence that young children were treated with callous indifference. Some scholars have devoted themselves to assembling veritable chambers of horrors, showing pictures of restraining devices that look like torture instruments and quoting the harsh precepts of some writers. While recognizing that they are not inventing, I would like to plead for a somewhat fairer historical balance. The emergence in the eighteenth century of practices and attitudes more congenial to our ways of thinking about child care makes it too easy to forget that for centuries people were apparently satisfied with what they were doing.

The most extreme form of indifference to children is to abandon them. That a poor unmarried mother should have been desperate enough to do so is understandable, especially in an age when illegitimacy was a terrible stigma and there were penalties for sexual misconduct. Every year, however, in all the larger European cities hundreds of babies were abandoned by married couples. Since it is not likely that they were all crazy, we must believe either that many of them, too, were desperate or else that they did not care. They were condemning the babies to a bitter fate, either early death or life first in an institution and then among the lowliest laboring poor. Most parents of abandoned children did not have much to offer their children and they could have felt that their only other choice was stretching their resources to the breaking point. Still, when they abandoned a child they were, for all practical purposes, ceasing to care for it.

Most parents, even very poor ones, did not abandon their children; they made a place for them in their busy, crowded households. It was not a central place, however. The treatment of babies and young children looks as though it was designed to keep them out of the way. What we notice first in pictures of infants is that they were swaddled. The baby was tightly wrapped in bands of cloth that confined the legs and arms, forming a neat package that was easy to pick up and move from place to place. Swaddling kept the baby warm in poorly heated rooms, since it could not throw off its covers, and prevented it from getting hurt without having to be watched all the time. During the day the swaddled infant spent hours in a cradle or basket, often near the fire. English court records of the fourteenth century tell of cases in which a chicken or a pig wandered indoors and knocked a burning ember onto the inflammable wood of the receptacle the baby was lying in or the cloth in which it was swaddled, with the result that, since no adult was close enough to hear its cries, the baby was badly burned.

Not every baby had a cradle, proverbial though that piece of furniture was. At night many babies slept with their parents—a convenient but potentially dangerous arrangement. Everybody in the Western world in this period was aware of overlaying. It was well known that infants were sometimes suffocated when adults rolled over on them in their sleep. As early as the thirteenth century church authorities condemned the practice, and several hundred years later there were French laws making death from overlaying a crime against the state. Nothing seems to have been effective in stopping parents from taking their babies into bed with them. It was apparently too convenient a habit to give up. Babies were accommodated within the limited space and warmth available in poor households. A more sinister motivation was hinted at in some of the church pronouncements on overlaying. Could it have been a half-intentional way of keeping down family size? At best, babies were terribly vulnerable, and it does not look as though parents went out of their way to minimize risks they could control.

In wealthier households some things were different. Babies were more likely to sleep in cradles and to have people looking after them. Soon after birth, an infant was likely to be put into the care of a wet nurse, either at home or in the nurse's household. Once past the swaddling stage, little children in wealthy households continued to pass most of their time with servants. A servant minded the baby much as he or she might mind the roast turning on the spit.

Children in all ranks of society up to about the age of seven were put in the care of whoever was available. It might be a servant, an apprentice, an older sister or brother, a neighbor—or any combination that was convenient. We can read about striking exceptions—royal princes and wealthy heirs who were carefully monitored by persons of rank and learning—but in general children seem to have been supervised as little as possible, although their physical movement was restricted. They had leading strings on their clothes, so that their efforts at walking could be controlled, and they sometimes used walkers on wheels that kept them confined as they moved about. Depictions of early childhood in the past rarely throw light on what was happening in really poor households. Some three- and four-year-olds wandered about freely enough to drown in ditches or be attacked by pigs and dogs on city streets.

It is a puzzling and dreary picture, but it will not do as a complete one. Unfortunately for the pursuit of completeness, the world of the young child was also the world of women. When men wrote about upbringing, they usually concentrated on formal education, which did not start until children (boys, that is) were old enough to be removed from "the company of women."[10] Pedagogical theorists tended to think that this time could not come soon enough. In the eighteenth century, William Cadogan, an English doctor, thought that even nursing had "been too long fatally left to the Management of Women," and he recommended "to every Father to have his Child nursed under his own Eye, to make use of his own Reason and Sense."[11] In the company of women, described as "foolish"[12] and "senseless," which was also the company of servants, "naughty girls," and "abandoned playfellows,"[13] the child was supposedly indulged, spoiled, and subjected to vulgar and immoral influences. That was how it looked to men dedicated to high ideals of morality and learning. They make early childhood sound like anarchy. But does it sound like constraint? Or indifference? These men chastised parents for taking pleasure in their children's mispronunciations and laughing at their innocent use of suggestive and blasphemous language. So some parents were clearly spending time with their children, even if only for their own amusement. Early childhood was a somewhat mysterious time, it would seem, when its needs, mainly physical, were catered to by women, and there was ambivalence about how much attention should be given to moral and mental development. One of the reasons widowers of modest means rushed to get married again was the necessity of having female care for young children. Exactly how a busy farmer's wife went about her job of caring for children is not known to us, but the job was at least partly recognized as necessary and valuable.

A closer look at some of the awful-sounding practices I have mentioned shows that they had another side. Swaddling was actually a lot of trouble. According to one set of seventeenth-century instructions, the mother or nurse first had to "place the child on a cloth or diaper. Then, with a wide bandage, starting at its chest, she makes one or two turns, keeping its arms at its sides and extending them so that the hands reach to the knees. Then it is again placed on the diaper. After that, a bandage goes around the whole torso. Then the knees are bent and part of the diaper is placed between them and along the legs, and the ankles are placed close together and wrapped in the diaper, which is afterward folded firmly together on top. This being done, she finishes bandaging the whole body, placing another cloth on top to keep it warm and secure."[14] There was a limit to how long the baby could stay swaddled in the same cloths, even if standards of hygiene were not what they are today. That means the process had to be gone through many times, perhaps three times a day in well-run households. It obviated changing diapers, but swaddling took longer than changing a diaper. One reason it was done was that it was supposed to be good for babies. Apart from keeping them warm and protected, it induced creatures that were barely human to assume the posture that distinguished men from beasts. Without such help they might be held back in their growth into proper adults. It was in line with this notion that animal-like behavior like crawling was discouraged. The "real" reason for an ancient custom like swaddling is almost impossible to discern, but it can be interpreted as an indication of concern, however that concern may have been tinged with hostility toward something frightening and alien in the baby's nature.

Even the abandonment of infants deserves a closer look. Parents did not usually drop their babies by the sides of roads or on private doorsteps. There were institutions for the purpose, at first shelters run by the houses of religious orders, then municipal and state hospitals set up for the specific purpose of receiving foundlings. Desperate parents could easily have persuaded themselves that a great institution was better able to take care of their children than they were. Sometimes they persuaded themselves that their fortunes would improve and they would be able to take their children back. In the eighteenth century the foundling hospital in Paris received a great many requests for the return of children. Harsh reality usually got in the way, since many of the children had long since died and for those still alive it was often difficult to ascertain their identity. Furthermore, the parents were presented with a bill for the children's entire upkeep. Needless to say, only a very small number of foundlings were ever reunited with their parents. Still, the hope kept being expressed, at least in the eighteenth century, which is the earliest period for which we have ample records of notes left with foundlings. A note pinned to the clothing of a newborn infant abandoned in Rouen a few months before the fall of the Bastille was typically couched in the language of eighteenth-century sentiment: "I was born today, January 7, of a legal marriage. My father and mother are suffering from extreme poverty and do not have it in their power to have me christened or to render me the services my tender youth requires them to give me. It is only with the most mortifying distress and acute sorrow that they abandon me and leave me here while they wait for heaven to grant them the favor of being in a position to call me back to the bosom of my family."[15] Neither literacy nor sentimentality was common in the preceding centuries, but I cannot help feeling that similar notes could have been written then, too. Even as a harsh decision was being made, concern for the child was not absent.

The fact that there were foundling hospitals says something about a general concern for infants. The sculptured medallions of babies by Andrea della Robbia at the Hospital of the Holy Innocents in Florence, dating to the fifteenth century, express tenderness and familiarity. The Innocents after whom the hospital was named were themselves a frequent subject of art. They were depicted as the babies of ordinary people, torn from the arms of grieving mothers by the soldiers of Herod. Another common subject of paintings was the allegorical figure of Charity, usually shown as a woman with two or three very young children in her arms. Earlier art had depicted Charity with a beggar, so it seems there was a change in the idea of who were proper objects of charity. This may have had more to do with a slackening enthusiasm for beggars than a growing concern for babies, but the movement to build institutions for foundlings and orphans nevertheless continued to grow. Some European towns supported foundling hospitals, and the royal government of France supported a very important one in Paris. It was not until the eighteenth century that a foundling hospital was opened in London, under private auspices. Joseph Addison chastised his countrymen for being slow to follow the lead of other countries in caring for the "multitudes of infants" who risked death because their parents were "either ashamed or unable to provide for them."[16] Earlier the charity mechanism that operated at the parish level in England had attempted to care for infants as it did for widows and old people. In some European towns and villages an effort was even made to get at one cause of abandonment by giving welfare payments to poor families with young children. In Rouen in the eighteenth century, for example, a poor family could receive a fixed amount for the first year of life of its third child and of every succeeding child.

Concern for small children began to take a somewhat different form in the eighteenth century. Central to this revision were two concepts: Innocence and Nature.

The association of innocence with childhood was not new. Children had always been called innocents, since they were not yet able to commit grown-up sins. Still, most Christians believed they came into the world with the stain of original sin and, what is more, with an alarming affinity to creatures that were not human. There was a link between the bestial and the demonic. Saint Augustine had said that "the innocence of children is in the helplessness of their bodies, rather than any quality of soul."[17] The first to proclaim the innocence of the newborn in unequivocal terms were Christians who denied the value of infant baptism. Yet this theological position apparently did not immediately cause them to treat their children differently from the way other Europeans treated theirs, and when the Quakers appeared over a century later it was still somewhat daring to hold that young children were totally innocent and could be trusted not to be an easy prey for the devil.

It took a big shift in the climate of opinion to impel people to see humanity as naturally inclined to good rather than predisposed to evil, and there were still plenty of people in the eighteenth century who held the hard-nosed opinion that this was sentimental poppycock. Children were the clearest beneficiaries of fashionable notions about noble savages and the perfectability of man. Of all humanity, they could most easily be thought of as uncorrupted. The concern of educated parents gradually turned from suppressing the devil and the beast in young children to preserving their innocence. Corrupting influences were often no different from old-style temptations to sin, so some parental behavior, especially toward older children, hardly changed at all, but the impulse to fend off outside influences that might spoil an almost perfect humanity meant that parents looked upon their children somewhat differently. They were on the way to idolizing them and worrying about them in ways that are familiar to us today.

A belief in the naturalness of babies and the goodness of nature led thinkers in the eighteenth century to reexamine age-old practices. Tradition was being called into question in all aspects of life, so why not the tradition of swaddling? John Locke, that pacesetter of the Enlightenment, typically looked to ancient models and to the experience of non-European peoples for evidence that children grew up stronger and healthier if they were untrammeled in infancy.[18] Jean-Jacques Rousseau took up the argument in Émile several decades later, depicting swaddling as the cruelest and most repressive of practices, to be understood solely as a convenience for the "mercenary women" who took care of others' children, for whom of course they had no natural affection.[19] It was as unnatural to bind and restrain human infants as it would be puppies and kittens, he said, making an analogy between people and animals that was still slightly disturbing to Western ears.[20] The other tradition that came under attack as unnatural was that age-old target of moralists, wet-nursing, which Rousseau linked directly with swaddling.

The technique of swaddling was gradually lost as the practice fell into disuse, even among those at the bottom of the social scale. Hardly anyone could remember why something that was more and more regarded as barbarous had ever seemed like a good thing. There was still resistance to allowing babies unconstrained movement, however, except by those in the most advanced circles.

By 1800 a view of motherhood as a full-time occupation dedicated to the health and character of young children was coming into focus. It is likely, however, that just about any mother in the whole 450-year span would have said she was concerned about her baby's welfare. She may very well have paid a great deal more attention to it than the baby's father did. But two influences tugged at women in all walks of life and kept them from caring for babies in ways that would match twentieth-century notions. First, few women were exclusively mothers; they had too many competing things to do for them to regard motherhood as a full-time occupation. Second, it was believed that what babies needed most of all, after food and warmth, was control and restraint. The concern of mothers can easily look like repression to us.

Natural Mothers or Substitute Mothers

Feeding is at the very center of infant care. Psychologists tell us it is the central experience of the child's existence, providing its first contact with other human beings and its earliest perception of the world around it. There has always been a polarity on this subject in the Western world. At one extreme is a belief, amounting at times to a kind of religious faith, that the proper and natural person to do the feeding is the baby's own mother, the corollary of which is that the only proper and natural food is the mother's own milk. At the other extreme is the persistent and frequent practice of someone else feeding the baby and even using something other than human milk. The polarity exists today in the United States. In the past the polarity was much sharper and it was more than just a difference between breast milk and formula or the issue of whether fathers should help with the feeding. The contrast was between keeping the baby in the mother's care and removing it to the care of another woman.

It is a subject on which a lot was said in the past, a lot that was emotional, hortatory, and abstract, as we have already seen. This sort of material obscures what was actually going on, since the behavior of the masses of people on the lower levels of society did not usually enter into the discussions. Western society was made up of the many who were nursed by their mothers and the few who were not. The ramifications of this difference between the lowly and the privileged on the very threshold of life are worth exploring. We are still gathering the facts, however, some of which have already been mentioned in connection with fertility, the relationship between husband and wife, and infant care in general. Little changed over the centuries. The wet nurse did not disappear from the Western world until long after 1800, not until bottle feeding was well established and provided parents with different options.

The use of substitute mothers in infancy is an ancient practice found all over the world. The way it was done in the West fitted into the hierarchical structure of society. Infants were generally of higher social rank than their nurses, and at the highest levels of society wet nursing was taken for granted. In some cities the practice also became the norm for people of less exalted rank, with the country, as usual, at the service of the city. The number of babies in the care of wet nurses in London and Paris increased as the population grew, and it has been estimated that toward the end of the eighteenth century only one of every ten babies born in Paris was nursed by its own mother.[21] As a result, wet-nursing as an institution had an impact on both city and country. In one rural area north of Paris there were said to be as many nurslings from the city as there were local babies. Practically every village household was involved, since the few that did not take in nurslings were likely to be of high enough status to put their own babies out to nurse.[22] What happened in Paris was not, however, replicated in every European city. There was a greater use of wet nurses by lower-class parents in Paris than in most other cities. At the upper end of the social scale, however, there were hardly any regional differences.

This business involving so many people worked in much the same way for hundreds of years. The basic arrangement was an individual one made between the father of a newborn child and the husband of a woman whose baby had died or was soon to be weaned. The newborn lived in the nurse's home, and the nurse—or her husband—was paid in cash once a month. In a variant of the basic arrangement the nurse was hired as a servant to live in the baby's household. This was usually more expensive and was common only among families of fairly high economic and social status, like those of merchants in fifteenth-century Florence and eighteenth-century Hamburg. In France it was pretty much limited to the nobility. The arrangement was not necessarily the same for every child in a family. Daughters and younger sons might be sent out and eldest sons kept at home.

A town of any size was likely to have some kind of nurses' registry, run either as a private business or by the government. The most famous of all, and apparently the largest, was the one in Paris, which was already in existence in 1350. By 1800 it had long been part of the central French bureaucracy. Governments supervised wet-nursing for two purposes. One was to control quality by checking on the health of the nurses and the kind of care they gave. One ordinance, for instance, prohibited them from having more than one nursling at a time and required them to notify parents immediately if their supply of milk gave out. The other purpose was to make arrangements for foundlings and orphans, recruiting nurses and transporting the babies to them. This was a rather big business in itself and produced copious records of great interest to historians, but it was an aspect of wet-nursing that did not affect most families.

It was thought desirable for a wet nurse to be a person of good moral character and stable disposition, not only because this made her a good caretaker but, even more, because milk was believed to transmit personality traits. As another form of uterine blood, it affected the kind of person the child would turn out to be at least as much as what happened in the nine months before birth. Michelangelo joked that he owed his calling as a sculptor to the fact that he had been nursed by a stone-cutter's wife, from whose milk "I sucked in the hammer and chisels I use for my statues."[23] At the very least, the nurse was supposed to be as much like the natural mother as possible. All this concern about the nurse's character, expressed over and over throughout Western history, seems to fly in the face of what most people did, however. In a period when it was commonly believed that coarseness and gentility were class characteristics acquired before birth or in earliest infancy, parents obviously made a compromise with the ideal the moment they handed a baby over to a poor, illiterate peasant woman. Where the demand was particularly high, wet nurses might be unmarried women, hence of dubious morality. In some cities, indeed, the placing of unwed mothers as wet nurses was one way of solving a welfare problem. Robustness and general good health were the qualifications most consciously sought. A pleasant disposition was also helpful, because anger or irritability might make the milk turn bad. A careful parent or agency would test the milk of prospective nurses, judging it on the basis of thickness, color, and taste. There were various theories, not all in agreement, about what constituted the best milk. Bad milk, in any case, might pose a threat to the baby's life.

Babies' experiences in the hands of their substitute mothers varied widely. The records of the institutions that supervised the care of foundlings show that the risks of substitute motherhood could be very high. In one French city in the eighteenth century, fully 90 percent of all foundlings died while staying with nurses. In the course of one nurse's twenty years in the business, during which she took care of twelve babies, not one survived.[24] A church official in seventeenth-century London, observing that "very few children prosper long in our parish, that are nursed in such places," commented, "He that loveth his dog would not put it in such a place to be brought up."[25] Foundlings unquestionably got the worst of it. They were handled carelessly on the way to the nurses in the country, frequently had to share a nurse with one or two other infants, and often were not suckled at all but fed substitute baby food prepared in a less than hygienic manner. It is best not to dwell too long on this slaughter of innocents. In any case, it was not what most parents doomed their children to. In the French town where almost all the foundlings died, babies who were not foundlings, but who were also placed with wet nurses under supervision by the authorities, had a better-than-even chance of coming home alive.[26] One reason for the difference could have been that the nurse was known to the parents. Contact between nurses and mothers seems to have been frequent, and the visit to the country by the city mother became a favorite subject of sentimental eighteenth-century paintings. Wet-nursing probably only intensified the normal perils of infancy. The nurse was usually a busy wife and mother, faced with many temptations to neglect the nursling in her charge. "Overlaid and starved at nurse" was often given as a cause of infant deaths in official lists in seventeenth-century London.

The baby stayed with the nurse until after it was weaned. Apart from the possible transmission of personality traits, their close association made the nurse an important figure in the child's development. Obviously she did more than feed the baby. She attended to the rigmarole of swaddling, fondled it (or not), gave it its first exposure to human speech, and saw it through the crises of teething and weaning that even the healthiest infants had to endure. The length of time they were together is uncertain. As usual, there was not a perfect match between theory and practice. Many authorities recommended at least two years of breast-feeding, but most wet nurses weaned their charges at around the age of one, and of necessity earlier if the nurse's milk gave out or she got pregnant. Weaning was usually quite abrupt and accomplished by various methods. In the eighteenth century in France a baby bottle was routinely distributed with each foundling, but many babies were apparently weaned with a spoon and some with a small dish fitted with a spout.

The wet nurses who lived in the households of the babies' parents were a small and relatively privileged group. They were better paid, they were probably better fed, and, since it was they, rather than the babies, who were separated from home, they had no competing demands on their time. Their charges were not only the children of the wealthiest and most prestigious people in society but were also likely to be the most privileged among those children. These distinctions suggest how complicated and contradictory the attitudes toward baby care must have been. It took one kind of concern to find a nice healthy nurse for one's infant daughter and send the baby away for two years, another to hire a woman to stay at home with one's son and heir. Although in France live-in nurses never became common, in the "enlightened" eighteenth century middle-class families elsewhere came to prefer them. The baby at home was likely to get care that approached the ideal. Its swaddling clothes were kept clean, it was fed when it was hungry, and attention was paid to it so it would not fret or cry.

Nevertheless, having a live-in nurse was not entirely without risks. The nurse might go against the rules and get pregnant or she might infect the baby with a disease. The correspondence of Madame de Sévigné in the late seventeenth century mentions the nurse of one of her daughter's children who was threatened with dismissal when her skin broke out in lesions like those of secondary syphilis. In spite of the mother's understandable fears, this case shows that the risks were not all to the child. The nurse protested that she could not possibly have a venereal disease, since she and her husband were decent people. We know from the correspondence that the baby had oddly formed teeth of a kind now associated with congenital syphilis, so the poor child may herself have transmitted the infection while suckling, and the ultimate source was probably her syphilitic father.[27]

The practice of wet-nursing was buttressed by an array of beliefs, prejudices, and practical needs. A wet nurse was a necessity if the natural mother was not present—something that happened often enough in those times of high childbed mortality. A wet nurse was also a necessity if the mother's own milk was insufficient. This reason was regarded with suspicion by moralists, as we have seen. Still, a frail woman was likely to have an inadequate milk flow, and if she happened to be sick as well it was doubly dangerous for her to do the nursing. In certain circles reasons of this kind were unnecessary, since no serious consideration was given to the possibility of mothers doing their own nursing.

The way wet-nursing spread among working people in cities is an indication that convenience was an important consideration. For city women who needed to have their hands, bodies, and time untrammeled so they could earn a living, the system was already in place, ready to expand as demand increased. For the more well-to-do there was the convenience of not having to make changes in their social and sexual life. Since it was supposed to be wrong for nursing mothers to have sexual intercourse, wet-nursing was, among other things, a moral convenience—something Catholic theologians often argued.

At a deeper psychological level, there was a lot of fear connected with nursing. The animal-like child seemed to be draining the mother of her vital forces—an image supported by the idea that milk was a form of blood, specifically menstrual blood, which first fed the child in the womb and then continued to feed it after birth. This is not the place to go into the terrors human beings have felt about menstrual blood, but it is appropriate to remind ourselves that Western culture is still not free of them. The fear of oral aggression would have been even stronger when babies started getting their teeth—a troublesome process for both child and mother. There were many ways in which nursing was frustrating, unpleasant, and unrewarding. Ironically, men may have felt more threatened than women, since men have had no little difficulty in coming to terms with female bodily functions.

The correct person to do what was in so many ways a lowly job was someone of lowly status. In a hierarchical society this could have been an important part of the attitude toward wet-nursing. Many important functions were assigned to people who were used to physical work, discomfort, and dirt. The growing of food, for example, which no one regarded as a trivial matter, was almost entirely in the hands of a class generally looked on with contempt. The contempt was mixed with a bit of gratitude, if not to the individual peasant then to a social order (often assumed to be the natural order) that provided peasants to work for their betters. An upper-class woman was not regarded as inadequate if she was not able to breast-feed, because the job was one suitable for a more animal-like creature. This was the same ambivalent attitude toward country matters that showed up in pastoral fantasies: simplicity and "natural" manners were idolized from a safe distance. In the eighteenth century, the practice of wet-nursing found a rationalization that was in harmony with a more frequently expressed concern for the child. The good of the baby was actually promoted by its being sent to a healthy nurse in the country. This may have had a special appeal to the growing numbers of city women who were adopting the practice.

In utter contrast to all this were the women who nursed their own babies and hardly thought about the alternatives. The historical record may give the impression that wet-nursing was pervasive, but numerically it was of minor importance. The contrast was between the few wealthy and privileged as against the many poor and socially inferior, the few city people as against the masses who lived and worked in the country.

Women in the country nursed their own babies, but, just like aristocratic ladies, they did not always have enough milk. Since they often suffered from malnutrition, they were even more likely to stop lactating. It was common to supplement breast milk with a traditional form of baby food, a pap or gruel made of bread warmed and softened in a liquid like water, milk, or even (in Germany) beer. Better-equipped households had a special pan for preparing the pap, for which there were various recipes. Many people had reservations about using animals' milk, which threatened to transmit the animals' characteristics, but there nevertheless seems to have been wide use of both cow's milk and goat's milk. As infrequently as poor people ate wheat, which was considered the luxury grain, they seem to have made a point of feeding it to babies. The main ingredient of pap was either white bread or fine wheat flour. In this way babies may not have gone hungry, but they were often not well nourished, and the supplemental food carried with it the danger of contamination. We have already seen how high the death rate was in the first year of life. In the town where 90 percent of the foundlings sent out to wet nurses died, babies who stayed with their own mother had about an 8-to-2 chance of surviving—close to the overall average, which seems appalling.[28] In addition, many children grew up with the deformities of rickets and scrofula, which can be caused by nutritional deficiencies. The babies of the poor were weaned slowly, gradually consuming more of the bread that would be their staple food for the rest of their lives and eventually making the transition to bread made of rye rather than wheat and dishes made with the cheaper grains—buckwheat, barley, and oats, and, after it was introduced from the New World, corn. Another New World import, the potato, began to catch on in the eighteenth century, when it was discovered that it was the cheapest of all staples to grow.

The majority of children thus had a different kind of care and feeding from the children of the privileged, since they were not taken from the embrace of their own mothers. How much time they actually spent being embraced by those preoccupied women we do not know. Live-in nurses probably gave babies more attention than either peasant wet nurses or peasant mothers did.

A small minority of upper-class women nursed their own babies. We know this because it was often noted as something remarkable and interpreted as an effort to give the babies a special advantage. What was most frequently mentioned was not that the baby would have the advantage of maternal affection or that the mother would satisfy her maternal longings but rather that contamination with what was socially and morally inferior would be avoided. Giorgio Vasari explained that Raphael, unlike the other artists he wrote about, was nursed by his mother because his father wanted him to learn "the family ways at home rather than in the houses of peasants or common people."[29] There were apparently a few other fathers who felt the same about their sons, especially their eldest sons.

Anyone who could read could find arguments against wet-nursing. All the official advice was in favor of mothers' feeding their own children. As we have seen, some of it was an attack on women's vanity and sensuality, but there was also some consideration of the benefit to the child or to humanity in general. Theologians argued for the obligations of parents to care for their offspring by using the natural means provided by God. Church authorities in Italy waged a largely unsuccessful campaign with the aid of art. It is an irony that those glorious Renaissance Madonnas embodied an ideal that was followed only by the lowly. Medical authorities, such as Rösslin, the author of the standard handbook for midwives, urged mothers to nurse their own children because wet nurses were often inferior people whose milk might be affected by their bad dispositions or transmit undesirable characteristics. A few moralists expressed concern about the forgotten child, the wet nurse's own baby, who was deprived of the care he or she was entitled to by nature. In the sixteenth century Montaigne said, "For a very slight profit, we tear . . . their own infants from their mothers' arms. . . . We cause them to abandon their children to some wretched nurse, to whom we do not wish to commit our own, or to some goat."[30] In the eighteenth century, many men with a scientific outlook were convinced that wet-nursing was a major cause of high infant mortality and urged mothers to breast-feed as a health measure.

The arguments of Rousseau were more like those of earlier writers. He thought that the central problem was the vanity and self-indulgence of well-to-do women. But he especially stressed the importance of doing what was natural ("Why go against the law of nature?"[31]), which, he said, brought untold benefits to the mother. Nursing gave women "the solid and permanent affection of their husbands, the truly filial tenderness of their children, the esteem and respect of the public, happy confinements without mishaps or consequences, [and] robust, vigorous health."[32] And another note crept into the discussion. Doing what nature intended us to do was connected with the cultivation of feelings, the life of the heart. Therein lay the greatest benefit for the child: "Where there is no mother, there is no child. Their duties are reciprocal. . . . If the call of the blood is not strengthened . . . , it will be extinguished in the earliest years, and the heart will die before it is born, so to speak."[33]

When women of fashion took up breast-feeding, the people around them were a little shocked, but they were usually impressed. The ambivalence on the subject left a great deal of room for approval. Nursing was a fad among the enlightened upper class that read Rousseau, but it was only a fad; its lasting effect was negligible. It may have corresponded to the needs of some women to be excellent mothers, but for many women it seems to have been more like the pastoral fantasies cultivated by Marie Antoinette when she played shepherdess in her artifical hamlet at Versailles. Rousseau himself was contradictory, like every other propagandist for maternal breast-feeding. A few pages after exclaiming about "the right of motherhood" and "the sweet duty" of nature, he gives some not particularly original guidelines for choosing a wet nurse. Before we succumb to the impulse to sneer, we should remember that many babies, among them Rousseau's Émile, did not have mothers of their own. Anyway, no moralist like Rousseau could resist the temptation to set the world straight on the correct way to do what so many people were doing, and doing so badly.

Anyone trying to imagine the life of babies in the past eventually comes up against a blank wall. Most of the information we have is about dead babies and absent babies. Burial records give us almost the only glimpse of the children of the poor and illiterate, and the literate men who might have told us about the others rarely laid eyes on them, since infants under the age of two were either away from home or in the exclusive care of women. There were exceptions and there was quite a bit of theory, pregnant with the possibility of revealing the truth but unreliable.

The extremely ambivalent structure I have described rests on a wealth of facts about two things in particular: the infant death rate and the workings of the wet-nurse system. Other aspects of early childhood are only slowly being illuminated. For the time being, the tension between concern and indifference on all levels of society remains striking. The contrast between rich and poor in the matter of maternal breast-feeding does, however, give hints of an important difference in the emotional development of children on different social levels. We will have to wait and see whether we can ever learn more about it.

8

Upbringing

Nowadays we like to think of childhood as a fairly long, pleasant period of dependence, in which adults shield children from danger, take care of their physical needs, and assure their happiness as their minds and bodies develop in accordance with their natural abilities. Although we are accustomed to hearing that lifelong psychological damage can begin in childhood, we persist in believing that it can be a period free from stress. How long the idyll lasts is not clear. Through elementary school? Through high school? Through college? Most of us recognize a difference between childhood and adolescence without being sure of the dividing line. Our culture does not have the benefit of coming-of-age rituals as some other cultures do, and the vestiges of such a ritual in the Jewish bar mitzvah are not terribly convincing today; the thirteen-year-old who solemnly announces he is a man continues to lead the life he did before. In any case, the stage after childhood is not thought of as true adulthood in most cultures. In our educational institutions and legal system it is treated as an extension of childhood, childhood in an attenuated form.

If the upper boundaries of childhood are unclear, the rest of it is a well-charted territory. Our interest nowadays is engaged by the tiny gradations in what we perceive as a complex development from birth to puberty. We feel obliged to provide the care and training appropriate at each stage, and no stage, however early, is without some kind of developmental challenge. The realm of childhood is complicated, important, and, to a great many of us, endlessly fascinating.

Childhood in the past was different, but there is much that looks familiar. There was a similar ambiguity about when childhood ends. There was probably less unanimity then than now about how to bring up children. We have already seen some of the ambivalence about very small children. When they turned into more recognizably human creatures, with the ability to walk and talk and manipulate materials, they were sometimes given responsibilities that we—and our laws—would regard as burdensome and inappropriate. Yet considerable effort went into preparing children for adult responsibilities and finding places for them in the adult world. If childhood was a sort of terra incognita that did not begin to be catered to as a condition with its own values and interests until the eighteenth century, it nevertheless always received attention of a sort.

Perhaps there is something universal about the ambivalences of childhood. Although very small children are naturally dependent, the dependence of older children is culturally determined, so "maturity" and "childhood" are social constructs rather than biological stages. Every society tends to do an incomplete job of keeping the two stages mutually exclusive. Childrearing also inevitably calls forth the ambivalence lurking in any relationship between those who wield authority and those who are subject to it.

The kinds of ambivalence associated with staying home or not and attending school or not have slightly less universal application. They reflect some important differences between Western society in the past and Western society in the present. A growing reliance on schools is a particular characteristic of the centuries we are looking at.

The notion of a hierarchy of rights and duties associated with status that permeated society between 1350 and 1800 was easily transferred to the way childhood was regarded. Another feature of that society was the tendency to learn by doing and through one-on-one relationships rather than by formal instruction—in other words, apprenticeship. A third feature was an age structure very different from what we are familiar with today. For example, in two different places two centuries apart for which there is a relative abundance of statistical information (early-fifteenth-century Tuscany and late-seventeenth-century England) more than half the population was under twenty-five. Children between five and fifteen would have been a highly visible presence. In the past there were about twice as many school-age children as middle-aged people, whereas nowadays there are roughly equal numbers of those two groups. The effect of such a proportion on the way children were brought up has not been explored, but it does not take much imagination to see that it must have given a certain shape to the experience of being a child.

Early Maturity or Prolonged Childhood

Because maturity in human beings is culturally defined, growing up is always accompanied by mixed signals. Reaching puberty means that physical parenthood is possible, but it rarely makes someone an adult in the legal or social sense. Taking on one kind of responsibility never automatically wipes out all forms of dependence. The signals of the past were no less confusing than those of the present. One obvious contrast between then and now is that our children are precocious as consumers, spending money in ways that would have seemed very strange to our ancestors, whereas children in the past tended to be precocious as producers.

There were fixed ideas about the significance of certain ages, often bolstered by the law. Similarly, the ages of six, eighteen, and twenty-one have certain associations for us. The most universally agreed-upon significant age throughout the four centuries we are looking at was seven, the point at which a child supposedly became teachable and trainable. Dividing the subsequent stages of life into seven-year periods had an attractive logic and was sanctioned by ancient usage, although it was only one among several ways of measuring the process of growing up and aging. In this scheme the time before age seven was a vague period of infancy, when, as we have seen, women were in charge. The period from seven to fourteen was the part of childhood that got the most attention. The seven years after that were not so clearly defined, except in neat theoretical and legal schemes. They were the period of "youth," and youth meant a lot of different things. After twenty-one came adulthood, which the makers of schemes often subdivided further, but this the law rarely did except when people over a certain age were categorized as too old to fulfill certain obligations. In many places that age was sixty. In colonial New England, for example, service in the militia was required for males between sixteen and sixty. Here the beginning of youth was moved ahead two years from fourteen to sixteen, possibly because of a tradition dominated by sixes instead of sevens. Roman law, which was influential even where it was not strictly followed, used the seven-year divisions, calling the three stages of the twenty-one years before adulthood *infantia, pueritia,* and *pubertas.*

The schematization into stages implied that each stage called for appropriate behavior. In graphic depictions there was little consistency about youth and young adulthood, however. Like Jaques in Shakespeare's *As You Like It,* the artists may have been making a point about old age and death rather than presenting an accurate picture of childhood and youth. Jaques's "seven ages" speech gives the early years short shrift and makes a precipitous leap from school to courtship:

> At first the infant,
> Mewling and puking in the nurse's arms.
> Then the whining schoolboy, with his satchel
> And shining morning face, creeping like a snail
> Unwillingly to school. And then the lover . . .

The truth is that no scheme clearly showed either what was expected of children and young people or what they actually did. There was less rigidity about the theoretical significance of certain ages than there is today. Practice varied from place to place and among social groups, and there was a bewil-

dering variety of individual behavior. To cut through the confusion I will con-
centrate on two extremes. First, I will show some ways in which maturity
came earlier than it generally does today, and then some ways in which adulthood was delayed longer than most of us would consider reasonable.

The age of fourteen was a far from rigid boundary, even in the law. Maturity of a sort could come at almost any time after the age of seven. It came as
early as nine in seventeenth-century England and New England, according to
some lawyers' handbooks, which said that nine was the "age of discretion,"
the age at which a person could be held responsible for such offenses as slan-
der. This later rose to fourteen and even sixteen before 1800, and is now a
largely unknown concept. In fifteenth-century Tuscany a boy as young as
eight or nine could be released from his father's legal authority, provided the
father himself formally allowed it. In sixteenth-century London heads of
households were required by law to have bows and arrows available for all
male occupants over the age of seven. In the records of some English legal
proceedings persons under twelve were identified by age, while those over
twelve were lumped together as adults. In France, a person of fourteen could
be tried as an adult for any crime. The canon law of the Roman church defined
the age of consent for marriage as twelve for females and fourteen for males.

The significance of age seven was probably not that what followed was so
clear but that what came before it was so vague. Around that age a number
of symbolic gestures made the point that the time of infancy, spent in the
world of women, was being left behind. Children under seven of both sexes
dressed alike, wearing skirts. Thus they did not assume the guise of males and
females until what we would consider an advanced age but, once they did, the
clothing they wore was almost identical to that of adults. Lower-class children
probably wore the cut-down hand-me-downs of older relatives. In paintings
rich children were usually depicted wearing elegant, formal garments that proclaimed status and dignity. Special clothes for seven-to-fourteen-year-olds are
relatively recent, hardly thought of before 1800. Another symbolic gesture
was leaving home. Children under seven rarely left home. (Could a boy in
skirts leave home?) In France even foundlings were supposed to stay with their
wet nurses until they were seven; a nurse continued to provide a home long
after a child was weaned, but when it reached the commonly recognized time
for starting to assume responsibilities it was handed back to the authorities.
For children who lived with their own families, leaving home between the
ages of seven and fourteen was common up and down the social scale. Rich
Italian girls were often sent to convents at age seven or so. Rich boys were
sent to be pages in noble establishments before they were fourteen, and they
sometimes embarked on military and naval careers at the age of twelve. As
we have already seen, servants in the country were often very young, and in
towns it was no great rarity for boys and girls under fourteen to be involved in
apprenticeship and indenture contracts. In 1797 a boy of nine named Asa
Sheldon left his father's farm in Massachusetts to live with another farmer; he

later called this "an important event in the history of a youth."[1] In his eyes he was no longer a child.

Whether they left home or not, many children did real work. Asa Sheldon had started working for farmers in his neighborhood when he was seven. About a hundred years earlier an Englishman recalled that he had begun to card and spin wool when he was seven "and grew so expert that at Eight Years of Age I could spin Four Pound a day which came to Two Shillings a Week."[2] Country boys under the age of twelve did such things as tend sheep, harvest grain, and act as millers' helpers. Country girls did the things grown women did; they gathered wood, took care of children, helped with cooking and laundry, and pitched in at harvest time. A report written in France not long after 1800, already somewhat sensitive to concerns about child development, nevertheless urged that a boy of seven do certain work that would prepare him to "take up the spade and hoe" when he reached fifteen. "Little tasks that required no physical strength" included tending a cow or a few sheep, gathering wood, fastening bundles of twigs, and getting practice at lifting loads.[3] Upper-class children could also expect to enter the world of serious work at an early age. The sons of Florentine merchants, after some schooling in reading, writing, and calculating on the abacus, joined their fathers' firms by the time they were sixteen, sometimes even seven or eight years earlier. Embarking on a military or naval career meant seeing real action at an early age, as twelve-year-old Prince Charles of England did at the battle of Edge Hill during the Civil War in the mid-seventeenth century. He was in the company of his father, but this was no recreational camping trip. It was war in deadly earnest, in which the king was fighting for his throne and his life.

All this suggests extreme precocity. We might assume that fourteen-year-olds who were hard at work, who earned money, and who ran great risks must have been adults in every sense. They were not. They were not even as mature physically as boys and girls of the same age today. Tantalizing bits of evidence suggest that both sexes reached puberty relatively late. The onset of menstruation seems to have been most common at fifteen or later. Boys' voices changed later, too, perhaps after sixteen or seventeen.[4] Beardless youths seem to have been very common, and although "youth" is an indeterminate period, that fact helps to explain why it may not have required too much imagination for theater audiences in Shakespeare's day to accept the spectacle of males taking female roles and plots hinging on transvestite disguises. The pace of maturation has stepped up considerably in the past hundred years, a period for which we have much more evidence than for all the preceding centuries. It is a knowledgeable guess that the conditions of health and nutrition prevailing in those centuries kept the average age of physical maturation high.

Real autonomy and independence did not automatically follow from "adult" obligations and activities. Young people were subject to full parental authority as long as they were under the parental roof, and the father's legal

authority usually continued after they left home. Those who no longer had
parents were often subject to a surrogate parental authority. The experience
of Asa Sheldon is instructive. When we last saw him he was an employed
"youth" of nine. When he was thirteen his father made a formal contract with
the man Asa had been working for; it was agreed that Asa would continue
working for him until he was twenty-one, at which time (and no sooner) Asa
would be paid one hundred dollars. In all this time the young man was subject
to two powerful authorities and had almost no freedom of movement.[5] In
many parts of the Western world, emancipation from paternal authority could
not take place unless the father agreed to it, at whatever age. It can be said
that childhood continued for precisely as long as one's father was alive. Under
the English poor laws, needy children could be taken from their parents' care
and placed as apprentices until the age of eighteen for females and twenty-
four for males. We have already seen that apprenticeship was theoretically a
parent-child relationship, so that even if the legal age of majority was said to
be twenty-one, a young man of that age apprenticed under the poor laws did
not have adult status.

To be an adult it was really necessary to be married. It was next to impossible for single people to be considered adults. Consistent with that, apprentices were not permitted to marry. The English poor-law apprenticeships,
which in many respects were not real apprenticeships but a form of indentured
bondage, did allow girls to marry—which automatically released them from
their contracts, transferring them from a master's authority to a husband's.
Typical of the mixed signals about maturity was the rule in Plymouth Colony
in the seventeenth century that all boys of sixteen were required to serve in
the militia but nobody under twenty had the right to vote on matters concerning the militia *unless he was married*. In Catholic countries the celibate
clergy was the largest exception to the rule that adulthood was impossible for
the unmarried. Taking the step into religious orders was seen as an analogue
to marriage insofar as the relationship with the family of origin was concerned.
Most of these notions about adulthood applied to men only. The adulthood
of women was an even more ambiguous matter. The only grown women who
could function as full legal adults were widows in certain localities and under
certain circumstances, but in France even a widow needed her father's consent to remarry if she was under twenty-five, just as though she were single.

Marriage was necessary but it was not always sufficient to break the bonds
of subjection to paternal authority. In upper-class families of southern Europe,
especially in joint households of married sons presided over by fathers, a man
could be married, over forty, a father himself, and still a dependent son, or *filius
familias*.

Since most people did not marry until their middle or late twenties, it is
plain that a sizeable chunk of the population drifted in a no-man's land
between childhood and adulthood, the ill-defined territory called "youth." It
was generally assumed that by fourteen, or at the latest sixteen, nobody could

any longer be considered a little child. On the other hand, before being established in the religious life or as the head of a household, a male over sixteen was necessarily a dependent of some sort. At the same time, he had a sort of freedom that would end when he assumed adult responsibilities. Youth implied certain characteristic behavior, apart from labor and subservience. Even at the end of the eighteenth century, there were traces of "youth-group" activity, and it seems likely that there had been more of it in previous centuries. Many of the village festivities, like charivaris and Maypole dances and midsummer bonfires, which may have descended from pagan times, were perpetuated and organized by youth groups. They seem to have been visible in towns, too, on certain holidays and special occasions.

Even apart from such organized activity, young people had a social life of their own, which was sometimes related to courtship but was frequently a spirited expression of male camaraderie and, in the opinion of the guardians of morality and order, all too likely to get out of bounds. Apprentices, journeymen, and other "bachelors" were expected to do a lot of drinking and carousing, even if they were often called to task for it. The qualification for participating was being a youth—an unmarried male, that is, not necessarily a young man of any particular age. Youth of both sexes constituted a large mobile population that formed only temporary attachments to households. Some journeymen and maidservants spent years moving about before they finally settled into marriage, the only conceivable end to youth.

Being called on to wield a bow and arrow at the age of seven and being considered a boy at the age of thirty if one was still single: these extremes of early maturity and prolonged childhood were characteristic of the entire period from 1350 to 1800. They made sense in their context, which is more important than any of the particular definitions of childhood and adulthood. The need to contribute to the work of the household made children into producers at an early age, and yet the recognized authority of household heads, especially fathers, kept grown people in the role of dependent children.

At Home or Away

Many children in the past spent part of their childhood away from their own homes. This seems to be in sharp contrast to today's norm, but before raising a lot of questions about it we should not exaggerate the contrast. Our children may live at home, but they are not educated at home. More than ever children today get information, training, and social skills outside the home. The particular arrangements keep changing, but if we take a long view we can see that there has been a continuous pattern in the Western world of sharing the responsibility of upbringing between the child's family and others. We may nurture in our bosoms the myth of a time when parents were the source of everything their children learned, before schools were compulsory and education got so complicated, but that is indeed a myth. A large part of upbringing has always taken place away from home.

In this division of responsibility lie the seeds of ambivalence. Individual choices have to be made about when a child should leave home; even if there really is no choice—when custom or law is absolute—there is room for mixed emotions. Leaving home at a relatively early age was the preindustrial norm, but it was not a rigid one. There were regional and class variations and over the centuries there was a slow process of raising the age and modifying the norm so that to send a child to the very best of boarding schools would eventually smack of cruelty. In 1800, however, the old norm, riddled with ambivalence and inconsistency though it was, was still in effect in all parts of the Western world and on all levels of society.

Children who stayed home generally did so because they were needed. A family of modest means working the land would use the free labor of at least some of its sons and daughters rather than hire outsiders. The designated heir in particular was likely to hang on indefinitely in anticipation of taking over one day. A few urban artisans trained their own sons, thus avoiding the expense and complications of apprenticeship, taking advantage of free labor, and assuring the succession to the business. In eighteenth-century America, Benjamin Franklin was one of these boys who was taught a trade by his own father, a candlemaker. He soon switched to another trade, printing, which he also could learn without leaving home because he was apprenticed to his brother. Rich merchants sometimes trained their own sons to enter the family business. This seems to have been the dominant pattern in Italy as early as the fourteenth century and may have been so from the earliest days of Italian commerce. In the thirteenth century the young Marco Polo had set out on his famous expedition under the tutelage of his father and uncle. There was a much greater tendency in southern Europe than in the north for prosperous families to keep children at home, in country and city alike. Among more modest country people all over Europe and in the New World as well, a definitive decision about staying or leaving was often postponed until marriage. Instead, children left and came back a number of times, nearly always to suit the convenience of their fathers and under arrangements made by them. Children left for a season to do planting and harvesting for others or to do other kinds of work in the off-season, returning home to do the seasonal farm work there.

Considering how limited the means of communication and transportation were, we can only be impressed by how much people moved about. If households were relatively less mobile than they are today, individuals were much more so, shifting from household to household. As we have seen, many parents thought nothing of sending newborn babies miles away from home to stay with wet nurses. Most parents took it equally for granted that at some point a growing child would leave home, possibly for good, and that he or she would take up residence in a number of places before settling down.

The similarity so apparent to us in all classes and regions appeared less uniform to contemporaries. What strikes us as a general compulsion to get children out of the house, in contrast to our own practice, took a number of different forms and had a somewhat different rationale depending on the parents' social status. The practice of wealthy aristocrats may have originated in ancient patterns that may or may not have had anything to do with the patterns followed by peasants. Still, for someone growing up between 1350 and 1800, one of the few things he or she could be sure of having in common with anyone of either inferior or superior rank was the experience of having left home before adulthood. Social and economic contrasts abounded, but this was not one of them.

The aristocratic pattern was for boys especially, but sometimes girls, too, to be sent to live in households where they learned how to be gentlemen and ladies by first learning how to be servants. They learned table manners and courtesy, and gained some experience of a wider world than that of their parents' homes. Books of etiquette, written for these rising social stars (like the fifteenth-century one in English called *The Babees Book*), were partly about how to eat and use one's napkin and partly about how to wait on one's master and his guests. Except among the highest nobility and royalty this system was fading in the years we are considering and hardly existed in Italy. Sending a child into a wealthier and more prestigious household than one's own continued to be regarded as desirable, but there was less shuffling of children among households of equal rank.

A page was an apprentice of a sort, but in the eyes of contemporaries true apprenticeship, formally arranged and legally recognized, properly belonged to city trades and professions. The normal pattern was for an apprentice to leave his home, and sometimes his city or country, and take up residence with a master for a fixed number of years, after which his education and upbringing were presumably complete. What made true apprenticeship different from the aristocratic pattern and from the pattern followed by lower-class people in rural areas was that the goal was specific. The boy became a shoemaker or a tailor or a lawyer or a banker, with marketable skills. During his apprenticeship, however, he resembled the aristocratic page in filling the role of a servant. Even in North America in the late eighteenth century and beyond, a prosperous merchant would send a young son out to serve as a cabin boy as the first step in training to become a junior partner in the father's firm.

The lower-class rural pattern was the least formal. Country children were expected to work and learn how to run a modest agricultural enterprise. If their parents needed their work, they stayed home. Poor farmers so often needed to get rid of extra mouths to feed, however, that it could look as though children were being sent to be servants out of dire necessity, not custom or desirability. For whatever reasons, the rural servant, usually a boy or girl of relatively tender years, was a common sight in every part of the Western world.

With all the confusion about the ages at which children were ready to do grown-up things, it is no wonder that there was no generally agreed-upon age for children to leave home. They were almost certain to be over seven, and would probably be at least fourteen when they left home for good. By the seventeenth century the appropriate age for apprenticeship was considered to be fourteen. Naval and military officers in the seventeenth and eighteenth centuries generally started their careers at fifteen. The timing of formal professional and vocational training therefore conformed to accepted ideas about the difference between childhood and youth. Still, many children left home before they were fourteen. Rich and poor alike, they left to do a less focused kind of learning and growing up, sometimes while waiting to be old enough to be apprenticed. Children were certainly learning and growing up—as they inevitably do—but their activity could look like just working. It is interesting to compare this with what was done with black slaves in the New World, since slave children would presumably have been treated by their masters only as productive labor, not individuals to be nurtured. In eighteenth-century Maryland, they lived with their parents at least until the age of seven, frequently until the age of ten. It was around this time that they usually started to work. They were taken from their parents' homes and sent to live elsewhere, either on the same plantation or on another one to which they had been sold. It would be wrong to minimize the terrible conditions of slavery, but European peasant children and even children in more privileged circumstances had similar experiences. They stayed home for seven years, unless they had been "privileged" enough to have spent their first two years in the home of a wet nurse, and then they could expect to leave home for short or long periods, starting any time and depending on what immediate employment was available and what future employment as adults was envisioned for them.

The merits of the system, such as it was, rarely came up for discussion. Up and down the social pyramid, leaving home seems to have been tacitly regarded as advantageous for children. A gentleman in fifteenth-century England left himself open to criticism if he denied his son the benefits of exposure to life in a noble establishment, where the boy would not only perfect his manners but also form lifelong associations that were valuable to his whole family. A poor farmer rejoiced at the prospect of sending his young daughter away to be a servant, knowing that she was far more likely to get a decent dowry from her master than from him. It was the really destitute who were forced to deny themselves such satisfactions; if they were reduced to begging, they would hold on to their children as helpful accessories.

Some people who routinely sent their children away, and some of those children, had mixed feelings. Signs of this crop up from time to time, often of no more significance than the tears that are shed nowadays on the first day of school. But some people were genuinely puzzled by why they were doing what was expected. Late in the eighteenth century the author Restif de la Bretonne told how his father sent off his daughters after he married for the second time, commenting, "These are natural arrangements, you see." One girl was sent to a relative, another became an apprentice, a husband was found for the third. Not too bad for any of them, but their father regretted their going, blaming it on the abnormal circumstance (but how abnormal was it?) of a stepmother in the household. The girls wanted to leave, apparently, and "natural arrangements" for females as well as males were familiar and to hand.[6] A favorite nursery tale in eighteenth-century America was "The Babes in the Wood," which is about sending children away from home and poignantly expresses the ambivalence of loving parents who reluctantly did what was "right."

In Italy people of means had different ideas from upper-class northerners about children leaving home. Some even kept their sons at home while they were apprentices, if the masters were in the same town. To them the practices of northern Europe were reprehensible. A comment by a Venetian ambassador to England in the sixteenth century, which has been quoted many times, throws an interesting light on what the English were up to and shows how vulnerable to criticism their practice was once there was a shift to another point of view:

> The want of affection in the English is strongly manifested towards their children, for having kept them at home till they arrive at the age of seven or nine years at the utmost, they put them out, both males and females, to hard service in the houses of other people, binding them generally for another seven or nine years. And these are called apprentices, and during that time they perform all the most menial offices, and few are born who are exempted from this fate, for every one, however rich he may be, sends away his children into the houses of others, whilst he, in return, receives those of strangers into his own. And on inquiring their reason for this severity, they answered that they did it in order that their children might learn better manners. But I, for my part, believe that they do it because they like to enjoy all their comforts themselves, and that they are better served by strangers than they would be by their own children.[7]

These hardhearted English (and the French, too) were not entirely in love with the system, and they eventually took to criticizing it themselves. Behavior may have changed little before 1800, but it seemed to need more and more justification, preparing the way for a present-day pattern in which children tend to live at home until their twenties. In the seventeenth century, William Penn castigated his contemporaries for taking equally bad care of their children and their souls. He could make a telling point about selfishness and shortsightedness because he himself had lost sight of any virtue inherent in a system of shared responsibilities: "They do with their Children as with their Souls, put them out at Livery for so much a Year. They will trust their Estates or Shops with none but themselves, but for their Souls and Posterity they have less Solicitude."[8] Quakers took an extreme position on individual responsibility (for souls and children), but Penn gave voice to a discomfort many non-Quakers also felt.

The aristocratic pattern was the first to crack. It has been suggested that the loss of political power by the landed aristocracy in Italy even before 1350 (and the absence of such an aristocracy in Venice) may be the reason the behavior of the English in the 1400s and 1500s looked so strange to the Venetian ambassador. When English aristocratic households were no longer the centers of power they had once been, they had less use as centers of training for the young. Country children continued to be servants in the homes of others and town children continued to live with the masters to whom they were apprenticed until the nineteenth-century factory system turned older economic arrangements into anachronisms. For the well-to-do another possibility and another institution was developing rapidly from the sixteenth century onward: the school.

Household or School

The central place of schools in the upbringing of children is firmly fixed today, but it took a long time for schooling to become so important. Schools had been around from ancient times, but in the 450-year period we are looking at their expansion and extension proceeded at a fast rate, reaching larger constituencies and taking on new tasks, until the educational empire of our own day was established.

By the end of the eighteenth century, however, school was not yet a necessary part of every child's upbringing. For certain segments of society it was already a significant option, and more and more children, even those at the very bottom of the social scale, were getting a taste of it. School was an alternative to learning in a household, and its rise constituted a social revolution, one that is by now so complete that it is hard to imagine a time when households were the primary centers of vocational and professional training.

Apprenticeship was at one time the model for learning every kind of skill. A "skill" was not only a craft like plumbing or carpentry, which are still learned in a modern watered-down version of apprenticeship, but also, among other things, music, painting, sculpture, textile manufacturing, and "business administration." The normal age at which to start an apprenticeship was, as we have seen, fourteen. This was sometimes stipulated by law, but it seems to have been observed with little rigidity. The normal length of an apprenticeship, also a matter treated with considerable flexibility, was seven years. Thus the period of life covered by apprenticeship fitted into one of the neat schematizations I mentioned earlier. An apprentice was a "youth," with all the ambiguities of that status. The period of apprenticeship more or less matched the long period of post-elementary schooling we have today (high school and college in the United States). Ideally, every child went through a seven-year period of dependency and training of one sort or another, and the ideal remains to this day. In practice, apprenticeship could start earlier and could last anywhere from a few months to seventeen years (the term of some contracts in eighteenth-century Philadelphia).

Since most apprentices lived in their masters' households, the master filled the double role of teacher and father. The double role existed even if, as sometimes happened, the apprentice lived with his own father. He might go out to a master's household by day or he might be apprenticed to his father (or brother, as Benjamin Franklin was). Apprenticeship contracts gave masters a large degree of paternal power. Standard American contracts in the eighteenth century required apprentices to obey all the masters' "lawful commands" faithfully, serve them dutifully, and preserve their house and trade secrets. They were forbidden to frequent taverns, gamble, "commit Fornication," or "Contract Matrimony."[9] In return, as all books of advice admonished, the master was to be a good father. In the words of one guild charter, "You will have to render account for this apprentice, and you must look after him as you would after your own child!"[10]

To be an apprentice was a mark neither of lowly status nor of privilege. It was roughly analogous to modern compulsory education, and indeed in some places the law did make apprenticeship compulsory. As experienced, however, it was different for people of different social status. Lowly foundlings were apprenticed as the final step in the authorities' supervision of their welfare, but whether they got much training is questionable. In both Europe and the New World they were often more like bonded servants than pupils. The seventeen-year apprenticeships in Philadelphia were probably of this sort. At the upper end of the social scale, well-to-do parents willingly paid high fees to place their children with wealthy masters—for instance, those in the great merchant guilds of London. The households of professionals like doctors, lawyers, apothecaries, and notaries, which were their business premises as well, usually contained apprentices. And until the seventeenth century, the "profession" of gentleman and the gentlemanly profession of war (on the officers' level) were likely to be learned in an apprenticelike situation under the tutelage of a master who headed a noble household.

Learning by doing, rather than formal instruction in a classroom, was the distinguishing mark of this pattern. But classroom learning also existed, particularly for reading and writing. Long before 1350, towns had an established pattern of modest day schools, which the French called "petites écoles" and the English "petty schools," to teach basic literacy to young children, some of whom went on to more advanced study but most of whom did not, retaining little more than the ability to sign their names and read with minimal ease. As time went on, primary or elementary schools were more available everywhere, even in country villages. Whether children went to school was usually left up to the parents and there seems to have been a lot of leeway about the age of the pupils, the regularity of attendance, and the length of schooling. Country children went to school only if they were not needed to work at home. Their education tended to be erratic and brief, even in a place that put a high value on literacy, such as colonial Massachusetts, where some children started school as early as the age of three.

In theory fathers were responsible for teaching their own children the rudiments of reading, but there is no doubt that wherever schools were available they were used. A committee report in Boston at the very end of the period declared that, although public funding of elementary schools was common, it was not desirable because "it ought never to be forgotten that the office of instruction belongs to parents, and that to the school master is delegated a portion only of the parental character and rights. In the retirement of domestic life, parents have opportunities to impart instruction, and to gain an influence over their children which the public teacher does not possess."[11] This may have been the advanced opinion of the time, but parents in Boston were no different from parents elsewhere in preferring others to take on the task of teaching their children. Starting in about 1600 elementary education became compulsory in some places in Europe.

It is impossible to talk about the history of schools without mentioning the part that religion played in their growth. Elementary education in particular, especially after the Reformation, was regarded as an inseparable mixture of literacy and religion. The educational system had always been associated with religion. Its main function in the Middle Ages had been the professional training of clerics, from the elementary choir schools up to the universities. This ecclesiastical connection persisted in later centuries in both Protestant and Catholic countries. With the confessional split of the sixteenth century came a new urgency for elementary education to be used as a tool of indoctrination in the competition between Protestants and Catholics. At the very time that parents were being exhorted to teach religion at home and conduct prayers in the household, schools were inculcating religion. Protestants wanted everyone to read the Bible, while Catholics wanted everyone to be able to resist heretical influences. Both wanted to train model Christians. In Catholic France, where there was a large minority of Protestants, rural elementary schools were openly directed at conversion, one of the results of which was that Huguenots were more strongly motivated than Catholics to keep up a high level of religious teaching at home.

Large numbers of people up through the eighteenth century got along without being able to read and write, and illiterate rural parents might never on their own have felt a need for children to spend time in school if there had not been pressure from the outside in the name of religion. In towns, where going to elementary school had always been the accepted occupation of certain classes of young children, it gradually became the accepted occupation for all children for at least a few years before they buckled down to serious work—which usually meant apprenticeship. French foundlings in the eighteenth century, removed from their nurses at the age of seven, went back to the institutions that had sent them out in the first place and, before being apprenticed, spent a few years learning reading, writing, arithmetic and, above all, as the regulations stated, religion and "the fear of God."[12]

Elementary schools were not a substitute for apprenticeship. They filled the time before apprenticeship, when most children were still at home. Eighteenth-century French social reformers thought school did not fill the time well enough. Since it rarely continued past the age of ten, the four or five years during which a boy waited to start his apprenticeship were, as one writer put it, "nearly always lost."[13] Developments in the nineteenth century were to remedy this, but for the time being elementary school was a short-term commitment.

The polarity of school and household came about because of a new phenomenon, the expansion of secondary schools. These were fairly elite institutions, originally intended to prepare pupils either for the university or the more literate professions. They taught what was considered true literacy (that is, Latin) and were sometimes called grammar schools because their main subject was Latin grammar. They remained elite institutions; what changed in this period was their clientele and, to some degree, their curriculum. The upper classes increasingly sent their children to school instead of to other households. Furthermore, notions changed about the kind of learning that was needed. Some schools that were founded in the sixteenth century included such gentlemanly skills as fencing and horsemanship, but more than anything else every gentleman was now assumed to need a solid literary education. This meant the kind of training in the classics that the fifteenth- and sixteenth-century humanists had developed, relying on Latin but changing the emphasis from exercises in syllogistic logic to the honing of literary skills. Paradoxically, in spite of the strong association between schools and religion, there was a growing secularization. Schools were no longer primarily devoted to training clerics. Some young men of the upper classes went on to universities but, in every part of the Western world, secondary school was usually an end in itself. In its various forms and under a variety of names (college, public school, high school, and the ones with a classical resonance like academy and gymnasium), it was out of the reach of most people.

Although to go to secondary school was a mark of privilege, it was apparently not taken for granted even in the wealthiest of families. There remained more than a vestige of the conviction that the training of youth should take place in a household instead of a specialized institution. Some wealthy parents hired tutors, sometimes several tutors with different specialties. More than a few books appeared in the seventeenth and eighteenth centuries promoting either schools or tutors and giving advice on how to choose them. A French work of 1740, for example, was entitled *Advantage of Education in Colleges over Education at Home.*[14] The preponderant drift was in favor of schools. One of their attractions was that they removed young people from their own homes, conforming in one respect to a reassuringly familiar pattern. Another attraction was that for all but the very wealthiest they were the only way to get a first-rate education of the right kind.

A formal education in school was more and more what distinguished a gentleman from a person who worked with his hands. A socially ambitious father who had not been to school himself would send a son to school to acquire the style of the social level to which he aspired. Apprenticeship was being slowly downgraded. According to one seventeenth-century social reformer, William Petty, it was a wasteful, inefficient system. He suggested in 1648 that books be written to give instruction in all the crafts and trades so that young people could avoid "the tedium of seven years' bondage."[15] Nobody at the time took him up on his suggestion. The winds of change were blowing from this direction, but the polarity persisted well past 1800: school for privileged youth and apprenticeship for the less privileged. Military officers, lawyers, and doctors were more and more likely as time went on to learn their skills in specialized schools.

Most of what I have said so far about schools refers to boys. The education of girls was not a central concern in these centuries, but its development was a reflection, if only a pale one, of the same trends. Rudimentary primary education was open to girls as well as boys, if the parents were willing to do anything about it. The religious motive applied perhaps even more to girls than boys. Rote learning of religion, at the expense of enhanced literacy, was frequently recommended for girls. Female foundlings were sometimes kept in the more protected environment of school to learn needlework instead of being sent out as "apprentices" to masters who might threaten their virtue. Where secondary schooling for girls was available, it was always separate from that of boys and rather different in content. Convent schools in Catholic countries and Protestant boarding schools for girls in England and on the Continent were still thriving in the eighteenth century and they sometimes provided a literary education almost as good as that offered to boys. More often they gave young ladies a superficial "finish" and constantly reminded them of their religious and marital obligations.

For girls in their teens there was a polarity similar to that for boys. Secondary school was for the privileged—in the case of girls, very few—while work in a household, sometimes combined with training, was the lot of the less privileged. The highly educated women we occasionally hear of in this period (writers like Margaret of Navarre in the sixteenth century, Madame de Sévigné in the seventeenth century, and Mary Wollstonecraft in the eighteenth century) were rarely the products of schools. They were either lucky enough to get superior instruction at home or motivated enough to educate themselves by building on their basic literacy.

Schools had many of the characteristics of households. Most secondary schools were boarding schools, sometimes far away from the pupils' homes, and they were expected to provide what well-run households did. That meant food and shelter, training in good manners, discipline, religious exercises, and a sound moral environment. Many boarding schools also had day pupils, but these were always considered inferior to the live-in pupils. Day pupils were deprived of the advantage of constant supervision by their masters and the opportunity to acquire in a hundred little ways what was expected of them in polite society. Besides, it cost more to be a boarder, so to be one demonstrated the superior status of a boy's family.

Even elementary schools had some characteristics of households. They were usually small and, although they functioned only in daytime, their premises were often actual households. In New England, for example, they might be "dame schools," classes conducted by women in their homes. Clergymen in both the Old World and the New gave lessons to little children in their homes.

But schools lacked some of the most obvious characteristics of a normal household. After a certain age, children of both sexes were not supposed to go to the same schools or even to have teachers of the opposite sex. Segregated education was the rule, the direct antithesis of the promiscuous mixing of classes and sexes in most households. This may have been one of the strongest attractions of schools for people who had so much uneasiness about sexuality. Another difference between school and household was that teachers were so often unmarried. The implication seems to have been that only a single person could devote himself or herself thoroughly to the care of the young. In any case, celibate teaching orders ran Catholic schools and unmarried schoolmasters and schoolmistresses taught in Protestant ones. Furthermore, schools were not supposed to be indulgent or suffused with tender affection, as perhaps some households were. Schools presented an idealized image of the right kind of household in which to bring up children, something few real households could be.

It was in the period between 1350 and 1800 that school started to be part of every childhood, in most cases a very small part early in life. For children of more exalted station school was becoming a dominant force in their lives, the place to which they went when they left the parental home for the first time. The majority of children, however, continued to spend the years after ten or so in a household, working and learning to work.

Conflict or Cooperation

If school was an idealized household, the model of childrearing was obviously different from what most of us recognize today. The attitude toward older children followed naturally from the attitude toward babies. More than anything else, children were thought to need discipline and control and, as they got older, they were expected to learn their place, which was, in general, inferior to that of all adults. Childrearing invited antagonism. It was often per-

ceived as a battle of wills. If today's model does not entirely deny this side of
childrearing, it emphasizes cooperation. Parent and child are assumed to have
common interests and goals; children need the guidance of adults and are willing to accept it when it is loving and affectionate. Egalitarian ideas have by
now extended to children, who are no longer considered inferior to adults.
Today the typical form of address to a mother by an American teenager of any
class is "mom" (probably preceded by "hey"). In the past it was likely to be
"madam," at least in the upper classes. But parents today still sometimes
behave in an authoritarian fashion and insist that children obey orders unques-
tioningly. The model, in short, is not followed perfectly. No model was followed perfectly in the past, either. The child was not always the defeated
party in the battle of wills and, more important, the battle did not rage inces-
santly and universally.

Only a few unusual pedagogues and, toward the end of the period, the
intellectuals of the Enlightenment questioned the general approach to childrearing, an approach based on some fundamental notions about the relationship of human beings to each other and to the universe. When everybody was
either someone's superior or inferior, rights and duties flowed from his or her
place in a hierarchical scheme. This left no room for anything like equal rec-
iprocity. Children in particular had few rights. Instead they had a mass of
duties to their parents. Nowadays, by contrast, it is parenthood that seems to
consist of nothing but duties. As for the place of human beings in the universe,
it was not a comfortable one. Life on earth was a constant battering by hostile
forces, physical and spiritual. A child, like any other mortal, was prey to disease, disaster, and the onslaughts of the devil. Physical nature, including what
was natural in human beings, was vulnerable and corruptible. Not harmony
with unreliable nature but the assistance of transcendent forces was what
could get people through the pains of mortal life to some ultimate rest and
reward.

I exaggerate, of course. But ideas about the treatment of children always
seem to be exaggerated versions of fundamental beliefs. Children play a special role in our view of our destiny and are a distillation of what we believe
most deeply about ourselves. That is one reason for ambivalence. It is also the
reason that there could have been what looks like such a sharp change from
the view that children were evil to the view that they were innocent. The
revolution in thought that was taking place throughout the period was making
it possible for people to feel they were part of a nature that they could understand and work with. When they no longer felt they were in conflict with
nature, they stopped looking upon their children as hostile forces. This change
was already detectible by 1800, but I hasten to add that it was far from complete. Fifty years later books were still referring to the "depraved nature" of
children.

Parents were cast in the role of rulers and children were their subjects.
Such a relationship could not be expected to operate smoothly. As John Calvin

put it, "Nothing is more contrary to human nature than subjection."[16] For every parent hovering close to the edge of tyranny there was a child on the brink of mutiny. Calvin was one of those who had rebelled in youth, so he knew what he was talking about. He remembered what the relationship could look like to a child: "Severity and petty strictness rouse children to obstinacy."[17] But most of the time he expressed the parent's point of view, complaining, in the typically hyperbolic tone of the time, "Do we find one child in a thousand who is obedient to his parents?"[18] At the end of his life he passed on this piece of wisdom: "There is always a certain conceit in youth that cannot be restrained and is full of contempt for others."[19]

In an era when so much of life was colored by religion, it is not surprising that filial rebellion often figured in religious conversions. Several of the great Reformation leaders, including Luther and Calvin, had conflicts with their fathers, and such conflicts were central to the experience of many Quakers and other sectarians. To feel that God was on one's side was extremely comforting, since the forces of society, including most of the institutions of organized religion, were on the side of parents.

Young people were believed to be difficult and getting worse all the time. Someone was always proclaiming that the "degeneracy" of the young was growing, whether in the fourteenth century or the eighteenth century. The remedy was the judicious use of corporal punishment, sanctioned in the Old Testament as an expression of parental love. "He that spareth his rod hateth his son," said the book of Proverbs. Even Quakers, who believed that children were innocent when they came into the world, quoted from Proverbs in their catechism: "Thou shalt beat him with the Rod, and shalt deliver his Soul from Hell."[20] Susannah Wesley, the mother of the founder of Methodism, summed up the good intentions behind what ran the risk of looking like cruelty: "As self-will is the root of all sin and misery, so whatever cherishes this in children insures their after-wretchedness and irreligion; whatever checks and mortifies it promotes their future happiness and piety."[21]

Disobedient children, especially those who stubbornly persisted or who countered violence with violence, were guilty of a crime against God and the state. A little book for children published in seventeenth-century France was called The Just Punishment of God against Children Who Are Disobedient to Their Mothers and Fathers, with the Pains They Will Suffer in Hell after Death.[22] Although parents had the authority to punish disobedient children themselves, in extreme circumstances the state could take over. In Pennsylvania, where Philadelphia, the City of Brotherly Love, was located, the punishment for assaulting or threatening a parent was six months' imprisonment at hard labor plus "thirty-one lashes ... , well laid on."[23] In Puritan New England, the laws prescribed death.

The power of parents over their children did not always lead to direct confrontation but could arouse resentment nonetheless. Poor parents decided when and where children would be sent to be servants or apprentices, often taking the wages for themselves. It was not so different for the rich, who tended to think in terms of grand family strategy, as in this piece of advice in a sixteenth-century French book on education: "Wealthy gentlemen with three children should place two in the army and middling nobles only one. The rest should enter either the Church or the Law, and only the eldest should have children. Marry few daughters, for that is the ruin of a noble house."[24] From all sides young people were reminded of their helplessness. Some grown men recalled vividly how frightening the world around them had seemed when they were children. There was a kind of terror imposed on children, not only by people close to them but also by forces beyond the control of human beings—devils, bogeymen, plague, famine, and war.

The feeling of helplessness was made all the stronger by parental behavior that to a child's eyes could look like indifference. When households broke up, as happened not infrequently, children were disposed of according to interests apart from their own immediate ones. In divorce and separation cases on the Continent and in the New World, children were hardly mentioned and their fate was not considered an issue. In England, where divorce was rare and occurred only in the upper class, children were automatically taken away from their (guilty) mothers and given to their fathers. Earlier, in fifteenth-century Tuscany, when a well-to-do father died, the mother often returned to her own parents' home, bringing her dowry with her but leaving her children behind with their father's family.

The common experience of losing a parent created conditions for the sharpest of conflicts. The orphan was proverbially the most deprived, the most abused, and the most pitiful of children. The stepmother was a made-to-order villainess, as we all know from fairy tales. I leave it to others to explore the fantasy element. The relations of natural parents with their children could be sufficiently strained to kindle at least covert hostility, but in stepparents and stepchildren the hostility could be more naked. Children who had lost both parents and were in the care of foster parents may have been even more subject to abuse than half-orphans, but the usual practice of putting orphans out to work at an early age and sending them away to learn a trade and become self-supporting as soon as possible does not seem so different from the treatment of most children.

Although brothers and sisters are natural allies in conflicts with their elders, we know how pervasive sibling rivalry can be. There were some special twists to it in the past, when inheritance was so important. To be the chief heir, for example, conferred a distinction from birth. This child, usually the eldest son, was less likely to be sent away to a wet nurse as an infant or to another household as a youth. A younger brother in the south of France in the seventeenth century penned these bitter words: "It is certain that in the share of my mother's heart I got no more than the minimum I was owed, and the prose of the eldest son was always preferred to the poetry of the younger."[25] The heir to even a tiny piece of land, whether designated by custom or the favor of his father, was a natural target for envy and resentment. He could also cultivate some resentment of his own, if he was made to feel his responsibilities early and, on top of that, knew that they included looking out for the welfare of his brothers and sisters. The different treatment of sons and daughters could also breed resentment.

It is not surprising that strangers in the household were also a source of conflict. The master-servant relationship was, after all, modeled on the relationship of parent and child. Other elements, like the economic aspect of the relationship, could eclipse the sense of personal obligation. In upper-class households, there was the element of class differences. Servants and apprentices often suffered from cruelty and neglect. In seventeenth-century London many apprentices sued their masters for mistreating them. Their parents complained that their children were not being trained and were instead put to work sweeping and fetching. For their part, masters complained of laziness, disobedience, and dishonesty. Apprentices were known to do the very things their contracts forbade. They drank, gambled, and stayed out late. They talked back and were disobedient, even though insubordination was a serious crime. Every kind of servant engaged in petty theft. In what must have seemed like a permanent state of war, each side tried to get away with what it could.

And yet, in spite of harsh precepts and recurrent conflicts, children were not inevitably deprived of affection and trust. The loving, even indulgent, father was proverbial. To be such a father must have been a fairly common impulse, or there would not have been so many warnings about the harm over-indulgence could do. There is a touch of déjà vu in the blame that was so often heaped on permissive parents when youthful rebelliousness erupted in public. As Calvin put it, "Mothers and fathers sometimes spoil their children by flattery. They indulge them so much that they as good as lead them to perdition."[26] A few fathers described their affectionate feelings. In a kind of love poem in Latin that Thomas More wrote to his bright and exemplary offspring he said, "Brutal and unworthy to be called father is he who does not himself weep at the tears of his child. How other fathers act I do not know, but you know well how gentle and devoted is my manner toward you, for I have always profoundly loved my own children and I have always been an indulgent parent—as every father ought to be."[27] A Frenchman of about the same time, Etienne Pasquier, said, "I am a father. When I say father to you, you can immediately judge the tyranny which nature exercises over me in favor of my children."[28] A seventeenth-century English clergyman, Ralph Josselin, said of his eight-year-old daughter that she was "a precious child, a bundle of myrrhe, a bundle of sweetness . . . a child of ten thousand, . . . [who] lived desired and dyed lamented, [and whose] memory is and will be sweete unto mee."[29]

Interest in sons tended to be especially evident. Fathers devoted much thought to their sons' futures, went out of their way to promote their prospects, and took extreme pride in their accomplishments. When a politically powerful man in sixteenth-century Paris created an important government position for one of his sons that was clearly not in the public interest, he justified his action on the grounds of his great love for his children. In return, sons exerted themselves to please their fathers, not out of mere duty but out of the belief that father and son shared common goals. The feeling of a deep community of interests was likely to be strengthened if the son entered the same profession as his father or became a co-worker in the same business. To Italians, who tended to work closely with their sons, the apprenticeship patterns of the North seemed to betray a lack of parental love, but we do not need to agree that this was so. Parents did not forget their children just because they had left home.

The severe discipline recommended in books was always justified as flowing from love. Eventually advice on upbringing took a different tack, as in the following from a book published in 1693: "Familiarizing oneself with one's children, getting them to talk about all manner of things, treating them as sensible people and winning them over with sweetness, is an infallible secret for doing what one wants with them."[30] Did this sound strange to contemporary ears or did it strike a responsive chord? Although it was much less authoritarian than most statements about childrearing at the time, it was still, as you have surely noticed, more manipulative than cooperative.

The emotional dynamics of lower-class families is a matter of guesswork, distorted by upper-class commentary, as in a suggestive remark by a French educational reformer in the early eighteenth century, Jean-Baptiste de La Salle, a man dedicated to the education of poor children, who, he says, "do just as they please, their parents paying no attention to them, even treating them in an idolatrous manner: what the children want, they want too."[31] That idolatry should be equated with "no attention" sounds odd until we recall the pervasive belief, especially among educational theorists, in the natural wildness and wickedness of children. "Paying no attention" meant not exerting firm control; the rest of the passage makes it unlikely that it meant indifference. The suggestion that lower-class people adored their children is interesting. It is not what we usually hear. Upper-class people did not generally admit to doing that until a century later.

Mothers were under fewer constraints than fathers. In the conventional roles assigned to southern French peasants, mothers were allowed to praise their children and defend them for the most egregious sorts of behavior while fathers had to be critical and impartially just. The supreme authority of the father placed the mother on a level closer to that of her children, and the intimacy of those first years of childhood in the world of women probably had a continuing effect, especially when added to the bond of nursing that was the usual experience of the lower classes. Mothers were proverbial sources of comfort and sympathy—a familiar enough idea. Thomas More, the indulgent father, described the kind mother sending her son off to the harsher atmosphere of school, telling him not to worry about being tardy: "She telleth him then that it is but early days, and he shall come time enough, and biddeth him: 'Go, good son, I warrant thee, I have sent to thy master myself, take thy bread and butter with thee, thou shalt not be beaten at all.'"[32]

The loss of a mother was universally regarded as a bitter blow. In seventeenth-century France, the fifteen-year-old son of a woman who was later canonized, Jeanne de Chantal, was in despair when his widowed mother announced that she intended to enter religious life. Knowing how strong his mother's religious vocation was, he could only make a dramatic gesture that gives a hint of the intensity of mother-son relationships. He lay down in the doorway of the house and cried, "I can't stop you, Mother, but you are going to have to walk over your own child."[33] This she did.

This woman's granddaughter, Madame de Sévigné, had a particularly intense relationship with her daughter, the recipient of almost all her famous letters. Mother-daughter relationships, it is fairly safe to say, could be more spontaneous and egalitarian than any other interactions of parents and children. Any correspondence between mothers and daughters that has survived tends to express in warm terms a host of shared interests and values. There is not a great deal of this correspondence, because most mothers and daughters did not need to write to each other, and until the eighteenth century even people who could write did not waste paper and ink on ordinary feelings or everyday matters. But when a fifteenth-century peasant girl named Joan of Arc recalled her fairly ordinary childhood, she singled out her mother with obvious affection as the one who had taught her the devotions that constituted her first experience of religion.

Apart from the almost subversive relationship with an indulgent mother or an ambivalent father unwilling to take on the heavier aspects of paternity, where was a young person most likely to find cooperation and sympathy? With equals—with people, that is, who were not threatening, who had similar interests, and who participated in activities regarded as unimportant. Equality had so little official standing in the preindustrial world that we find it mainly at the periphery of life, especially in games and play. Even hard-working peasant children played, and they continued to engage in what was regarded as carefree juvenile recreation until they became adults, that is, got married. Apprentices had the reputation of playing harder than they worked, and the bond they felt with each other was reinforced by their antagonism toward their masters.

In both rich and poor households playmates included servants, who were usually young themselves. One sixteenth-century reminiscence of a middle-class boyhood in a German town included confessions of such "mischief" as squabbling with sisters, minor vandalism in the company of schoolmates, and accidentally shooting a maid in the eye with an arrow when she obligingly presented her backside as a target.[34] The participation of servants is especially striking in upper-class households, where the servants' official social inferiority was overlooked in their unofficial relations with the children. The suspension of social barriers extended beyond the household, since in many small towns and country villages the children of the better-off played with the children of peasants. The interpenetration of social classes and the experience of equality in the years when people were growing up must have conditioned their perceptions of the hierarchical structure that they would later become part of. The structure remained intact for a long time, so these childhood experiences cannot be said to have destroyed it. But they were fertile ground for ambivalent feelings.

Brothers and sisters were often playmates, and in households where the oldest son wore the mantle of heir apparent the other children were united in a bond of shared inferiority. The fraternal feeling adults often expressed later in life were suffused with a warmth that came from the childhood experiences of equality and pleasure. Not for nothing was *fraternité* adopted as part of the slogan of the French Revolution.

The proverbially pathetic orphan had a fairly good chance of benefiting from whatever tendencies there were in childrearing toward cooperation and sympathy. Relatives of both the father and mother were in most places supposed to take responsibility, and among poorer people it was common for an orphan to live with an aunt or uncle, who often felt considerable affection for the child. Although adoption was virtually unheard of, such foster parents assumed all the more obvious parental obligations. Half-orphans, too, were sometimes taken in by aunts or uncles if the surviving parents remarried. But the commonest situation for a half-orphan was to remain with a widowed mother. The normally warm bond would be strengthened and, where there was little or no property involved, there would be little interference from relatives. Rich half-orphans, on the other hand, easily became pawns in remarriage negotiations, and the expression of concern over their helplessness was sometimes a mask for exploitation.

The ambiguous situation of orphans highlights the ambivalence about bringing up children in general. On the one hand orphans were easy victims, on the other hand they awakened the compassion of everyone. In 1783 a girl dressed in rags was found in an empty room in a French town with a note pinned to her clothes that read, "I was born paralyzed. I am 20 years old. I cannot put myself to bed or feed myself. I have no father or mother, brother or sister, which has caused those in whose charge I am now to leave me in this place so that I may get the kind of help I need. I have never talked. . . ."[35] It is not hard to understand why someone would have refused the burden of caring for this girl. She was never going to be able to work for her keep or be anything but a drain on a poor household's resources. And yet—why bother to write that note? Why the device of writing in the child's own voice (which we have seen before)? Surely an appeal was being made to the reserves of sympathy in all human beings. At the very moment of turning his back on her, someone had tried to see things through her eyes. Is it too much to believe that, under less extreme circumstances, adults mixed sympathy with the responsibility they took for the young people in their charge?

One of the reasons patterns of childrearing changed slowly is that circumstances tended to recur. The resentful child grew up to become an authoritarian parent, and the cycle started all over again. Because of low life expectancy, one thing missing in most children's lives was the tempering presence of grandparents. Relationships with parents were in some ways extremely intense, an intensity that was not reduced by the presence of nonrelatives in the household, since servants fitted into the same structure of authority. Children rarely saw a father's authority questioned in the household or observed a father having to play the role of a son.

Most of what we know about how it felt to be brought up in households of the past comes from biographies of unusual individuals. The rules laid down by theorists and moralists, which cannot be taken as descriptions, give us an idea of what people thought was important and problematic. These meager hints convey a strong impression that childhood (the years from seven to fourteen) was not a carefree time. On the other hand, bits and pieces of other kinds of evidence give an impression of extraordinary variety in the ways children spent their time and the relationships they had with those around them. We need to remember that children in the past were being prepared for neither democracy nor technology, as our children presumably are. Even in the English colonies of North America, even in so-called "democratic" pockets in the Swiss mountains, it was essential for children to learn how to obey the orders of superiors and to acquire skills appropriate for a predominantly non-industrial, low-tech economy.

IV

Relatives Past,
Present,
and Future

The household has a concrete existence and is therefore relatively easy to talk about, even if there are many unanswered questions about it. The subject of the family does not end with the household, however. We do not define a family by coresidence alone. Included in our present-day image of "family" is something that goes beyond the household and colors our perception of life inside it.

That something is kinship. I have already discussed the relations of kin and nonkin in the household. In this part the framework is no longer the household but a nexus of relationships that individuals and society recognize without its necessarily taking any physical form.

There is a lot to say about kinship, but we are still ignorant about many of the ways it worked in the past. We know most about the connection between living and dead kin, because the processes of inheritance left so much documentation. Before wading into that fathomless ocean on which society seemed to float, however, I would like to look at the relations among living kin, near and distant.

9

Kinship

Kinship in our own lives gets little conscious attention, perhaps because we take it for granted. Anthropologists first noticed how important it was in cultures other than our own; some sociologists and historians in turn became curious about kinship in the Western world. They discovered it was something very complex, with endless local variations and changes over time.

Historians are trying to find out how kinship worked in the past and how it differed from what it is now. Many feel that the history of the family is hopelessly distorted and incomplete with kinship left out. One reason I think family history is still in its infancy is that this gap is just beginning to be filled in.

There are really only two questions that need to be asked about kinship: Who are my relatives? What do my relatives and I have to do with each other? Each one of us can come up with answers from our own experience, but most of us will discover that the answers are not obvious, and they become less obvious the more we think about them. For example, I have a first cousin in Europe who would seem to qualify as a relative, and yet I have never seen him or heard from him; if he died I would probably not know about it. (He is the son of my immigrant father's long-lost sister.) If he suddenly materialized, however, and called on me for help, I would feel obliged to listen to him, even if one of the first things he would have to tell me would be his name. There were as many ambiguities in the past as there are today: great variety in who qualified as a relative, in the things relatives were expected to do, and in the relatives a given individual felt closest to.

Some things have changed. One reason kinship seems peripheral today is that it no longer performs certain functions. The connection between kinship and government, for example, has changed profoundly, even if vestiges of the past crop up from time to time. Politically powerful clans today are but feeble shadows of the ruling dynasties that used to be. Today there is much less emphasis on family pedigree, even at the highest social levels. This is a tendency that has been evolving for hundreds of years, and, during the four centuries we are looking at, it was cause for considerable ambivalence. Nowadays kin tend to be defined informally in terms of relationships with each other as individuals, from both the paternal and maternal sides, instead of being qualified by descent, however remote, from a formally recognized male line, as was often the case in the past.

Not every question about kinship in the past has an answer, so the following pages deal with only a few basic matters: the size and extent of kinship groups, biological and legal definitions of kinship, the importance of kinship compared to that of other relationships, and the ways in which kinship affected individual lives.

Wide or Narrow

The number of relatives a person has is only partly a matter of fertility. A great deal depends on perception: who is known and who matters. It used to be said that everyone was descended from Adam and Eve or, slightly more realistically, Noah and his wife, but nobody ever took that seriously on a practical level. After so many centuries the descendants of Noah were so distantly related to each other that, to all intents and purposes, they were not related at all. The same conditions apply on a smaller scale. Unless relatives are kept track of over several generations they are lost. A distant relative is no relative if the relationship is not recognized or recorded. So a kinship group has certain natural limits: the limits of living memory. Relatives who are alive at any one time will recognize grandparents or great-grandparents in common, but rarely great-great-grandparents. Consequently, third and fourth cousins tend to be borderline kin and are likely to be overlooked. Another limiting factor is distance. Cousins and in-laws who move, either spatially to another town or country or socially to another status, often cease to exist as kin.

Large kinship groups tend to be widely extended; they are no more characteristic of the past than small, narrowly extended ones are characteristic of the present. On the contrary, wide and narrow groups coexisted in the past and continue to do so. Many of us know of large clannish families that hold regular reunions and even have formal organizations with officers and bylaws. Although such families are found on all levels of society, wide kinship today usually goes along with wealth and power. It was the same in the past. There was a correlation between size of household and extent of kin, not because the extended kin of the wealthy lived together but because having a lot of relatives went along with high status, like having a big house. Poorer people had smaller households and narrower kinships. There is thus a polarity that parallels what we encountered when we looked at the size of households. Some people belonged to huge, extended kinship groups, while most people in the past seem to have had no more kin than most people do today.

Large kinship groups were a sign not only of wealth but also of aristocratic rank. This is hardly surprising, since being an aristocrat was so much a matter of birth. Keeping track of connections was essential. The remoter kin of aristocrats tried to share in reflected glory by pressing the advantage of any shred of kinship. In 1602 a minor French noble, the seigneur de Brantôme, age sixty-two, drew up a list of his living relatives. It included, as he put it, "my nephews, grandnephews, and great-grandnephews in the Breton style," and he stretched it enough to squeeze in all his relatives of princely rank. There were 258 names on the list, of which 73 were classified as spouses.[1] To know the names and exact relationships of so many people is no mean feat. He no doubt regarded the effort as worth it. It is conceivable that a list compiled by one of Brantôme's princely relatives would have been even longer, so close was the correlation between rank and kinship size. Florentine patricians, for example, were likely to be well acquainted with their third and fourth cousins.

Prosperous people of all ranks had more relatives than the really poor. It was, after all, literacy and property that made the reckoning of kin feasible and meaningful. Various sixteenth- and seventeenth-century diarists, mostly men of the merchant and professional class, made reference to about eighty living relatives each—which may be less than the number any of them would have included in a self-aggrandizing list. The childless Samuel Pepys, who lived in a three-person household, was one of these diarists.

Kinship spread over a wide geographical area is also typical of high social status and is seen most clearly in the international family ties of royalty. But rank and money are not the only conditions for keeping up with absent kin, either today or in the past. Outsiders in a society tend to have far-flung kinship, as long as they have some means of maintaining ties, like letter-writing. The kinship of European Jews, especially the more prosperous among them, was almost as international as that of royalty. There was nothing unusual about the son of a Jewish merchant in Hamburg in the seventeenth century marrying the daughter of a rabbi in Warsaw, thus setting up ties among in-laws, grandchildren, and grandparents that would last for at least a couple of generations. Immigrants, even lowly workers, tried not to sever their old ties, most of which were with kin. To move from country to city, which was such a common experience throughout these centuries, stretched the ties but, far from breaking them, often strengthened them. Immigrants over long distances seem to have acted in similar ways. Swiss and German glassworkers who went to France in the eighteenth century kept in close touch with relatives back home, and the early settlers of New England sent letters by slow boat to family in the old country. The tendency of deracinated people to cling to dispersed kin is strikingly demonstrated by the behavior of Afro-American slaves on eighteenth-century North American plantations. They were somehow able to maintain connections with kin in many different locations, in spite of being moved around and separated from each other against their will.

Kinship reached the zenith of extent and numbers in the Roman Catholic church's view of what constituted an exogamous group, all the people who, because they were "close," were not allowed as marriage partners. The church's definition of kinship was so wide as to run the risk of including almost everyone in an individual's acquaintanceship, especially if that individual lived in a small village. In canon law, kin comprised all blood relatives to the fourth degree, which by the method of computation that the church used meant extending out to third cousins in the same generation. It also meant extending down to great-great-grandchildren, great-grandnephews, and great-grand-nieces. The "Breton style" Brantôme referred to was apparently similar. But blood kin were not the whole story. In-laws were also included as exogamous kin. A widower could not marry his sister-in-law (his wife's sister) or even his widow's second cousin once removed. In addition, the church reckoned god-parents and their children as kin and even, as became apparent in some con-troversial cases, the relatives of persons who had illicit sexual relations with each other. For example Henry VIII's marriage to Anne Boleyn was for a time in danger of being delayed because he had had an affair with her sister. In the church's view it made no difference if one knew who these out-of-bounds rel-atives were or not, as long as they fell into the forbidden categories. Marrying a relative in ignorance was as good a ground for annulment as the most willful incest. Some degrees of relationship were, however, more forbidden than oth-ers. It was not impossible, for example, for second or third cousins to marry as long as they got permission (a dispensation) ahead of time. The point of all this is not that the canon law on marriage was complicated and sometimes arcane but that it was based on an extraordinarily generous and inclusive view of kin-ship. It was almost as far-reaching as the recognition in some inheritance laws of the period that *any* relative, up to any degree, had a claim.

For most people there was a huge gap between this theoretical conception of limitless kinship and their own experience. There is abundant evidence that hardly anyone was as generous as canon law about the number of relatives admitted into his or her reckoning. For one thing, marriageability was not a criterion by which ordinary people defined nonkin. As we have seen, relatives often preferred to marry each other, within much closer degrees than the canon law stipulated. The Catholic church's proliferation of forbidden degrees was something the Protestant Reformers attacked, claiming that it was unreal-istic and only an excuse for church authorities to profit from the selling of dis-pensations. Most Protestant churches narrowed the range of kin who could not marry. Catholics meanwhile continued to marry according to customary notions of appropriate spouses and to ask for dispensations accordingly. What determined the size of a group of kin for most people was not a set of abstract rules but certain living realities. It was the different perspectives

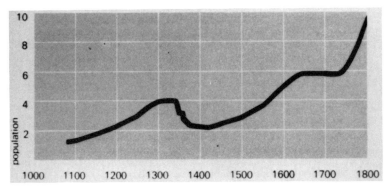

FIGURE 28   Long-term population trends in England and Wales, 1000–1800 (population given in millions). Note the sharp fall around 1350, the plateau in the seventeenth century, and the explosive rise from the middle of the eighteenth century. This pattern was pretty much that of western Europe as a whole.

FIGURE 29 *(left, below)*   "Man that is born of woman is of few days." Holbein's 1538 woodcut shows death walking off with a little boy, who waves good-bye to his distraught peasant mother. This is part of a "dance of death" series.

FIGURE 30 *(right, below)*   The Massacre of the Innocents was a popular subject in art. In this classicizing illustration for a 1591 edition of the Gospels in Arabic, the babies are plump and cuddly, the mothers fierce in their resistance.

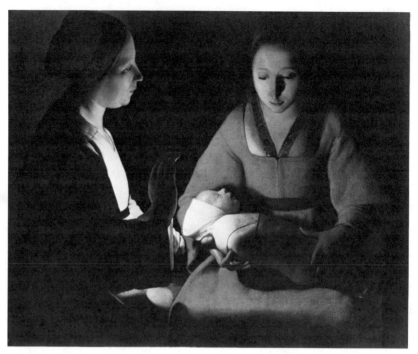

FIGURE 31 A young mother in the seventeenth century holds her sleeping newborn, carefully wrapped in swaddling clothes. Only the head is exposed.

FIGURE 34   In this idyllic scene a fashionably dressed eighteenth-century couple retrieves their baby from a wholesome wet nurse and her husband in the country.

FIGURE 32 *(facing, left)*   The Virgin suckles her child. This fifteenth-century version of one of the most widespread images in Western art is from Spain.

FIGURE 33 *(facing, right)*   The "law of nature," as interpreted by Rousseau, is being followed by this relaxed aristocratic couple enjoying the untrammeled play of their scantily clad children. The little girl seated at the table is somewhat more decorous.

FIGURE 35 Twelve ages of man (and woman), depicted in late-seventeenth-century clothing and with a dour sensibility common in the period. The ascending side and the declining side are balanced in their imagery: in both the first and last ages the pair is lying down, in the second and penultimate ages the pair uses props to help them walk, and so forth. "Adolescence" goes from 10 to 19 years, and the age of "Discretion" is not reached until 40, a decade after "Nubility."

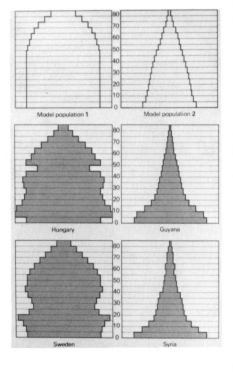

FIGURE 38   Young agricultural servants in England in the late eighteenth century. This kind of work was the commonest form of "education."

FIGURE 36 (facing, left)   A Dutch boy in the seventeenth century, appropriately dressed as a young child in a skirt, is shown about to try his hand at golf.

FIGURE 37 (facing, right)   A depiction of one demographic difference between industrialized and nonindustrialized societies in the 1960s. The graphs show the relative numbers of persons of various ages (the numbers indicate ages). Before 1800 most of Europe was like model population 2 and, accordingly, like modern undeveloped areas. The bulk of the population was under 20.

FIGURE 39   The wrong way to bring up children, according to the verses the artist put at the bottom of this sixteenth-century German woodcut. They begin with the familiar words, "He who spares the rod . . ." Compare this with the Rousseau idyll in Figure 33.

FIGURE 40   The huge kinship of a distinguished family: a fifteenth-century view of the legendary relatives of Jesus. They include the sisters and brothers-in-law of his mother Mary, as well as her nephews, who are his first cousins. The complicated family relationships are typical of the period. Jesus, his mother Mary, and his grandmother Anne are the focus here (along with the eucharistic bread in a basket and wine in a chalice). Mary's two half-sisters (by two different fathers) are behind Mary's maternal cousin Elizabeth. Although female relatives fill the foreground, all the young cousins of Jesus are male, as are the relatives standing nearest the altar.

FIGURE 41   Kinship obligations in the church hierarchy: a new cardinal comes home to share his honor with his family. The figures in this mid-fifteenth-century scene, apart from retainers and servants in the background, are the cardinal, Francesco Gonzaga, in the center; his father, the ruler of Mantua, a skilled family strategist who, in addition to overseeing Francesco's ecclesiastical career, negotiated many marriage alliances with other Italian ruling houses; and Francesco's three young nephews. The oldest of the nephews became the husband of Isabella, of the powerful Este family, and eventually succeeded to the rule of Mantua.

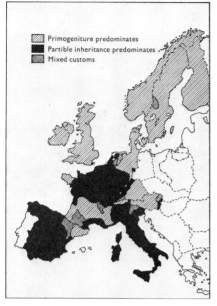

FIGURE 42 *(left)*   A simplified map of the pattern of inheritance customs in western Europe. Simplified though it is, it shows how complicated the situation was. Note the dramatic contrast between Britain, dominated by primogeniture, and Germany and northern France.

FIGURE 43 *(right)*   The linking of generations in the ancestry of Jesus. The forefather from which this family tree derives is Jesse, who was the father of King David. This is a royal line and, like most such genealogies, a strictly male one, except for Jesus's mother, the Virgin Mary.

FIGURE 44   The political importance of both household and kinship is epitomized in the Great Hall of Montacute House in England. The interiors of the sixteenth-century mansion bespeak wealth and power, and the portraits proclaim the owners' pedigree.

FIGURE 45 *(left, below)*   The permanent imprint of a family on a public monument, one of the fountains of Rome. The coat of arms is that of the Albani family, to which Pope Clement XI, in whose reign the fountain was built, belonged.

FIGURE 46 *(right, below)*   Giuliano de' Medici on a bronze medal ordered by his brother Lorenzo the Magnificent to commemorate his assassination by the Pazzi, a family who were longtime political rivals of the Medici in Florence.

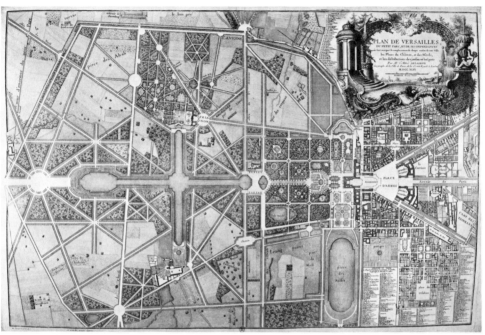

FIGURE 47 "The most magnificent house in the world" and its huge grounds: Versailles in 1746. The main building is on the Place d'Armes on the right, opposite the pair of stables.

FIGURE 48   A house that inspired the building of Versailles: Vaux-le-Vicomte and its gardens in the seventeenth century. Nicolas Fouquet's ambition, which led him to endow this showplace with royal splendor, ultimately led to his downfall.

FIGURE 49 *(facing, above)*   Ancestor worship in the sixteenth century: the ancestors of the Lumley family of Northumberland, carved in the style of medieval recumbent figures and placed in a parish church by order of a devoted descendant.

FIGURE 50 *(facing, below)*   The archetype of the good son: Aeneas carries his father Anchises to safety from the destruction of Troy. This engraving in a 1582 book is labeled "The Duty of Children to Parents."

FIGURE 51 A highly charged sentimental view of family roles by the eighteenth-century French painter Greuze. The mother, who is probably breast-feeding her youngest, is awash in a sea of affectionate children and is the object of admiration by her own mother (or a nurse) and her husband, just returned from the outdoor masculine activity of hunting. A maid stands in the shadows at the extreme left.

of rich and poor, highborn and lowborn, that created the difference in numbers.

The ordinary villager had a very limited perspective. There was considerable moving about from village to village and from village to city, but the means of communication were slow and restricted. Most people got about on foot, and few were truly literate. The kin who counted most were the ones who were visible, those who could be seen in one's household from time to time, who lived within walking distance in the same village or a nearby one. The experience of multigenerational households in the mountainous regions of southern France is instructive. For the period of time during which a household contained grandparents, parents, and children, there was a strong likelihood that all were aware of the children's second cousins, if there were any, since they would be the grandchildren of the sisters or brothers of someone living in the house. This was a large network of kin, but it was not stable. When the grandparents died, the more distant ties were loosened. In other places, where the average household consisted of no more than two generations and where most couples started new households, distant ties were loose to begin with. Then as now, second cousins had a real existence only if the relationship was reinforced by continued contact, as might happen if the cousins were neighbors.

In general, the kin who really mattered were those with a direct link to one's parents, either generationally or laterally: the parents' parents, the parents' siblings, and the parents' children (one's own siblings and half-siblings). In spite of any presuppositions we may have about extended families, there seems to have been a strong practical emphasis everywhere on this "nuclear" basis of kinship. The English poor laws, which were based on the premise that dependents were the responsibility of their relatives, limited the obligation to parents and grandparents. If parents were too poor to care for their children, the responsibility fell to the grandparents. The records of poor relief everywhere show, however, that other relatives frequently stepped in to help. Almost always these were relatives with direct sibling connections, either brothers and sisters of the needy or their aunts and uncles. For example, a certain Robert Greene in the 1630s "tooke in his sister with 3 or 4 Children as an Inmate in case of necessity who being displaced were enforced to lye in the church porch."[2] Aunts and uncles were highly visible kin everywhere, outweighing all other kin in importance. By an obvious extension, first cousins became part of the picture. But it is striking how abruptly relatives beyond first cousins fell into the shadows. The wills of people of modest means, when they mentioned kin outside the household at all, rarely went beyond nieces and nephews. In an interesting English will of the early nineteenth century (a little later than our period but a product of the same rural social patterns) a yeoman in his nineties mentioned thirty people, but every one of them was a very near relative or a direct descendant, the most distant kin being nephews and great-grandchildren.[3]

It can be argued that wills do not reveal anything about kinship except how people want to dispose of property. It would be more helpful, to be sure, to know who turned out for important social occasions, like weddings and funerals. As far as lower-class people are concerned, what little we know about such occasions confirms the impression that kinship was not very wide. Even higher up on the social scale, for example among prosperous merchants and lesser nobility in seventeenth-century Bordeaux, the usual limit of extension was out to second cousins, and it was that wide only when kin came together with the intention of affirming their collective identity as a family. More telling, perhaps, is the experience of some noble families in seventeenth-century England. At the lower levels of the nobility, especially among newly created baronets, awareness of kinship seems to have had so much in common with that of the lower classes that some families became extinct sooner than they had to. That is, they made no great effort to keep track of relatives beyond first cousins, even though more distant relatives may have existed and would have been able to inherit the family titles.

Huge extended families, a major component of our contemporary myth about families in the past, did exist, but they were exceptional. They were a feature of the most visible, most powerful, and wealthiest sector of society, the one that has left the most graphic evidence and takes up the most space in history books. Other people seem to have had far less motivation and fewer means to surround themselves with an army of kin. In this respect they seem to have been a lot like us.

Blood or Marriage

Kinship is a social convention. Like adulthood, it is partly biological, but the biology is filtered through value systems and social usage. The "blood" aspect of kinship is not a simple matter of common genetic heritage; it also involves legitimation and exclusion. The research of anthropologists in remote cultures has shown that there are many methods of reckoning blood kin and several different methods have been used in Western culture. The kind of kinship that is created by marriage is entirely a social convention and not biological at all.

Blood kinship and in-law kinship are based on two different principles. Blood kinship is something a person is born into. It is thought of as permanent, a bond that sometimes seems almost mystical. It is backward-looking and has an existence independent of any individual's life. In contrast, in-laws are acquired after a good deal of life has been lived. They are located in the present, forming a temporary association clustered around a particular marriage. The two kinds of kinship can become blurred for the children of that marriage, who are the blood kin of all the in-laws. In some places there is a tendency for people to consider themselves primarily the blood kin of one side (usually but not necessarily the father's) and only temporarily allied with the other side. On the other hand, some people feel that they belong only to the temporary cluster around their parents; being part of a permanent blood-linked group is only incidental. The term "kindred" is sometimes used for the particular configuration of kin that ceases with an individual's death. Marriage partners play different roles in these two images of kinship. One requires that a spouse (usually but not necessarily the wife) be absorbed by the family into which he or she marries and function as an almost invisible instrument for passing along the blood. The other gives equal prominence to husband and wife and to the kin each comes supplied with.

Both images are in evidence today, and both were in evidence throughout the four centuries and more that we are looking at. Most of us today lean toward the second image, in which blood kinship is confined to the cluster around our parents. In the past the first image (that of the permanent blood group) was much more prominent. Although the two images were not engaged in any kind of open war, there was more tension between them than there is today. Theory often proclaimed the principles of one image, while practice followed those of the other.

In the mid-eighteenth century an article in the French *Encyclopédie* defined "family" as kinship—a rather recent meaning. Earlier, as we have seen, it had chiefly meant household. The definition went on to embrace both images of kinship: "All those descended from the same stock and who therefore have the same blood. . . . Family commonly refers to a group of several persons united by the ties of blood or affinity."[4] This is an ambiguous statement and it probably reflects the ambivalence of the man who wrote it. The ambiguities are multiple. "The same blood" contrasts with "blood or affinity"—blood kin versus kin by marriage. At the same time "the same stock" and "ties of blood" contrast the single permanent line of the first with the changing clusters of the second.

The *Encyclopédie* writer was living in a world in which kinship sometimes meant one thing and sometimes another. He may have felt that blood was more important than the "common" linking of blood and affinity, but he had to include both. To do otherwise would have been to falsify the experience of his readers. Neither they nor their ancestors for hundreds of years back lived in a simple society with a single rigid tradition. By the fourteenth century several different social and legal systems had merged in western Europe, and the process of accommodation among them was still going on in the eighteenth century. We can see it happening in inheritance practices and in the way the various kinds of kinship ties were cultivated in different circumstances and for different ends.

The notion of blood kinship was inseparable from the concept of European nobility. "Blood" and its near synonyms *race* (France), *raza* (Spain), and *nazione* (Italy) were used as emblems of pride by those who claimed ties to the wealthy and powerful. It was here that patrilineal descent ruled supreme. The blood flowed through the males and wives did not count in the reckoning. Patrilineal kinship carried some weight lower down the social scale as well, since it received legal recognition and was embedded in certain social practices. Its clearest manifestation was in surnames. Fixed surnames as we know them hardly existed before 1350, and it was only gradually that men switched from identifying themselves by their connections to their fathers through the use of simple patronymics (e.g., "John, son of Henry," "Martin, Peter's son," "William fitz [fils de] Gerald"), which some were still doing in the fifteenth century, to taking names that connected them not merely with their own fathers but with all their fathers' male relatives. European Jews came very late to surnames, and some were still using patronymics in the eighteenth century ("Moses ben Jehudah"). Surnames made it possible for kinship through male blood to be identified by a simple label and the theoretical invisibility of a wife was shown by her assuming the same label as her husband although her own "blood" gave her no right to it.

In some places (usually ones that were remote from centers of government, like Corsica and the Scottish Highlands), patrilineal descent groups were formally organized as clans and continued to be so organized beyond 1800. There were also traces of clanlike structures in some cities. In one Castilian city, Valladolid, for example, all municipal offices in the sixteenth century were in the hands of two lineages, each consisting of five "families." Only men could be members and they had to have blood kinship with one of the families through their fathers. The structure was so intricate that kinship was only the starting point, but without it nobody could be elected to membership or allowed to take an oath of loyalty.[5] Powerful lineages, consciously and quasi-formally constituted, bearing such famous surnames as Contarini, Medici, and Strozzi, were prominent in the republican city-states of Italy.

The almost obsessive concern with male blood lines masked the fact that there was also a tendency to take blood kinship on the female side very seriously. This was especially true in the places that had never been integrated into the ancient Roman Empire—which means most of Europe. A wife often kept a link with her own blood relatives although she gave up their name. Even today, given and middle names can proclaim the link between a mother's kin and her children, counterbalancing the paternal surname. The pull of kinship ties on an individual could be at least as strong from the maternal side as the paternal side, in spite of the fact that the individual was going to pass along to his or her children membership in the paternal line only. For the time being at least, he or she had membership in two lineages. As late as the seventeenth century, there were different words in German for aunt and uncle depending on whether one was referring to the mother's or the father's siblings. The terminology brings to light a distinction the English language no longer requires us to make. Not only does it show awareness of a two-sided kinship, but when one pair of terms was dropped, it was the one for paternal kin (Vetter and Base). Oheim and Muhme were transferred to all aunts and uncles. The mother's kin must have been extremely important for those terms to have prevailed.

The mother's kin and the father's kin have a relationship to each other, that of affinity. The brothers and sisters of a married couple make their first appearance as kin not in the roles of aunts and uncles but as brothers-in-law and sisters-in-law. Although they have roles in the future as the consanguineal kin of a new generation, there is hardly a culture that does not recognize that they are important from the beginning. Even today the attractiveness of a woman may be enhanced by the prospect of a close association with her brother or her father. In the past, people on all social levels had no compunctions about admitting such a motivation. In the sixteenth century, Rabelais's idea of a happy marriage was one arranged by a father in accordance with his own tastes and interests. Good fathers, he said, did not want to lose daughters "on whose breeding and education they had spared no cost" to worthless suitors they knew nothing about, but hoped, rather, "in an opportune and convenient time to establish them by marriage with the sons of neighbors and ancient friends."[6] In the late seventeenth century, a high French noble, the duke of Saint-Simon, described how disappointed he and a good friend had been when they were unable to work out a marriage between him and the friend's daughter. "My only consolation," said the friend, "is the hope that one day your children and mine will be able to marry each other."[7] A peasant with no sons might very well feel that his daughter's husband was at least as important to him as to her. A son-in-law meant hope for the household's continued existence on its land, and he often acquired the legal standing of a real son.

The creation of in-laws forged new connections and also reenforced existing ones. Interconnection through marriage was an almost obligatory feature of any social group with common interests. The master glassblowers among the immigrant glassworkers in France in the eighteenth century were quick to marry the daughters of local French merchants. The people with local prestige felt they had a claim to the new wealth in their community, and the new industrialists, for their part, felt they were entitled to share the prestige. (The ordinary glassworkers married immigrants like themselves or people back home.) In England the ability of the Protestant clergy to marry, acquired at the Reformation, initiated a pattern of marriages among the families of higher-ranking churchmen, who also married into the landed gentry, eventually forming what was in effect a single class. In France there was a slow amalgamation through marriage of the new nobles "of the robe" and the older, more exalted nobles "of the sword."

Marriage links also reaffirmed ties of blood kinship. This happened in many parts of the Western world, in disregard of the church's traditional teaching that everyone should reach out as far as possible for a marriage partner. In French mountain villages, it was not unheard of for a sister and brother to be sister-in-law and brother-in-law as well, or even for the weddings of a pair of brothers to a pair of sisters to take place on the same day. Less startling and even more common in such villages was the tightening of affinal kinship by marriages between distant in-laws and marriages between cousins in the next generation. The merchant class of Boston in the eighteenth century used a similar strategy to consolidate the power of the famous "Brahmin" families. It was almost taken for granted among Cabots, Lowells, and Higginsons that two brothers-in-law, who were likely to be business associates, would arrange a marriage between their children, and even paired brother-sister marriages of the French village type were no great rarity. A particularly striking example of this kind of behavior occurred in Paris in the sixteenth century when two daughters of a well-to-do man took husbands who were not only brothers but also brothers-in-law of the women's father through his second marriage.[8]

If marriage links helped to proclaim the solidarity of a group, it is not hard to see that marriage might be a way for an outsider to enter the group. Two famous examples from the world of politics illustrate how mobility was connected with the choice of in-laws. In France in the seventeenth century, one middle-class man began a successful career as a financier with the help of his father-in-law's wealth and connections. That man's son was Jean-Baptiste Colbert, who became the chief minister of Louis XIV and acquired a noble title. His political relationships were intertwined with marriage connections and his daughters eventually reached the pinnacle of society by marrying dukes.[9] In England in the eighteenth century, William Pitt got started on a political career through the relatives of his brother's wife. That was how he acquired his political patron, Richard Temple, a titled lord and member of an influential family with connections by marriage to another influential family, the Grenvilles. Pitt worked closely with this cluster of kinsmen, finally becoming a power on his own. His eventual marriage to a Grenville was an affirmation of his social and political position.[10]

The process of acquiring in-laws demanded attention, whether one was the chief minister of a kingdom, like Colbert or Pitt, or the owner of a parcel of land in a remote village. It often demanded the attention of all who were reckoned as kin, not only the parents or guardians of a couple-to-be. Unmarried relatives were normally thought of as instruments for forming alliances that could benefit their kinfolk. One reason so many secular laws and legal contracts required parental consent is that families believed they had a right to exclude undesirable in-laws. The most desirable son-in-law or daughter-in-law was one who brought wealth, status, or both, hardly ever in his or her own person but through his or her kin. An undesirable in-law was one with shameful connections or one who seemed likely to squander a family's resources. Peasant families also made such "dynastic" marriages in rising to become dominant in village affairs. Their marriages often fitted in with strategies for consolidating and expanding property: whether to marry late or never to marry or to marry the possessor of neighboring fields. Poorer people and landless workers, who had less to bargain over, nevertheless had occasion to consider the in-laws who would come along with a future spouse. A brother-in-law in the same craft could be the reason for the choice of a bride. Needless to say, a father-in-law with a shop or some land could be important in a young man's life.

The terms for affinal relationships in use today emphasize their parallelism with consanguineal relationships. In English, "in-law" is tacked on to a term for a close blood relative, and other modern languages have words for affines constructed along similar lines. The "law" in question is the old canon law of the Roman church, and each term reveals at a glance a close relationship that harbors the danger of incest. The church was eager to show that a relationship through marriage, even if distinguishable from a blood relationship, was just as real and deep. This apparently struck a responsive chord in Europeans, who by the fourteenth century had pretty much abandoned an older vocabulary of special terms for in-laws in favor of this simple scheme. It did not mean that affinal kin became either less important or more important but rather that people were perfectly willing to assimilate into the vocabulary of consanguinity a group of people who were already so important that they had previously been honored with a vocabulary of their own. One group of Europeans who still use that vocabulary are Yiddish-speaking Jews, who have retained the terms the Germans used in the Middle Ages and, in addition, have a special term for the relationship the parents of the bride and groom have to each other. Ancient Romans had also used special terms: *socer* and *socrus* for father-in-law and mother-in-law, *gener* and *nurus* for son-in-law and daughter-in-law. The newer terms suggested not only a special relationship but also an intimate one. A *belle-mère* obviously has more in common with a *mère* than a *socrus* has with a *mater*.

No wonder the *Encyclopédie* was so ambiguous about what constituted a "family." Powerful institutions and traditional practices supported the notion that blood in a single line was possible to identify and created an ineradicable bond, but the energy expended at all social levels on acquiring connections through marriage proclaimed the importance of family bonds of another kind.

Relatives or Others

The most important people outside the household today are not necessarily related either by blood or by marriage. Nonrelatives, whether friends, colleagues, or neighbors, may be the ones we prefer to spend time with or call upon for help. Some of us think it is faintly old-fashioned to confine oneself to the company of kinfolk. In an individualistic age, there seems to be total freedom to establish relationships on our own, apart from family considerations and family approval. How individualistic most of us really are in this respect is debatable, but it is nevertheless part of the common mythology of the family that in the past kin provided most of the human contact anyone wanted. The truth seems to be not so clear-cut. Alongside a strong reliance on kin went a reliance on other kinds of networks, whose functions overlapped those of kinship networks, as they do today. Some evidence even suggests that one effect of nineteenth-century industrialization was to expand rather than reduce the role of kinship in the lives of the poor. For the high-born and wealthy, its role has probably diminished, mainly because now different meanings attach to the status derived from birth.

My unknown cousin in Europe has little reality for me compared to a friend I have known for twenty years. I chose that friend, we have interests in common, and we renew the relationship by constant association. Yet an ambivalence surrounds friendship. The claim on one's loyalties by relatives is not easily ignored and friendship often risks being ranked lower than kinship, even if it gives greater personal satisfaction. There is every reason to believe that this ambivalence is not a totally modern phenomenon, although the modern emphasis on individualism may have made it more common. Another kind of ambivalence shows up in the common tendency to clothe nonkin associations in kin terminology. A "brotherhood" or "sisterhood" or "fraternal organization" awakens more emotional commitment than a mere club. What may seem like a sentimental confusion of categories today when Elks or labor unions are concerned can be a source of serious conflict if fictitious families demand greater devotion than its members give to their real families. There were many voluntary, dedicated nonkin organizations in the past, which some contemporaries felt were a threat to the principles of kinship and family. The appeal of religious orders to some individuals was precisely that the orders were a means of escaping from family bonds.

People in the past certainly had opportunities to form individual friendships but, by their very nature, such friendships were private and, except for extremely rare exchanges of correspondence that have been preserved, hidden from the eyes of historians. Nonkin ties in the past are detectable mainly in the behavior of groups—which may give the impression that there was less individual choice than there actually was.

Every baptized Christian had godparents, a set of fictitious relatives to whom there was, at least in theory, a lifelong attachment. In the eyes of the church they were truly kin. There were prohibitions against marrying them modeled on the prohibitions against marrying in-laws. For the child's parents, the choice of godparents offered a variety of possibilities not unlike those involved in the choice of in-laws. In some places local notables were routinely asked to be godparents of quite humble people. The paternalistic aspect of lordship was reinforced by these individual relationships, which were, however, more symbolic than intimate. After appearing at the baptismal font, many godparents faded from the scene, playing almost no part in the lives of their godchildren. To be the godfather of many children conveyed a prestige not unlike that of having a large following of clients and often amounted to the same thing. It was much more common for godparents to be on the parents' own social level. Whatever the basis of the parents' choice, there were times when it was clearly not perfunctory and, well into the period we are looking at, some parents were eager to provide their infants with a superabundance of godparents. In some places girls had two godmothers each, in addition to a godfather, and boys had two godfathers. The Council of Trent in the sixteenth century declared that each child should have only one pair of godparents, a reasonable spiritual parallel to the parents provided by nature.

Godparents were often chosen from among the parents' friends and colleagues. Being asked to be a godparent, then as now, was a tribute to past associations and a commitment to continuity. Multiple godparents and godparents from different social categories widened the circle of personal ties. Many people seemed to feel they needed to add to their "real" kinship, whether quantitatively or qualitatively, and they seized the opportunity by means of godparentage. Not surprisingly, connections did not stop with the godparents themselves. The godparents' kin were implicated as well. It was fairly common for marriages to occur between the kin of godparents and godchild—for instance, between a godchild's brother and the godfather's niece. As in most aspects of kinship, ordinary people drew no hard lines between kinds of kinship and seemed to want to blur the lines whenever possible.

Another kind of spiritual kinship was found in religious organizations. Convents and monasteries used family terminology: "father," and "mother," "sister," and "brother." Lay people also had spiritual "fathers" and "brothers." In Catholic countries every priest, especially one hearing confession, was a spiritual father, although the use of this title when addressing a priest came later. There was a widespread tendency for men engaged in common pursuits to join together as spiritual brothers. They called their groups confraternities and they formed them for religious purposes—to support churches, build chapels, conduct services, and take part in processions. Found mainly in towns, confraternities were often offshoots of craft and merchant guilds; the link of spiritual brotherhood was forged by men who already had associations with each other. Village guilds, which flourished for a time in the English countryside, translated general community ties into kinship terms, with members calling each other brothers and sisters. Their functions were almost identical to those of the urban confraternities.

Confraternities soon disappeared from Protestant countries and lost much of their importance in Catholic ones as well, but some of the impulse behind them persisted in the notion of occupational and collegial brotherhood. Unlike youth groups, they could be lifelong associations. The Freemasons, who emerged in the seventeenth and eighteenth centuries, incorporated many of the elements that had been present in the confraternities and directed them to the service of somewhat different religious ideas. There were Freemasons in both Europe and the New World, and much has been written about their influence on intellectual and political life. For our present purpose, they serve as an excellent illustration of the considerable power of nonfamilial ties, ties that were emotional and close.

One important network of nonrelatives generally managed to do without kinship terminology: neighbors. In villages with formal guild organizations, neighbors were of course aware of the analogy to kinship, but even without the terminology the most striking thing about neighbors is that they often appear in historical evidence precisely where we would expect to find relatives. Groups of neighbors frequently acted as surety in legal proceedings. They were witnesses to wills and were named as executors. Occasional accounts of funerals indicate the presence of neighbors in large numbers. To be sure, very close relatives were usually visible, too, but more distant relatives (and nonhousehold kin in general) were not. Neighbors stepped in to back up the household kin.

The shared activities of everyday life in city neighborhoods and in villages with common land meant that ties with neighbors were not just for special occasions. Welcome or not, the interconnectedness of members of the community was felt in many ways. One was the surveillance of morals. The right of neighbors to demand conformity to community standards was not an abstract idea, carried out by impersonal forces. Individual neighbors criticized misconduct, reprimanded wrongdoers, and came to the rescue of victims of family violence or other misfortune. They reported misconduct to the authorities or, when called upon to testify in marriage, divorce, and separation cases, revealed knowledge of the most intimate details of life in other people's households. Not only was such behavior generally accepted, but, as we have seen, groups of neighbors also sometimes took it upon themselves to express their disapproval in charivaris. Neighbors did not have to be related in order to act like their brothers' keepers.

Neighbors were important on all levels of society. They may have been most important for those on the middling and lower levels, who, as we have seen, tended not to have large and extensive networks of kin. Having said that, and with due regard to the extremely significant relationships that people had with nonkin, we cannot escape the impression that a lot of people preferred to rely on kinfolk when they could. In mountainous areas where village communities hardly existed, neighbors who were not also kin counted for very little. A sense of isolation seems to have strengthened the role of kinship, as it may still do in today's very large cities. Immigrants took a while to become integrated in a neighborhood. They tended to keep looking back to their place of origin and made efforts to recruit relatives both as a way of being helpful to them and as a way of easing their own isolation. This was what immigrants to America did as late as last week, and it was already being done in the fourteenth and fifteenth centuries by countryfolk who moved to towns. In the early days of industrialization in eighteenth-century England, the decision to leave the country and work in a textile mill may ultimately have been based on impersonal economic forces, but in each individual's drama there was usually a brother or a cousin already in the mill who made the suggestion and prepared the way.

Godparents were frequently not only kin but also close kin. The opportunity for expanding the circle of connections was sometimes rejected in favor of reinforcing already existing ties, just as happened with certain kinds of close marriage. In many places in France in the seventeenth century, the almost automatic choice was a relative from each side of the child's family and a grandparent whenever possible. The godparents' duty of protecting their godchildren and giving them spiritual guidance was far more likely to be carried out by relatives. In some places godparents gave their own names to the infant, so there was the additional advantage of preserving family names. But the utility of godparentage is perhaps best demonstrated by cases in which an in-law who might have been lost through the death of a spouse was retained in the spouse's family. For example, in sixteenth-century Paris, the uncle of a young woman who died asked her husband's second wife to be godmother to his child.[11] We are not sure why he did it, but it is likely that he wanted to cement his bond with a man who had been a valued in-law.

The tug of kinship also operated in work relationships. There were southern French villages in which crafts and occupations were practically the monopolies of certain families. As we have seen, Italian boys were frequently trained by their fathers and uncles and taken into family businesses. One thing that has changed very little over the centuries is the way in which entrepreneurs choose their partners. Perhaps it is starting to change now and more people are choosing partners only for their abilities and objective qualities. On the other hand, nobody is surprised when a man goes into business with his brother or his brother-in-law. In the past such a move was taken for granted, and it made no difference whether the business was a "traditional" or a "modern" one.

The nature of historical evidence is such that it tends to rob ordinary people of their individuality. They usually show up in lists and, what is more, lists arranged in groups, especially family groups. No wonder we get the impression that people associated mainly with relatives or with people organized into familylike structures. I am far from making a case for the overwhelming importance of kin in the past as opposed to the present. On the contrary, once we cut through our contemporary rhetoric about individualism and unlimited choice of lifestyle, the similarities are striking. For some of us today blood runs very thick indeed, and we tend to subordinate all else to considerations of family. Conversely, for some people in the past, connections with relatives outside the household were of minor importance and were subordinated to personal and work relationships with nonkin.

Welcome Support or Burdensome Obligations

Behind the behavior we have been looking at lay negative and positive feelings about kinship and a structure of benefits and obligations. The functions of kinship are both practical and emotional. Everyone recognizes the practical value of having a well-placed relative who can further a career, come to the rescue, or get things wholesale. It still helps to have "connections." Even relatives without pull or prestige can be asked for temporary shelter or small loans. If they live far away, they can act as guides and hosts when we come to visit. The emotional side of kinship, apart from individual ties of affection, is twofold: the feeling of belonging to a group where membership is unquestioned and the feeling of vicarious pride (or shame) in members' accomplishments and status. In a way, nothing has changed since long before 1350, but most of these functions have assumed different forms over the years.

The subject is shot through with ambivalence. Today there is a tendency to minimize the importance of kin, as though every interaction between relatives were a matter of personal choice. Even people whose lives are thoroughly wrapped up in their extended families often claim that it is only because their relatives are so nice. Owing a great deal to relatives makes people feel uncomfortable: the comfortable feeling of belonging is offset by a nagging guilt at not having earned something on one's own merits. The seeds of this ambivalence are in all of us today, since we cannot escape the contradictions in the rival attractions of security and freedom.

When seen as a tissue of obligations and expectations, kinship is naturally divided into two categories of persons: beneficiaries and providers, that is to say, takers and givers. In the perverse way of all human activity, givers often feel they are getting a great deal when they give and takers feel they are being asked to give something in the very act of taking. Without minimizing this subtle interaction, there is some justification in looking separately at those who, in the main, stand to benefit from the operations of kinship and those on whom demands are made. Today ambivalence is felt most strongly by takers, those who benefit from kinship and are not sure they should. In the past ambivalence seems to have been felt more strongly by the givers, those who were expected to shelter, advance, or make sacrifices for others. This is another way of saying that the obligations of kinship used to be greater and in some cases were more formalized. The formal obligations, particularly the legal ones, were the first to disappear. By the time the United States was established, they were hanging by a thread almost everywhere in the Western world, poised to be cut down sooner or later in the course of the following century. Informal obligations remained strong for a long time, however, and are still strong in a few places today.

No blood relatives outside the conjugal or household nucleus matched those inside in visibility and in their role as beneficiaries as much as nephews did. "Doesn't he do anything for you?" the narrator asks the title character of *Rameau's Nephew*, and then goes on to say that Rameau is "a bad father, bad husband, and bad uncle."[12] Having an uncle to turn to modulated the sometimes harsh authoritarian presence of the father and in any case provided an alternative adult male role model. Maternal uncles were at least as important as paternal uncles; the mother's brother was the usual link to whatever advantages could come from her family line. Childless aunts and uncles were a potential resource for younger sons disadvantaged by primogeniture. In powerful circles a young orphan suffered no particular career disadvantage from losing his father if he was the nephew of a well-placed man. I speak primarily of nephews because power and wealth were usually in male hands and it is easier to find out about men, but nieces could benefit in similar ways. In the upper strata, a generous aunt or uncle could make the difference between a merely adequate dowry and a brilliant one (and hence the difference between spinsterhood or life in a convent and an enviable social position). For girls on every social level, aunts and uncles were mentors, employers, and even surrogate parents. Ten-year-old Marie de Rabutin, later to become Madame de Sévigné, found a comfortable home and the opportunity for a fine literary education with her maternal uncle.

This glowing picture of family responsibility and affection needs to be moderated by the recognition that these relationships could create tensions, too. A nephew's expectations of help from an uncle were sometimes built on animosities and rivalries in the older generation and could lead to jealousy and conflict among his own siblings. Whether harmonious or troubling, a significant part of the drama of family life was played out on the not entirely obvious plane of extraconjugal, nonhousehold kinship.

Marie de Rabutin's uncle was a well-to-do Catholic clergyman, a man ideally placed to be of service to a niece or a nephew. The unmarried clergy in Catholic countries are the most outstanding examples of devotion to kin in this period. Most priests seem to have stayed in touch with their sisters and brothers and taken an interest in their children. To be the nephew of a priest was to have, at the least, a useful connection. The higher the priest's position, the more useful the connection.

At the very highest levels, the prospects for nephews were limitless. The so-called Renaissance popes, presiding over a glittering court life in a restored Rome from the middle of the fifteenth century into the seventeenth century, assiduously followed this pattern of family devotion. They distributed appointments and privileges to relatives and made it almost a rule to name nephews as cardinals. A cardinal then was as much a temporal as an ecclesiastical prince and controlled huge amounts of wealth and power. To benefit his kinfolk, a pope often had to work fast while he had the chance, dispensing red hats and noble titles to boys who were barely out of childhood. In a political crisis like the one in France at the end of the sixteenth century, when the country was in danger of falling under Protestant rule, Pope Sixtus V was prepared to maneuver a nephew onto the French throne. If he did not succeed, he nevertheless managed to do extraordinarily well by the family of his sister, whose grandchildren included a cardinal, a millionaire, and wives of papal princes, one an Orsini and another a Colonna (the acme of the old Roman nobility).[13]

In the highly charged atmosphere of Protestant-Catholic conflict in the seventeenth century, the practice got a bad name, nepotism, from *nepos*, Latin for nephew. The word has continued to have evil connotations. It was used by opponents of the papacy to suggest highly improper behavior. In the eyes of anti-Catholics, the impropriety was that the popes were treating the church as though it were family property. Neither Protestant nor Catholic laymen could possibly claim that they themselves avoided nepotism. Most of them were thoroughly aware of its importance in secular affairs. A nephew was not only a legitimate claimant to an inheritance if there was no direct issue (Francis I, for example, was the nephew of his predecessor on the French throne, and his own grandnephew, Henry IV, became king after the last of Francis's grandsons died without issue), but nephews also were almost universally regarded as proper recipients of many kinds of favors a man could bestow in his lifetime, including jobs, property, and political backing.

Relatives less special than nephews also assumed that they were entitled to ask better-off kin for help. The needy and the improvident in general were thus another category of beneficiaries. This was especially true outside the mainstream of society. Although Jewish communities had their own charitable institutions, a Jew was expected to turn to relatives first. Black slaves in America, who were even more outside the mainstream, sought refuge in kinship whenever they were in trouble. A runaway usually followed a route that led from kin to kin or to benefactors suggested by kin.

In general, however, one of the differences between the less fortunate and the more fortunate was that the latter had rich and powerful relatives. They could be failures in their own endeavors, but if they belonged to a successful family, even if to a somewhat distant branch of it, they had a safety net. Kinfolk did not invariably deliver on this expectation, however, and it was not a perfect welfare system. Lower down on the social scale, where the awareness of extended kin was weakest, help was more likely to be given to individuals who were known, whether relatives or not. The safety net existed mainly for those on the upper rungs of society and those who claimed kinship with them.

Merely being a member of a kinship group could be its own reward. If bearing a proud name still means something, it used to mean much more. For one thing, it usually signified political power, which in so many places was based on landed wealth regarded as the possession of families rather than of individuals. Being on the losing side in a civil war was less damaging if one had kin on the winning side. An individual or two might be destroyed, but the family as an aggregate survived. It is even possible that people anticipated the outcome by making sure that there would be family members in both camps. In a time of political and religious conflict it was said of one wealthy Englishman that "nothing in Newcastle can prevail against him, being both in affinity and consanguinity with both factions there."[14] Writing of a similar time in France, a nobleman remarked that "it was a perfect moment to advance one's relatives, and it was wise for those who could not come out on top to help others to do so. . . . If the reputation could not be one's own, at least it belonged to the family as a whole."[15]

Honor went with power. Not only was family honor something people thought about a great deal, but the legal system was their ally in upholding it. Hence the various laws stressing family control over individual inheritances and individual marriages, which helped to consolidate wealth and power and kept out the "unworthy" and "dishonorable." In the sixteenth and seventeenth centuries the French monarchy issued a series of decrees on marriage the purpose of which was to avoid "shameful and disgraceful" acts that "tarnished the honor" of families. In the eighteenth century the monarchy collaborated with families through the device of the *lettre de cachet*, suppressing kin who might bring shame to their families through crime or immorality or mental incapacity by putting them into prison without trial. The handful of prisoners in the Bastille on July 14, 1789, were just such representatives of good families being kept from bringing shame to their kin.

The greater the reputation of a family, the more was expected of its members. It might not be a pleasurable experience to be approached as the source of bounty, but it was an obligation nonetheless. The busiest providers of the benefits of kinship were the rich and powerful heads of great families, who were assumed to have an unending obligation to everyone else in the family. The duke of Buckingham in 1626, defending the favors that James I had conferred on his relatives, said he thought "he were to be condemned in the opinion of all generous minds, if, being in such favor with his master, he had minded only his own advancement and had neglected those who were nearest unto him."[16]

The heads of great families were expected to keep a sort of permanent open house for kinsmen and also be the guardians of the family's power and honor. This called for a lot of effort. A Florentine patrician, Giovanni Rucellai, expressed it almost feverishly: "Duty requires helping [our kinsmen], not even so much with money, as with sweat and with blood, and by any means one can, even to giving your life for the honor of the house and its members."[17] This was the burden assumed by any eminent lawyer or royal bureaucrat who had at his disposal preferments and connections and marriage prospects. We know from the correspondence of the mighty that a great deal of thought and effort went into the placement and advancement of younger kin and the arrangement of advantageous marriages. Hence the recurrent rise of new dynasties, like the Du Plessis and La Portes (Cardinal Richelieu's relatives), the Colberts, the Pitts, and less well-known names in finance, commerce, the law, and (especially in England) the Protestant clergy. Napoleon Bonaparte at the very end of the period followed the same kinship imperatives on the grandest of scales, as the genealogical chart on page 198 shows. When he got to the top he parceled out kingdoms and duchies to brothers and brothers-in-law (first carefully arranging for his sisters to marry his colleagues and sup-

The Bonaparte Family

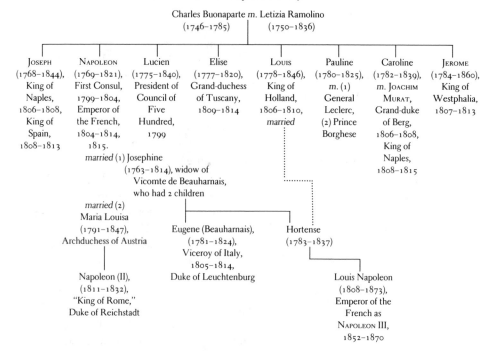

Charles Buonaparte *m.* Letizia Ramolino
(1746–1785)   (1750–1836)

JOSEPH (1768–1844), King of Naples, 1806–1808, King of Spain, 1808–1813

NAPOLEON (1769–1821), First Consul, 1799–1804, Emperor of the French, 1804–1814, 1815.
married (1) Josephine (1763–1814), widow of Vicomte de Beauharnais, who had 2 children
married (2) Maria Louisa (1791–1847), Archduchess of Austria
Napoleon (II), (1811–1832), "King of Rome," Duke of Reichstadt

Lucien (1775–1840), President of Council of Five Hundred, 1799

Elise (1777–1820), Grand-duchess of Tuscany, 1809–1814

Louis (1778–1846), King of Holland, 1806–1810, married

Pauline (1780–1825), *m.* (1) General Leclerc, (2) Prince Borghese

Caroline (1782–1839), *m.* JOACHIM MURAT, Grand-duke of Berg, 1806–1808, King of Naples, 1808–1815

JEROME (1784–1860), King of Westphalia, 1807–1813

Eugene (Beauharnais), (1781–1824), Viceroy of Italy, 1805–1814, Duke of Leuchtenburg

Hortense (1783–1837)

Louis Napoleon (1808–1873), Emperor of the French as NAPOLEON III, 1852–1870

porters). It was his nephew, Louis Napoleon, the offspring of a marriage between his brother and his stepdaughter, who became the second French emperor long after Napoleon I died.

Naturally enough, the burden was sometimes resented. An English nobleman, the earl of Banbury, wrote at the end of the period, "Our numerous connections find much work for Civility, Bowing-Bowing, Sister by affinity, Law and Connection, Brother-by-Age, Hospitality and Marriage. Lord Help us as where will it all end our mighty etceteras of Blood and Affinity."[18] Providers on all levels of society could easily slip into a kind of paranoia about being taken advantage of. One Florentine patrician, Bernardo Rucellai, wrote snappishly in 1484 of a relative, "As I told you on another occasion, I am a kinsman of Piero di Cardinale when it's necessary."[19] An eighteenth-century French peasant who grudgingly provided refuge to some needy kin had the feeling he had to draw the line somewhere because if he acknowledged all his cousins he would end up running an inn.[20] French folk sayings are full of resentment against relatives beyond the immediate family.

Aunts and uncles, the potential benefactors of all those expectant nephews, did not necessarily welcome their obligations. They could not easily escape, however. They were frequently named in wills as guardians and executors, and in areas where dowries were required by law, as in Italy, the obligation to provide one almost always passed to an uncle if a girl's father died. Southern French proverbs abounded in references to the insatiable demands of nephews. Sometimes good-natured, sometimes not, there was something inevitable, even eternal, about the grousing of those who felt the pressure of kinship obligations.

Basking in the glory of a prestigious family exacted a price: the subordination of individual interests to the good of the group. It was rarely a matter of choice and it bred its resentments. Being a kinsman could bring curses as well as benefits. A sufficiently serious misstep by a prominent family member could have consequences for his relatives, whether they liked it or not, putting them under a collective cloud. Less dire but more pervasive was the weight of family responsibility that hung over young people, especially "privileged" young people, when they were making decisions about their futures. Career choices and marriage choices alike were affected by what would be useful to one's kin. A young Frenchman in the sixteenth century confessed that he had not really wanted the prestigious bishopric his father had maneuvered to get for him. He would have much preferred a life of adventure as a knight of Malta, but he knew that his being a bishop could be used "for the fortune, the honor, and the good of our house all together."[21]

A recurrent cliché in the abundant literature on marriage was the soft-hearted father who let his daughter make an inappropriate marriage; equally common was the cliché of the hard-hearted father who made his daughter place family interests and family honor above true love. In general, parents and children seem to have accepted their obligations to kin and to have seen their value, but the behavior of widows, who had greater independence than single people of either sex, hints at a desire to shed these burdens. Widows often resisted pressures to go along with collective kin strategy, refusing to remarry or choosing men with whom their relatives had no desire to be allied.

The burden on all members of the kinship group assumed its most dramatic form in feuds and vendettas. To be involved in a family feud was a mark of privilege, even if it was only the privilege of belonging to the most important family in a remote mountain settlement. Feuds in the period are interesting, not because they involved great masses of people, but because of the influence they still exerted on the prominent and powerful. The tit-for-tat bloodshed of the Capulets and Montagues eventually disappeared, but not all at once, even in the centers of European civilization. The Pazzi conspiracy in Florence at the end of the fifteenth century, in which Lorenzo de' Medici's brother was killed, was the bloody culmination of a political struggle between families. In sixteenth-century France the Montmorency family and the Guise family vied constantly for the highest political stakes. A hundred years later in France the Colberts and Le Telliers were also rivals for the attractive political rewards the king could bestow, but by then the struggle, while just as serious, was less violent. By the end of the eighteenth century real blood feuds were relegated to areas beyond the reach of central governments. That the Bonapartes of Corsica were involved in such a feud is consonant with the dynastic ambitions on the world stage of their most famous member.

The ambivalence about kinship obligations eventually acquired a new vocabulary, that of individualism. By around 1700 a London merchant who was called on to bail out an improvident nephew deeply in debt might justify his reluctance on the grounds of high moral principle. Why should he not be generous to those he thought deserved to be helped rather than those who deserved to suffer the consequences of their misdeeds? Shouldn't individual initiative lead to individual success or individual failure? The merchant was likely to feel quite responsible for those immediately dependent on him, the "family" of his household, but the occult bonds of more distant kinship were losing their hold on him. A pious woman, Elizabeth Bury, wrote in her commonplace book that the constant obligation to help poor relations made her run the risk of "dishonouring GOD, by intangling myself in Debts, or in denying what Help might be in my Power to the Afflicted."[22] Reluctance was often accompanied by a feeling of discomfort. Samuel Marriott earned his family's wrath when he invested in the Corporation of the City of London instead of his brother's manufacturing business. He said he realized he was rejecting "higher Duties . . . , such as Trust & Familiarity and venturing our Lives and Fortunes."[23] Giovanni Rucellai's words about the duty of helping kin by sweat and blood are echoed in this guilty acknowledgment.

In contrast to some tribal societies, in which kinship is clearly defined and, however complicated it may seem to us, limited to a finite number of persons in a restricted geographic area, an open-ended, almost formless view of kinship has evolved in Western society. Tribal societies often have strict rules prescribing marriage between certain kinspeople and forbidding it between others. By the period we are looking at, and possibly for a long time before, most people in the world of European civilization followed no such neat rules. Only the prohibitions against "incest" were observed, and sometimes none too tidily. Although it is impossible to overlook kinship as a force in people's lives, it is also impossible to pin it down. Not only did it operate differently in different social groups, but, all too often for the comfort of historians, it also operated in subtle and informal ways. We know that then as now there was a sense in which "family" went beyond the household. Perhaps it is enough to be reminded of that, and to keep an eye out for kinship's multiform, contradictory manifestations in changing social, political, and economic circumstances.

The widest view of kinship has to include the dead as well as the living. The relationship of the living to the dead has changed considerably in the past two hundred years, and it is this change that has probably most affected the relations among living kin, especially at the top of the social scale.

10

The Linking of
Generations

Anyone who has ever been part of a family knows about the extension of families backward to the past, to ancestors, and forward to the future, to posterity. The time frame may be short or long. It is almost never so short as to be limited to a single generation, the link between parents and children; when children become parents themselves, they inevitably become part of a three-generation chain. A four-generation chain (great-grandparents to great-grandchildren) can exist without much record-keeping or institutional underpinning. Longer chains, like wider kinships, take more effort and more resources. They require the cultivation of memory and, with respect to posterity, long-term planning.

The links between generations are forged by inheritance. Apart from biological matter, which even plants inherit, all manner of things can be inherited by human beings. Laws and customs determine what they are. Some inheritance takes place at birth and remains throughout a person's life. Things inherited in this way are usually intangible. Other inheritance takes place later, often when an older person dies and passes a (usually) tangible resource on to someone younger.

Inheritance provides one of the contrasts between our time and the centuries before industrialization. What used to be a pervasive principle has become limited, and what was a public concern has become a private one. It is still common for people to inherit property, and there are laws that protect the rights of heirs, but modern Western society does not entirely approve of inherited wealth, and it is not considered necessary to inherit something in order to get on in the world. Inherited wealth is regarded with some suspicion and is heavily taxed. By contrast, in the past *everything* tended to be inherited.

There were three main categories of things that were inherited: material, social, and personal. Material legacies are real property and other wealth. In the past, although land was bought and sold, its normal route from one person to another was by inheritance. This alone explains why inheritance loomed so large in people's lives. Not only outright ownership of land but also the mere right to use it could be inherited, and it was often this right, rather than ownership, that peasants passed along to their heirs. Wealth of any kind, even if it was acquired by purchase or as a gift, tended to become hereditary sooner or later.

Social legacies included name, status, and occupation. What is today only sometimes inherited used to be always inherited, and what is now given to heirs by choice used to be the heirs' legal right. Only surnames now have the legal standing that all these social assets used to have. At the highest levels of society, titles as well as names were inherited. An indication of how things have changed is the fact that, in modern Britain, most new titles conferred by the state, such as knighthoods and life peerages, are not hereditary, while in the past much of their value lay in the very fact that they were hereditary. Status in the past was enshrined in the law and regarded as hereditary and fixed. A slave, a serf, a bourgeois, a gentleman, a lady, or a noble was usually what he or she was from birth. Although nobody was born a clergyman, many churchmen very nearly inherited their clerical status because they held positions that were virtually hereditary, like a whole gamut of other inherited occupations, jobs, and offices. Peasants who held village "offices" usually inherited them, from mayor and reeve to shepherd and woodward. Even the man whose job in one French town was transporting infants to wet nurses was likely to be the son of the previous holder of the job.[1] In eighteenth-century France, at the same time that nobles of ancient family were claiming their exclusive right to certain high offices, shepherds in the countryside were insisting, sometimes in violent demonstrations, that their jobs were strictly hereditary.[2]

Personal assets include physical traits and intangibles like character and health. In the past there was a tendency to minimize environment and upbringing and put all the emphasis on inheritance. To be granted the status of burgher in many a European town, a man had to offer proof of "good birth" and the absence of disease in both his parents, specifically the dreaded disease of leprosy. A nobleman in theory was not merely someone who was lucky enough to have parents who filled a certain social niche at the time of his birth but someone who actually inherited *nobility*, a quality of character that resided in the blood. Slaves were servile and peasants were boorish because it was in their blood to be so. Deeply entrenched notions about the connection of class and character and the inheritability of both propped up the hierarchical structure of society and persisted into later, supposedly more democratic, times as ingredients of racism.

When kin shared a family's honor or shame it was not just a vague feeling but, especially in the case of direct descendants, a hard fact with practical consequences. A person convicted of a capital crime was not only deprived of his life and personal honor but was also likely to be stripped of his property, which, along with titles or other signs of status, was barred from going to his heirs. Cutting off the ability to transmit by inheritance was understood as a terrible punishment. In a way, the practice confirmed universal inheritability by making the punishment itself hereditary. The ominous-sounding term for this was "corruption of blood." It is significant of a changing outlook that Article III of the U.S. Constitution in 1787 specifically ruled out corruption of blood, even for high treason. It lingered on in the Old World, however.

This chapter is mostly about tangible resources transmitted at death. There was a variety of ways to transmit them, all of them involving choices, some which were not easy, either for the person in the older generation or the one in the younger generation. Near unanimity about the rightness of inheritability did nothing to eliminate the ambivalence that surrounded certain aspects of it. Some of that ambivalence is still with us. Should a person be free to write any kind of will he or she desires or should inheritance follow well-worn paths? Should all the offspring inherit equally or should one heir be preferred? Should sons and daughters be treated differently? In addition to these ever-present questions, two other subjects in this chapter are rooted almost entirely in the conditions of the past. One is how continuing inheritability affected what an heir could do with what was inherited. This is so important that I put it first. At the end I take up the second subject: inheritance from mothers, which may be overlooked when we are dealing with a world that was so dominated by fathers.

By the time the American Declaration of Independence was written, inheritability had lost something of its luster. If it was self-evident that all men were created equal, then it was no longer accepted that unequal status and character were inborn. The principle of heredity was under attack in the eighteenth century and the attack gathered adherents as time went on. There had long been some theoretical opposition to the idea of a social order built on inherited distinctions and there were always people who noticed the discrepancies between what nobles were supposed to be and what they actually were, not to mention the achievements of a few people whose merit could not be explained by the usual notions of heredity. Christianity always had a strong commitment to egalitarianism, to the notion that all souls are created equal and remain equal before God. Nevertheless, inheritability as a universal principle lost ground very slowly. In the wake of the American Revolution, laws in the United States prohibited most kinds of inherited status, but not all— slavery is one example. In the wake of the French Revolution, attitudes to inherited status fluctuated for decades. Other European countries continued to cling to familiar ways. By 1800 the ways of inheritance as they affected most people had changed little from 1350.

Ownership or Stewardship

Today when children inherit their fathers' estates, they assume that they are the owners and can do whatever they like. After all, that is what inheritance is, isn't it? Well, no, say some present-day French farmers. When asked what they think they can do with land they have inherited, they say that it was not really given to them personally and is not theirs to dispose of.[3] In the sixteenth century, Montaigne said the same thing: "The estate is not properly ours, since by a civil ordinance and independently of us it is destined to certain successors. And although we have some liberty beyond that, . . . it is abusing this liberty unreasonably to make it serve our frivolous and private fancies."[4]

In this view of inheritance, the individual counts for little. The heir is a steward rather than an owner. Ideally, the estate passes through his hands untouched. Rather than use it or even add to it, his first duty is to preserve it. It does not take much imagination to see that this ideal might be fertile soil for ambivalence, as Montaigne's words suggest. Throughout the past the concept of a patrimony to be preserved existed in uneasy balance with the concept of personal ownership. Since not only property but also status, name, and honor were legacies to be preserved, the balance tended to tip in favor of stewardship.

Still, the records of the past are full of people who seemed to have had different goals from the simple preservation of patrimonies. Any number of people wasted their inheritances and ended up selling or mortgaging their patrimonies. And for every seller, there was a buyer who was changing *his* patrimony by enlarging it. Legal technicalities supposedly stood in the way of treating inherited property like property acquired in other ways, but the law could not eliminate the temptations. There were numerous court cases in which people were accused of selling ("alienating") what they had inherited. At the lower end of the social scale, it was usually hard times rather than extravagance that created the need to do so. In England the rise of a wealthy class of farmers, the yeomen, can be traced to the dealing in land that went on at a lively rate in the fourteenth and fifteenth centuries. Although part of their increased wealth came from a multiplicity of inheritances from relatives whose normal heirs had fallen victim to plague, the freeing up of land from servile obligations in this period made it easier for it to be put onto the market and for prosperous farmers to get their hands on what poorer farmers were forced to sell.

In our own time the notion of stewardship is implicit when one parent dies and the other holds property intended to pass eventually to the couple's children. In the past control over some of a dead spouse's property usually passed into the hands of the surviving spouse, but the survivor's behavior was often not in the least stewardlike. Husbands used to controlling their wives' property simply continued doing what they had always done when they became widowers. One wealthy widower in sixteenth-century Paris blithely ignored his wife's will in a way that seems shocking but was apparently rather typical. Instead of giving her property to their children, as he was supposed to do, he kept it in his own hands for thirty-six years, while his children grew to maturity and middle age.[5] More often the parent who survived was the mother, and her stewardship was put to the test if she remarried. Not infrequently a lower-class widow would give total control of her inherited land to her second husband and the land would eventually pass to his children, not to her first husband's. Even if she inherited only a lifetime right to the income from the property (a common arrangement), she might channel its benefits toward her new husband and their new family. In circles where large amounts of property were involved, widows could sometimes upset dynastic calculations. One English-woman in the seventeenth century refused to go along with her husband's suggestion that they work out an arrangement to make sure their children would get a considerable part of the large estate she expected to inherit from her father. She did not, as she put it, want to "draw the cradle upon her head"—that is, put their interests ahead of her own.[6] In the middle of the six-teenth century a rich widow in Paris had caused a scandal by giving everything she owned to a young husband whom she loved with what was viewed as a foolish passion. Her seven children were left with a relatively meager pittance. To contemporaries this was an extreme example of what they thought they saw happening all the time.[7]

The law almost always came down on the side of stewardship. The official response to the scandal of the Parisian widow was a new law in 1560, a royal edict whose preamble stated that it was designed to prevent "the devastation of good families." Henceforth a widow was not allowed to bring to a new marriage anything that had come from her dead husband and, furthermore, she could not give more of her own property to her second husband than she gave to each of her children. Although the edict spoke of the "infirmity of the sex" and spawned an outpouring of misogynistic commentary, its provisions were soon extended to widowers.[8] Laws of this sort would not have been needed if the virtues of stewardship had been universally accepted.

Some obligations clinging to inheritances were almost impossible to avoid, all of them reminders that collectivities took precedence over individuals. This was not, by the way, what the Christian church advocated, especially in pre-Reformation days. It encouraged unmarried or childless people to leave their wealth to the church and ignore obligations that extended beyond the conjugal group. Large religious donations of this sort were not common, how-ever. Kinsmen kept a watchful eye on property that was in danger of slipping out of the family's hands. In some places they had a legal right of first refusal (called *retrait lignager* in French), on the assumption that patrimonial property was ultimately theirs, not the individual owner's. Since the normal way to retain property in the family was to bequeath it to one's children, the obliga-tion to descendants was the strongest of all. Even under the old laws, the chil-dren of the infatuated Parisian widow were entitled to something and the new law was really just a refinement of a basic principle. But the absence of direct descendants (a common enough situation) brought other family obligations into play. Many marriage contracts stipulated that, in case a couple had no issue and the wife died, the property she had received from her kin would be returned to them, carefully separated from the husband's patrimony, which would be returned to *his* kin if he died first. It was almost as though the couple had never existed. Under the customary law of Paris, the childless widow of an innkeeper who had deserted her years before he died was required to hand over a share of the inn to her husband's relatives although she had been running it by herself for a long time. The claims of kin were considered sacrosanct even in the fluid conditions of the English countryside during the years after the Black Death. Landlords tended to favor tenants' distant kin from distant places over nearby nonkin, and people who held land they had not inherited risked being dispossessed by heirs who might appear out of the blue.

Widows were the quintessential stewards. The majority of them did not remarry and, no matter what system of inheritance they were living under, their hold on property was temporary. In every part of Europe, especially in the large rural population of moderate means, a widow was likely to come into possession of all her husband's property. She might have been a sharer of community property all along or her husband might have left her everything in his will. In either case, she was supposed to be holding it for her children, who would automatically take over when they came of age or she died (depending on what rules were being followed). A common way of indicating the tentative nature of her possession was to give her the right of usufruct, that is, only the right to what the property produced. The minimum usufruct was to a third of the husband's property, a minimum found, with slight variations, in the laws of every region. This was, for example the dower right of English common law, recognized in the colonies of the New World. A widow's "thirds" were often pitifully inadequate. Many husbands felt they could safely provide more generously for their wives, in New England as elsewhere, because of the assumptions about stewardship. Even so, dowers did not often include valuable landed property. Men wealthy enough to leave generous cash settlements usually preferred to do so.

People went to considerable lengths to make sure that their heirs would behave like stewards. Every legal system allowed special arrangements that went beyond the transfer from one generation to the next. Under a variety of legal forms with many names (*fideicommissum, substitution*, entail, strict settlement, *mayorazgo*), a document placed conditions on a legacy so that the heir was bound to bequeath it exactly as ordered. The document might also impose similar conditions on a whole series of heirs for several generations down the line. (This was only on the higher levels of society. The masses who worked the land usually did not have complete control over the little they inherited, which ultimately belonged to their landlords.)

An inheritance of this sort could look very different to the heir and to the man who made the arrangement. The latter was likely to feel that he was virtuously protecting his patrimony and his perhaps hard-won acquisitions while taking admirable care of his posterity. The heir was likely to feel oppressed. In contrast to his father or whoever made the arrangement he had almost no freedom of action. No wonder the legal profession was often asked to exercise its wits in undoing such arrangements. Not until after the period we are looking at, however, did the theoretical right to make them come to be outlawed. For centuries, the "dead hand" of an ancestor lay heavy on many a prominent person's wealth.

Stewardship of property could hardly be separated from stewardship of memory. An heir was the guardian of his family's collective memory. Visible embodiments of memory like tombs, chapels, and portraits were family property that an heir was obligated to take care of. He owned none of them, except perhaps pictures and other works of art in his home, and even those he was under severe moral constraints not to sell. Coats of arms occupied a place midway between the tangible reality of chapels and the intangible symbolism of names. To be a guardian of the family arms was synonymous with being a guardian of the family honor—or its "name," as it was so often put.

Names themselves were a precious patrimony, closely associated with family status. To have a surname at all had at first been a prerogative of the upper classes. The prospect of losing a name always threatened, even at the very top, and men sometimes worked out elaborate schemes to keep it from happening. These schemes had much in common with entails on property. If there was no direct male heir a typical procedure was for a man to designate as his heir a son of his daughter or his sister (the ever-present nephew), attaching the condition that the heir had to adopt the man's name (and arms, if there were any). Prominent men in France and England did this throughout the period. The long-term history of noble families in Hesse shows that it could really work; Hessian estates rarely passed from father to son and yet family names were preserved.

Given names were also part of a patrimony. Using certain names generation after generation was another way of preserving the collective memory. This was something even lower-class people could do and in some peasant communities there were stable family lines that consistently passed along the same property and the same given names for hundreds of years. The puzzling practice of parents' giving the same name to more than one child may have had something to do with the wish to ensure the name's preservation. Sometimes the same result was achieved by invariably using the names of godparents who were also relatives. An heir did not necessarily get his father's name. In some places he was more likely to get his grandfather's name or the name of some important member of the family who had died. In Renaissance Florence, the only time a boy was named after his father was when the father had died before the child was born.

In the transmission of family memory as in the transmission of family property, some people felt profoundly responsible while others felt profoundly distrustful that heirs would carry out their responsibilities. In the early part of the period people carefully spelled out the memorial masses they wanted said for them and often provided funds to endow special chaplains for the purpose. They sometimes left money so their orders for these memorials would be on permanent display in the church. Descendants were supposed to see that such family duties were performed, but why take chances?

There is a fine line between preserving collective memory and honoring the memory of individuals. Tombs and sarcophagi were sometimes grandiose monuments to individuals. And was a portrait an expression of personal vanity or a contribution to the family heritage? Michel de l'Hôpital's will in the sixteenth century stated that he wished his daughter's sons to add his surname to theirs so that his personal achievements might be an inspiration to them.[9] Montaigne fretted at the French practice in which a noble family's head used the name of one property and younger sons bore titles based on the names of other properties because it could lead to the obliteration of family consciousness.[10] There was confusion as to whether a title shed glory on the individual who bore it or on the family as a whole. History students are not the only ones who need to be reminded that the first duke of Marlborough's surname was Churchill, that the earl of Somerset was a Seymour, or that "Chatham" and "Pitt" were the same person. In England, at any rate, unlike France, only one person inherited a noble title; all other family members used the surname.

The ideal of stewardship infused the practice of inheritance, but it was an ideal tempered by the realities of life: *all* the realities, including political and social conditions and the quirks of personality.

Individual Decisions or Strict Rules

The patterns most people follow when they transmit property to the next generation are embodied in the rules for disposing of the property of people who die without leaving wills. Our system of law imposes some limits on wills (for example, it is difficult to exclude a wife or child entirely), but it allows a great deal of freedom. Even so, most wills nowadays are routine.

In the past more or less the same thing was true. What was different was that there were many regional and social variations in the basic rules. One variation was that wills were common in some places but almost never used in others. Another was that in some places estates were supposed to be divided up and in others were supposed to be transmitted intact. Within regions there were also variations of a sort that seemed natural in a society in which status was legally recognized: inheritance rules were different for nobles and commoners.

Every region had a horde of legal professionals familiar with the local rules and ready to guide their clients along well-worn paths. They were also ready to help their clients get around the rules, which throughout the period were repeatedly strained to the utmost.

When a large amount of property was to be disposed of, there were nearly always elaborate written instructions but they were not necessarily in the form of a last will and testament. Marriage contracts and dowry arrangements supplemented wills or took their place. Even quite lowly people in some places participated in this profusion of paperwork. Historians have been studying the rules of inheritance for a long time but not until recently have they started to study actual wills and contracts to see how the rules enunciated in law codes, collections of customs, and legal commentaries were applied. Neither the rules nor the documents tell a complete story. They played together, each tuned to the other, in a complex harmony with occasional dissonances.

The systems of inheritance in the Western world between 1350 and 1800 were a confusing patchwork and it was not always clear which was the right law to follow. In some places, for example, one had a choice among ancient Roman law, the law or customs of one's province, and the customs of one's small locality. Even in a relatively centralized country like England, the common-law rules of inheritance existed alongside rather different rules that prevailed in some counties (with colorful names like Borough English and Kentish gavelkind). This made for a rather orderly sort of chaos. The basic patterns were well enough known for considerable regularity to emerge, although certain ambivalences kept recurring at points where two systems seemed to collide.

The main focus of inheritance was real property, land in particular. There was a common underlying pattern. Land that had been inherited was supposed to pass into the hands of the children of the person who had title to it. A surviving spouse had some rights, but not, except in a few places, the right to permanent title, as the children did. If there were no children, the land went to the nearest blood relative of the deceased. The main divergence was that in some areas the land had to be given intact to one heir (impartible inheritance) and in others it had to be divided among the heirs (partible inheritance).

Other forms of wealth (so-called movable or personal property) were subject to less rigid rules. Personal property could be sold, for example. But at least some of it was supposed to be left to one's children, with the surviving spouse getting most of the rest. Many laws specified the proportion that a widow was entitled to, over and above her dowry, most often a third or a half.

There were rules about the inheritance of nonproperty, too. Where nobles were concerned, these could be the strictest rules of all. A man who held a title or an inheritable office was supposed to pass it to his eldest son. The status of nobility or gentility itself was inherited at birth by all his children. Where political office and status overlapped, as they did, for example, in England and some Italian city-states, sons inherited the right to sit in certain governing bodies. It was a much-coveted right, and some men resorted to concocting false genealogies. Not only was legitimate birth of the right sort required, but sometimes, as in Venice, the status of the mother as well as that of the father was taken into account. In most places it took more than one generation of inherited status to be able to claim such rights. In the last days of the Old Regime in France some positions were open only to men who could prove they had four generations of nobility behind them.

The rules of inheritance exerted a strong moral force. Agricultural tenants were usually safe in assuming that their children would take over their tenancies. Furthermore, no matter how much local variation there was, even to the point of stark contrasts between neighboring communities, children knew what form their inheritance was likely to take. In southern France, for example, the main rule was that a father could dispose of his land as he wished and so fathers were expected to make wills. Southern French farmers almost always did make wills, even if they had very little to pass on and even if the wills merely confirmed certain local patterns, such as primogeniture. In a southern French city like Toulouse, a man who was dissatisfied with the terms of his inheritance knew that there was not much he could do, since a court of law would regard a father's will as sacrosanct, but a man in the same situation in Paris knew there was a chance his father's will could be overturned if it flouted certain local rules.

Rules were put to the test in unusual circumstances, most commonly when there were no direct heirs or the normal heirs were under age. These "unusual" circumstances were not really so unusual, as we would surmise from the prevailing conditions of birth and death. An almost universal form of rule-bending, as we have seen, was to leave everything, whether temporarily or absolutely, to the widow. Wills expressed anxiety about leaving things to chance. The wills of rich and poor alike provided for underage children, especially if the property they were being left did not clearly come under customary rules. In one English village all through the sixteenth and seventeenth centuries, it was the poorest men who most often made wills, men with little or no land, sometimes with only a cottage and grazing rights on the common. Those in the village who were in secure possession of land under local custom rarely made wills.[11] If an inheritance was to go to one or more adult sons in the normal way but there were also children who were under age, a will often went into minute detail about the heirs' responsibility to those children. When there were no children at all, some people felt the need to make wills in which all they did was order the normal thing, that is, the property was to go to the nearest blood relatives.

Other people wanted to circumvent the normal process. A man might name a favorite nephew or two in a will, sometimes a nephew of his wife when his own nephew would have been the normal heir. Some people skipped over their nearest relations and chose distant relatives or strangers whom they "adopted." One version of skipping over blood relatives was to make a daughter's husband the chief heir (having had some say in his selection, it is safe to assume). Since the occupant of a house was so often assumed to be its rightful owner, one way of fiddling with inheritance was to install a prospective heir in one's home during one's lifetime. Some wealthy Parisians resorted to arbitrarily labeling personal property as real property in order to restrict its alienability or, conversely, gave themselves or their children greater freedom in handling real property by labeling it personal property. Almost anything was possible, provided that nobody with a clear right under the prevailing rules complained.

One exceptional circumstance that came up from time to time was the presence of illegitimate children. In most places bastards had no legal rights, so they were entirely dependent on the generosity of their fathers. We do not know what happened to most bastards, but we know that some of them were well provided for. It should be pointed out again that illegitimacy was not common throughout these centuries. The bastards of some high-born men were visible because their fathers chose to recognize them and could do so without social disapproval (an instance of the difference between the privileged and the unprivileged in parts of the Western world). But in England, where the common-law dictum was, "Once a bastard, always a bastard," even the privileged could not make their illegitimate children into legitimate heirs, while in some parts of Germany even lower-class people openly acknowledged their bastards. There were examples on all levels of society of bastards who were allowed to inherit or were given things that became inheritable from them. Henry VIII in the early sixteenth century in England and Louis XIV in the early eighteenth century in France bestowed noble titles on bastard sons and attempted to arrange their succession to the throne (neither king had a direct legitimate adult male heir at the time). In peasant communities, too, the feeling that a bastard was preferable to someone who was not a direct descendant caused the occasional bending of rules. Bequests of personal property, always subject to fewer restrictions than real property, found their way into wills, sometimes even the wills of wives of the fathers of bastards. One noble Venetian lady left "to the natural child of the above husband of mine 10 gold ducats and if anything should happen to him, this will go to his mother."[12]

The power and authority of fathers were restricted by some rules of inheritance. When powerful fathers chose to modify them, they were often successful, however. One of the appeals of Roman law, which was being revived in this period and which served as the inspiration for much new law, was that it gave fathers absolute liberty in disposing of their property. This Roman "liberty" contrasted not only with customs that had come down from the Middle Ages but also with the restrictions imposed on some estates by entail and other such devices. The very liberty of fathers to impose such restrictions had the effect of restricting the liberty of later fathers. It was a commonplace that liberty enhanced the authority of fathers over their households and offspring. Francis Bacon in the early seventeenth century regretted the foregone certainty about their inheritance that made some sons "disobedient, negligent and wasteful, often marrying without the Father's consent and growing insolent in vice."[13] In the next century, some American Quakers felt that the rule in William Penn's charter establishing rights of inheritance for all sons robbed fathers of the power to reward "Virtue, obedience, and sweetness" and punish "Vice and refractoryness."[14]

To keep one's potential heirs guessing could be an effective weapon. As far as we can tell, however, final decisions rarely upset expectations. For instance, in southern France a father's much-vaunted Roman liberty amounted to little more than the power to decide that an eldest son might be too unruly or incompetent to take over the property, and so another son or perhaps a nephew would be named as heir. Of course, to sons this could look like tremendous arbitrary power.

In the mingling of traditions that took place in the New World, the testamentary power of fathers led to a few oddities. One seventeenth-century settler in a Massachusetts village, who had been born into the English gentry, chose to hand over his entire estate to his eldest son, almost alone in his community in adopting primogeniture and impartibility instead of the Massachusetts hybrid that was like the Pennsylvania rule of equal shares for all sons and a double share for the eldest.[15]

A common way of modifying the rules was to give things away during one's lifetime. It was the usual way to undo the all-or-nothing effect of primogeniture, and it was the method of choice in providing for daughters. In some circumstances sons received portions that were like dowries. Generally speaking, receiving a portion made one ineligible to inherit, although under some rules a child could give up the portion when the parent died and he or she could become part of the pool of those entitled to the estate (where division was the custom). Among small landholders and tenants, no matter what the rules, it was common for only one child to inherit the house and land and for the other children to receive portions when they moved away. The wills of prosperous people frequently had nothing to say about the transmission of property but were concerned only with tokens of gratitude and instructions for funerals and memorial services. It was in marriage contracts and deeds of gift (donations *inter vivos*) that the transmission of property was arranged. The more that was siphoned off during a father's lifetime, the less he kept control of. For the very rich, the power to get around customary restrictions on inheritance was apparently worth the loss of some control. For the less prosperous, giving things away in one's lifetime could be dangerous. We have already seen the elaborate precautions that some elderly farmers took when they handed over their property while they were still alive. In the early days of New England, long-lived farmers seem to have had little incentive to give away property. Instead they let sons live on sizeable subdivisions while they themselves retained legal possession.

Simply to say that rules were regularly flouted is to miss the point of the interaction between rules and individual decisions. The most seemingly egregious bending of the rules could be done in the name of a higher principle, most often that of stewardship. There were other principles that came into play as well, ones that we today may find easier to understand. These included parental affection, resulting in the ambivalences described in the next two sections.

One Heir or Something for Everyone

Most of us assume that it is the duty of parents to provide for all their children. Our society's ideas about equality tend to make us feel that favoring one child to the detriment of other children is unfair, if not repugnant. At the same time, we know that dividing up certain kinds of property or putting them in the joint possession of several owners can be disastrous. The newspapers have carried stories about the disintegration of businesses because of conflicts among inheriting children. The challenge is to find a balance between not ruining the property and not ruining the children.

The challenge was the same in the past. Most of the complications and legal devices were ways of dealing with it. Nowhere was the search for a balance totally abandoned in favor of keeping property intact. There was a strong legal and customary prejudice in favor of fairness for all children in many parts of Europe, and there were also widely recognized ways of achieving fairness under the rules that dictated single, undivided inheritance.

To modern eyes one form of privileged inheritance, primogeniture, stands for all that was unfair and arbitrary in the past. To be born to the position of sole heir can seem as unjust an advantage as to be born a noble or as unjust a disadvantage as to be born a slave. The way that people regarded primogeniture in the years between 1350 and 1800 is a clue to much of what they thought. This was the period of its ascendancy. The practice grew and spread in the sixteenth and seventeenth centuries, displacing older patterns of inheritance, and reached its peak in the eighteenth century, to remain in some places and on some levels of society throughout the next century. As it reached its peak, it came more and more under attack. At the end of the eighteenth century, the laws of the new American republic in North America, like those of the French republic in the same period, rejected it. To say that this was a welcome change for all Americans and Frenchmen would be far from the truth. Old habits die hard, and this habit was congenial to many.

There was a pervasive ambivalence in practically all behavior connected with the division of inheritance. In the European patchwork of rules, some areas favored partible inheritance, others impartible inheritance. In some areas of impartible inheritance, the heir was supposed to be the eldest son, in some the youngest (ultimogeniture), and in some any one person chosen by a testator. But the rules themselves betrayed ambivalence. In the American colonies, where an estate was supposed to be divided into equal shares, the eldest son was entitled to a double share. In some parts of France, the privilege of the eldest son was similarly both affirmed and tempered. It would be nice to be able to explain these rules in terms of economic conditions and a clear pattern of historical development, but that would not be easy, since they were a legacy of centuries of change, movement, and conquest. There were basically two legal strains. One went back to ancient Rome and favored testamentary freedom and impartibility. The other went back to various Germanic tribes and favored partibility and equality. By the fourteenth century traces of both strains could be seen everywhere, even though there was still a rough division between north and south, partibility belonging to the north and impartibility to the south.

In many places there was a strong impulse to divide peasant property equally. This was often prescribed by law in the northwestern part of the Continent, including most of southwestern Germany. Where there were several options, as in England, people often chose to divide equally. An Englishman in the sixteenth century named John Copland possessed only a single strip of land in an open field, along with twenty sheep and two cows, which probably grazed on the village common. In his will he left each of his two sons ten sheep and one cow; one son got a large brass pot, the other a small brass pot and, presumably to even things out, the tiny piece of land.[16] A German bureaucrat in the early eighteenth century complained about the persistence of partibility: "The children divide the inherited holdings, meadows and lands without permission, split the holding, make two homes out of one or even live in the sheds, and likewise divide the payments which they owe for labour services among themselves, which causes great confusion in the registry."[17] The impulse toward equality often ran counter to the convenience of landlords and sometimes perilously close to the ridiculous.

But in any number of places peasants seemed to consider carefully whether division was advisable. If a farmer in England or Ireland was prosperous enough to provide more than one child with the basis for a decent living, he was fairly likely to do so. The eighteenth century in Ireland, the period of the potato's dominance, was a time of widespread partible inheritance, because the potato made it possible to live off a relatively small piece of land. When the potato crop failed, most Irish farmers went back to an earlier pattern of impartible inheritance. Richer farmers, however, had been reluctant to divide their property even in the heyday of the potato, apparently hoping to improve the economic and social status of their lineages. In England, a prosperous farmer named Edward Colyn left a will in 1509 in which he stipulated that each of his five children would get sixteen sheep. There were two houses with adjoining land, one of which he left to his eldest son, the other (after the mother's death) to the youngest. As a final provision in this example of a finely tuned egalitarian document, a large amount of cash was to be taken from the value of the estate and divided into five equal parts.[18] After a couple of generations, the Colyns might no longer be the possessors of estates large enough to divide, and by the eighteenth century many of England's yeomen had sunk in the social and economic scale as the result of such divisions. The settlers of New England, possessing more land than most of them had ever dreamed of having in the villages they came from, were able to divide their estates without running any such risk.

There was a rather different tradition of equal peasant inheritance in parts of northern Italy (Tuscany, Lombardy, Venice) and central France. In these places the danger of fragmentation was avoided by joint ownership. This meant keeping the land intact and all the heirs working it together. It also often meant that they all lived together in the same house, as we have seen, in what was called a community, a *fraterna*, or a *frérèche*. Community arrangements of this sort were recognized in law and continued to exist among the better-off peasantry at least into the eighteenth century. Their effectiveness as a corrective to fragmentation may have been due to the fact that the egalitarian principle was subordinated to the principle of impartibility. That is, the condition for keeping one's equal share was coresidence; moving away meant losing one's share.

Extremely wealthy landowners handled inheritance with the same ambivalence but on a larger scale. Division among all children was not uncommon. The law in some places required an equal distribution of all property that was not classified as noble. Even if a parent attempted to do some juggling by handing over property (a portion) during his or her lifetime, every child so favored was entitled to participate in the eventual division of the estate as long as the portion was put back in the estate. The law sometimes made it possible to favor one child above the rest as long as the others were not altogether excluded, but in a locality that has been carefully studied (the Bordeaux region in southwestern France), hardly any parents chose to take full advantage of the option, preferring to treat children equally.

The rules of noble inheritance in France were quite ambivalent. However favored an eldest son was, he could never inherit the entire estate if there were other children. At least one-third had to go to them, in equal parts. It takes only a moment's calculation to realize that by this process the size of a noble holding would be reduced over several generations. In the Paris region in the sixteenth century, it took only fifty years for a share in a certain seigniory to shrink to one-sixth of one-seventh of one-third of the original estate. Another seigniory in the same period, which belonged to the brother of the scholar Guillaume Budé, was divided among Budé's eight nieces and nephews, one half to the eldest nephew and one-fourteenth (one-seventh of one-half) to each of the rest.[19]

There were strategies by which noble families avoided this downward progression, including the constant acquisition of new property by purchase and marriage. One strategy was to avoid siphoning off wealth by whatever means presented themselves. A family of Burgundian nobles in the seventeenth century, the Saulx-Tavanes, made extraordinarily good use of this strategy by a combination of luck and planning. Of eleven children who survived to adulthood only two ended up with their full shares, apart from the eldest son, who received his two-thirds. Five of the children (three daughters and two sons) entered the religious life and were given relatively small portions, as was usual in such cases. Two other sons never married and presumably never received their shares. The remaining daughter was given a dowry when she married, but she died childless and her dowry, along with some of her husband's property, went back into the estate. This left two married sons, who got what they were entitled to but far less than if there had been only three children to begin with.[20]

The tendency to equal division was for a long time particularly strong in cities, where of course personal property, not land, formed the bulk of estates. The laws of Paris and London favored equal division. Wealthy Parisians hired professionals to work out meticulous divisions—a delicate matter when it came to putting cash values on a variety of objects—and engaged in formalized rituals that proclaimed their devotion to the principle of equality. When the heirs gathered for the distribution of the shares, it was traditional to call in a small child off the street to draw lots, on the premise that, since all the shares had exactly the same value, chance was as fair an arbiter as any other. The law of London allowed more leeway to a testator than the law of Paris, but at least one-third of an estate had to be divided among all the children.

Even rulers of political territories followed the principle of a fair division among all children. In the ninth century Charlemagne had "destroyed" his empire by dividing it among his three sons, but the practice was not unique to him. The fragmented political map of eighteenth-century Germany, an area of three-hundred-odd principalities, is testimony to that. The most fragmented part of Germany was where the custom of partible inheritance was strongest. Hence the proliferation of hyphenated Hesses (Darmstadt, Cassel) and Saxonies (Weimar, Gotha, Coburg). It was often the luck of the demographic draw that determined the political fate of a territory. A ruler with one son or no sons was more likely to leave his territory intact than one with several sons.

The demographic lottery saved France from something of the same fate as Germany's. In the middle of the fourteenth century the French king, John II, carved up his kingdom among his four sons, bestowing on all but the heir to the throne grants of land called appanages. They were Burgundy, Orleans, and Berry, rich territories whose names reverberate in the cultural history of the period. The appanage was a sort of entail, by which the land would revert to the crown if there were no direct male successor. In the case of Burgundy, there was not only a century-long series of male successors, but they were all extremely able, ambitious men. By the middle of the fifteenth century the duke of Burgundy had become one of the most powerful rulers in Europe. He was on the verge of acquiring the title of king in his own right and posed the greatest threat, along with the English king, to the power of the king of France. Luckily for France, in 1477 Charles of Burgundy died without leaving a son. Like the other appanages earlier, Burgundy was reincorporated into

France (without the territory the dukes had acquired in the course of their rule; it went with Charles's daughter when she married one of those lucky Habsburgs) and the practice of granting appanages was abandoned.

One duke of Saxony agonized over his decision to partition his already partitioned portion of Saxon territory and the words of his will in 1573 reflected his inner conflict. He said he was convinced in the end that partition was God's will. A duke of Hesse, who made the opposite decision, said that it fell heavily on his conscience to prefer one son.[21] The comforting phrase "share and share alike" often appeared in English wills. French wills used phrases like "an equal love," "a fair and just division," and, with a touch of ambivalence, "a desire to promote harmony." One French will in the sixteenth century explained that an equal division was a way of avoiding "any future occasion for lawsuits."[22] Royal appanages had been explained in similar language, being granted out of a desire "that our children, after our death, should live in love and peace and that any occasion for discord should be taken from them."[23] Whether done out of love or fear, partition obviously had a strong moral and emotional appeal.

Against this appeal stood the rising tide of primogeniture. German princes did not automatically divide their territory, however strongly precedent favored their doing so. Wealthy London merchants chafed at the longstanding legal requirements of partibility and after the first quarter of the eighteenth century the city's requirements stopped being enforced. The model for the transmission of wealth by the upwardly mobile was becoming a tightly controlled consolidation in the hands of one successor. In England this was the pattern followed by the landed nobility, and in many other places it became the pattern of royalty, nobility, and the very wealthy in general. Yet partible inheritance not only persisted but also took on a politically ideological coloration. The program of legal reform during the English Commonwealth included the abolition of primogeniture, and the proponents of republicanism in the eighteenth century continued to advocate its abolition. Montesquieu felt that there was something fundamentally antithetical to republicanism in primogeniture. Thomas Jefferson praised the abolition of both entails and primogeniture in Virginia, because it would prevent "the accumulation and perpetuation of wealth in select families . . . substituting equal partition. . . . Every fibre would be eradicated of antient or future aristocracy and a foundation laid for a government truly republican."[24] Not for the first time in human history was something being widely attacked at the moment of its greatest success.

It was hard to deny the advantages of impartible inheritance. It preserved the identity of a piece of property and, when rights and duties went along with the property, they were easier to keep track of and more certain to continue. At the bottom of the social scale, it suited the convenience of landlords for tenants to keep the size of holdings constant, both for administrative purposes and for efficient exploitation of the land. Much higher up on the social scale, the rationale for impartibility was linked to the military origins of land tenure.

A fief was in theory land granted by a lord to a military officer as payment for the officer's perpetual readiness to serve, and the officer's heir was supposed to assume both the duty and the land. Vassals were doing homage to their lords for such feudal territory throughout this period, a formality that remained one of the clearest marks of the old nobility, even after the military duty itself faded away. Along with this went the fact that a large piece of real estate was an unmistakable sign of wealth and hence of power and prestige. Said one Englishman at the end of the sixteenth century, "If I shall leave my land and living equally divided amongst my children . . . then shall the dignity of my degree, the hope of my house, . . . be quite buried in the bottomless pit of oblivion."[25] The growing use of cash for the portions of the other children made it easier for wealthy men to pass land intact to a single heir. Even where the laws continued to require division, heirs themselves would agree not to take land they were entitled to. Upwardly mobile men were repeatedly learning the lesson that impartibility was desirable. Its rightness was reflected in the routine acceptance of the single heir's prerogatives. "The peasant has only one child," says a German proverb. In southern France the heir was often referred to as l'enfant, as though he had no sisters and brothers and, indeed, as though it were a royal title.

Primogeniture was for a long time only one among several patterns of impartible inheritance, and its origins are no clearer than those of any other pattern. In the sixteenth and seventeenth centuries various arguments were used to justify it. The authority of the Bible was used, although ancient Hebrew inheritance practices were not all that easy to fathom. "Nature" was appealed to; people tended to believe that there was a natural superiority in the first fruits, and the first fruit of a marriage was likely to be the product of youth and vigor, not to mention purity, since the couple, or at least the wife, could have conceived in the final moment of virginity. These arguments were somewhat fatuous, since often the child who ended up as the eldest was not the first-born, and if the first-born was a female she had to defer to a younger brother. To the lawyers who were pushing for primogeniture much of its appeal lay in the fact that it was clear and convenient. It was convenient to have a designated heir, and many kinds of legal difficulties were avoided if the designated heir was determined by one simple rule. It did not hurt that the rule conformed to deeply felt notions about the superiority of men to women and of age to youth. One of the greatest appeals of primogeniture, however, was its association with nobility and royalty. Centuries of crowns and titles succeeding to eldest sons seemed to demonstrate the utility of primogeniture and gave it cachet.

Primogeniture spread down from the top and out across wider geographical areas. Its greatest triumph was in England, where as early as the fourteenth century peasants were substituting it for a variety of earlier rules. By the middle of the seventeenth century, it had become the universal rule for the gentry, even in Kent, which for a long time had been a pocket of partible inheritance.

In the eighteenth century nonaristocratic landowners of substance almost invariably used primogeniture and, as we have seen, wealthy townfolk like the merchants of London were eager to do the same. In France the movement toward universal primogeniture was slower and the situation remained somewhat more ambiguous, although the privileged position of the eldest son was widely accepted. It was in Germany that primogeniture had to overcome its greatest obstacles, because it was not included in the traditions of so much of the ruling class. An important step was taken in 1356, when the so-called Golden Bull revised the constitution of the German federation that went by the name of the Holy Roman Empire. Of the seven rulers who had the right to elect the emperor, four were laymen; they were required to pass their right, along with the territory on which it was based, to their eldest sons. This became a model, but its adoption throughout the Empire was never complete. The advances of primogeniture between 1350 and 1800 were made in a dynamic, turbulent, ambiguous context. While there were some who regarded it as being unambiguously right, others embraced it reluctantly or not at all.

Primogeniture was rarely simple or pure. The more land a father had, the better he was able to leave some to several children without having to divide up a central, patrimonial parcel. He could thus have it both ways. Even a poorer man might have several kinds of land, some that came under strict inheritance rules, some that did not. Property that was not in the form of land was likely to go to the so-called nonheirs. But the biggest complication in primogeniture was that the privileged heir acquired, along with his inheritance, obligations to the sisters and brothers who were left out of the inheritance as well as to the widowed mother. Many of the primogeniture rules specified the rights of younger children, and more often than not the heir was burdened with honoring them. It was he who had to pay out portions and dowries as the occasion arose. Any payments of this sort made during the father's lifetime would already have reduced the value of what the heir received. What is more, an estate might be encumbered with heavy debts, so that the heir was worse off than siblings who had been given straightforward gifts of cash and goods. Younger sons of peasants were supposed to move out when they married, or else not marry and work for the father and then the heir. But when they moved out they did not usually leave empty-handed and when they stayed they could strain the resources of a poor farm.

At the very top of the social scale, the situation was no simpler. The most throughgoing form of primogeniture was that practiced by the English aristocracy. No English law required the patrimony to be nibbled at, as French laws did, even allowing younger sons to acquire titles along with certain lands and forming what were called cadet branches of noble houses. In England younger sons were proverbially pathetic, proverbially loose cannons, in search of fortunes to make or marry. Overseas colonization in the sixteenth and seventeenth centuries was touted as a way of solving the younger-son problem, and younger sons were specifically appealed to in the efforts to settle Ireland and Virginia. But younger sons were not always cast adrift. They were provided with substantial cash portions, to be paid out of the future income of the estate. A standard procedure that had evolved by the eighteenth century was called the strict marriage settlement. It was drawn up at the time of the heir's marriage and provided that the estate would pass intact to him on his father's death and subsequently to his eldest son. At the same time provisions were made for all the other children by what in effect were mortgages on the estate. Thus the typical aristocrat in eighteenth-century England was the possessor of land he could not sell or pass on as he wished and the earnings of which were in large measure out of his control.

Nevertheless the prestige of being the heir and becoming the head of a peasant household or an aristocratic house was undeniable. Republican theorists may not have liked it, but it suited a lot of people that this prestige should not be earned by merit but acquired by natural right, by what could be interpreted as divine providence, just like the accession to a throne by a five-year-old boy who happened to be the eldest son of its previous occupant. Many people seemed to be willing to accommodate their impulse (supported by some ancient traditions) to be fair and considerate to all their children within this framework of a single, primary inheritance. The pervasive ambivalence surrounding the matter had as much to do with notions of power and status as it did with economic considerations.

All the Children or Sons Only

An obvious feature of primogeniture is its sexual bias. If a daughter ever inherited where its rule held sway, it was only because there was no son and because special allowances were made. Treating sons and daughters differently was not, however, limited to primogeniture. Partible inheritance was often restricted to sons. Even today, when most systems of inheritance favor equal rights for all children, there are lingering traces of the notion that a substantial legacy requiring full-time attention (a big business, for example) should go to sons. There is an ambivalence that pulls people away from thoroughly accepting the dominant doctrine of equality.

Ambivalence in the past pulled away from a different doctrine, according to which only men ran things, owned things, and ruled over people. Yet there were always some women who headed businesses, possessed wealth, and occupied the seats of government. These women could be found up and down the social scale because, in a society in which almost everything was inherited, women participated in the inheritance process. They did so sometimes overtly, sometimes indirectly. We have already seen that widows were important as heirs. Daughters inherited from their fathers, just as their brothers did, and not, as in some non-European societies, only from their mothers. Ambivalence grew out of the clash between the desire (and obligation) to maintain a patrimony in a male line and the desire (and obligation) to provide for daughters. Certain situations were categorized as exceptional no matter how often they occurred. Certain routine methods of transmission from one generation to the next avoided the formal label of inheritance (dowries in particular). Daughters were also sometimes true heirs.

The bulk of the population, making a living on the land, assumed that it was necessary for land to be in male hands. Whether inheritance was partible or impartible made no difference. What was needed was male labor and what was deemed natural and desirable was male control. Some laws specifically excluded daughters from inheriting land, but in the absence of such laws peasants tended to exclude daughters anyway. A group of English villagers in the early sixteenth century believed that daughters in their region had never been able to inherit, that "they never knew any man's daughter was adjudged to any customary tenement," even though the records of the previous century show that this was not true.[26]

As farming was a male prerogative, so was fighting. The land and titles associated with the warrior nobility had to descend to sons. Nobility was almost by definition a masculine condition, even though wives and daughters were noble by their relationship to the titleholders. The rare occasion when a woman achieved high political power through heredity was a matter for comment. It was hard for contemporaries to accept it as really normal when queens ruled in England, Spain, Italy, and Sweden, as they did at times in these centuries. Aristocratic titles tended to go in search of distant male heirs rather than pass to more closely related females. When judicial, administrative, and legislative offices were transmitted by inheritance, as was common, daughters were ineligible. Apart from considerations of land, wealth, and office, women did not in a sense possess the very blood through which heredity flowed. A family line could survive only through sons.

The usual way to pass along property to a daughter was in the form of a dowry. Dowries were no mere wedding presents and seeing them as an aspect of inheritance helps explain why they were so important. In the heartland of primogeniture, an English nobleman, Lord Delamer, wrote in the late seventeenth century: "To provide convenient matches for your daughters if you can, is without doubt your Duty, as also to give them good portions, but not such as will make your eldest sonne uneasy, for that is to give them more than comes to their share."[27] Everyone recognized the obligation to give daughters their share and in some places the share was guaranteed and specified by law. The dowry bore a relationship to what was transmitted by inheritance at the time of the father's death. It might involve forfeiting all right to inheritance, be given as an advance on inheritance, or be the occasion for a voluntary renunciation of inheritance. A marriage contract was the usual occasion for such a renunciation, paradoxically making the contract a deal between the bride and her father rather than between a husband and a wife. Younger sons received portions, too, sometimes actually called dowries. Daughters' dowries were sometimes bigger than sons' portions, but in any case were likely to be calculated according to an overall proportionality. The relationship of dowry to inheritance is glaringly clear in some famous cases in which dowries were not paid and, as a consequence, claims to inheritance were revived. Louis XIV took his country to war in 1667 over such a claim, which he made on behalf of his wife, whose dowry had not been fully paid and who he said should therefore be given the Netherlands after her father, the king of Spain, died.

The time for granting dowries and portions was when a child married or entered into what might be considered the equivalent of marriage. A portion was given when a child went into monastic life or left home for good. The ancient Roman theory was that the dowry was a contribution to the support of a household, but it seemed to function more as a personal share of family property. Although wives did not have control of their dowries, they often gained control when they became widows, and in some places a widow returned to her parental home with her dowry intact (especially if she had no children), ready to take it out again if she remarried.

Dowries could consist of any kind of property, including land. The impulse to keep parcels of land intact and in the hands of men, however, usually led parents to limit dowries to cash, household furnishings, and livestock. Here are two examples of how fairly prosperous farmers in widely separated places in the seventeenth century juggled their options. William Ingleby, a yeoman in northeastern England, drew up a will in 1632 in which he provided some flexibility for his executors when his two daughters would marry: both were to get large amounts of land and money if their mother and two uncles consented to their marriages but no land if they married without such consent, although the cash payments were to be the same.[28] When Marie Bonnal of Ribennes, a mountain village in southern France, married in February of 1695 she received 600 *livres* in cash (her minimum share of her parents' property as legally mandated), a heifer worth 12 *livres*, a blanket, five fat ewes, two shrouds, and a pine chest with a lock.[29] Cash dowries in the upper classes could be huge, enough to provide the foundation for a mercantile fortune or to purchase large amounts of land and so make a difference to the wealthiest of aristocrats.

Among the privileged classes, dowries ballooned in size and importance throughout the centuries we are looking at. So-called dowry inflation was partly an economic phenomenon, the result of the operation of supply and demand, but it was also partly due to the longstanding use of dowries to transmit status. A woman's dowry was as much an expression of her family's status as were abstract notions of blood and honor. To obtain a wife with a large dowry did not necessarily make a man richer. In fact, it could be a zero-sum game. The constant preoccupation with dowries would probably cause him to turn his wife's dowry into a dowry for a sister or a daughter, thus constantly recirculating the money for the same purpose. English aristocrats used their wives' dowries to buy land to replace land tied up to provide dowries and portions under strict settlements. The careful calculations in wealthy people's wills and in their long drawn-out marriage negotiations may look like parsimony, but they were often strategies for maintaining the family's eminence. As a Venetian in the fourteenth century put it, there was "a right amount for a patrician girl" to have as a dowry. When he wrote his will before the birth of his second child it seemed proper for him to destine the child for a convent if it was a girl, so that Lucia, the daughter he already had, would be sure to get a really distinguished dowry. Lucia would get less if the baby turned out to be a boy, but the whole prestige of the house would not be riding on her then.[30] He was not the last upper-class man in these centuries to realize that, if he wanted to provide a prestigious dowry for one daughter, his other daughters had to remain single and, as it were, be canceled out of the inheritance.

Daughters were real heirs, on an equal footing with sons, under some rules of partible inheritance. Sometimes a daughter might inherit even under a rule of impartible inheritance. She then became a female version of the heir, an heiress—in other words, an anomaly. An heiress was not a rarity, however. Having a son who survived to adulthood was something no couple on any social level could count on.

Among the majority of the population who lived and worked on the land, heiresses presented an opportunity to noninheriting sons, because the fathers of heiresses were almost invariably looking for suitable sons-in-law. In a sense, the heiress's position was illusory. Her legal right to property did not necessarily give her real control over it. Her father was likely to arrange for control to be put into the hands of the son-in-law, sometimes even "adopting" him. If the father died before the daughter married, his will might instruct his widow or some other relative to supervise the heiress's marriage choice.

Inheritance by sons-in-law was not only common, it was also sometimes considered preferable to inheritance by sons, especially in places where an heir could be freely chosen. Sons might be incompetent, they might be disobedient, and they might even choose to move away. In a mountainous region of southern France where almost half the wills left the property to female heirs, we can assume that their husbands were the real beneficiaries. We have already seen how dynastic preoccupations higher up the social scale sometimes caused sons-in-law to take their wives' surnames so as to give the impression of unbroken family lines.

If inheritance passed *through* heirs rather than *to* them, this was doubly true of heiresses. Royal heiresses, the women who actually wore crowns in countries where there was no law of strict male succession (the main example of such a law was the so-called Salic law in France), may seem to be an exception, but it is well to remind ourselves that one queen who wielded a great deal of power, Elizabeth of England, spent a large part of her life playing a wily game of eluding marriage, for she was, like all heiresses, the target of ambitious suitors.

The inferior social and legal position of women did not leave them out of the inheritance picture. It simply gave them a special place in it.

From Father or from Mothers

If women own property, they can presumably pass it on to their children. Yet children today do not expect to inherit in a significant way from their mothers, in spite of the fact that women in the United States own a great deal of property. When most of us think of inheritance we think of parents' property as their common possession, the bulk of which passes first to the surviving spouse and then from him or her to the children. The idea of separate maternal and paternal legacies hardly exists. On the other hand, when we turn from major bequests, like the family home, a family business, investments, and bank accounts, to more personal, individual things like jewelry, books, and household items, it seems unexceptional that they should be inherited from mothers. And we have no difficulty at all in accepting the fact that we inherit intangibles from our mothers, among them looks, character, and kinship connections.

There is, in other words, an imbalance between mothers and fathers as sources of inheritance. In the past, not surprisingly, fathers were the main source of inheritance, but mothers were the source of more than we would expect. Just as the period between 1350 and 1800 was one in which primogeniture was slowly replacing older forms of inheritance, so, too, was it a period in which older patterns of maternal inheritance were disappearing. And just as primogeniture was never wholly triumphant, neither was purely paternal inheritance.

Almost every new development in these centuries reinforced the tendency for everything to descend from fathers. As the use of surnames spread through all ranks of society, for example, they usually came to children from their fathers, not their mothers (unless they were illegitimate). Before surnames became common, documents had identified people by patronymics, and many surnames were based on them. In Tuscany, where surnames were for a long time associated with high status, the patronymic form stressed the connection with forefathers venerated as founders of lineages. Surnames had a variety of other origins as well (places, occupations, personal characteristics), but whatever the origins, once they became fixed they passed to succeeding generations through fathers.

In some places, especially in the upper classes, first names also tended to come from fathers, or at least from fathers' kinship groups. Names, even girls' names, "ran in families." Lineage-conscious men gave their fathers' or grandfathers' names to their heirs. Toward the end of the period, as can be seen from the names of kings, alternation (Francis-Henry-Francis, Philip-Charles-Philip) gave way to outright repetition (four Philips in Spain, four Louis's in France, four Georges in England). We really cannot say much about how humbler people named their children. A handful of saints' names formed the pool that everyone dipped into and, with perhaps 25 percent of the male population of Europe named John (or Jean or Giovanni or Juan or Johann), we can never be sure by what calculation each bearer of a name acquired it.

There was little doubt in most people's minds that wealth and status came from fathers—and probably character and personality as well. If a man married down, there was no question that his children would share his status, not the mother's. If a man married up, it took some doing—special arrangements in a marriage contract, for example—for the children to get any formal benefit from the mother's status. Married women, as contrasted to widows, rarely wrote wills. When women died before their husbands, their children were not likely to inherit anything that amounted to much. That was mainly because, as we have seen, land was so rarely in the hands of women. When a mother died, there was no major transfer of property and authority such as took place when a father died. With a few exceptions, the most the children would get was half of what had legally belonged to her, the rest going to (or, more accurately, staying with) the father. A good part of what had "belonged" to the mother was her dowry, over which her husband had had full control and which, if it had been given in a series of cash payments, might not even still exist at the time of her death. One of the bases of the popular stereotype of stepmothers was that the children of the first wife often had occasion to suspect that they were not getting what little they were entitled to as their maternal inheritance.

Although outweighed by the inheritance that came from fathers, maternal inheritance was not without significance. This was, after all, a social system in which bilateral kinship played a big part. Mothers mattered less as individuals than as conveyors of tangible and intangible legacies from grandparents and ancestors. A seventeenth-century Englishman commented, "It was the greatest honour that can betide a family, to be often linked into the female inheratrices of ancient stocks."[31] Instead of being totally absorbed into their husbands' families, women were sometimes thought to retain identification with their lineages. The patchwork of European inheritance rules included a few in which the lineage identification was paramount. In them anything that the mother had received from her family (including her dowry) went to her children and none of it to their father.

In the process of becoming fixed, surnames in some places reflected the primacy of lineage over marriage (at least in death, since in Spain, France, and Italy married women were often listed in burial registers under their fathers' surnames). For a long time children in the English countryside got their surnames from their mothers, especially if the mother was the person who had inherited the land. In France it was not uncommon for country women to be known by their mothers' surnames. French noble heiresses were able to pass along to their sons certain titles (the names of lands they had inherited) that they themselves were not permitted to use. Present-day Spanish surnames, which include the mother's maiden name, are a vestige of these older practices. Given names could also be carriers of a mother's legacy. In superpatriarchal Florence one of a woman's sons was likely to be named after her father, even if all the other children were named after her husband's relatives. In the English-speaking world in the eighteenth century, just at the time when primogeniture was making its most rapid advances, maternal-family given names and surnames were being used as children's middle names.

Serfdom, in the part of western Europe where it persisted for a while in this period, was a condition inherited from either parent, but in a few places the child of a serf father and a free mother inherited her status. "The womb frees and ennobles [*ventre affranchit et ennoblit*]," according to some customary laws in effect in France through the sixteenth century.

Married women who wrote wills were usually quite wealthy and had personal property to dispose of. Their wills were generally different from men's wills in revealing almost no dynastic motivation. They did not pass along land and houses, the basis of economic and political power, but parceled out bequests to people they wanted to reward for love or service. The beneficiaries often included female relatives outside the household and serving women inside the household. The greatest concern women showed, however, was for their daughters. They added their own contributions to the dowries the fathers were obliged to provide (an indication of the close relationship between size of dowry and a desirable lot in life). In seventeenth-century Bordeaux, many women who wrote wills during their husbands' lifetimes left greater shares to daughters than to sons; it is perhaps unnecessary to say that fathers in Bordeaux tended to favor sons when *they* left unequal shares. Women's wills were personal documents that bore little resemblance to the grand testaments disposing of family property envisioned in Roman law.

The unmistakable fact of maternal inheritance did not fit comfortably into the growing tendency to see paternal inheritance as the only kind that mattered. When Europeans made family trees they were almost always patrilineal. The fiction was adopted that a person was descended only from his father, who in turn was descended from his father, and so on all the way back in a straight line that was purely male. The contributions of wives, even more of wives' families, were blotted out. The making of genealogies was very popular among those with pretensions to status in these centuries, and they all followed the rule of fictitious patrilineal filiation. In fact a man's status might owe everything to a history of advantageous marriages. There are eighteenth-century genealogies in which the earliest forefathers were very humble men who married women who had money or were the daughters of men who started their sons-in-law on successful careers. The genealogies do not tell us that. They merely note the wives' names and go on to the eldest sons in the next generation. These men in turn were sometimes failures or wastrels rescued by advantageous marriages—another crucial fact omitted by the genealogies. Patrilineal surnames made all this seem natural. At the same time that everyone was avidly pursuing good marriage alliances and making the most of them, the contributions of mothers to their children's official ancestry were systematically suppressed. This is not to say that mothers and the families they came from did not loom large in most people's lives. Resistance to the father's monopoly of control over the household inheritance remained strong, and the mother's family often behaved as though her children belonged to them at least as much as to the father.

The bilineal character of inheritance remained a permanent part of the European tradition. Having two sources of inheritance and two kinship groups made for complexity and, inevitably, a certain degree of ambiguity. The ambiguity was compounded by the growing preference for patrilineality, which never entirely superseded bilineality but instead made a variety of accommodations to it. A lot depended on where you were on the social ladder, or where you wanted to go.

Making sense of the complexities of inheritance is never easy and there is a lot more we need to learn about how it worked. It is obvious that knowing what was in the laws is not enough. Behavior had a way of blurring laws and responding to other imperatives. Some of these imperatives arose from practical economic considerations, others arose from feelings about particular people, and still others arose from convictions about what was right and what families ideally should be.

V

Ideas
and
Ideals

There is nothing important in our lives that is not surrounded by a cluster of ideas and ideals. "Ideology" has taken on an evil odor in recent times, but in its dictionary meaning of "a coordinated body of ideas or concepts" it can certainly be applied to the family.

The body of ideas or concepts about the family that is widely accepted today is tied in with notions about individualism and individual worth and it starts from a central preoccupation with children. Judicial decisions are usually good places to look for ideological statements, and child-custody cases are particularly revealing. Perhaps nothing told us more about family ideology in the late twentieth century than the Baby M "surrogate mother" case of the mid-1980s. The main question in that vexing case, in which a woman who was paid to bear a child for a childless couple refused to let them have the child, was what was best for the child's happiness. There was also talk of "rights," among them the right of a biological mother to her child, no matter what her legal position, and the right of people to be parents, no matter by what means. The desirability of having children for emotional gratification was taken for granted.

Nearly everything about the case, least of all the advance in reproductive technology, would have been impossible in the past. People simply did not think about the family that way. How they did think about it may be divided into two parts: ideas about the family's political role and ideas about the family's emotional role. That a whole chapter is required for the political role of the family should come as no surprise to anyone who has read this far, but it may still seem strange that so little was thought about the kind of emotional role we assume to be the family's. Like us, people in the past concentrated on some aspects of the family more than others. Household management and inheritance, for instance, received more attention than babies and conjugal companionship. The family ideology of the past should be seen as belonging to a view of society that has undergone drastic transformation.

11

The Political Role
of the Family

The first place to look for ideas about the political role of the family is the writings of political theorists. Such ideas existed in greater abundance in the period we are considering than in present-day political theory. There were also widely held ideas that were not in perfect harmony with formal theories. Today, too, there are discrepancies between the deceptive neatness of theories and the often unconscious, contradictory, and subversive principles on which people act, even though what is now called political science relies heavily on surveys, polls, and statistics.

The long European tradition of formal political theory starts with Aristotle's *Politics*, which in 1350 had been available to western Europeans for about a hundred years. Writers of the most diverse sort throughout the period echoed what Aristotle said about the family. His dicta on the family actually survived beyond the period in which his intellectual authority was supreme, and were still being echoed by writers who did not intentionally use him as a guide. When political writers—as varied as Jean Bodin, Thomas Hobbes, John Locke, and Jean-Jacques Rousseau—attempted to formulate universal principles, they almost always drew on him. Some theory about the family is also found in works that focused on two central political institutions of western Europe: nobility and monarchy. This theory usually went back not to Aristotle but to the Stoics, by way of Cicero, and was sometimes part of the polemics of actual political controversies.

The family was never the most important element in any of this formal theory. We have seen, however, that marriage, the household, kinship, and inheritance had political implications. People seem to have been guided by ideas that either never got mentioned in formal theories or were much more complex and pervasive than the theoretical works suggested. This is a situation that cries out for the talents of a Claude Lévi-Straus, someone who can read the structure beneath the messages conveyed in people's actions and casual comments. It will take a lot more work by historians before the structure is fully revealed.

What follows is an exploration of the most oft-repeated ideas about the relationship of the family and the state in the centuries before 1800. It includes some things that have been said in earlier chapters. Since no human being makes every thought and action conform to a coordinated body of ideas, there is at least as much ambivalence in this chapter as in the others.

Household or Kinship

"Family" is itself an ambiguous term. For a long time its predominant meaning was "household," but it could also mean "kinship." This ambiguity still enters into thinking about the family and encourages a certain kind of political double-talk. Politicians say "family" to evoke both the image of the familiar nuclear-family household and the mythic nostalgia of an endlessly extended kinship. The political rhetoric of nationalism has always had a tendency to refer to nations as kinship groups. Most references to "family" in twentieth-century political speeches are emotive, focusing on the family as a nurturing environment. In the past the emotive side was not the one that figured in political thought. Both household and kinship were thought of as collectivities, engulfing the individuals they contained. Where for us politics is about individuals engaging in certain kinds of activities and families belong to individuals' private lives, in the past "family" meant a corporate entity with a political role of its own.

In political theory the meaning of family as household (the older meaning) was by far the more common one. Following Aristotle, most writers said that the household was the precursor of the state; it was a form of political organization that existed before the state and out of which the state evolved—an idea that is still pretty much accepted today. "It was out of the association formed by men with ... women and slaves," said Aristotle, "that the first household was formed. ... The next stage is the village. ... The final association, formed of several villages, is the city or state."[1] In the sixteenth century, Jean Bodin was saying pretty much the same thing: "The first companionship, that of man and wife, is thought to be the most ancient of all. ... The tie of human association has been extended from one home into several families, into villages, towns, cities, and nations. ... So domestic society has expanded into political society."[2] John Locke in the seventeenth century said: "The *first society* was between Man and Wife, which gave beginning to that between Parents and Children; to which, in time, that between Master and Servant came to be added."[3] Rousseau in the eighteenth century agreed that "the earliest of all societies, and the only natural one, is the family."[4] For some theorists the household was not only the precursor of the state but also a model of how it worked, a state in miniature, or, as one early-seventeenth-century Puritan divine, William Gouge, termed it, "a little commonwealth."[5] Thomas Hobbes at about the same time called it "a little monarchy,"[6] and Aristotle had recognized that it was a model congenial to monarchists ("Rule over children is royal . . . , and this is the prototype of royal rule"),[7] although he himself rejected the analogy.

A few theorists claimed a third, and much more important, role for the household: it was, or should be, the fundamental unit of the state. The most familiar version of the theory is in Thomas More's *Utopia*, which describes an ideal government based on households of more or less uniform size. "Every thirty families choose annually an official" who rules over them, and these officials elect the one supreme governor.[8] A less familiar (and less extreme) version is in a work by a German writer of the early seventeenth century, Johannes Althusius, who advocated a kind of federal republic. He starts with the domestic unit, as Aristotle did, and then goes on to say that "the community is an association formed by fixed laws and composed of many families and collegia living in the same place. . . . The members of a community are . . . associations of families and collegia, not the individual members of . . . associations."[9]

The persistence of Aristotle's influence may have owed something to the fact that society gave the appearance of being made up of households. If individuals were not in households, they were in institutions that resembled or imitated households. Rulers tended to deal with households, through household heads, rather than with individuals. Churches kept records of parishioners and assigned pews by households.

Kinship is barely mentioned in most political theory. Aristotle recognized the conjugal basis of the household and its filial consequences, and so did those who echoed him, but that is about as far as they went. One exception was Althusius, who, unlike other writers, thought the interaction of kin was an important aspect of politics. His definition of kinship has the ring of authenticity derived from observation: "The kinship association is one in which relatives and in-laws are united for the purpose of communicating advantages and responsibilities. This association arises from at least three persons, but it can be conserved by fewer. Frequently it consists of a much larger number."[10] In other works of political theory, kinship was usually brought in only by implication in discussions about whether power should be based on birth.

Power was often based on birth, so the disapproving tone of these discussions shows a disjunction between practice and theory. Whatever ambivalence people may have had about inherited status, they had to be preoccupied with kinship if they were interested in power. The very word "house," which would seem to denote household, became a synonym for kinship or lineage in almost every language. In many contexts family meant the ties of blood over generations and not a group of living persons sharing a common residence.

Nearly every time Shakespeare used the word "family" (and he used it rarely) it was in connection with kinship and political power: a "noble family," "the family of York," and three passages in the first act of *Titus Andronicus* that link the honor of a family with its political standing.[11] The most venerated family of all, that of Jesus, while sometimes depicted as a modest nuclear household, was frequently shown in timeless glory with extended kin.

Political theory and political practice more or less agreed on the family as household, but in most theory kinship did not come under the rubric of "family." In practice, both household and kinship were important, and either one might be implied in "family."

King as Father or Father as King

"Rule over children is royal," Aristotle said. For many people at all times this has been a compelling metaphor. It still has a certain appeal, although thinking of fathers as kings is now less acceptable than it used to be. The idea that kings are like fathers is sturdier, but it was already under attack at least three hundred years ago. When the metaphor worked in both directions (explaining both monarchy and paternity), its charm lay in its reconciliation of the ordinary with the remote. A king might move in a world most people never participated in, but he became comprehensible when thought of as a father. At the same time, the flesh-and-blood man who was one's father acquired stature and authority. The metaphor may have had least appeal to people at the top of the social scale, who preferred images of shared power and group sovereignty, although they liked it well enough when it applied to their own relationship with tenants, serfs, and servants. In many places the less privileged and less sophisticated continued to cling to the image of the monarch as a father well into the twentieth century. Writers engaged in political polemics often conceded the point that fathers were kings and concentrated their fire instead on the other half of the metaphor.

It was easy to think of the father as a king because what he ruled over seemed to be a political microcosm. Running a household was a complex job in which many kinds of activities were involved and a variety of persons participated. Fathers ruled not only over children but wives and servants as well. Thomas Hobbes said a family (he was thinking of a "great" family) was "a little monarchy—whether that family consist of a man and his children, or of a man and his servants, or of a man and his children and servants together."[12] Almost everything about households seemed to confirm the idea of a single supreme ruler with an unquestioned, possibly divinely ordained right to rule. Judeo-Christian doctrine held that the husband was the head of the wife. He was God's deputy and the obedience due him was a natural religious duty. It was generally agreed that the household's pattern of authority was based on the conjugal relationship. Even Locke, who was at some pains to dislodge the monarchical image of the family, conceded that "it . . . being necessary, that . . . the Rule should be placed somewhere, it naturally falls to the Man's share, as the abler and stronger." Furthermore, it was "easie, and almost natural for Children . . . when they were Men [to] find [no] greater security to their Peace, Liberties, and Fortunes, than in the *Rule of a Father*."[13] The roles of husband, father, and household head all came together in one royal figure, the personal embodiment of the household and the sole occupant of the top rung of a hierarchical ladder. Impelled by paternal love and religious piety, the ideal father was capable of wise decisions and deserving of respect and obedience. His unquestioned authority, like that of a king, assured orderly relations among those subject to his rule. He did not really need to be anyone's actual parent, but the fact that he usually was the biological father of some of those under his authority seemed to guarantee that, however absolute his rule, it would be benign.

Locke was not comfortable with the inevitability of the father's royal rule. He said that "*Conjugal Society* is made by a voluntary Compact between Man and Woman"[14] and pointed out that "in this power the *Mother* too has her share with the *Father*." When the father "quits his Care of [his children] he loses his power over them, which goes along with their Nourishment and Education, to which it is inseparably annexed."[15] Rousseau stated the same idea a little more forcefully, saying that "children remain attached to their father only so long as they have need of him for their own preservation. As soon as this need ceases, the natural bond is dissolved. The children being freed from the obedience which they owed to their father, and the father from the care which he owed to his children, become equally independent. If they remain united, it is . . . voluntarily."[16] Republican ideology undermined the royal metaphor for the family.

Everyday ideas about the converse analogy, that kings were like fathers, were routinely expressed in the paternal images that sprang to the lips of subjects and underlings. Addressing a barrage of criticism at his sovereign, Louis XIV, François Fénelon could say, "Your people, whom you should love as your children and who thus far have been so enamored of you, are dying of hunger."[17] The assumption was that as a loving father a king was of necessity a good ruler and could not be held responsible for bad policies, which were blamed on evil advisers.

Formal monarchist theory was built on more rigorous arguments. Single rule was said to be natural and to be effective in maintaining a prosperous, orderly society. Thus Bodin: "If we should inspect nature more closely, we should gaze upon monarchy everywhere. . . . What is a family other than the true image of a state? Yet this is directed by the rule of one, who presents the true picture of a king."[18] "Natural" almost always meant "in harmony with divine law." An earthly king was an analogue to God the Father and Ruler of the Universe and, besides, he received his power from God, as all fathers did.

The full-blown theory of divine right was forged amid political conflict in the turbulent years of the sixteenth and seventeenth centuries. It was an aggressive theory, not flaccid conventional wisdom. Out of one of the bitterest conflicts, the English Civil War, came the most thoroughgoing statement of the fatherhood of kings, Robert Filmer's *Patriarcha, or the Natural Power of Kings,* which is best known nowadays as the springboard for Locke's *Two Treatises of Government,* the first part of which is a systematic attack on Filmer. Filmer said that the power of all kings derived from the father of mankind, Adam:

> God gave to Adam not only the Dominion over the Woman and Children that should Issue from them, but also over the whole Earth . . . , so that, as long as *Adam* lived, no Man could claim or enjoy anything but by Donation, Assignation, or Permission from him. . . . In the dispersion of *Babel,* we . . . find the Establishment of Royal Power, throughout the Kingdoms of the World. . . . The Nations were distinct Families, which had Fathers for Rulers over them; . . . God was careful to preserve the Fatherly Authority, by distributing the Diversity of Languages, according to the Diversity of Families.[19]

There was another sense in which kings were thought of as fathers, one less loaded with religious and other emotion. This was the king as housekeeper. Royal government was assumed to be like a household and continued to be thought of in this way even after the growth of bureaucracies and standing armies should have made the idea obsolete. Kings were supposed to live off their own estates, like other landholders, and to manage them in such a way that they stayed out of debt while continuing to live in a suitably grand manner. It took a long time for the fiction to be abandoned that taxation was exceptional, necessary for extreme emergencies only, and that asking the country for money was a sign of poor household management or wicked extravagance or both. This was one of the chief complaints against England's Richard II when he was forced to abdicate in 1399. It was said that he could have lived "honourably from the issue of his kingdom and from the patrimony belonging to his crown," but "great sums of money were owed . . . for the victuals of his household."[20]

The stubborn persistence of the metaphor of the father-king is connected with our disposition to think in analogies. Even when we seem to have moved very far away from family images in politics, ancient political imagery has a place in some modern views of family relationships. Parents are often perceived, at least on deeper levels of consciousness, as kings and queens, and the Oedipus complex is, in a way, the replaying in the individual psyche of a drama about a ruler.

Birth or Merit

If the commonest way of thinking about the household in political terms was to compare it to a royal government, the commonest way of thinking about kinship in political terms was to consider the connection between blood and power. A literary tradition, which went back to antiquity, discussed the opposition between the inner assets of "virtue" or "merit" and exterior assets such as wealth, family connections, and inherited rank. Some of the writing has a rarefied tone, as though barely connected with the real world, but at times it betrays an intensity that must have come from the writers' personal concerns. Every writer had to make sense of the fact that the world placed inordinate value on inherited status and yet also made room for some mobility. Western society throughout these centuries was precariously set in an ambiguous territory midway between a closed caste system and a system of unlimited opportunity. The thrust of formal theory was against the claims of birth, but people generally acted as though birth were everything. The legal structure seemed to say they were right. The rejection of this legal structure by so many revolutionary governments toward the end of the period makes considerable sense when we recognize the ambivalence in the thought of the preceding centuries. The ambivalence persisted for decades longer, even, if the truth be told, in the United States, but especially in countries that did not go through a revolution around 1800, like England, or that overturned revolutionary laws and restored inherited privilege, like much of the Continent.

Individual merit could occasionally carry a man far, even in the fourteenth century, especially in certain fields of endeavor. The most commonly recognized opportunities were in the church, for whose clergy it rejected not only inherited offices but also, in one important ecclesiastical tradition, marriage itself, the indispensable mechanism of kinship. A poor boy of lowly birth could become a priest, and he might even, against all the odds, become pope. It happened, though not often. Outside the church, men could advance themselves on the social scale through learning and industry, and on the basis of their achievements might eventually acquire the enviable status of burgher (bourgeois), with the right to participate in the oligarchic rule of a town. European towns may have been full of desperately poor and powerless people, but they nevertheless continued to beckon the ambitious. That was the message of the popular story of Dick Whittington, the poor boy who became lord mayor of London.

Some kinds of rulers got their positions by being elected. Many churches elected their officers, and it was fairly common for the governments of villages and towns to be elected, including those of several independent city-states that continued to exist well into the seventeenth century. At the highest pinnacles of power a few important positions, among them the king of Poland, the Holy Roman Emperor, and the pope, were filled by elections. They were not widely based, democratic elections, but they were elections nonetheless and they were a familiar alternative to inherited rulership.

In formal theory there were two kinds of attacks on birth. One came from writers who attacked monarchy, especially during the French religious wars at the end of the sixteenth century and the English Civil War of the next century. The other came from writers who attacked the nobility. Machiavelli summed up the antimonarchist argument when he said, "Kingdoms which depend entirely upon the virtue of one man endure but for a brief time, for his virtue passes away with his life, and it rarely happens that it is renewed in his successor."[21] François Hotman, the author of the late-sixteenth-century *Francogallia*, urging an elected monarch in France on the model of what he claimed was the ancient Gallic practice, said it was "a great mistake . . . to seek birth before quality in a prince." Like other antimonarchists, he was more concerned with how kings exercised power than with whether or not they were elected, and he made a plea for shared authority: "Real authority . . . ought to be controlled by the nobility and men of distinction," who were, as he put it, "authorized by the people."[22]

Without saying so outright, Hotman was clearly willing to accept birth as a qualification on some levels of government. But not so Machiavelli, and not so Thomas More, who ridiculed pride in noble ancestry, saying that the most important thing a man can have is honor, which cannot be passed on to one's descendants.[23] A fifteenth-century Italian work translated into English as *Declamation of Nobleness* said that to regard nobility as hereditary was "a vain supposing," because if a man failed to be as virtuous as his "worshipful ancestors" it was especially "shameful and abominable."[24] A couplet considerably less worshipful of ancestors had some currency in England from the fourteenth century on:

> For when Adam delved and Eva span,
> Who was then the gentleman?

Although it was possible to think about political power in the abstract without paying much attention to birth, it was impossible to think about really achieving power without taking birth into account. Political offices had a way of becoming hereditary, as Hotman had to concede. This advocate of an elected monarchy, seeing that his faction had a chance of achieving power through hereditary succession, revised his text to say that "the crown of France became hereditary by custom [and] passed through the eldest sons by male descent."[25]

Apart from particular offices, one's general standing in the world was assumed to come from birth. Wealth helped, of course, but the notion of wealth was rarely at odds with the notion of birth, in spite of what the theorists said. Wealth was something to pass along to heirs and to dispense in proclaiming one's standing and ancestry. Writers who theorized about true nobility as often as not ended up accepting the nobility of nobles, saying, for example, that "the inward ornaments and virtue . . . shine and glitter in a nobleman" more than in anyone else, especially "a person rural or of very base lineage."[26] Cardinal Wolsey was attacked as unworthy because he was "a wretched poor man [of] greasy genealogy."[27] Wolsey was vulnerable as no aristocrat could ever be. Aristocrats were protected, as it were, by their ancestors, whom they gathered about them and displayed as a reminder to the rest of the world of what truly counted. They were convinced, as one sixteenth-century English gentleman, Laurence Humphrey, put it, that the common people venerated "renoune and fame of auncestry."[28] "New men" tried to make themselves look as much like persons of inherited status as they could. An observer of the English scene in the late sixteenth century sardonically enumerated the steps to be taken by a would-be gentleman who, having reached the point of being able to live "without manual labor, . . . shall for money have a coat and arms bestowed upon him by the heralds . . . and thereunto being made so good cheap, be called master, which is the title men give to esquires and gentlemen, and reputed for a gentleman ever after."[29]

The association of blood and power was of such long standing that to many it seemed like a fact of nature. That is not to say they liked it. It was obviously resented by many, and was attacked and discredited by some. Before the end of the period even some beneficiaries of the system felt uncomfortable about it, at least as a principle that could be thoughtfully defended. The French aristocrats in the National Assembly on August 4, 1789, made a dramatic gesture of renouncing many of their hereditary privileges. A short while later, Thomas Paine wrote, "The punyism of a senseless word like *Duke* or *Count* or *Earl* has ceased to please."[30] And yet at the very same time, Edmund Burke was praising what he called "a natural aristocracy," which sounded a little like a meritocracy and a lot like the advantages of birth and breeding, since it included being "bred in a place of estimation" and seeing "nothing low and sordid from one's infancy."[31]

State Concern or State Neglect

States ancient and modern have pursued policies based on assumptions about the state's interest in the family. The emergence of an acknowledged "welfare state" in recent times is an example. Any decision to intervene reflects ideas about what the family is and should be as well as ideas about what a state is and should be. Most present-day democracies have a goal of promoting the health and happiness of children. Although there is no agreement on the best way to reach it, the goal is almost universally accepted. In the past, by contrast, the health and happiness of children were not matters of state policy. One of the assumptions of the modern welfare state is that the same family values apply to rich and poor alike, and it can perhaps be said that a lot of the disagreement about welfare policy is about whether the policies themselves create a difference between rich and poor. The hierarchical societies of the past had no such worries. They had avowedly different ways of dealing with upper-class families and lower-class families, paying attention to them and ignoring them in different ways.

For most of the period we are looking at, the legal systems of all states were involved in family matters simply by being involved in the registration and enforcement of contracts. As we have seen, written contracts were in many places a much more prominent feature of marriage and inheritance than they are today. There were also laws about how property could be disposed of, laws that affirmed certain norms of marriage arrangements, dowries, and the devolution of property to subsequent generations. Although the formation of marriage was at first a private or at least a religious matter, the state's role grew. A late-seventeenth-century French treatise justified the state's role in marriage on the ground that families were "the columns on which the state rests and the seminaries of its subjects."[32] Most of the laws on marriage in this period were aimed at strengthening the control of parents. When England in the eighteenth century finally abandoned the old canon law that permitted so-called clandestine marriages, it was after years of debate about the danger of too much freedom for young people. Behind that lay a concern about protecting the wealthy and powerful. The danger was misalliance, as the preambles to several French marriage laws made abundantly clear.

The state acted as the ally of families in the top layers of society, whose needs were seen as identical with those of the state. As the French Edict on Second Marriages of 1560 put it, "The desolation of good families [causes] the diminution of the strength of the state."[33] The preamble to a late-eighteenth-century North Carolina law abolishing entail made a point of rejecting the long-established idea that "good" families should have a special role: "The wealth and importance of particular families [gives] them an unequal and undue influence in a republic."[34] An instance of unequal and undue influence is the way the French monarchy in the eighteenth century cooperated with certain families by means of the infamous *lettres de cachet*. Normal judicial procedures were dispensed with to avoid embarrassment, and troublesome individuals who threatened the reputation of important families or who refused to accept the authority of family heads, usually in marital matters, were put under lock and key by a special royal writ. The state assumed the role of guarding the honor of families (that is, the traditional values of important kinship groups) and not the rights of individuals.

When the state intervened in lower-class families it seemed to operate under a different set of assumptions. It is not so easy to decipher what they were, but they did not include a general concept of "family." Instead, the state tried to keep children alive one way or another, by providing charity to parents or by placing children in institutions. In both France and England help was given to people "surcharged with children" and, as we have seen, to children without parents. It was, after all, necessary to have a large number of hewers and tillers. A booming population was supposed to be the sign of a happy, prosperous society. In spite of the burden of poor relief, writers in the seventeenth and eighteenth centuries continued to equate small populations with poverty and large populations with wealth. One French writer after another in the eighteenth century deplored what he believed to be a decline in the birth rate, uncertain whether this was a sign of his country's moral failings or its economic weakness. Thomas Malthus of course had other ideas. In any case, state intervention in the affairs of poor families had to do with numbers and procreation, not honor and corporate identity.

States in the past neglected some aspects of the family almost entirely. They had no interest in the upbringing of children, except for some concern about preventing the growth of heresy and helping those in danger of starving or becoming beggars. When families broke up, as they so often did, no judge or social agency provided guidelines for the placement of the children. Disputes about a child's custody (in a divorce case, say, or after the death of a father who belonged to a prestigious family) tended to be resolved without considering the child's happiness or some principle such as a child's need to be with its mother. Internal household discipline was no concern of the state, either, even when it was extremely harsh. This was one of the respects in which household heads were absolute monarchs. Laws supported their authority when it was threatened by insubordination, but victims of domestic tyranny were relatively unprotected. Abused wives went to court throughout these centuries, but even when a string of neighbors testified to recurrent acts of cruelty, courts tended to send the women back to their husbands with pious wishes that things would improve. Public attitudes to cruel masters and abusive parents were rather complex, but the state was expected to remain aloof.

Some traces of the *values* that underly present-day policies can be found in the past, but they had nothing to do with politics, which was bound up in blatant class bias and reverence for authority. The whole notion of "family policy" has changed radically.

Active Households or Passive Households

Politically speaking, households can have both active and passive functions. In the United States today households are not assigned a political function that can be called active. When we say a family has political power we usually mean that individuals in politically important positions happen to be related to each other, or else that an economically powerful kinship group has an influence on politics. Households are irrelevant to our notions of political power, but they are not totally irrelevant in politics, since they have passive political functions. The word household appears on income-tax returns, in census data, and in welfare legislation. In the past, by contrast, the household had a number of active political functions. In these as in so much else, status made a difference. A handful of households at the top of the social scale exercised most of the active political power. Still, the notion that a household could play an active political role was present on all social levels.

Since the household was regarded as the fundamental unit of society (something on which theory and practice were in agreement), it was a common habit of thought to bypass individuals and speak of society as consisting only of households. When anyone wanted to know the population of a political jurisdiction, it was natural to count by households. Being counted is still one of the household's passive political functions. Unfortunately for historians, the way that was done in the centuries before 1800 often yielded only the number of "hearths," with no explicit clue to the number of persons around each hearth. There may have been common assumptions about the size of households, but we know neither what they were nor whether they bore any relationship to reality. In his *Utopia* Thomas More pursued the notion of a society of evenly matched households to a logical extreme: "That the city neither be depopulated nor grow beyond measure, provision is made that no household shall have fewer than ten or more than sixteen adults. . . . This limit is easily observed by transferring those who exceed the number in larger families into those that are under the prescribed number."[35] Nobody pretended that real households were evenly matched, but counting by households remained the rule, even after due consideration was given to the actual numbers within households. Gregory King, a remarkably acute observer of the economic and social fabric of England in 1696, spoke only of households and considered it worth his while to estimate the normal size of households on various social levels as an aid to grasping the dimensions of society. When census takers in eighteenth-century France referred to "inhabitants," they meant heads of households, all others being grouped under them.

Taxes were almost always assessed by household. They were sometimes based on the size of the house, sometimes on the number of people in the house, and sometimes on household income. In almost every case the person liable for the tax was the household head and no one else. It is because of the tax collectors' diligence in counting that we have such a good idea of what households were like in certain parts of Europe, the most notable example being Florence and its surrounding territory in the fifteenth century, to which I have alluded several times.

The notion that society was made up of households also accounted for their active role. While some political theory concerned itself only with rule from above and assumed that households were only passive objects of that rule, other theory and most practice recognized a more complex interaction. The significant figure in this interaction was, again, the household head. The household was embodied in its head. On the lowest level of politics, in many country villages, every household had a voice and, when the occasion arose, a vote—but always through its head. Being a household head was more important than being a father or even a man, since widows who were household heads sometimes participated in community decisions. Traces of this pattern are detectable in France at the time of the calling of the Estates General in 1789. The voting law varied according to locality, providing for general male suffrage in many places, but in other places the vote was limited to heads of households, some of whom were women.

On the higher levels of society, the household had a number of other political functions. More than metaphorically it was a miniature state. The relationship of peasants to their lord in a manor or seigniory was not very different in kind from the master-servant relationship, however different it may have been in detail. Many lords presided over courts that heard local civil and criminal cases. This political power that came with lordship was often acquired simply by buying and occupying a house and an estate that comprised a political jurisdiction. It was more important politically to be the head of a particular household than to have the right ancestors.

Household symbolism was assiduously cultivated. Every château, country house, town mansion, and palazzo was a political statement, by virtue of its location, its size, and its magnificence. Fortified castles and battle-ready towers disappeared in this period, but the symbolism of buildings was as strong as ever. Louis XIV saw a political threat in the lavish expenditure that Nicolas Fouquet made on his house and gardens at Vaux-le-Vicomte. In the end, Fouquet's symbolic political power, strong as it was, could not protect him against the superior power of a real king. The livery worn by the superabundance of servants in great houses was descended from the livery of earlier armed retainers and was as much a political symbol as the coats of arms it was based on or a country's flag. The dedication to largesse and hospitality of the rich and powerful was a way of affirming their status as well as of gathering adherents. Newly created cardinals in Rome as a matter of course set about building palazzos and putting on expensive entertainments, to which they invited both local dignitaries and important foreign visitors. Even if a cardinal's kinship with the pope was all he had to start with, he could build a considerable "house" of his own on that basis. "The more authority a Gentleman hath in the shier, the more is the resort unto him," said an Englishman in 1579.[36] A century later another Englishman, pining for the good old days, summed up the political significance of the great household in the most benign terms: "Every Nobleman's House in the Country was like the Court of a Prince, and every moderate Gentleman's Hospitality was Noble; when they were highly respected by their subordinate Neighbors and their united Hearts able and willing to do God and their Country better service."[37]

Size had something to do with it. Although the present-day nostalgia for the supposed big families of the past has almost nothing to do with the political role of the family, a case can be made that if there was any ideological commitment to big families in the past it had more to do with politics than with notions of personal happiness. To be poor and have a big family was to be "surcharged with children" and live on the brink of disaster. To be prosperous and have a big family was something else. A peasant with enough land to guarantee the future prosperity of a large number of sons (to take a very simple illustration) was someone to be reckoned with. The land and the sons together made him important in village politics. Large households, whether filled with children or with a variety of nonrelatives, were at the very heart of being rich and powerful. A fifteenth-century Florentine patrician said, "We pay salaries over the years to various strangers and feed and clothe servants, not because we wish only to take advantage of their services, but because we want to have more people in our house."[38] The number of inhabitants Gregory King assigned to the average household of a lord was forty. Greatness and bigness were easily assimilated to each other.

The biggest and most powerful households of all were those of kings. Just as the estates of lords were part of their households, so an entire realm could be thought of as an extension of the king's household. The royal household was the politically active household in its purest form, and the earliest bureaucracies were set up like household staffs. Nobody believed that the royal household was the only politically active one, however, no matter how much some absolutist theorists wished that it were so.

Good Family or No Family

"Family" has become more socially neutral than it used to be. Every family is potentially a good family. We may be a little vague about what "good" means, perhaps a little less vague about what a bad family is, but in either case we are not talking about politics. On the other hand, there is a whisper of an older political meaning attached to "good," an association with aristocracy, wealth, and prestige. People still speak of the "best" families in this old-fashioned way.

Almost everything we know about the ideology of the family in the past comes from those who possessed political power or were interested in possessing it. They were members of the "best" families and for them "family" was a word with political overtones. Whether people of lesser rank had similar ideas we are at a loss to say. The social system required the majority to behave as though they accepted "family" as an attribute of the few. To have a family was to be one of those who mattered. It went beyond having a mother and father and sisters and brothers and a roof over one's head. In other words, it had almost nothing to do with most of what this book is about. In the eyes of their contemporaries most people did not have families worth mentioning.

All the synonyms of "family" (house, line, casa, race) had the potential of meaning something privileged and powerful. A family was all the good things rolled into one: kin, property, honor, and ancestors.

Ancestors and blood kin were basic to the idea of family as good family. If you were lucky enough to be born with enough of the right sort you had it made, provided you upheld your side of the bargain, which was to act in the collectivity's interests. Yet birth was not the only way to have a family. You could acquire one by wealth and by reputation, which often went hand in hand. What you needed was a little patience, because it took time to build a family. You had to use your wealth and your talents to reach the point of seeming to rely on neither. Everyone knew how essential wealth was. *Familia, id est, substantia* ("Family, that is to say, wealth") was a truism among lawyers and a central family obligation was to watch over the upkeep and disposition of property. Making money directly in commerce and industry was a way of accumulating enough wealth to have a family. Using your talents was another. The seventeenth-century painter Georges de La Tour, for example, was the progenitor of a good provincial family whose members happily overlooked any artistic gifts that may have been passed on to them as they enjoyed the status the artist's work had helped to buy.[39] As the sixteenth-century English recipe for becoming a gentleman pointed out, you needed to be able to "live without manual labor," and there were a number of ways to attain that condition: law, the university, "physic and the liberal sciences," "service in the room of captain in the wars, or good counsell given at home, whereby [the] commonwealth is benefitted."[40] With the foundation of *substantia* it was already possible to be reckoned a family, but marriage alliances moved the process along. You proclaimed who you were by whom you married. And if you married into a long pedigree your son was in the enviable position of combining the two most secure attributes of a family: wealth and ancestors.

The notion that good families were important politically appears again and again in various political and legal documents, although not in the great theoretical works of Western political thought. The desolation of good families was said to cause "the diminution of the strength of the state." The image of families as columns on which the state rested was often invoked. The Spaniard Martín González de Cellorigo wrote in 1600: "The greatness of these realms is founded on great and illustrious houses, as if on great and immovable pedestals; if they were divided, the prop which supports the monarchy . . . would be lost."[41] The discussion of primogeniture thus took on a political cast. A French legal commentator pointed out that the "public interest is served by the conservation of families, the possessions of which should be conserved and distributed to the males, who uphold the splendor and dignity of the house whose name and arms they bear."[42]

The cooperation of king and good families implied in these statements was supposed to be enhanced by another function of families: they were not only "the columns on which the state rests" but also "the seminaries of its subjects." What these seminaries taught was obedience. "The natural reverence of children toward their parents is the bond of the legitimate obedience of subjects toward their sovereign," said a French royal decree in 1639.[43] The English Puritan William Gouge around the same time said, "A familie is . . . as a schoole wherein the first principles and grounds of government and subjection are learned."[44] Jean Bodin, claiming that the state was made up of families, said that if they were "well-governed" the state would function well.[45] The Connecticut writer James Lockwood in 1754 spoke of "the great Trust reposed in" the heads of families and confidently asserted that if "Family-Religion & Discipline were thoroughly . . . maintained . . . the Civil State would prosper and flourish from Generation to Generation."[46]

Several meanings of "good" are competing in these statements, as are several meanings of "family." Behind them can be discerned a yearning for social stability. In reality, great families did not always function as supports of the state in these centuries or provide models of good government and obedience. When great families got to be very powerful they were sometimes threats to the state's rule, and when great families were engaged in rivalry with each other they were threats to the state's tranquility. Not until well into the seventeenth century were such threats taken as anything but serious, and even as late as 1800 in places where blood feuds continued they needed to be taken as very serious. Nobody who thought about politics was likely to forget the role played by great families in the Wars of the Roses, the French religious wars, the Fronde, and the English Civil War. A practical ruler had little choice but to respect the families whose goodness could be measured by the extent to which they forbore to do the harm they were capable of.

From the point of view of those at the top, however that was defined, society consisted only of themselves. Everyone else was an accessory. Thomas More bewailed the fact that the nobodies seemed to accept the role of accessories. The common people, he said, had been brought up to cherish a system of inherited privilege in which the dazzling attributes of the nobility were "the true glories of the commonwealth." Among those attributes were of course the greatness and goodness of their families, and the lower orders seemed to be just as impressed by "quality" as the quality themselves were.

In the microsocieties that were not usually noticed by those at the top the same dynamics may have been at work. Village and parish politics was dominated by certain families, which seem to have had something of the wealth and continuity that characterized good families. Large numbers of people may have accepted an ideology of the family that put them in the position of having no families and excluded them from politics at any level. The best evidence for this supposition is the path that ambition so often took. In villages and cities alike men seemed to turn their attention to acquiring families as soon as they were in a position to do so. If we could peek into the fantasy life of peasants and servants and laborers in the past we would be better able to say how much they shared with their betters the idea that "family" went along with privilege. We might begin by thinking about those fairy tales in which peasants marry princesses.

Aristotle gave no place to ancestors in his political theory and was followed by a stream of theorists who did not quite know what to do about them. It was possible to think about politics and the family in the past without considering any definition other than "household." But what stands out in the political life of these centuries is the ideological use that people with political power made of all aspects of the family. The elite took pride in their families. It was the elite who could count their ancestors—count them and name them—while ordinary persons were lucky if they knew their grandfathers' names. The elite punished those who injured their family honor. Their homes were centers and symbols of power. And those who craved political power seemed to know that it had to comprise all these things.

This ideology took a long time to change, but by now it seems barely comprehensible, especially in a New World whose leaders have generally made a virtue of rejecting it. Our own ideology of the family is no longer one in which a political role is prominent.

1 2

The Emotional Role
of the Family

Today the emotional role of the family receives most attention. Things that could be done by other institutions (like feeding, sheltering, and "socializing" the young) are said to be done by the family in such a distinctive way that not to grow up in a family is to be deprived of something vital to emotional health. Even people who may not think that families are necessarily good pay them the tribute of blaming them for a great deal of psychological damage.

I am including in the emotional role of the family everything that its political role is not: how families affect individuals rather than what families as collectivities do in society. Every aspect of the family that I have described so far, from household tasks to the inheritance of property, had an emotional component, and I have said something about emotional responses to circumstances and rules, in particular the contradictory and mixed responses that come under the heading of ambivalence. This chapter is about *ideas*, ideas about feelings associated with the family.

Most institutions (army, school, church, political party) have two emotional aspects. They are the settings for emotional events, but they are also abstractions that, as ideas, awaken emotional responses. A family is a setting for personal relationships, for the acquisition of habits and values, and for pleasant or unpleasant activities. "The family," whether it means every family or just your family or my family, is an abstraction that calls forth feelings of veneration or loathing, of acceptance or rejection.

The atmosphere nowadays seems to be saturated with ideas about the family. We come across them in odd places, like a newspaper obituary of the head of a large corporation: "In a very real sense, everybody in the auto industry is part of the same family, sharing the same dreams and challenges and fighting the same battles in the competitive arena that is today's marketplace.

That family lost one of its leading members today."[1] Whatever that means, it is assuredly a statement about emotions, about how people in families feel. "Family" is constantly used as a metaphor. Although, as with so many emotive words, the meaning is vague, I venture to say that most of us think we get the drift.

With metaphorical uses of "family" in the past we feel less sure that we are getting the drift. We are on uncertain ground partly because the emotional role of the family was not thought of as its only role. The main reason, however, is that after 1800 a new ideology of the family came into being that blotted out most of the older ideas and ideals and altered the significance of those that remained. Among the most prominent features of this ideology is nostalgia. Family values are said to be old-fashioned, even timeless, and are assumed to derive from what the family was like before industrialization and its attendant ills. For anyone who wants to know what ideas of the family were really current in the centuries before 1800 this is a formidable challenge.

It takes a leap of historical imagination to see a world in which the new ideology was taking shape but had not yet crystallized. We are at the mercy of evidence supplied in almost every case by privileged, articulate people. There is a possibility that the gulf between "good families" and other families was particularly wide when it came to the way their emotional role was perceived. It is tempting to speculate that lower-class ideas about the family were more recognizably modern than upper-class ones, even though the first evidence of such ideas is in upper-class written sources. Until we can make the inarticulate speak, we are limited to the ideas of a rather small group. We can console ourselves by saying that its influence was greater than its size, but that is only an assumption. No one knows for sure how such ideas travel.

Home or House

The word "home" packs such an emotional punch today that sellers of real estate use it to refer to empty buildings. Most of us know better. We say a home is a place with a family in it. It is the emotive synonym for household, summing up almost everything we mean when we say "family." Almost but not quite. There is hardly anyone who would not also include kin outside the household in his or her idea of family. "House" is an old-fashioned word for this, a wonderfully ambiguous word related to the symbolic value of prestigious households. It is not much used today, but there are still significant emotions attached to relatives we do not live with, even distantly connected ones, ones no longer alive, and ones we have never met. It is not always clear what is meant when someone says "I love my family" or "I am proud of my family." Ambiguity keeps clinging stubbornly to the word.

The words "house" and "home" are a shorthand for two ways of thinking about the family, but it needs to be pointed out that they did not go through history as a pair. "House" is almost a dead word, used today only to refer to things grand and historical. People in the past did not use "home" in the emotionally loaded way we do. The Romance languages do not even have an equivalent word for "home" and have to call other words into service for expressing the modern concept.

As I am using the words, "home" is a specific place that can be measured and described, containing a finite number of occupants, all known to each other. It cannot last, because people are born, move out, and die, and even the exteriors and interiors of buildings change with fortune or fashions. A "house," on the other hand, is as close to being intangible as anything made up of people can be. It extends backward and forward in time and has no spatial limits. Its members, even all its living members at any given moment, do not necessarily know each other. It is not surprising that two such different entities evoke different emotional responses. As an abstraction, "home" has a familiar emotive power, but the emotive power of "house" is all but forgotten. One reason why "house" is archaic today is that the values and feelings associated with home have come to dominate the way people think about kinship.

It is hard to pin down when this change in attitude took place. In the nineteenth century the articulate elite were still writing about "house," though with a difference: they were less likely to be thinking of that concept when they used the word "family" instead. There is some debate among historians about whether this was a typically nonaristocratic, and hence "bourgeois," attitude or whether it started in the aristocracy and trickled down. Although there is a neat logic to the notion that aristocrats would cling to the values of lineage ("house") longer than those without much of a house to call their own, certain influences on the aristocracy in the eighteenth century interfered with the neatness of that logic. The fashionable ideas of the Enlightenment, for one thing, encouraged the appreciation of domestic expressions of intimacy, spontaneity, and individuality. A shift assuredly took place, but it is not clear how and why.

One characteristic of home is that a person experiences it directly and on a daily basis. Feelings about it are apt to be on a fairly small, intimate scale. The idea that a family is people who know each other well and have deep feelings about each other is such a cliché today it may be hard to believe that it was rarely expressed in earlier times. Thomas More may have been talking about it when he described some of the economic arrangements in Utopia: "Those who have given out of their stock to any particular city without requiring any return from it receive what they lack from another to which they have given nothing. Thus, the whole island is like a single family."[2] He could have been thinking of close relations in a household—but not necessarily. Our impulse is to assume that More must have meant what we would mean, especially since we know that most people had the experience of living in small, closely knit households. Actually, it was not until much later that less ambiguous statements about the emotional quality of home life began to appear.

In the eighteenth century Rousseau and Diderot liked to contrast the wholesome joys of parenthood and domesticity with the licentiousness of which they accused their contemporaries. When couples late in the century had an opportunity to record their reasons for wanting to marry, they conjured up images of domestic happiness and contentment that were missing from such declarations in earlier years. Some historians have suggested that a real change in domestic life was responsible for this change of attitude, but (as in the case of the attitude toward babies) we should not discount the possibility that certain feelings had existed for a long time without finding voice in the sort of writing we are forced to rely on. In the sixteenth century, for example, priests were for the first time being advised in confessors' handbooks to pay attention to the obligations of parents to young children; before then the emphasis had been on the duties of children to parents. Yet we know very well that, for laymen, concern for young children was not a new idea in the sixteenth century.

Although it is fairly certain that people had strong ideas about the feelings members of a household should have for each other, there was a paucity of general ideas about this before the eighteenth century. More's remark may be a hint of what was going on in people's minds. He may indeed have meant household ("home"), not kinship, in this passage, since he usually used the word "family" to mean household. Perhaps, too, the founders of religious sects in the sixteenth and seventeenth centuries were reflecting ideas about the closeness and immediacy of home life when they decided to call themselves the Family of Love, the Church of the Brethren, the Moravian Brethren, and the Children of Light.

Since groups of any kind, especially small ones, tended to organize themselves along the lines of households, we may infer that certain ideas were abroad about the benefits of doing so. Almost nothing was said about these benefits, however, so we can only speculate. It may be that households were considered efficient. The ideal household head was almost invariably described as a good manager whose account books were in order and whose subordinates obeyed him. An even stronger idea may have been that of inevitability or naturalness. Or perhaps the impulse to reproduce the household was based on a craving for what was familiar and, for that reason, comfortable. When general ideas about the warmth and comfort of home began to emerge in the eighteenth century, they were also applied to institutions that resembled households, but we cannot be certain that such ideas existed before they were expressed. Indeed, the impulse to organize along household lines seems to have become weaker just as people were giving more conscious thought to home as a unique center of the emotions, set off from the rest of the world.

The tendency to follow the household model persisted through the eighteenth century, however. The form of the early textile industry was an outgrowth of both artisans' workshops in town and cottage industry in the country. Schools tried to be like homes. The Quaker founders of a new school for poor children in London in the eighteenth century said that the pupils were to dress alike and think of themselves as one family. They said they wanted social differences to be overlooked.[3] Family meant equality to them: the venerable notion that all the children in a family were equal.

Naturalness and inevitability implied that being part of a household was a necessity. In the past the oddness of being a loner could be fraught with danger, especially if one were old, poor, and female. That may sound like a familiar contemporary problem, but I am talking about ideas, about suspicion and fear, not lack of food and shelter. In the heyday of witchcraft persecution (starting in the fifteenth century and climaxing in the late seventeenth century) unattached women were particularly suspect. It was all too easy to think that a woman without a husband and deprived of a father's supervision was, in the sort of family metaphor that sprang so readily to people's lips, married to the devil. Anyone who wanted a place in society on any level had to locate herself or himself in a household. Not that it had to be a permanent home, just a structure of which he or she was a part for the time being.

When we turn from hard-to-find ideas about "home" to ideas about "house" we have plenty to look at. "House" was a subject that came up often. The only book I know of in this 450-year span that purports to be about the *family*—not marriage, not household management, not fatherhood—was written by a Florentine patrician obsessed with the status of his lineage. Leon Battista Alberti wrote *Della famiglia* in the early fifteenth century. His purpose, he said, was "to investigate carefully what exalts and ennobles families."[4] When one of the interlocutors in his dialogue asks the chief speaker what he means by family, the answer is, "Children, wife, other relatives, retainers, and servants."[5] This comes just as he is about to launch into advice on running a household. Most of the work is not about the household, however; three of its four books are about entirely different things. The fourth book, on friendship, is often published separately because editors consider it unrelated to the rest. I am not so sure that it is. It says a lot about how the choice of the right friends can advance family interests. The "family" that gets most of Alberti's attention is big. It is bigger than life, on a completely different scale from the prosaic interactions of the household. It is definitely a "house," a large group of men (no women in Alberti) with the same surname who share a history and a reputation. If you want to learn about the correct thoughts and feelings of someone who belonged to a "good family," consult Alberti. Members of good families in the eighteenth century saw themselves much as he saw himself. When they talked about their houses they also employed grandiloquent language, using words like "greatness," "splendor," "dignity," "honor," and "glory."

Feelings of pride and a deep sense of obligation to this awe-inspiring institution were expressed over and over in memoirs, letters, and wills. The French nobleman who accepted "the onerous condition of bishop" because he saw the need to contribute to "the fortune, the honor, and the good of our house" was stating a commonplace. Alberti has a character in his book say, "Members of our family always returned [from tournaments] with great honors and praise. . . . Just think how pleased I was to see the favor our Alberti family justly enjoyed," and he adds how much he wanted "to go forth with the others and be admired and praised."[6] In another place someone exclaims, "It is my duty to do everything within my power, even risk my own life, for the honor of our house and our family."[7]

Underlying these feelings were two ideas about kinship: the tie of kinship was unique and kinship was permanent. Almost never stated overtly, these ideas appeared again and again. There is a possibility (at least, the little evidence we have does not rule it out) that people lower down the social scale had these ideas, too, since they could be attached to kinship without necessarily being associated with great wealth or political power.

Kinship was unique because it was a biological tie. As members of noble families were always saying, what counted was blood. Being born with a family's blood was what made one a member, and nothing could change that. It was a concrete physical fact that was at the same time mystical. We still say "Blood is thicker than water" and understand why people protect unworthy relatives. "Never believe your own relatives will deceive you," says someone in Della famiglia. "Is there a member of your family who would not rather deal with you than with strangers?" That is as it should be, he says. "It is more useful and praiseworthy to do good to your own family than to strangers."[8] When the subject of affection among kin comes up, Alberti's interlocutor compares it to "the warmth and affection one feels among his fellow-citizens [, which] is greater than that which one feels among foreigners."[9] Is this perhaps a ray of domestic warmth creeping in? Is he talking about familiarity? Not really. He says, "The light of glory and prestige will shine more brightly for one who is in the midst of his family, feared and trusted for many reasons, than for one who is alone or in the company of strangers." There is not much logic in Alberti. He keeps saying kinship is special because it is special. But his conviction was deep. This widely shared conviction may have been what led men to borrow the aura of kinship for their brotherhoods and fraternities and the church to create the spiritual kinship of godparentage. Deep down, however, everyone recognized that there was only one real kinship, the one that alone had the virtue of being sealed by blood.

Because blood flowed from the past and into the future, kinship could seem to transcend time. It had a permanence that was precious in a world of corruption and decay. Being part of a continuum was something members of great houses often talked about. "Preserving the family" was a recurrent phrase. It meant doing everything possible to keep up a house's wealth, reputation, and numbers. The glory of individuals became part of the permanent glory of the house. "We do not marry for ourselves, whatever we say," said Montaigne. "We marry just as much or more for our posterity, for our family."[10] Someone in Della famiglia says to a bachelor kinsman, "It will be very harmful to our family if it does not have the many children it expects from you. I think one should suffer all discomforts and inconveniences rather than allow the family to be reduced to just a few members and have no one to take the father's place and name."[11]

There is more than a trace of anxiety in these exhortations to think of the house's future. Permanence was comforting, but it required eternal vigilance—too much vigilance, in the eyes of some religious men, who were afraid that the emotional commitment to preserving families showed an insufficient trust in God. "It is not good to be too solicitous in . . . thinking to perpetuate a man's name and family," said Sir Hugh Cholmley in the seventeenth-century, as he observed the growing practice of fixing lines of inheritance far into the future. "God gave lands to men and if men could make lands continue in their families for ever this would be a stop to the providence of God."[12] Men in all walks of life were trying to do just that—make lands continue in their families forever.

People in the past had much more to say about "house" than about "home." There was barely a glimmer of the emotional aspect of home that we know so well. The mystical power of kinship did not color the picture of the household, which in its ideal form was depicted rather as an efficient provider of shelter, food, and certain kinds of instruction. The ideal house, on the other hand, was the carrier of values of the most highly charged sort: antiquity, honor, and dignity. Kinship on a smaller scale, that within the dimensions of the household, was generally overlooked when writers in the past waxed enthusiastic about the family.

Religion in the Family or Religion of the Family

The association of religion with the family is an ancient one. People today who promote what they consider the values of religion talk a lot about family values. When religion loomed larger in most people's lives, it pervaded ways of thinking about every event and every institution. In a sense, the religious role of the family was its emotional role. It was the one most often articulated and it was expressed in behavior as well, especially symbolic behavior. People spoke about religious activities that took place in the household, but they also spoke about religious views of the family: the theology of the family, as it were. Beyond that, some of them spoke of the family as the quasi-religious object of a cult of its own.

Christianity as an organized religion has not always had a harmonious relationship with the family. Unlike Judaism, it kept almost no rituals that took place in private homes. The esteem that monasticism and priestly celibacy enjoyed implied a denigration of marriage and parenthood. One of the battlegrounds in the struggle between the church and lay rulers in the Middle Ages had been the family, the regulation of marriage in particular. The church's view, culminating in the official recognition of marriage as the seventh sacrament in 1439, was that laymen should not be guided by the expedients of dynastic strategy, marrying close relatives as they wished and divorcing them when more advantageous alliances presented themselves. The medieval struggle continued in a more muted form through the sixteenth, seventeenth, and eighteenth centuries. The will of a wealthy Florentine in 1508, for example, expressed a fear that, through the action of some devout heir, his family wealth might fall into the hands of a "monastery or church."[13] Something of a change came with the confessional split of the Reformation, since Protestants claimed to have a positive view of marriage and the family. The Catholic view at the time was actually not very different. The absorption of marriage into the sacramental structure of the church carried an implication of the family's spiritual nature, and in practice the Catholic clergy took at least as great an interest in family relations as the Protestant clergy did. In spite of the continued value placed on monasticism in Catholic countries, there was a widespread feeling throughout the Western world that the family was a Christian institution.

The writings of clergymen may be full of professional bias, but they were widely sold and read, not only by other clergymen but also by serious, literate laymen, and so are good sources for ideas about the family. Here are the titles of some seventeenth-century English books intended as manuals for household heads: *The Practice of Piety, Carter's Christian Commonwealth, A Godly Form of Household Government, A Christian Family Builded by God,* and *The Whole Duty of Man.* The last, published in 1658, was a best-seller well into the next century.

It was generally agreed that the family was divinely sanctioned. Sacrament or no sacrament, the blessings of God were bestowed on every legitimate marriage. Ordinary people were no strangers to this idea, which was reflected in the reason some French couples gave for wanting to marry. They often used the phrase "the glory of God and their salvation." "Holy matrimony" was an institution filled with great spiritual potential. It was in the religious context that the clearest statements were made about the desirability of having many children. Saint Augustine had said that the first "good" of marriage was children—a sturdy idea that managed to survive alongside other notions about what made marriage valuable. A Puritan minister in the early seventeenth century stated the matter baldly, saying that the larger the family the more the parents had been blessed by God.[14] The Anglican liturgy of churching included the words, "Children are an heritage and gift that cometh of the Lord. Happy is the man that hath his quiver full of them."[15] Mindful of this, an Englishwoman in 1762, expecting her twelfth child, wrote, "I have resolved not to grumble! After all, are not my pretty babes a blessing?"[16]

Sanctioned by God though it was, the family was not intrinsically so holy that it would inevitably promote religious values. There was little veneration of the family in what clergymen wrote. Instead, they treated the family as an opportunity given by God for promoting Christianity. One seventeenth-century title, *The Protestant Monastery,* encapsulated the notion that all Christians, not only those in religious orders, could pursue a life of piety and prayer. The Protestant monastery was the household. A well-run, decent household was also a place of prayer. In spite of the implied attack on Catholic values, this idea was embraced in only a slightly different form by the clergy in Catholic countries as well. Everyday life had always been punctuated by pious gestures, and in the period of the Reformation, which included the parallel Catholic movement that some call the Counter Reformation, a great emphasis was put on the father's role as a religious leader and on daily prayer in the household. The twentieth-century dictum "The family that prays together stays together" shows how much the idea of family prayer has changed, having become a way to strengthen the bonds between close relatives. In the seventeenth and eighteenth centuries the idea was rather that the family that prayed together *prayed.* Prayer was not an instrument for holding families together. The family was an instrument for promoting prayer.

Ben Jonson in the seventeenth century sang the praises of the country seat called Penshurst, where the children

> are, and have beene, taught religion. Thence
>   Their gentler spirits have suck'd innocence.
> Each morne, and even, they are taught to pray,
>   With the whole household, and may, every day,
> Read in their vertuous parents noble parts,
>   The mysteries of manners, armes, and arts.[17]

The home as a place for raising children, which is so familiar an idea to us, appears here in its typical premodern guise. Children would learn how to be good adults by being taught religion and imitating the virtues of their parents. The ideal parent was a paragon of virtue. A German manual for household heads, published as late as 1807, was still declaring that the father "is the model of every manly virtue, so that all the male occupants of the household have only to observe him to develop in the noblest and manliest way possible."[18]

The idea of the household as the setting for religious worship and instruction was in perfect harmony with the dominant Catholic and Protestant thought of the time. "Family" in this case was the family-as-household and servants were supposed to be included with relatives in these activities. Kinship was not what mattered.

But kinship did matter, and it was linked with religion in ways that were less in harmony with the religion that the clergy represented. The disharmony was not terribly noticeable because there had been so many accommodations with Christianity, but a certain intensity of feeling betrayed the continued existence of this different kind of religious commitment. The Englishman who worried about the lack of reliance on God's providence seemed to sense it.

Members of families that could call themselves houses had religious feelings about their families. If religion means worship and ceremony, there was, for one thing, the cult of ancestors. Something very like the worship of these dead took place in the church itself. There was a proliferation of family chapels, always known by the families' names. Because of the families' expenditure on their decoration, especially in art-conscious Florence, some of their names are known to tourists today: Brancacci, Gondi, Strozzi, Pazzi. The funerary monuments of the family members buried in them were highly visible. Alberti, ever mindful of the family even when writing on architecture, said, "Care ought to be taken of the dead body, for the sake of the living, and for the preservation of the name to posterity, there can be no means more effectual than sepulchres."[19] A certain Lord Lumley filled a church in Nottingham with a row of recumbent effigies, extending from the Saxon founder of his house down to his own father.[20] Such an all-out effort, which required faking a few ancestors, was not unique.

The same lord also made the hall of his castle a family shrine. It was hung with fifteen specially painted portraits of his ancestors, pride of place going to the Saxon founder, represented by an equestrian statue in full armor. On the wall was an inscription: "Worship not that which passes away."[21] Lord Lumley was probably impervious to irony; the memory of his ancestors was not going to pass away if he could help it. Every noble castle and every princely palace had its portrait gallery, with the pictures usually arranged in chronological order, like a genealogical chart. Vasari tells us that in Florence there was a custom of making "inexpensive casts of the heads of those who died; and so one can see in every house . . . , over the chimneypieces, doors, windows, and cornices, endless examples of such portraits, so well-made and natural that they seem alive."[22]

Christians prayed for the souls of the dead, especially their own dead. Those in a position to do so ordered masses for the dead to be said in church, a practice that grew to such proportions by the sixteenth century that it came under attack by those who called for church reform. Some masses were established for all the ancestors of a particular house, confounding the Christian concern for individual souls with veneration of a family.

These were not the only forms of ancestor worship. People carefully preserved the names of their ancestors, breathing new life into them as they bestowed them on the newborn. They preserved the memory of ancestors by drawing up genealogies that were sometimes fleshed out in family memoirs with accounts of ancestors' deeds and words, which the writers usually claimed were intended as models of behavior for the living but in which the hagiographic tone often overshadowed the practical didactic intent.

Ancestor worship called forth many emotions. One, of course, was pride in being part of something that had political and social power. Even deeper feelings were connected with the quest for immortality, which participants in the religion of the family pursued on a track separate from Christian doctrine.

A fifteenth-century Florentine said, "Men desire sons, grandsons, and descendants to attain immortality in their seed."[23] This simple statement by a Renaissance admirer of the pagan classics sounds as if it is about biology. But in fact men expected their descendants to preserve not only their seed but also their memory. Edward Gibbon said, in the cool tones of the Enlightenment, "A lively desire of knowing and of recording our ancestors so generally prevails that it must depend on the influence of some common principle in the minds of men. We seem to have lived in the persons of our forefathers; it is the labor and reward of vanity to extend the term of this ideal longevity."[24] It was a terrible threat indeed when some relatives said to an old man who was about to disinherit them, "As thou treatest us in life so shall we treat thy memory after death!"[25] The author of Della famiglia, who never married and had no direct descendants, concluded the preface to his book with an emotional appeal to the "young Albertis": "Pay heed to what our fathers, most learned, erudite, and refined men, thought ought to be done . . . for our family. Read my work and love me."[26]

Sharing the same ancestors created something like a religious bond among living blood relatives. If, along with worship and ceremony, religion means sacrifice and communion, the family had its own web of sacred obligations. By participating in the cult of their ancestors, kinsmen shared a responsibility to give the dead their due and appease their ghosts, of whom there was a genuine fear that was fairly common. The powerful feelings evoked by the dead were colored by ambivalence; it was not always easy to distinguish adulation from fear. Family plots in cemeteries were a relatively late development that provided to those lower down on the social scale a less costly version of the family chapel.

People claimed to be guided by a spirit of selflessness when it came to furthering the welfare of their relatives and preserving a heritage for posterity. Like individual persons, individual conjugal units were of less importance than the house. This seems to have been the most common sentiment uttered about the family. It was an idea that justified a passionate pursuit of honor and wealth. Women and men alike were supposed to make sacrifices for the good of the house. Adultery of either husband or wife may have been a Christian sin, but the adultery of a wife was considered a heinous crime against the honor of a house, and in a strange way the whole mighty structure rested precariously on what was seen as the fragile character of women. Self-sacrifice apparently gave meaning to people's lives, even though we have every right to believe that hypocrisy, too, was widespread. The young bishop who dreamt of being a knight of Malta was not the only one who believed that his own ambitions were trivial compared to the needs of his family. Many a younger son accepted the unpleasant necessity of deferring to a sole heir. When the inheritance laws of the Massif Central region were changed during the French Revolution, many of the intended beneficiaries were apparently unconvinced that it was an improvement and colluded in schemes to assure that patrimonies would remain intact instead of being shared among several heirs as the law intended.[27]

A religious aura surrounded the family in the past, both the aura of official religion and the aura of beliefs that rivaled it in intensity. Apart from a stray remark like Joan of Arc's about how her mother had taught her to pray, we have no clue to whether the mass of people perceived any such aura, however. It was the assumption of sentimental artists late in the period that the humble peasant's abode was a haven of piety as it was supposed to be (hardly reliable evidence). Ordinary people were exposed to the mysteries and glories of kinship as it applied to good families and even had a little share in it when they wore the livery of those families or received largesse from them, but we do not know whether they had similar beliefs about their own families.

Individual Relationships or Standard Roles

Our experiences in families seem to be intensely personal. Each relationship with another family member has its own unique mixture of positive and negative feelings, of contacts and avoidances. At the same time, none of us are oblivious to the requirements of family roles. Fathers are supposed to act one way, brothers another. When a father says, "I'm a big brother to my son," or a girl says, "My mother and I are really like sisters," they are recognizing norms in the very act of tampering with them.

The emotional significance of the family has come to reside more and more in personal interactions rather than the feelings and beliefs connected with the religious aspect of the family that we have just looked at. A feeling not unlike religious emotion, based on an extremely positive view of these interactions, has come to the fore.

> And here being thus together,
> We are an endless mine to one another;
> We are one another's wife, ever begetting
> New births of love; we are father, friends, acquaintance;
> We are, in one another, families.
> I am your heir and you are mine. This place
> Is our inheritance.[28]

This is Shakespeare in *The Two Noble Kinsmen*, sounding rather modern in his only reference to "family" that is not political. He seems to be saying that a family is an assortment of individuals tied to each other by frequent contact and a shared concern about the future ("I am your heir"). Nothing here about power, public image, glory of ancestors. In their adversity the speaker must rely on his cousin as he would on the people in his household, his near relations, and his neighbors. The "friends" and "acquaintances" are perhaps not so modern, since they represent the intrusion of nonkin, but this passage comes about as close as anything in the early seventeenth century to a general statement about the emotional significance of the family. The passage operates on the small scale of personal interactions and embraces household and kin without distinction.

Using the word "family" when talking about such things was as rare in the past as it is common today, although talking about them was not rare. Ideas about family roles were constantly being expressed. Whether the subject was a nonspecific role like "kinsman" or a specific one like "father," "brother," "wife," and so on, it was freighted with expectations that were for the most part good, although there were some roles of which the worst seemed to be expected: "stepmother," for example. Expectations formed the basis for a wide range of emotional responses. At one extreme was the possibility of fulfillment and delight, at the other the possibility of disappointment and rage.

This is the stuff of literature, the split between appearance and reality, ideals and behavior. Imaginative literature in the Western world has often dealt with family relationships, and in dramatic literature from the sixteenth century on the distortion of family roles was a favorite subject. Dramatists and poets can tell us, if anyone can, what people thought about the emotional role of the family. I rely mainly on Shakespeare, on the assumption that his large output and wide, lasting appeal are something of a guarantee of the currency of his ideas. If Shakespeare had not been as interested as he was in how family members behaved to each other, we probably would not be reading him still. Like so many other writers in these centuries, he perceived the whole world as a tissue of family relationships. I am not advocating that we read him or any of his literary contemporaries as a reliable source of realistic observations. Rather, he is a mine of ideas, all presented with emotional coloring—exactly what we are looking for.

There is another class of writing, less enjoyable to read, that can be considered together with imaginative literature. It comprises the normative statements about family roles in religious confessors' handbooks, advice to householders, moral polemics, and educational theory. I have already referred to works of this sort from time to time. They can help us interpret the literary work, often by drawing our attention to the fact that literary works focused on some relationships to which the advice-givers paid little attention. Toward the end of the period there was an increasing abundance of another kind of writing: personal letters and diaries. They show us people in the midst of playing family roles, responding to them, and even from time to time telling us what they thought about them.

What emerges from all these sources does not add up to a full-blown ideology, like the ideology that appeared in the period after 1800, which assumed that a family was centered on a romantically involved couple whose responsibilities were clearly divided between husband and wife and whose children were emblems of love warmed by orderly affection. Much of what scholars today say about the nineteenth century stresses the newness of this image, but it is possible to see many of its elements in the centuries before 1800.

The balance between "individual relationships" and "standard roles" was skewed in most of what was written before 1800. The proper performance of standard roles got much more attention than love and friendship between the individuals in a family. Alberti may not have been typical but, since he was one of the few who were not silent, we can take note of the fact that for him the model of disinterested personal affection was friendship, which he exhorted kinship to imitate. "If," says one of the interlocutors in *Della famiglia*, "you must share every thought, possession, and fortune with your friends and undergo inconveniences, hardships, and fatigue for those who love you, you certainly owe much more to your father. . . ."[29] because he is your father, not because you and he feel like friends.

Still, there are occasional glimmers of the idea that being in a family meant being able to let one's guard down in an atmosphere of warmth and intimacy. They come late in the period, when a sharp line was being drawn between family and servants, who were now being housed in segregated quarters and were supposed to appear only when summoned by a bell. As we have seen, the houses of the wealthy were being built with family dining rooms and sitting rooms separated from public reception areas. At the very end of the period, an obscure Virginian wrote, "When relations whom we love visit us we have no reserves, ceremony is discarded, & what is all important, they visit us in times of Trouble and Sickness, when common acquaintances are apt to neglect us."[30]

"Relations whom we love" tips the balance away from standard roles to individual relationships. If people in earlier times thought that such relationships were among the satisfactions provided by family life, they did not say so. I suspect they had the experience without conceptualizing it as people did later. The *idea* of finding emotionally satisfying personal relationships in the family emerged only slowly. It seems to have started with marriage, which was talked about mainly as a means to family formation, but it was hard for any sexual relationship to be completely untouched by the ideas of romantic love found in the chivalric literature that was already widely diffused before 1350 and the Petrarchan poetry that flourished throughout the period, both of which spread even more with the development of printing. By the end of the seventeenth century, the sister-in-law of Louis XIV could observe that if men wanted loving relationships with their wives (and she assumed they did) there were better ways than making lots of babies: "Trust, respect, and tenderness are a hundred times more apt to produce the affection and harmony that are so desirable in marriage."[31] Marriage was becoming a relationship thought of as an end in itself, or at least as one whose end was emotional satisfaction. "Happiness" and "peace" were the words that people used. Ordinary French couples, when asked why they wanted to marry, more and more often stated that they were in search of happiness and peace.

Before long, these things were connected with the family in general. "How often when travelling in dark nights & bad roads did I reflect on the peaceful happy circle I had left behind," wrote one Virginian in the early Republic. "Without thee and the rest of our beloved family & a few friends," wrote another, "this world would cease to have a charm for me. To these do I look for the little happiness which may be destined for me in this life."[32] A religious aura associated with these feelings was starting to surround the family. Wetenhall Wilkes in 1740 had declared that married love was "the completest image of heaven we can receive in this life."[33] Later, people sometimes thought of heaven as an image of the family—in the words of an American in 1808, "the happy seats above where there will be no sorrow, no more pain, no more parting, there we [the man, his wife, and their family] shall live together in everlasting love."[34]

It is a far cry from these late effusions, well on the way to nineteenth-century ideology, to the tone of earlier literature on family relations. There the balance was tipped in favor of standard roles, and the subject most often addressed was how roles might be bungled and distorted. If good role-players were depicted, they were invariably set against bad role-players: no Griselda without her cruel husband, no Cordelia without Goneril and Regan, no good son like Sheridan's Charles Surface without Joseph Surface. The extreme horror of Jacobean drama derived not only from the relentless depiction of physical cruelty but also from what was, to put it mildly, inappropriate role playing. The duchess of Malfi was done in by a most unnatural brother. This was shocking stuff, as were all the patricides, fratricides, adulteries, and rejections of children in imaginative literature.

The relationships most commonly depicted were almost never treated as dynamic interactions of individual personalities. Rather, they were performances—good, bad, sincere, perfunctory. The conjugal relationship was a matter of husbands and wives following or not following appropriate role patterns, the relationship of parents and children a matter of what fathers and mothers were supposed to be like and what sons and daughters were supposed to be like, and the fraternal relationship a matter of what brothers and sisters owed each other and how they honored their obligations.

In the conjugal relationship the role of the wife got more attention than that of the husband. It was on her that the happiness of a marriage was said to depend, perhaps because the writers almost always took a man's point of view. In Alberti, who always spoke of the family as essentially masculine, this attitude was particularly exaggerated. A wife was, above all, supposed to be fertile, "a woman suited to childbearing,"[35] someone who was "prolific and [would] bring peace and honesty to your house."[36] One of the interlocutors in Della famiglia says he told his wife shortly after they were married, "Three things will please me above everything else. The first is . . . that you will never wish for any other man in this bed but me." In other words, the first requirement after fertility was that she not misuse her sexuality. Being chaste was one way, presumably, that she brought honesty to the house. As for "peace," this speaker says the second thing that will please him is for her to care for the family "modestly in peace and tranquillity." He concludes by saying that she should see to it that "our household goods would not be wasted."[37] Says another speaker, "The woman shall preserve what the man brings home."[38]

Ben Jonson commends Penshurst for being in the charge of a lady who is such a good manager that a royal visitor could drop in without advance notice: ". . . not a roome but drest, / As if it had expected such a guest!" But, like Alberti, Jonson is mindful of the wife's sexual function: "Thy lady's noble, fruitful, chaste withall. / His children thy great lord may call his owne; / A fortune, in this age, but rarely knowne."[39] A wife was supposed to be fruitful, efficient, and submissive, but the quality that provoked the most emotional comment was chastity. It was closely linked to the other wifely qualities, especially submissiveness. She subordinated herself to her husband and kept things running smoothly. The last thing a wife was supposed to be was exciting. In the words of Della famiglia, "We must . . . seek a woman suited to childbearing and pleasant enough to be our constant companion" (my emphasis). The image of the ideal wife in all such utterances was remarkably consistent.

Jonson could not resist the cynical observation that chastity was "in this age but rarely known" and the dramatic situations in Shakespeare remind us that men were not confident that wives would be what they wanted them to be. Wifely qualities are often put to the test in Shakespeare's plays. Many of the women in Shakespeare are of course not yet wives and there is a considerable contrast between the role of lover and that of wife. Courtship, a common subject in the plays, seems to be less about getting a wife, as wives were usually portrayed, than about another side of the relationship between the sexes. It was when a woman became a wife that the familiar role requirements appeared. The wives in Shakespeare, with few exceptions, are submissive and chaste, sometimes heroically so. The least submissive is the proverbial shrew Kate, who is at the center of a comedy that exudes the values and atmosphere of a charivari, a noisy entertainment aimed at putting things back into their proper order. The merry wives of Windsor seem not to be submissive but in fact are, and they are impeccably chaste. It is their husbands who are uneasy about their wives' chastity, like husbands in some of the more serious plays. The wives in those plays are treated unfairly by their husbands, and they respond with extraordinarily reassuring demonstrations of submissiveness and chastity. "I must be patient," says Hermione in The Winter's Tale,[40] and defends herself from the charge of adultery by saying to her husband: "I lov'd him as in honour he requir'd; / . . . with a love even such, / So and no other, as yourself commanded."[41]

Desdemona has the same reassuring combination of qualities. "Whate'er you be, I am obedient," she says[42] and an onlooker remarks, "Truly, an obedient lady," when he hears her say to Othello, "I will not stay to offend you."[43] Emilia undercuts the reassurance by reminding the men in the audience that "the ills we do, their [men's] ills instruct us so," but Desdemona is the one who has heroic stature and embodies the ideal. She is content to be what she is supposed to be:

> If e'er my will did trespass 'gainst his love,
> Either in discourse of thought or actual deed,
> Or that mine eyes, mine ears, or any sense
> Delighted them in any other form,
> Or that I do not yet, and ever did,
> And ever will (though he do shake me off
> To beggarly divorcement) love him dearly,
> Comfort forswear me! Unkindness may do much;
> And his unkindness may defeat my life,
> But never taint my love.[44]

In the relationship between parents and children fathers and sons got the most attention. A good father was strong, wise, and honorable. A good son was respectful and obedient. The conversations in Alberti's *Della famiglia* take place while such a good father is on his deathbed. He is described as loving his sons "more than anyone else."[45] "I believe," says one of the speakers, "there is no love so powerful, so constant, so complete, and so great as to equal a father's love for his children."[46] Later, someone says the duty of an "upright, good, prudent father" is to risk everything "for the honor of our house and our family." Not surprisingly, the duty to the house in general, rather than to individual sons, receives emphasis in Alberti, and such a father is called "the model of family love."[47] Sons, like wives, were supposed to be submissive. The Bible commanded everyone to "honor thy father and thy mother," and for a long time commentaries on this Commandment had almost nothing to say about the obligations of parents to children. This gradually changed, but the generally recognized qualities of a good father did not, since they could easily be understood to include concern for children.

When mothers were mentioned in normative works, they were hardly differentiated from fathers. If the father was the model of every manly virtue, the mother was the model of every womanly virtue, and it was usually left at that. The responsibility for "parenting" was the father's. Of course, what we call parenting is not exactly what people in the past were usually talking about. They may have been aware of a more motherly kind of parenting, but they rarely mentioned it, except in connection with very little children, who were not a common subject for discussion. Expectations about the mother's role can be glimpsed indirectly in some aspects of the cult of the Virgin Mary, especially her role as merciful intercessor.

The attitude toward disobedient, disrespectful sons, as expressed in drama, was akin to the attitude toward anything that upset the natural order. Daughters in Shakespeare tend to be more reliable than sons. *The Tempest* has a particularly warm, harmonious, idyllic father-daughter pair and Timon of Athens addresses his daughter as "cordial of mine age"[48] and "dearer than my soul."[49] Hamlet is a good son, bent on avenging his father's death and ready at any moment to sing his praises ("Where every god did seem to set his seal").[50] He struggles to be obedient, since he has received a "dread command" from his father's ghost.[51] His fault (which makes the play more complex and interesting than an ordinary revenge play) is that he is not as quick to act as the impetuous and less intelligent Laertes, son of a father on whom every god had not set his seal, yet convinced that any "drop of blood that's calm proclaims me bastard"[52] and ready to show himself his "father's son in deed / More than in words."[53]

Although obedience is almost always the note sounded in the parent-child relationships in Shakespeare, much depends on how fathers play their roles. When the disappointing son, Prince Hal, turns into the reassuringly reformed King Henry, he addresses a father-surrogate as follows:

> You shall be as a father to my youth;
> My voice shall sound as you do prompt my ear,
> And I will stoop and humble my intents
> To your well-practis'd wise directions.[54]

Fathers who do not give "wise directions" can upset the natural order as much as disobedient sons can. The romantic comedies of the two centuries after Shakespeare often turn on the foolish decisions of deluded parents. There are many such examples in Molière and Sheridan, very few in Shakespeare. *King Lear* is the magnificent, ambiguous exception. Cordelia is punished for properly understanding the filial role: "You have begot me, bred me, lov'd me; I / Return those duties back as are right fit, / Obey you, love you, and most honour you."[55] This will be quite enough when Lear becomes helpless and dependent and the exaggerated protestations of his other daughters have shown themselves to be false. Meanwhile Lear suffers for his unwise directions. The play hovers on the brink of the dangerous idea that he deserves what he gets, which contributes to the mysterious power of this disturbing work. It is brought back from the brink by the unremitting wickedness and generally unnatural behavior of Goneril and Regan, who are no better wives than they are daughters, and by the more accessible situation of Gloucester and his two sons. Gloucester is a worthy father. Edgar is a worthy son. Edmund, the unworthy son, is a bastard. Everyone is reassuringly true to type in this trio, and the worthy father, no less than Lear (the unworthy father?), suffers from filial disloyalty.

Lear, which is, I suppose, the most "family" of all Shakespeare's plays, also has something to tell us about sisters and brothers. This is one subject that the normative literature passed over in relative silence. Writers of that literature

tended to talk about authority in the household or obligations to the abstract
entity of "house," neither of which directly involved the relationship of siblings to each other. The speech about "family" in *The Two Noble Kinsmen*
does not mention brothers or sisters. Still, they were a subject hard to avoid
anywhere else, either in literature or life. Their relationships were fraught with
ambivalence, being associated with both cooperation and competition, often
in the same breath. Ideal brothers loved each other selflessly, real brothers
were likely to vie for parental favors. Alberti says little, taking it for granted
that the fraternal relationship is an extremely close one. The dying father in
Della famiglia hands over the care of his sons to his brother with his last
breath.[56] One of the speakers says that brothers should live together under the
same roof.[57] Shakespeare's plays show a number of warm, loving relationships
between brothers, which often extend to each other's children, so that uncles
are shown to be as important as they surely were in reality. Sisters and brothers
are also shown in close relationships, full of concern for each other, as in
Twelfth Night, and sometimes too easily making assumptions about their obligations to each other, as in *Measure for Measure*.

The dark side of the fraternal relationship is, however, much more evident
in Shakespeare. Bad brothers seem to have had an endless fascination for audiences. To be a bad brother was a clear sign of villainy and, conversely, villains
were bad brothers. Plots take their starting points from fraternal betrayals and
usurpations, as in *The Tempest* and *As You Like It*. Bad brothers move the
action along in *Much Ado about Nothing*, *Lear*, and, of course, *Richard III*.
Richard is a perfect villain in every one of his family roles, but most strikingly
as a brother and, in the role that is its corollary, as an uncle. The ghosts of the
princes murdered in the Tower cry out, "Thy nephews' souls bid thee
despair."[58] He sums up his treachery to his brothers as follows: "The sons of
Clarence have I pent up close, / His daughters meanly have I match'd in marriage, / The sons of Edward sleep in Abraham's bosom."[59]

Referring to people by their family roles instead of their names is a constant reminder of implied obligations. What the obligations of a brother are is
constantly suggested, more often by how they are honored in the breach. Here
is a sampling of such loaded statements: "False to thy gods, thy brother, and
thy father." (*Lear*, V, iii, 134); "That a brother should be so perfidious!" (*The
Tempest*, I, ii, 67); "Tell me / If this might be a brother." (*The Tempest*, V,
i, 130–131); "He . . . bars me the place of a brother." (*As You Like It*, the opening speech of the play by Orlando); "A secret and villainous contriver against
me his natural brother." (*As You Like It*, I, i, 150); "Your brother (no, no
brother! yet the son— / Yet not the son—I will not call him son / Of him I
was about to call his father)." (*As You Like It*, II, iii, 119–121); "I am his
brother, and I love him well." (*Richard III*, I, iv, 232); "Who spoke of brotherhood? Who spoke of love?" (*Richard III*, II, i, 108); "Brother, for in that
name doth nature plead—" (*Titus Andronicus*, I, i, 373).

To be a brother, a wife, or a son was to accept a role with set duties and a predetermined place in the family structure. Every one of these roles was nevertheless the focus of deep feeling, especially when its requirements were ignored. I think there is more to be said about the feelings people thought were connected with family relationships, but we have to become more accustomed to detaching ourselves from our present-day ideas on the subject before that can be done.

Several decades into the nineteenth century a European traveler in the United States thought he perceived an important difference between the Old World and the New in the hold that the family had on people's loyalties. In contrast to France, he said, the United States had no tradition of powerful families who might resist the ambitions of a tyrant, and instead relied on strong communities and a belief in the importance of the individual. Alexis de Tocqueville was a political thinker, and his was a political perspective, but he chose to use the vocabulary of emotion when he spoke of the family:

> As long as family feeling was kept alive, the opponent of oppression was never alone; he looked about him and found his clients, his hereditary friends, and his kinfolk. If this support was wanting, he felt himself sustained by his ancestors and animated by his posterity. But when patrimonial estates are divided, and when a few years suffice to confound the distinctions of race, where can family feeling be found?[60]

Where indeed? The implication is that only "good families" had family feeling—a message that comes to us from countless sources in the four hundred and more years preceding this statement. Defined in Tocqueville's terms, it was a feeling from which most people in the past were excluded. I have suggested that they might not have been excluded from a whole array of other family feelings that were, however, rarely characterized as such.

A statement like Tocqueville's illustrates how hard it is to get beyond the intellectual and class bias of even the best writers if we want a really broad picture of the past. He may have been blind to the values and feelings of some of his own fellow countrymen whose traditions had more in common with Americans than he thought. His is a useful statement, however, because it is so backward-looking. At the very moment when a different set of ideas about family life was crystallizing he summed up the older ideas in terms so lapidary they could be carved on a tombstone.

Epilogue: Toward the Twenty-first Century

About eight generations of human beings have been born since the period covered in this book. Two hundred years is a long time, long enough for changes to have taken place in the relationships and institutions that come under the heading of "family." The Western family in 1800 was more like what it was in 1700 than what it would be in 1900. The typical family in 1800 was rural. Although cities were already quite large and acted as magnets that pulled immigrants from the country, most people lived on the land. Thomas Jefferson thought of America as a nation of farmers, and for him as for others it looked as if it would always be that way. Most households were centers of economic activity, in city and country alike. Factories were few, and where they did exist they tended to be modeled on household organization. The Age of Steel may have been on the horizon, but the village blacksmith, who was often a part-time farmer, plied his trade, still an important one, in a shop adjacent to his living quarters. Food and clothing were not necessarily produced in one's own household, but they were produced in *someone's* household. Family relations in 1800 could still be described as "patriarchal." It is a much-abused word these days, but if it suggests the power of fathers, it is the right word for what was expected of a well-run household: the father gave orders and made decisions, and everyone else obeyed.

Families that fit this 1800 model are next to impossible to find in the Western world today. Most people live in cities, household activity has little to do with economic production, fathers are no longer the absolute rulers they once were, and inheritance is far less important as a method of conveying wealth and power. These are big changes. It would be ridiculous to expect them to have happened quickly or in a straightforward, uncomplicated way. As one who has spent a lot of time looking at families before 1800, I harbor a slight suspicion that some of the changes have not been as radical as they seem to be, but there can be no doubt that certain developments of the last two centuries left their mark.

Factory production all but eliminated the household production of manufactured goods. The office building joined the factory as a place where individuals spent large portions of the day. Shifts in political power diminished the advantages of inherited status, as the new lords of industry became the rivals of the old landed nobility and suffrage was eventually extended downward to lower levels of society. The good family, as Tocqueville saw so clearly, no longer had a tight grip on society and on the minds of men.

Science and technology, especially in the twentieth century, extended Western life expectancy, with effects on family forms, family functions, and family finances that have not yet been clearly calculated. Parenthood as a consequence of sexual activity is no longer inevitable, thanks to a variety of effective contraceptive methods and an increasing acceptance of their use. It would be naive to believe that every child born in the Western world today is a wanted child, but with modern technology every child *could* be.

By the middle years of the twentieth century, the balance of the Western world's population had shifted to cities and to appendages of cities, the suburbs. Gone were the rural character of the typical household and the common association of the household with economically productive work. Do we yet know what urbanization has done to the family? It may have intensified the emotional aspects of family life, since city institutions tend to take on many of the functions of the preindustrial household. Perhaps urbanization has created the impression of fragility in family structure, since families in cities do not have the potential cement of shared productive work in an inherited homestead.

The high rate of divorce intensifies the impression of fragility. Divorce is a very recent phenomenon. Not until the years following World War II did people come to believe that, contrary to earlier received wisdom, an ordinary, decent life was possible after divorce. Divorce has contributed to an emphasis on individual satisfaction in marriage, and it may have something to do with the increasing frequency with which couples set up households without getting married.

The most interesting developments since 1800, and perhaps the most profound ones, are in the ways in which we think about the family. What you and I usually mean when we say "family" is something that comes to us from the nineteenth century, not from time immemorial. As family life has been changing, a new set of ideas has been forged about its unchanging nature. The household was transformed into Home Sweet Home, which was imagined to embody old, eternal values, the very values that humanity was in danger of losing in the new industrial age. The charm of hominess was a discovery of that age and so was the notion that hominess was something old and worth struggling to preserve.

Home was, above all, a nest for the young. This seemingly obvious idea came into its own in the nineteenth century, when a single model of family life came to be applied to everyone. The bourgeois family—neither the supposedly ceremonial, status-ridden aristocratic family nor the supposedly sloppy, subsistence-driven lower-class family—was an ideal toward which aristocrats and proletarians could strive, and indeed they do seem to have felt its influence.

The work of Sigmund Freud in the early twentieth century made important contributions to a revised middle-class ideal of the family. It shone light into dark places that propriety would have liked to keep hidden and revealed conflict and suffering beneath the surface of the earthly paradise of home, but in other respects Freud simply amplified the nineteenth-century image. He gave his attention to what were already regarded as the family's most important aspects. He examined the intense emotional involvement of family members with each other, showing that the "family romance" was a very complicated matter; above all, he looked at the experience of children, already the household's most important occupants, pushing the critical years of their upbringing back to early infancy.

I think there will always be household groups, more or less based on kinship, that carry on some of the functions that households and kin did in the past. It is hard to see exactly what those functions will be, however, or what shape households will take. We are already seeing the beginning of legal recognition of families—in the sense of households—that are not in any way based on marriage or conventional heterosexual arrangements. We can even see the possibility of the end of kinship, if the Chinese attempt at promoting one-child families should ever prove successful and be taken up elsewhere. The mind struggles to imagine future generations with no sisters and brothers, aunts and uncles, or cousins.

Will anything of the experience of families in earlier centuries go into the making of the families of the twenty-first century? The family today is not all newness and modernity—and I am not talking about the "traditional" things that turn out to be not very old. The legacy of the Western family is long and complex and, while some of it may be consciously rejected, it is unconsciously present whenever we do the ordinary things we do "without thinking." Beliefs and actions are no more perfectly matched today than they were in the past.

In a sense, we are all peasants today. We are certainly not all aristocrats, even though we would probably like to claim the refined sensibilities of which the upper classes used to think they were the sole possessors. We may call ourselves middle class, but most of us live on too restricted a scale to resemble the prosperous bourgeoisie of the nineteenth century or the burghers of old. Of course we do not earn our living like peasants and we do not usually live in the country, but we do live in relatively confined quarters, in close intimate contact, and with practically no stake in the ancestry and prestige of our kin. We take care of our own children, including all their physical needs. All classes and both sexes are more and more united in this, at least as an ideal. Why else would the heir to the British throne, of all people, want to be photographed carrying his infant son in a canvas sling? In the past he might have posed with him for a formal portrait emblematic of lineage, but today he presents himself as an informal, loving dad.

The ideology of the family has been completely transformed. "Family" no longer has anything to do with power and wealth. They are irrelevant to the association of the family with affection, which is equally accessible to all. I do not mean to imply that there are no class differences in family behavior today, but when it comes to *thinking* about what is essential to the family the assumption is that we are all the same.

We find it hard these days to think about the family without being confronted with what look like insurmountable problems. Knowing about the variety of past centuries may give us some comfort. It will probably do nothing to change the minds of those for whom "family" has become a conservative rallying cry. For them, an image of the family formed out of elements culled from the nineteenth- and twentieth-century myth of the traditional family is a standard by which contemporary experience is measured and usually found wanting. We are probably in for a time of controversy about what government policy on the family—that is, "society's attitudes"—should be. From history we learn this small certainty: many things are possible.

NOTES

Chapter 1

1. Cited in Jean-Louis Flandrin, *Familles* (Paris, 1976), p. 11.

2. Keith Wrightson, *English Society 1580–1680* (London and New Brunswick, N.J. 1982), p. 42.

3. Ann Kussmaul, *Servants in Husbandry* (Cambridge, 1981), pp. 86–87.

4. Audiger, *La Maison réglée ou l'Art de diriger la maison d'un grand seigneur . . .* (Paris, 1692), pp. 1–2. Cited in Cissie Fairchilds, *Domestic Enemies* (Baltimore, 1984), p. 12.

5. Richard Gough, *The History of Myddle*, ed. David Hey (Harmondsworth, 1981), p. 14.

6. Fairchilds, p. 19.

7. J. William Frost, *The Quaker Family in Colonial America* (New York, 1973), p. 140.

8. William Whately, cited in Wrightson, p. 69.

9. Pierre Goubert, "Family and Province," *Journal of Family History* 2 (1977), 187–88.

10. Alain Collomp, "Alliance et filiation en haute Provence," *Annales E.S.C.* 32 (1977), 460.

11. Alexander Keysser, "Widowhood in Eighteenth-century Massachusetts," *Perspectives in American History* 8 (1974), 104.

12. Margaret Spufford, "Peasant Inheritance Customs and Land Distribution in Cambridgeshire," in Jack Goody et al., eds., *Family and Inheritance* (Cambridge, 1976), p. 174.

13. David Gaunt, "The Property and Kin Relationships of Retired Farmers," in Richard Wall et al., eds., *Family Forms in Historic Europe* (Cambridge, 1983), pp. 259–60.

14. Michael Mitterauer and Reinhard Sieder, *The European Family* (Chicago, 1982), p. 167.

15. Richard M. Smith, "Some Issues Concerning Families and Their Property," in R. M. Smith, ed., *Land, Kinship and Life-Cycle* (Cambridge, 1984), pp. 74–75.

16. Philip J. Greven, Jr., "Family Structure in Seventeenth-century Andover," in

Michael Gordon, ed., *The American Family in Social-historical Perspective* (New York, 1978), p. 30.

17. Spufford, p. 175.

18. Linda Auwers, "Fathers, Sons, and Wealth in Colonial Windsor," *Journal of Family History* 3 (1978), 136.

Chapter 2

1. Jean-Louis Flandrin, *Familles* (Paris, 1976), p. 96.

2. M. W. Barley, *The English Farmhouse and Cottage* (London, 1961), p. 133.

3. John Demos, *A Little Commonwealth* (Oxford, 1961), pp. 33–34.

4. Cited in Fernand Braudel, *Capitalism and Material Life* (New York, 1975), p. 216.

5. Cited in Barley, p. 261.

6. Richard Gough, *The History of Myddle* (Harmondsworth, 1981), p. 77.

7. *Boswell's Life of Johnson* (London, 1961), p. 185.

8. Marc Bloch, *Les caractères originaux de l'histoire rurale française* (Paris, 1968), pp. 60–61.

9. Cited in Barley, p. 125.

10. Tomb of Sir William Broughton, cited in Felicity Heal, "The Idea of Hospitality in Early Modern England," *Past & Present* no. 102 (Feb. 1984), 93.

11. Cited in Heal, p. 79.

12. Robert Forster, *The House of Saulx-Tavanes* (Baltimore, 1971), p. 114.

13. Ibid.

14. Heal, p. 89.

Chapter 3

1. Michel Terrisse, "Le rattrapage de nuptialité d'après peste à Marseille," in *Sur la population française au XVIIIe et au XIXe siècles* (Paris, 1973), p. 578.

2. From an episcopal court case in fifteenth-century Troyes, France, cited in Beatrice Gottlieb, "Getting Married in Pre-Reformation Europe" (Ph.D. diss., Columbia University, 1974).

3. From the diary of a seventeenth-century apprentice, Roger Lowe, cited in Keith Wrightson, *English Society 1580–1680* (London and New Brunswick, N.J., 1982), p. 82.

4. Jean-Marie Gouesse, "Parenté, famille et mariage en Normandie," *Annales E.S.C.* 27 (1972), 1145.

5. Cited in Ivy Pinchbeck and Margaret Hewitt, *Children in English Society* (London, 1969), p. 56.

6. Referred to in Pinchbeck and Hewitt, p. 49.

7. Gouesse, p. 1141.

8. Roger Schofield, "The Relationship Between Demographic Structure and Environment," in Werner Conze, ed., *Sozialgeschichte der Familie* (Stuttgart, 1976), p. 152.

9. Benjamin Franklin, *Poor Richard Improved*, cited in J. Potter, "The Growth

of Population in America," in D. V. Glass and D. E. C. Eversley, eds., *Population in History* (London, 1965), pp. 643–44.

10. Franklin, *Observations* (1751), cited in Potter.

11. Silvia M. Arrom, "Marriage Patterns in Mexico City," *Journal of Family History* 3 (1978), 380.

Chapter 4

1. Paolo Sarpi. In his *Historie of the Council of Trent*, trans. Nathaniel Brent (London, 1629), p. 757.

2. Cited in John R. Gillis, *For Better, For Worse* (Oxford, 1985), p. 141.

3. Martin Luther, *Von den Ehesachen* (1530), in *Werke*, vol. 30, pt. 3 (Weimar, 1910), 212.

4. Christiane Klapisch-Zuber, "An Ethnology of Marriage in the Age of Humanism," in Klapisch-Zuber, *Women, Family, and Ritual in Renaissance Italy* (Chicago, 1985), pp. 247–60.

5. Cited in Gillis, p. 137.

6. Christiane Klapisch-Zuber, "The 'Mattinata' in Medieval Italy," in Klapisch-Zuber, pp. 261–82.

7. Cited in A. de Ruble, "François de Montmorency," *Mémoires de la Société de l'histoire de Paris* 6 (1879), 221.

Chapter 5

1. Benedicti, *La somme des pechez* (1584), no. 30, cited in Jean-Louis Flandrin, *Familles* (Paris, 1976), pp. 126–27.

2. Lawrence Stone, *The Family, Sex and Marriage in England* (New York, 1979), p. 137.

3. Martin Ingram, "Ridings, Rough Music and the 'Reform of Popular Culture,'" *Past & Present* no. 105 (Nov. 1984), p. 98.

4. François Lebrun, *La vie conjugale sous l'Ancien Régime* (Paris, 1975), p. 80.

5. Cited in Stone, p. 222.

6. Ingram, p. 98.

7. Etienne Pasquier, cited in David Hunt, *Parents and Children in History* (New York, 1972), p. 69.

8. *A Letter of Genteel and Moral Advice to a Young Lady* (1740), cited in Stone, p. 218.

9. Cited in Stone, p. 139.

10. Hermann von Weinsberg (1553), cited in Steven Ozment, *When Fathers Ruled* (Cambridge, Mass., 1983), pp. 65, 68.

11. Lebrun, p. 84.

12. Cited in Keith Thomas, "The Double Standard," *Journal of the History of Ideas* 20 (1959), 196.

13. *Christiani matrimonii institutio* in *Opera omnia*, vol. 5 (Leyden, 1704), col. 633.

14. Michel Terrisse, "Le rattrapage de nuptialité d'après peste à Marseille," in *Sur la population française* (Paris, 1973), p. 568.

Chapter 6

1. Hélène Bergues et al., *La prévention des naissances dans la famille* (Paris, 1960), p. 248.

2. Cited in André Armengaud, *La famille et l'enfant en France et en Angleterre* (Paris, 1975), p. 49.

3. See Angus McLaren, *Reproductive Rituals* (London and New York, 1984), pp. 13-14.

4. Ibid., p. 21.

5. Nicholas Culpepper, *Directory for Midwives* (1656), cited in McLaren, p. 38.

6. T. R. Malthus, *An Essay on the Principle of Population* (1798), pp. 20-21, cited in J. Potter, "The Growth of Population in America," in D. V. Glass and D. E. C. Eversley, eds., *Population in History* (London, 1965), pp. 631-32.

7. Jean-Baptiste-Pierre de Sénancour, *De l'amour considéré dans les lois réelles et dans les formes sociales de l'union des sexes* (Paris, 1806), cited in Bergues, p. 305.

8. Cited in Judith S. Lewis, *In the Family Way* (New Brunswick, N.J., 1986), pp. 228-29.

9. Cited in Armengaud, p. 61.

10. Louis-Sébastien Mercier, *L'an 2440, rêve s'il en fut jamais* (London, 1771), cited in Bergues, p. 281.

11. Lewis, p. 239.

12. T. H. Hollingsworth, "A Demographic Study of the British Ducal Families," in Glass and Eversley, p. 372.

13. Hubert Charbonneau, *Vie et mort de nos ancêtres* (Montreal, 1975), p. 222.

14. See Lewis, p. 123.

15. Cited in Lewis, p. 211.

16. Cited in J. William Frost, *The Quaker Family in Colonial America* (New York, 1973), p. 72.

17. Philippe Hecquet, *De l'indécence aux hommes d'accoucher les femmes*. See François Lebrun, *La vie conjugale sous l'ancien régime* (Paris, 1975), p. 113.

18. Steven Ozment, *When Fathers Ruled* (Cambridge, Mass., 1983), p. 102.

19. Valentine Seaman, *The Midwives Monitor, and Mothers Mirror*, cited in Catherine M. Scholter, "'On the Importance of the Obstetrick Art,'" *William and Mary Quarterly*, 3d ser., 34 (1977), 430.

20. Charles White (1793), cited in ibid., 437.

21. Ibid., 441.

22. Claire Tomalin, *The Life and Death of Mary Wollstonecraft* (New York, 1974), pp. 220-26.

23. Cited in Tomalin, pp. 226, 270n.

24. *Elizabeth in Her Holy Retirement*, cited in Scholter, p. 428.

25. Late seventeenth century. Cited in Jean Donnison, *Midwives and Medical Men* (New York, 1977), pp. 13, 205n.

26. See Jean-Louis Flandrin, *Familles* (Paris, 1976), p. 209.

27. Letter of September 15, 1797, cited in Ralph M. Wardle, *Mary Wollstonecraft, A Critical Biography* (Lawrence, Kan., 1951), p. 307.

28. Cited in Peter Laslett, *The World We Have Lost*, 2d ed. (New York, 1971), pp. 115-16.

Chapter 7

1. Iris Origo, *The Merchant of Prato* (London, 1957), pp. 200–201.

2. *Les caquets de l'accouchée*, cited in Hélène Bergues et al., *La prévention des naissances dans la famille* (Paris, 1960), p. 315.

3. Cited in Christiane Klapisch-Zuber, "Childhood in Tuscany at the Beginning of the Fifteenth Century" in Klapisch-Zuber, *Women, Family and Ritual in Renaissance Italy* (Chicago, 1985), pp. 94–116.

4. Steven Ozment, *When Fathers Ruled* (Cambridge, Mass., 1983), p. 167.

5. See A. Tenenti, "Témoignages toscans sur la mort des enfants autour de 1400," *Annales de Démographie Historique* (1973), 133–34.

6. Klapisch-Zuber, "Childhood in Tuscany."

7. Cited in Bergues et al., p. 153.

8. Cited in Ivy Pinchbeck and Margaret Hewitt, *Children in English Society* (London, 1969), p. 301.

9. Giorgio Vasari, *The Lives of the Artists: A Selection*, trans. George Bull (Harmondsworth, 1972), p. 71.

10. Sir Thomas Elyot, *The Book Named The Governor*, ed. S. E. Lehmberg (London and New York, 1962), p. 19.

11. William Cadogan, *An Essay upon Nursing* (1748), cited in Angus McLaren, *Reproductive Rituals* (London and New York, 1984), p. 53.

12. Elyot, p. 18.

13. Desiderius Erasmus, *The Education of a Christian Prince*, trans. Lester K. Born (New York, 1965; reprint of 1936 ed.), p. 143.

14. Guillemeau (1649), cited in François Lebrun, *La vie conjugale sous l'ancien régime* (Paris, 1975), p. 124.

15. Cited in Jean-Pierre Bardet, "Enfants abandonnés et enfants assistés à Rouen," in *Sur la population française* (Paris, 1973), pp. 37–38.

16. Cited in Pinchbeck and Hewitt, p. 179.

17. *Confessions* 1.7, cited in David Herlihy, *Medieval Households* (Cambridge, Mass., 1985), p. 27.

18. Joseph E. Illick, "Child-rearing in Seventeenth-century England and America," in Lloyd de Mause, ed., *The History of Childhood* (New York, 1974), p. 318.

19. Jean-Jacques Rousseau, *Émile*, ed. François and Pierre Richard (Paris, 1961), p. 15.

20. Ibid., p. 16.

21. Cissie Fairchilds, *Domestic Enemies* (Baltimore, 1984), p. 215.

22. Jean Ganiage, "Nourrissons parisiens en Beauvaisis," in *Sur la population française*, pp. 273, 287.

23. Vasari, p. 326.

24. Jean-Louis Flandrin, *Familles* (Paris, 1976), pp. 195, 196.

25. Cited in Thomas R. Forbes, *Chronicle from Aldgate* (New Haven, 1971), p. 199.

26. Flandrin, p. 196.

27. Emile Gérard-Gailly, *Madame de Sévigné* (Paris, 1971), pp. 111–14. Corroboration of medical hypothesis from Dr. Morelly Maayan.

28. Flandrin, p. 196.

29. Vasari, p. 285.

30. Montaigne, *Essais*, II, viii, 26–27. Cited in David Hunt, *Parents and Children in History* (New York, 1972), p. 104.

31. Rousseau, p. 20.

32. Ibid., p. 19.

33. Ibid.

Chapter 8

1. Cited in Joseph F. Kett, "The Stages of Life," in Michael Gordon, ed., *The American Family in Social-historical Perspective* (New York, 1978), pp. 174–75.

2. Cited in Keith Wrightson, *English Society 1580–1680* (London and New Brunswick, N.J., 1982), p. 113.

3. Cited in François Lebrun, *La vie conjugale sous l'Ancien Régime* (Paris, 1975), p. 136.

4. Herbert Moller, "Voice Change in Human Biological Development," *Journal of Interdisciplinary History* 16 (1985), 239–53.

5. Kett.

6. Jean-Louis Flandrin, *Familles* (Paris, 1976), p. 48.

7. Daniele Barbaro, *Italian Relations* (1551), in Molly Harrison and O. M. Royston, eds., *How They Lived*, vol. 2 (Oxford, 1963), pp. 167–68.

8. Cited in J. William Frost, *The Quaker Family in Colonial America* (New York, 1973), p. 144.

9. Frost, p. 138.

10. Cited in Michael Mitterauer and Reinhard Sieder, *The European Family* (Chicago, 1982), p. 105.

11. Cited in Carl F. Kaestle and Maris A. Vinovskis, "From Apron Strings to ABCs," in John Demos and Sarane Spence Babcock, eds., *Turning Points* (Chicago, 1978), pp. 49–50.

12. Alain Molinier, "Enfants trouvés, enfants abandonnés et enfants illégitimes," in *Sur la population française* (Paris, 1973), p. 472.

13. Cited in Roger Chartier et al., *L'éducation en France* (Paris, 1976), pp. 222–23.

14. Cissie Fairchilds, *Domestic Enemies* (Baltimore, 1984), pp. 204–5.

15. Cited in Steven R. Smith, "The London Apprentices," *Past & Present* no. 61 (Nov. 1973), 151.

16. *Commentary on the Epistle to Titus* in Opera, ed. G. Baum, E. Cunitz, and E. Reuss (Brunswick, 1863–1900; reprint 1964), vol. 52, p. 421.

17. *Commentary on Paul's Epistle to the Ephesians* in Opera, vol. 51, p. 229.

18. Ibid., p. 228.

19. "Farewell to the Members of the Senate," in Opera, vol. 9, p. 890.

20. Frost, p. 84.

21. Cited in Ivy Pinchbeck and Margaret Hewitt, *Children in English Society* (London, 1969), pp. 274–75.

22. Lebrun, p. 137.

23. Cited in Frost, p. 136.

24. Marshal Gaspard de Saulx (d. 1579), cited in Robert Forster, *The House of Saulx-Tavanes* (Baltimore, 1971), p. 4.

25. Cited in Yves Castan, "Pères et fils en Languedoc," *XVII* *Siècle* nos. 102–103 (1974), 39.

26. *Sermons on the Epistle to the Ephesians*, no. 43, in *Opera*, vol. 51, p. 783.

27. Leicester Bradner and Charles A. Lynch, eds. and trans., *The Latin Epigrams of Thomas More* (Chicago, 1953), pp. 230–31.

28. Cited in Barbara B. Diefendorf, *Paris City Councillors in the Sixteenth Century* (Princeton, 1983), p. 120.

29. Alan Macfarlane, *The Family Life of Ralph Josselin* (Cambridge, 1970), p. 221.

30. Abbé Goussault, *Le portrait d'une honnête femme*, cited in Philippe Ariès, *Centuries of Childhood* (New York, 1962), p. 132.

31. *Conduite des écoles chrétiennes* (1720), cited in Ariès, p. 131.

32. Cited in Ariès, p. 129.

33. Emile Gérard-Gailly, *Madame de Sévigné* (Paris, 1971).

34. Steven Ozment, *When Fathers Ruled* (Cambridge, Mass., 1983), p. 155.

35. Jean-Pierre Bardet, "Enfants abandonnés et enfants assistés à Rouen," in *Sur la population française* (Paris, 1973), p. 39.

Chapter 9

1. Jean-Louis Flandrin, *Familles* (Paris, 1976), p. 32.

2. Tim Wales, "Poverty, Poor Relief and Life-Cycle," in R. M. Smith, ed., *Land, Kinship and Life-Cycle* (Cambridge, 1984), p. 383.

3. Dennis R. Mills, "The Nineteenth-century Peasantry of Melbourn," in Smith, p. 514.

4. Cited in Flandrin, p. 12.

5. Bartolomé Bennassar, *Valladolid au siècle d'or* (Paris, 1967), pp. 407–8.

6. Rabelais, *Book 3*, ch. 48.

7. Flandrin, p. 28.

8. Barbara B. Diefendorf, *Paris City Councillors in the Sixteenth Century* (Princeton, 1983), p. 294.

9. René Pillorget, *La tige et le rameau* (Paris, 1979), pp. 108–9.

10. Ibid., pp. 205–6.

11. Flandrin, p. 35.

12. Denis Diderot, *Rameau's Nephew*, trans. Jacques Barzun and Ralph H. Bowen (Indianapolis, 1956), pp. 12, 14.

13. Jean Delumeau, *Vie économique et sociale de Rome dans la seconde moitié du XVI* *siècle* (Paris, 1957), vol. 1, pp. 460–61.

14. Cited in Mervyn James, *Family, Lineage, and Civil Society* (Oxford, 1974), p. 158.

15. "La vie de Gaspard de Saulx, Seigneur de Tavanes," in C. B. Petitot, *Collection complète des Mémoires*, ser. 1, vol. 25 (Paris, 1822), p. 10. I am indebted to John Nordhaus for this reference.

16. Cited in Linda Levy Peck, "'For a King Not to Be Bountiful Were a Fault' . . . ," *Journal of British Studies* 25 (1986), p. 56.

17. Cited in Francis W. Kent, *Household and Lineage in Renaissance Florence* (Princeton, 1977), p. 154.

18. Cited in Judith S. Lewis, *In the Family Way* (New Brunswick, N.J., 1986), p. 158.

19. Cited in Kent, pp. 296–97.

20. Yves Castan, *Honnêteté et relations sociales en Languedoc* (Paris, 1974), pp. 244–45.

21. Cited in Diefendorf, p. 129.

22. Cited in Margaret R. Hunt, "English Urban Families in Trade" (Ph.D. diss., New York University, 1986), p. 43.

23. Cited in Hunt, pp. 45–46.

Chapter 10

1. Jean-Pierre Bardet, "Enfants abandonnés et enfants assistés à Rouen," in *Sur la population française* (Paris, 1973), pp. 31–32.

2. Marc Bloch, *Les caractères originaux de l'histoire rurale française* (Paris, 1968), p. 184.

3. Martine Segalen, *Historical Anthropology of the Family* (Cambridge, 1986), p. 67.

4. Cited in Robert Wheaton, "Affinity and Descent," in Robert Wheaton and Tamara K. Hareven, eds., *Family and Sexuality in French History* (Philadelphia, 1980), p. 118.

5. Barbara B. Diefendorf, *Paris City Councillors in the Sixteenth Century* (Princeton, 1983), pp. 284–85.

6. Ralph A. Houlbrooke, *The English Family 1450–1700* (London and New York, 1984), p. 100.

7. Diefendorf, p. 289.

8. Ibid., p. 290.

9. Ibid., p. 277.

10. Jean-Louis Flandrin, *Familles* (Paris, 1976), pp. 18–19.

11. Margaret Spufford, "Peasant Inheritance Customs and Land Distribution in Cambridgeshire," in Jack Goody et al., eds., *Family and Inheritance* (Cambridge, 1976), pp. 170, 172–73.

12. Novella Contarini (1405), cited in Guido Ruggiero, *The Boundaries of Eros* (New York, 1985), p. 175n.

13. Cited in Lloyd Bonfield, *Marriage Settlements, 1601–1740* (Cambridge, 1983), p. 16.

14. J. William Frost, *The Quaker Family in Colonial America* (New York, 1973), p. 135.

15. Philip J. Greven, Jr., "Family Structure in Seventeenth-century Andover," in Michael Gordon, ed., *The American Family in Social-historical Perspective* (New York, 1978), p. 32.

16. Mervyn James, *Family, Lineage, and Civil Society* (Oxford, 1974), p. 20.

17. Cited in Lutz K. Berkner, "Inheritance, Land Tenure, and Peasant Family Structure," in Goody et al., p. 83.

18. Barbara Hanawalt, *The Ties That Bound* (New York and Oxford, 1986), p. 77.

19. Diefendorf, pp. 271–72.

20. Robert Forster, *The House of Saulx-Tavanes* (Baltimore, 1971), p. 7.

21. Joan Thirsk, "The European Debate on Customs of Inheritance," in Goody et al., pp. 189–90.

22. Diefendorf, pp. 268–69.

23. Cited in Denys Hay, *Europe in the Fourteenth and Fifteenth Centuries* (London, 1970), p. 98.

24. Cited in J. P. Cooper, "Patterns of Inheritance and Settlement by Great Landowners," in Goody et al., p. 195.

25. *A Health to the Gentlemanly Profession of Serving Men* (1598), cited in James, p. 26.

26. Christopher Dyer, "Changes in the Size of Peasant Holdings," in R. M. Smith, ed., *Land, Kinship and Life-Cycle* (Cambridge, 1984), pp. 291–92.

27. *The Works of the Right Honorable Henry Late Lord Delamer* (1694), cited in Bonfield, p. 103.

28. Keith Wrightson, *English Society 1580–1680* (London and New Brunswick, N.J., 1982), p. 75.

29. Pierre Lamaison, "Les stratégies matrimoniales dans un système complexe de parenté," *Annales E.S.C.* 34 (1979), 724.

30. Stanley Chojnacki, "Dowries and Kinsmen in Early Renaissance Venice," in Robert I. Rotberg and Theodore K. Rabb, eds., *Marriage and Fertility* (Princeton, 1980), p. 46.

31. Sir Simon D'Ewes, *Autobiography*, cited in H. J. Habakkuk, "Marriage Settlements in the 18th Century," *Transactions of the Royal Historical Society*, 4th ser., 32 (1950), 27.

Chapter 11

1. Aristotle, *The Politics*, trans. T. A. Sinclair (Harmondsworth and Baltimore, 1967), p. 27 (1.2).

2. Jean Bodin, *Method for the Easy Comprehension of History*, trans. Beatrice Reynolds (New York, 1969), pp. 212–14.

3. John Locke, *Two Treatises of Government*, ed. Peter Laslett, rev. ed. (New York and Toronto, 1965), p. 362 (*Second Treatise*, 77).

4. Jean-Jacques Rousseau, *The Social Contract and Discourse on the Origin and Foundation of Inequality among Mankind*, ed. Lester G. Crocker (New York, 1967), p. 8.

5. William Gouge, *Of Domesticall Duties* (1622), cited as the epigraph to John Demos, *A Little Commonwealth* (Oxford, 1970).

6. Thomas Hobbes, *Leviathan Parts I and II* (Indianapolis and New York, 1958), p. 167.

7. Aristotle, p. 50 (1.12).

8. Thomas More, *Utopia*, ed. Edward Surtz, S.J. (New Haven, 1964), pp. 61–67.

9. *The Politics of Johannes Althusius*. An abridged translation of the third edition of *Politica methodice digesta, atque exemplis sacris et profanis illustrata* and including the prefaces to the first and third editions, trans. Frederick S. Carney (London, 1965), p. 35.

10. Ibid., p. 25.

11. Scene 1, ll. 239, 345, 451.

12. Hobbes, p. 167.

13. Locke, pp. 364, 360–61 (*Second Treatise*, 82, 75).

14. Ibid., p. 362 (*Second Treatise*, 78).

15. Ibid., p. 352 (*Second Treatise*, 64, 65).

16. Rousseau, p. 8.

17. François Fénelon, *Letter to Louis XIV* in *Introduction to Contemporary Civilization in the West*, 3d ed., vol. I (New York, 1960), p. 881.

18. Bodin, p. 271.

19. Locke, pp. 185, 285 (*First Treatise*, 14, 143, 144).

20. Brian Tierney, ed., *The Middle Ages*, vol. 1, 2d ed. (New York, 1973), pp. 323, 324.

21. Niccolò Machiavelli, *The Prince and The Discourses* (New York, 1950), p. 148 (*Discourses* 1.11).

22. François Hotman, *Francogallia*, ed. Ralph E. Giesey, trans. J. H. M. Salmon (Cambridge, 1972), pp. 220-21, 154-55 (chs. 6, 1).

23. In his translation of the *Life of Pico della Mirandola*. See More, *Utopia*, trans. and ed. Robert M. Adams (New York, 1975), p. 57n.

24. Buonaccorso da Montemegna (1428), cited in Quentin Skinner, *The Foundations of Modern Political Thought*, 2 vols. (Cambridge, 1978), vol. 1, p. 81.

25. *Francogallia*, editor's introduction, pp. 95-96, 100-101.

26. *The Nobles, or of Nobility* (1563), cited in Skinner, vol. 1, p. 238.

27. John Skelton, cited in Skinner, vol. 1, p. 240.

28. Humphrey, cited in Mervyn James, *Family, Lineage, and Civil Society* (Oxford, 1974), p. 32.

29. William Harrison, *Description of England* (1577, 1587), cited in Peter Laslett, *The World We Have Lost*, 2d ed. (New York, 1971), p. 33.

30. *Rights of Man*, cited in R. R. Palmer, *The Age of the Democratic Revolution*, vol. 1 (Princeton, 1959), p. 54.

31. Cited in Palmer, vol. 1, p. 54.

32. *Treatise on Marriage* (1670), cited in Alain Lottin, "Vie et mort du couple," *XVIIe Siècle*, nos. 102-103 (1974), 60.

33. Cited in Barbara B. Diefendorf, *Paris City Councillors of the Sixteenth Century* (Princeton, 1983), p. 290.

34. Cited in Toby L. Ditz, *Property and Kinship* (Princeton, 1986), p. 164.

35. More, ed. Surtz, pp. 75-76.

36. *Cyvile and Uncyvile Life* (1579), cited in Felicity Heal, "The Idea of Hospitality in Early Modern England," *Past & Present* no. 102 (Feb. 1984), 74.

37. George Wheler, *The Protestant Monastery* (1698), cited in Heal, p. 66.

38. Leon Battista Alberti, *The Albertis of Florence*, trans. Guido A. Guarino (Lewisburg, Pa., 1971), p. 120.

39. Anne Reinbold, "Le sablier de Georges de la Tour," *Annales de l'Est*, 5th ser., 29 (1977), 95-126.

40. Harrison, in Laslett, p. 33.

41. Cited in J. P. Cooper, "Patterns of Inheritance and Settlement by Great Landowners," in Jack Goody et al., eds., *Family and Inheritance* (Cambridge, 1976), p. 249.

42. Cited in Diefendorf, p. 228.

43. Cited in Diefendorf, pp. 169-70.

44. Cited in Demos, p. xix.

45. Cited in René Pillorget, *La tige et le rameau* (Paris, 1979), p. 13.

46. James Lockwood, *Religion in the Highest Interest of a Civil Community* . . . (1754), cited in Ditz, p. 120.

Chapter 12

1. Roger B. Smith, quoted in obituary of Henry Ford II, *The New York Times*, September 30, 1987, p. B5.

2. Thomas More, *Utopia*, ed. Edward Surtz, S.J. (New Haven, 1964), p. 83.

3. J. William Frost, *The Quaker Family in Colonial America* (New York, 1973), pp. 102–3.

4. Leon Battista Alberti, *The Albertis of Florence*, trans. (of *Della famiglia*) Guido A. Guarino (Lewisburg, Pa., 1971), p. 27.

5. Ibid., p. 188.

6. Ibid., p. 165.

7. Ibid., p. 249.

8. Ibid., p. 208.

9. Ibid., p. 193.

10. Cited in Barbara B. Diefendorf, *Paris City Councillors in the Sixteenth Century* (Princeton, 1983), p. 155.

11. Alberti, p. 56.

12. Cited in J. P. Cooper, "Patterns of Inheritance and Settlement by Great Landowners," in Jack Goody et al., eds., *Family and Inheritance* (Cambridge, 1976), p. 206.

13. Lorenzo Capponi, cited in Francis W. Kent, *Household and Lineage in Renaissance Florence* (Princeton, 1977), p. 147.

14. Samuel Hieron (1614). See Robert V. Schnucker, "Elizabethan Birth Control," in Robert I. Rotberg and Theodore K. Rabb, eds., *Marriage and Fertility* (Princeton, 1980), p. 79.

15. Cited in Judith S. Lewis, *In the Family Way* (New Brunswick, N.J., 1986), p. 202.

16. Cited in Lewis, p. 229.

17. Ben Jonson, "To Penshurst," *The Forrest*, ii.

18. Christian F. Sintenis, *Das grössere Buch für Familien*, 2 (1807), cited in Ingeborg Weber-Kellermann, *Die deutsche Familie* (Frankfurt am Main, 1974), p. 75.

19. Alberti, *Ten Books of Architecture*, cited in Kent, p. 259.

20. Mervyn James, *Family, Lineage, and Civil Society* (Oxford, 1974), pp. 109–110.

21. Ibid.

22. Giorgio Vasari, *The Lives of the Artists: A Selection*, trans. George Bull (Harmondsworth, 1971), p. 239.

23. Matteo Palmieri, *Della vita civile* (ca. 1530), cited in Kent, pp. 252–53.

24. Gibbon's *Autobiography*, epigraph to Kent.

25. Cited in Kent, p. 99.

26. Alberti, *The Albertis* . . . , p. 34.

27. Pierre Lamaison, "Les stratégies matrimoniales dans un système complexe de parenté," *Annales E.S.C.* 34 (1979), 725–26.

28. Act II, sc. ii.

29. Alberti, p. 46.

30. Cited in Jan Lewis, *The Pursuit of Happiness* (Cambridge, 1983), p. 206.

31. Cited in Hélène Bergues et al., *La prévention des naissances dans la famille* (Paris, 1960), p. 155.

32. Both cited in Jan Lewis, pp. 204–6.

33. Wetenhall Wilkes, *A Letter of Genteel and Moral Advice to a Young Lady* (1740), cited in Lawrence Stone, *The Family, Sex and Marriage in England 1500–1800* (New York, 1979), p. 218.

34. Cited in Jan Lewis, p. 193.

35. Alberti, p. 121.

36. Ibid., p. 126.

37. Ibid., pp. 219–20.

38. Ibid., p. 118.

39. Jonson, "To Penshurst."

40. Act II, sc. i, l. 106.

41. Act III, sc. i, ll. 64–66.

42. *Othello*, Act III, sc. iii, l. 89.

43. Act IV, sc. ii, ll. 258–59.

44. Act IV, sc. ii, ll. 152–61.

45. Alberti, p. 46.

46. Ibid., p. 51.

47. Ibid., p. 249.

48. *Timon of Athens*, Act I, sc. i, l. 166.

49. Ibid., Act III, sc. i, l. 102.

50. *Hamlet*, Act III, sc. iv, l. 61.

51. Act III, sc. iv, l. 108.

52. Act IV, sc. v, l. 117.

53. Act IV, sc. vii, ll. 126–27.

54. *Henry IV Part 2*, Act V, sc. ii, ll. 118–21.

55. Act I, sc. i, ll. 98–100.

56. Alberti, p. 164.

57. Ibid., p. 194.

58. Act V, sc. iii, l. 155.

59. Act IV, sc. iii, ll. 36–38.

60. Introduction to *Democracy in America*, in *Introduction to Contemporary Civilization in the West*, 3d ed., vol. 2 (New York, 1961), p. 507.

BIBLIOGRAPHY

This is not intended as an exhaustive list. The books and articles are ones that I not only found useful but also can recommend as particularly enjoyable, illuminating, or provocative.

Alberti, Leon Battista. *The Albertis of Florence: Leon Battista Alberti's Della Famiglia.* Trans. Guido A. Guarino. Lewisburg, Pa., 1971.

Anderson, Michael. *Family Structure in Nineteenth Century Lancashire.* Cambridge, 1971.

Ariès, Philippe. *Centuries of Childhood; A Social History of Family Life.* New York, 1965.

———. *Western Attitudes toward Death.* Baltimore and London, 1974.

Armengaud, André. *La famille et l'enfant en France et en Angleterre du XVIe au XVIIIe siècle: Aspects démographiques.* Paris, 1975.

Auwers, Linda. "Fathers, Sons, and Wealth in Colonial Windsor, Connecticut." *Journal of Family History* 3 (1978).

Barley, M. W. *The English Farmhouse and Cottage.* London, 1961.

Bardet, Jean-Pierre. "Enfants abandonnés et enfants assistés à Rouen dans la seconde moitié du XVIIIe siècle." In *Sur la population française* (Paris, 1973).

Baulant, Micheline. "The Scattered Family: Another Aspect of Seventeenth-century Demography." Trans. of "La famille en miettes." In Forster and Ranum (Baltimore, 1976).

Beales, Ross W., Jr. "In Search of the Historical Child: Miniature Adulthood and Youth in Colonial New England." *American Quarterly* 27 (1975).

Behrens, C.B.A. *The Ancien Régime.* London, 1961.

Belmont, Nicole. "The Symbolic Function of the Wedding Procession in the Popular Rituals of Marriage." Trans. of "La fonction symbolique du cortège dans les rituels populaires du mariage." In Forster and Ranum (Baltimore, 1976).

Bennassar, Bartolomé. *Valladolid au siècle d'or: Une ville de Castille et sa campagne au XVIe siècle.* Paris, 1967.

Bergues, Hélène, et al. *La prévention des naissances dans la famille: Ses origines dans les temps modernes.* Paris, 1960.

Berkner, Lutz K. "Inheritance, Land Tenure and Peasant Family Structure: A German Regional Comparison." In Goody et al. (Cambridge, 1976).

―――. "The Stem Family and the Developmental Cycle of the Peasant Household: An Eighteenth-century Austrian Example." *American Historical Review*, 77 (1972).

―――and John W. Shaffer. "The Joint Family in the Nivernais." *Journal of Family History* 3 (1978).

Berlanstein, Lenard R. "Illegitimacy, Concubinage, and Proletarianization in a French Town, 1760–1914." *Journal of Family History* 5 (1980).

Bernard, R.-J. "L'alimentation paysanne en Gévaudon au XVIIIe siècle." *Annales: Économies, Sociétés, Civilisations* 24 (1969).

Bideau, Alain. "L'envoi des jeunes enfants en nourrice: L'exemple d'une petite ville: Thoissey-en-Doubes 1740–1840." In *Sur la population française* (Paris, 1973).

Biraben, Jean-Noël. "La médecine et l'enfant au moyen âge." *Annales de Démographie Historique* (1973).

Bloch, Marc. *French Rural History: An Essay on Its Basic Characteristics.* Trans. by Janet Sonheimer of *Les caractères originaux de l'histoire rurale française* (first ed., 1931). London, 1966.

Boswell, John. *The Kindness of Strangers: The Abandonment of Children in Western Europe from Late Antiquity to the Renaissance.* New York, 1988.

Braudel, Fernand. *The Structures of Everyday Life: The Limits of the Possible.* Trans. Siân Reynolds. New York, 1981.

Burguière, André. "The Charivari and Religious Repression in France during the Ancien Régime." In Wheaton and Hareven (Philadelphia, 1980).

―――. "The Marriage Ritual in France: Ecclesiastical Practices and Popular Practices (Sixteenth to Eighteenth Centuries)." Trans. of "Le rituel du mariage en France." In Forster and Ranum (Baltimore, 1976).

Campbell, Bruce M. S. "Population Pressure, Inheritance and the Land Market in a Fourteenth-century Peasant Community." In Smith (Cambridge, 1984).

Carr, Lois Green, and Lorena S. Walsh. "The Planter's Wife: the Experience of White Women in Seventeenth-century Maryland." In Gordon (New York, 1978).

Casey, James. *The History of the Family.* Oxford and New York, 1989.

Caspard, Pierre. "Conceptions prénuptiales et développement du capitalisme dans la Principauté de Neuchâtel (1678–1820)." *Annales: Économies, Sociétés, Civilisations* 29 (1974).

Castan, Yves. *Honnêteté et relations sociales en Languedoc (1715–1780).* Paris, 1974.

―――. "Pères et fils en Languedoc à l'époque classique." *XVIIe Siècle* nos. 102–103 (1974).

Chambers, J. D. "The Course of Population Change" and "Population Change in a Provincial Town: Nottingham 1700–1800." In Glass and Eversley (London, 1965).

Chamoux, Antoinette. "L'allaitement artificiel" and "L'enfance abandonnée à Reims à la fin du XVIIIe siècle." *Annales de Démographie Historique* (1973).

Charbonneau, Hubert. *Tourouvre-au-Perche aux XVIIe et XVIIIe siècles: Étude de démographie historique.* Paris, 1970.

Chartier, Roger, Marie-Madeleine Compère, and Dominique Julia. *L'éducation en France du XVIe au XVIIIe siècle.* Paris, 1976.

Chojnacki, Stanley. "Dowries and Kinsmen in Early Renaissance Venice." In Rotberg and Rabb (Princeton, 1980).

Cipolla, Carlo M. "Four Centuries of Italian Demographic Development." In Glass and Eversley (London, 1965).

Cody, Cheryll Ann. "There Was No 'Absalom' on the Ball Plantations: Slave-naming Practices in the South Carolina Low Country, 1720–1865." American Historical Review 92 (1987).

Collomp, Alain. "Alliance et filiation en Haute Provence au XVIIIᵉ siècle." Annales: Économies, Sociétés, Civilisations 32 (1977).

Cooper, J. P. "Patterns of Inheritance and Settlement by Great Landowners from the Fifteenth to the Eighteenth Centuries." In Goody et al. (Cambridge, 1976).

Cott, Nancy F. "Divorce and the Changing Status of Women in Eighteenth-century Massachusetts." In Gordon (New York, 1978).

———. "Eighteenth-century Family and Social Life Revealed in Massachusetts Divorce Records." Journal of Social History 10 (1976).

Crawford, Patricia. "Attitudes to Menstruation in Seventeenth-century England." Past & Present no. 91 (May 1981).

Croix, Alain. Nantes et le pays nantais au XVIᵉ siècle: Étude démographique. Paris, 1974.

Darrow, Margaret H. "Popular Concepts of Marital Choice in Eighteenth-century France." Journal of Social History 19 (1985).

Davis, Natalie Zemon. "Ghosts, Kin, and Progeny: Some Features of Family Life in Early Modern France." In Rossi et al. (New York, 1978).

———. Society and Culture in Early Modern France. Stanford, 1975.

De Mause, Lloyd, ed. The History of Childhood. New York, 1974.

Demos, John. "Developmental Perspectives on the History of Childhood." In Rabb and Rotberg (New York, 1973).

———. A Little Commonwealth: Family Life in Plymouth Colony. New York and London, 1971.

———. "Old Age in Early New England." In Gordon (New York, 1978).

———, and Virginia Demos. "Adolescence in Historical Perspective." Journal of Marriage and the Family 31 (1969).

Diefendorf, Barbara B. Paris City Councillors in the Sixteenth Century: The Politics of Patrimony. Princeton, 1983.

Ditz, Toby L. Property and Kinship: Inheritance in Early Connecticut, 1750–1820. Princeton, 1986.

Donnison, Jean. Midwives and Medical Men: A History of Inter-Professional Rivalries and Women's Rights. New York, 1977.

Dupâquier, Jacques. "Naming-practices, Godparenthood, and Kinship in the Vexin, 1540–1900." Journal of Family History 6 (1981).

———, and Marcel Lachiver. "Les débuts de la contraception en France ou les deux malthusianismes." Annales: Économies, Sociétés, Civilisations 24 (1969).

Dyer, Christopher. "Changes in the Size of Peasant Holdings in Some West Midland Villages 1400–1500." In Smith (Cambridge, 1984).

Elshtain, Jean Bethke, ed. The Family in Political Thought. Amherst, Mass., 1982.

Fairchilds, Cissie. Domestic Enemies: Servants and Their Masters in Old Regime France. Baltimore, 1984.

———. "Female Sexual Attitudes and the Rise of Illegitimacy: A Case Study." In Rotberg and Rabb (Princeton, 1980).

Febvre, Lucien. Amour sacré, amour profane: Autour de l'Heptaméron. Paris, 1971; first published 1944.

Finlay, Roger A. P. "Population and Fertility in London, 1580–1650." Journal of Family History 4 (1979).

Flandrin, Jean-Louis. Les amours paysannes: Amour et sexualité dans les campagnes de l'ancienne France (XVI⁰–XIX⁰ siècle). Paris, 1975.

———. "La cellule familiale et l'oeuvre de procréation dans l'ancienne société." XVII⁰ Siècle nos. 102–103 (1974).

———. "Contraception, Marriage, and Sexual Relations in the Christian West." Trans. of "Contraception, mariage et rélations amoureuses dans l'Occident chrétien." In Robert Forster and Orest Ranum, eds., Biology of Man in History: Selections from the Annales: Économies, Sociétés, Civilisations (Baltimore, 1975).

———. Families in Former Times: Kinship, Household, and Sexuality. Trans. by Richard Southern of Familles: Parenté, maison, sexualité dans l'ancienne société. Cambridge, 1979.

———. "Repression and Change in the Sexual Life of Young People in Medieval and Modern Times." In Wheaton and Hareven (Philadelphia, 1980).

Forbes, Thomas Rogers. Chronicle from Aldgate. Life and Death in Shakespeare's London. New Haven, 1971.

Forster, Robert, and Orest Ranum, eds. Ritual, Religion, and the Sacred: Selections from the Annales: Économies, Sociétés, Civilisations, trans. Elborg Forster and Patricia M. Ranum (Baltimore, 1976).

Fourastié, Jean. "De la vie traditionelle à la vie 'tertiaire': Recherches sur le calendrier démographique de l'homme moyen." Population 14 (1959).

Friedman, Alice T. House and Household in Elizabethan England: Wollaton Hall and the Willoughby Family. Chicago, 1989.

Frost, J. William. The Quaker Family in Colonial America: A Portrait of the Society of Friends. New York, 1973.

Gallet, Michel. Stately Mansions: Eighteenth Century Paris Architecture. Trans. James C. Palmes. New York, 1972.

Ganiage, Jean. "Nourrissons parisiens en Beauvaisis." In Sur la population française (Paris, 1973).

Garden, Maurice. "Les verriers de Givors au XVIII⁰ siècle: Les origines d'une population ouvrière spécialisée." In Sur la population française (Paris, 1973).

Giesey, Ralph E. "Rules of Inheritance and Strategies of Mobility in Prerevolutionary France." American Historical Review 82 (1977).

Gillis, John R. For Better, For Worse: British Marriages, 1600 to the Present. Oxford, 1985.

Glass, D. V., and D.E.C. Eversley, eds. Population in History: Essays in Historical Demography. London, 1965.

Goldthwaite, Richard A. "The Florentine Palace as Domestic Architecture." American Historical Review 77 (1972).

Goode, William J. The Family. Englewood Cliffs, N.J., 1964.

———. "The Theoretical Importance of Love." American Sociological Review 24

(1959), 38–47. In slightly revised form in Goode's *Explorations in Social Theory* (New York, 1973).

Goody, Jack. *The Development of the Family and Marriage in Europe.* Cambridge, 1983.

———. "Inheritance, Property, and Women: Some Comparative Considerations." In Goody et al. (Cambridge, 1976).

———, Joan Thirsk, and E. P. Thompson, eds. *Family and Inheritance. Rural Society in Western Europe, 1200–1800.* Cambridge, 1976.

Gordon, Michael, ed. *The American Family in Social-historical Perspective.* 2d ed. New York, 1978.

Gottlieb, Beatrice. "The Meaning of Clandestine Marriage." In Wheaton and Hareven (Philadelphia, 1980).

Goubert, Pierre. "Legitimate Fecundity and Infant Mortality in France during the Eighteenth Century: A Comparison." *Daedalus* 97 (1968).

———. *Louis XIV and Twenty Million Frenchmen.* Trans. Anne Carter. New York, 1970.

———. "Recent Theories and Research in French Population between 1500 and 1700." In Glass and Eversley (London, 1965).

Gouesse, Jean-Marie. "Parenté, famille et mariage en Normandie, aux XVIIᵉ et XVIIIᵉ siècles: Présentation d'une source et d'une enquête." *Annales: Économies, Sociétés, Civilisations* 27 (1972), 1139–54.

———. "Le refus de l'enfant au tribunal de la pénitence (en Basse-Normandie aux XVIIᵉ et XVIIIᵉ siècles)." *Annales de Démographie Historique* (1973).

Greven, Philip J., Jr. "Family Structure in Seventeenth-century Andover, Massachusetts." In Gordon (New York, 1978).

———. *Four Generations: Population, Land, and Family in Colonial Andover, Massachusetts.* Ithaca, N.Y., 1970.

Gutman, Herbert. *The Black Family in Slavery and Freedom, 1750–1925.* New York, 1976.

Habakkuk, H. J. "Marriage Settlements in the Eighteenth Century." *Transactions of the Royal Historical Society,* 4th ser., 32 (1950).

Hair, Paul. "Bridal Pregnancy in Rural England in Earlier Centuries." *Population Studies* 20 (1966). Also "Bridal Pregnancy . . . Further Examined." *Population Studies* 24 (1970).

———, ed. *Before the Bawdy Court: Selections from Church Court and Other Records.* London, 1972.

Hajnal, John. "European Marriage Patterns in Perspective." In Glass and Eversley (London, 1965).

———. "Two Kinds of Pre-industrial Household Formation System." In Wall et al. (Cambridge, 1983).

Hanawalt, Barbara A. *The Ties That Bound: Peasant Families in Medieval England.* New York and Oxford, 1986.

Hatcher, John. *Plague, Population and the English Economy, 1348–1530.* Atlantic Highlands, N.J., 1978.

Heal, Felicity. "The Idea of Hospitality in Early Modern England." *Past & Present,* no. 102 (Feb. 1984).

Hecht, J. Jean. *The Domestic Servant Class in Eighteenth-century England.* London, 1956.

Helmholtz, R. M. *Marriage Litigation in Medieval England*. New York, 1974.

Herlihy, David, and Christiane Klapisch-Zuber. *The Tuscans and Their Families*. Abridged trans. of *Les Toscans et leurs familles*. New Haven, 1985.

Higman, B. W. "African and Creole Slave Family Patterns in Trinidad." *Journal of Family History* 3 (1978).

Hollingsworth, T. H. "A Demographic Study of the British Ducal Families." In Glass and Eversley (London, 1965).

Homans, George C. *English Villagers of the Thirteenth Century*. New York, 1970; first published 1941.

Hoskins, W. G. *The Midland Peasant: The Economic and Social History of a Leicestershire Village*. London, 1957.

Houlbrooke, Ralph A. *The English Family 1450–1700*. London and New York, 1984.

Howell, Cicely. "Peasant Inheritance Customs in the Midlands, 1280–1700." In Goody et al. (Cambridge, 1976).

Hunt, David. *Parents and Children in History: The Psychology of Family Life in Early Modern France*. New York, 1970.

Illick, Joseph E. "Child-rearing in Seventeenth-century England and America." In De Mause (New York, 1974).

Ingram, Martin. "Ridings, Rough Music and the 'Reform of Popular Culture' in Early Modern England." *Past & Present*, no. 105 (Nov. 1984).

James, Mervyn. *Family, Lineage, and Civil Society: A Study of Society, Politics, and Mentality in the Durham Region, 1500–1640*. Oxford, 1974.

Jones, Paul V. B. *The Household of a Tudor Nobleman*. University of Illinois Studies in the Social Sciences 6, no. 4 (Dec. 1917).

Kaestle, Carl F., and Maris A. Vinovskis. "From Apron Strings to ABCs: Parents, Children and Schooling in Nineteenth-century Massachusetts." In John Demos and Sarane Boocock, eds., *Turning Points; Historical and Sociological Essays on the Family* (Chicago, 1978).

Katz, Jacob. "Family, Kinship and Marriage among Ashkenazim in the Sixteenth to Eighteenth Centuries." *The Jewish Journal of Sociology* 1 (1959).

Kent, Francis William. *Household and Lineage in Renaissance Florence: The Family Life of the Capponi, Ginori, and Rucellai*. Princeton, 1977.

Kett, Joseph F. "The Stages of Life." In Gordon (New York, 1978).

Keyssar, Alexander. "Widowhood in Eighteenth-century Massachusetts: A Problem in the History of the Family." *Perspectives in American History* 8 (1974).

Kirshner, Julius, and Anthony Molho. "The Dowry Fund and the Marriage Market in Early Quattrocento Florence." *Journal of Modern History* 50 (1978).

Klapisch-Zuber, Christiane. *Women, Family, and Ritual in Renaissance Italy*. Trans. Lydia Cochrane. Chicago, 1985.

Kulikoff, Allan. "The Beginnings of the Afro-American Family in Maryland." In Gordon (New York, 1978).

Kussmaul, Ann. *Servants in Husbandry in Early Modern England*. Cambridge, 1981.

Lamaison, Pierre. "Les stratégies matrimoniales dans un système complexe de parenté: Ribennes en Gevaudan (1650–1830)." *Annales: Économies, Sociétés, Civilisations* 34 (1979).

Laqueur, Thomas. *Making Sex: Body and Gender from the Greeks to Freud*. Cambridge, Mass., 1990.

Laslett, Peter. "Characteristics of the Western Family Considered over Time." *Journal of Family History* 2 (1977).

———. *The World We Have Lost.* 2d ed. New York, 1971.

———, ed., with the assistance of Richard Wall. *Household and Family in Past Time.* Cambridge, 1972.

Leach, Edmund. "Complementary Filiation and Bilateral Kinship." In Jack Goody, ed., *The Character of Kinship* (Cambridge, 1973).

Lebrun, François. *La vie conjugale sous l'Ancien Régime.* Paris, 1975.

Le Roy Ladurie, Emmanuel. "Family Structures and Inheritance Customs in Sixteenth-century France." In Goody et al. (Cambridge, 1976).

Lewis, Jan. *The Pursuit of Happiness: Family and Values in Jefferson's Virginia.* Cambridge, 1983.

Lewis, Judith Schneid. *In the Family Way: Childbearing in the British Aristocracy, 1760–1860.* New Brunswick, N.J., 1986.

Lindemann, Mary. "Love for Hire: The Regulation of the Wet-nursing Business in Eighteenth-century Hamburg." *Journal of Family History* 6 (1981).

Lottin, Alain. "Vie et mort du couple: Difficultés conjugales et divorces dans le Nord de la France aux XVIIe et XVIIIe siècles." *XVIIe Siècle* nos. 102–103 (1974).

Macfarlane, Alan. *The Family Life of Ralph Josselin, a Seventeenth-century Clergyman: An Essay in Historical Anthropology.* Cambridge, 1970.

———. *Marriage and Love in England: Modes of Reproduction 1300–1840.* Oxford, 1986.

Mandrou, Robert. *Introduction to Modern France, 1500–1640: An Essay in Historical Psychology.* Trans. R. E. Hallmark. New York, 1975.

Marvick, Elizabeth Wirth. "Nature versus Nurture: Patterns and Trends in Seventeenth-century French Child-rearing." In De Mause (New York, 1974).

Meuvret, J. "Demographic Crisis in France from the Sixteenth to the Eighteenth Century." In Glass and Eversley (London, 1965).

Mills, Dennis R. "The Nineteenth-century Peasantry of Melbourn, Cambridgeshire." In Smith (Cambridge, 1984).

Mitterauer, Michael, and Reinhard Sieder. *The European Family—Patriarchy to Partnership: From the Middle Ages to the Present.* Trans. of *Vom Patriarchat zur Partnerschaft: Zum Strukturwandel der Familie.* Chicago, 1982.

Moller, Herbert. "Voice Change in Human Biological Development." *Journal of Interdisciplinary History* 16 (1985).

Morgan, Edmund S. *The Puritan Family: Religion and Domestic Relations in Seventeenth-century New England.* Rev. ed. New York, 1966.

Morineau, Michel. "Révolution agricole, révolution alimentaire, révolution démographique." *Annales de Démographie Historique* (1974).

Noël, Raymond. "L'état de la population de Mostuejouls (Aveyron) en 1690." In *Sur la population française* (Paris, 1973).

Ortigues, Edmond. "La psychanalyse et les institutions familiales." *Annales: Économies, Sociétés, Civilisations* 27 (1972).

Ozment, Steven. *When Fathers Ruled: Family Life in Reformation Europe.* Cambridge, Mass., and London, 1983.

Peller, S. "Births and Deaths among Europe's Ruling Families since 1500." In Glass and Eversley (London, 1965).

Perrenoud, Alfred. "Malthusianisme et protestantisme: 'Un modèle démographique weberien.'" *Annales: Économies, Sociétés, Civilisations* 29 (1974).

Piponnier, Françoise. "Les objets de l'enfance." *Annales de Démographie Historique* (1973).

Plakans, Andrejs. *Kinship in the Past: An Anthropology of European Family Life, 1500–1900.* New York and Oxford, 1984.

Potter, J. "The Growth of Population in America, 1700–1860." In Glass and Eversley (London, 1965).

Quetel, Claude. "Lettres de cachet et correctionnaires dans la Généralité de Caen au XVIIIe siècle." *Annales de Normandie* 27 (1978).

Rabb, Theodore K., and Robert I. Rotberg, eds. *The Family in History: Interdisciplinary Essays.* New York, 1973.

Ramos, Donald. "City and Country: The Family in Minas Gerais, 1804–1838." *Journal of Family History* 3 (1978).

Ravensdale, Jack. "Population Changes and the Transfer of Customary Land on a Cambridgeshire Manor in the Fourteenth Century." In Smith (Cambridge, 1984).

Razi, Zvi. "Family, Land and the Village Community in Later Medieval England." *Past & Present* no. 93 (Nov. 1981).

Rebel, Hermann. "Peasant Stem Families in Early Modern Austria: Life Plans, Status Tactics, and the Grid of Inheritance." *Social Science History* 2 (1978).

Riché, Pierre. "L'enfant dans le haut moyen âge." *Annales de Démographie Historique* (1973).

Ross, James Bruce. "The Middle-class Child in Urban Italy, Fourteenth to Early Sixteenth Century." In De Mause (New York, 1974).

Rotberg, Robert I., and Theodore K. Rabb, eds. *Marriage and Fertility: Studies in Interdisciplinary History.* Princeton, 1980.

Roux, Simone. "L'habitat urbain au moyen âge: Le quartier de l'Université à Paris." *Annales: Économies, Sociétés, Civilisations* 24 (1969).

———. *La maison dans l'histoire.* Paris, 1976.

Rossi, Alice S., Jerome Kagan, and Tamara K. Hareven, eds., *The Family* (New York, 1978).

Scholten, Catherine M. " 'On the Importance of the Obstetrick Art': Changing Customs of Childbirth in America, 1760 to 1825." *William and Mary Quarterly*, 3d ser. 34 (1977).

Shanly, Mary Lyndon. "Marriage Contract and Social Contract in Seventeenth-century English Political Thought." In Elshtain (Amherst, Mass., 1982).

Skinner, Quentin. *The Foundations of Modern Political Thought.* 2 vols. Cambridge, 1978.

Slater, Miriam. "The Weightiest Business: Marriage in an Upper-gentry Family in Seventeenth-century England." *Past & Present*, no. 72 (Aug. 1976).

Smith, Daniel Scott, and Michael S. Hindus. "Premarital Pregnancy in America 1640–1971: an Overview and Interpretation." In Rotberg and Rabb (Princeton, 1980).

Smith, Richard M. "Some Issues Concerning Families and Their Property in Rural England 1250–1800." In Smith (Cambridge, 1984).

———, ed. *Land, Kinship and Life-Cycle.* Cambridge, 1984.

Smith, Steven R. "The London Apprentices as Seventeenth Century Adolescents."
    Past & Present, no. 61 (Nov. 1973).

Spufford, Margaret. "Peasant Inheritance Custom and Land Distribution in
    Cambridgeshire from the Sixteenth to the Eighteenth Centuries." In Goody et
    al. (Cambridge, 1976).

Stone, Lawrence. *Crisis of the Aristocracy 1558–1641*. Oxford, 1967.

———. *The Family, Sex and Marriage in England 1500–1800*. London, 1977;
    abridged paper ed., New York, 1979.

Sur la population française au XVIIIe et au XIXe siècles: Hommage à Marcel Reinhard.
    Paris, 1973.

Sussmann, George D. "Parisian Infants and Norman Wet-Nurses in the Early Nine-
    teenth Century: A Statistical Study." In Rotberg and Rabb (Princeton, 1980).

Taylor, Peter, and Hermann Rebel. "Hessian Peasant Women, Their Families, and
    the Draft: a Social-historical Interpretation of Four Tales from the Grimm Col-
    lection." *Journal of Family History* 6 (1981).

Terrisse, Michel. "Le rattrapage de nuptialité d'après peste à Marseille (1720–21)." In
    Sur la population française (Paris, 1973).

Thirsk, Joan. "The European Debate on Customs of Inheritance, 1500–1700." In
    Goody et al. (Cambridge, 1976).

Thomas, Keith. "The Double Standard." *Journal of the History of Ideas* 20 (1959).

Thompson, E. P. "The Grid of Inheritance: A Comment." In Goody et al. (Cam-
    bridge, 1976).

———. " 'Rough Music': Le charivari anglais." *Annales: Économies, Sociétés, Civil-
    isations* 27 (1972).

Tomalin, Claire. *The Life and Death of Mary Wollstonecraft*. New York and London,
    1974.

Trumbach, Randolph. *The Rise of the Egalitarian Family: Aristocratic Kinship and
    Domestic Relations in Eighteenth-century England*. New York, 1979.

Ulrich, Laurel Thatcher. *A Midwife's Tale: The Life of Martha Ballard, Based on Her
    Diary 1785–1812*. New York, 1990.

Van de Walle, Etienne. "Recent Approaches to Past Childhoods." In Rabb and Rot-
    berg (New York, 1973).

Vann, Richard T. "Nurture and Conversion in the Early Quaker Family." *Journal of
    Marriage and the Family* 31 (1969).

———. "Wills and the Family in an English Town: Banbury, 1550–1800." *Journal of
    Family History* 4 (1979).

Vinovskis, Maris A. "Angels' Heads and Weeping Willows: Death in Early America."
    In Gordon (New York, 1978).

Wales, Tim. "Poverty, Poor Relief and the Life-Cycle: Some Evidence from Seven-
    teenth-century Norfolk." In Smith (Cambridge, 1984).

Wall, Richard. "The Age at Leaving Home." *Journal of Family History* 3 (1978).

———. "Real Property, Marriage and Children: The Evidence from Four Pre-indus-
    trial Communities." In Smith (Cambridge, 1984).

———, Jean Robin, and Peter Laslett, eds. *Family Forms in Historic Europe*. Cam-
    bridge, 1983.

Walzer, John F. "A Period of Ambivalence: Eighteenth-century American Child-
    hood." In De Mause (New York, 1974).

Wells, Robert V. "Demographic Change and the Life Cycle of American Families." In Rabb and Rotberg (New York, 1973).

Wheaton, Robert. "Affinity and Descent in Seventeenth-century Bordeaux." In Wheaton and Hareven (Philadelphia, 1980).

———. "Family and Kinship in Western Europe: The Problem of the Joint Family Household." *Journal of Interdisciplinary History* 5 (1975).

———, and Tamara K. Hareven, eds. *Family and Sexuality in French History.* Philadelphia, 1980.

Williams, W. M. *The Sociology of an English Village: Gosforth.* London, 1964; first published 1956.

Wrightson, Keith. *English Society 1580–1680.* New Brunswick, N.J., 1982.

———. "Kinship in an English Village: Terling, Essex 1500–1700." In Smith (Cambridge, 1984).

Wrigley, E. A. *Population and History.* New York, 1969.

———. "Reflections on the History of the Family." In Rossi et al. (New York, 1978).

Zonabend, Françoise. "Baptismal Kinship at Minot (Côte d'Or)." In Forster and Ranum (Baltimore, 1976).

ILLUSTRATION CREDITS

1. Thomas de Keijser, *Family Portrait*. Copyright © Bildarchiv Preussischer Kulturbesitz, Berlin, 1991. Kriegsverlust, vormals Kaiser Friedrich-Museum Berlin.

2. Joseph Van Aken, *An English Family at Tea*. Tate Gallery, London/Art Resource, New York.

3. S. H. Grimm, "Charity Distribution in Durham." By permission of the British Library.

4. "A Scheme of the Income and Expense of the Several Families of England . . . In Charles Davenant, *The Political and Commercial Works*, II (London, 1771), facing p. 184. General Research Division; The New York Public Library; Astor, Lenox and Tilden Foundations.

5. Floor plan, Somersby. In M. W. Barley, *The English Farmhouse and Cottage* (London, 1961), p. 81.

6. "November." The Pierpont Morgan Library, New York. M.399, f. 12v.

7. David Allan, cottage interior. In Allan Ramsay, *The Gentle Shepherd* (London, 1880), facing p. 116. General Research Division; The New York Public Library; Astor, Lenox and Tilden Foundations.

8. Miniature from Gilles Romain, *Le livre du gouvernement*. Bibliothèque Nationale, MS 5062, f. 149v.

9. John Blagrave, "Map of the Manor of Feckenham, Worcestershire." *Geographical Magazine* 18 (June 1945).

10. "As the Church is Now 1701." Shropshire Record Office 1525/1.

11. Andrea del Sarto, *Marriage of Saint Catherine*. Gemäldegalerie Alte Meister—Staatliche Kunstsammlungen Dresden.

30. "The Massacre of the Innocents," woodcut by Leonardo Norsino after Antonio Tempesta. In *Evangelium Sanctum Domini* . . . (Rome, 1590). Spencer Collection; The New York Public Library; Astor, Lenox and Tilden Foundations.

31. Georges de la Tour, *Le nouveau-né*. Musée des Beaux-Arts et d'Archéologie de Rennes.

32. Pedro Campaña, *Virgin with Child*. Copyright © Bildarchiv Preussischer Kulturbesitz, Berlin, 1991. z. Zt. Gemäldegalerie Dahlem/ Westberlin, vormals Kaiser Friedrich-Museum, Berlin.

33. J. B. Simonet after Jean Michel Moreau, "Voilà la règle de la nature." The Metropolitan Museum of Art, Harris Brisbane Dick Fund, 1930 (30. 67. 2).

34. Etienne Aubry, *Les adieux à la nourrice*. Sterling & Francine Clark Art Institute, Williamstown, Massachusetts.

35. "Misère humaine, ou Les passions de l'homme en tous ses âges." Bibliothèque Nationale.

36. Wybrand de Geest, *Portrait of a Boy*. Rijksmuseum Amsterdam.

37. "Age Pyramids." In E. A. Wrigley, *Population and History* (1969). By permission of McGraw-Hill Publishing Company.

38. George Morland, *Cowherd and Milkmaid*. Tate Gallery, London/ Art Resource, New York.

39. "La mauvaise éducation." In Georg Hirth, ed., *Kulturgeschichtliches Bilderbuch aus drei Jahrhunderten*, 2d ed., II (Leipzig, 1890?), p. 458. Art & Architecture Collection, Miriam & Ira D. Wallach Division of Art, Prints and Photographs; The New York Public Library; Astor, Lenox and Tilden Foundations.

40. Geertgen tot Sint Jans, *Holy Kinship*. Rijksmuseum Amsterdam.

41. Mantegna, *L'Incontro*. Soprintendenza per i Beni Artistici e Storici di Mantova. Photograph by Antonio Quattrone.

42. "Inheritance Customs in Western Europe." Adapted by Joan Thirsk from Wilhelm Abel, *Agrarpolitik*, 3d ed. (Göttingen: Vandenhoeck & Ruprecht, 1967), p. 170.

43. Jan Mostaert (attr.), *The Tree of Jesse*. Rijksmuseum Amsterdam.

44. The Great Hall, Montacute House. The National Trust.

45. Fountain in Piazza della Rotonda, Rome. Print Collection; Miriam & Ira D. Wallach Division of Art, Prints and Photographs; The New York Public Library; Astor, Lenox and Tilden Foundations.

46. A-990 b *Giuliano de' Medici*, 1478, Giovanni di Bertoldo, c. 1420–1491. National Gallery of Art, Washington, Samuel H. Kress Collection.

47. "Plan de Versailles . . . par M. L'abbé Delagrive." Bibliothèque Nationale.

48. Israel Silvestre, *Vaux-le-Vicomte*. Art & Architecture Collection, Miriam & Ira D. Wallach Division of Art, Prints and Photographs; The New York Public Library; Astor, Lenox and Tilden Foundations.

49. Effigies of Lumley ancestors at Chester-le-Street. Mervyn James, *Family, Lineage, and Civil Society: A Study of Society, Politics, and Mentality in the Durham Region, 1500–1640* (Oxford: Clarendon Press, 1974).

50. "Pietas filiorum in parentes." Rare Book and Manuscript Library, Columbia University.

51. Greuze, *La mère bien-aimée*. Carlos Munoz de Laborde, Marquis de Laborde.

INDEX